It Did Happen Here

It Did Happen Here

Recollections of
Political Repression in America

Bud Schultz
Ruth Schultz

WITH A FOREWORD BY VICTOR NAVASKY

University of California Press
Berkeley   Los Angeles   London

University of California Press
Berkeley and Los Angeles, California

University of California Press, Ltd.
London, England

© 1989 by
The Regents of the University of California

Printed in the United States of America
2   3   4   5   6   7   8   9

Library of Congress Cataloging-in-Publication Data

It did happen here.

    1. Political persecution—United States—History.
I. Schultz, Bud.   II. Schultz, Ruth.
JC599.U518   1989   323.4'9'0973   88–27855
ISBN 0-520-06508-5 (alk. paper)
ISBN 0-520-07197-2

The paper used in this publication meets the minimum requirements of
American National Standard for Information Sciences—Permanence of Paper
for Printed Library Materials, ANSI Z39.48–1984.♾

To our children

Contents

Preface

Political repression is the nether side of the American tradition of constitutional liberties. It has become institutionalized in American life, an unwelcome legacy from the sometimes brutal, sometimes hysterical attacks on political dissidents. Every branch and every level of government has participated in suppressing free expression. Unfortunately, before we distance ourselves sufficiently from one assault on constitutional rights, we fall victim to the next. Keeping alive memories of those grim experiences is one antidote against their recurrence.

In *Political Repression in Modern America,* Robert Goldstein offers this definition: "Political repression consists of government action which grossly discriminates against persons or organizations viewed as presenting a fundamental challenge to existing power relationships or key government policies, because of their perceived political beliefs." In this volume, we bring together the stories of persons who have been grossly discriminated against because they challenged existing power relationships or government policies. Although some express their beliefs as they tell their stories, this is not a book about the merits of their views. Rather, it is about the right to advocate and organize, free of government interference, for the purpose of political or economic redress. It is about political repression in America, told by those who experienced it, stood up to it, and therefore can tell its story from a unique and valuable perspective.

Every repressive act has a technique and a target. In a future volume, we intend to focus on the targets, examining the ramifications of government interference with movements for social and economic justice. The primary focus of this book is on techniques, on the ways government discriminates against political dissenters. The stories presented in the first part describe some forms of protest prohibited by repressive government actions and introduce the repressive techniques that are examined more closely in subsequent sections. The second part sets forth the particular contributions of the legislative, executive, and judicial branches of government to the suppression of beliefs and activities that challenge established views or government policies. In the third part, the ugly extremes of police-state actions are considered. Finally, the fourth section concludes with the stories of people who lost so much to win vindication.

We came to respect the persons we interviewed for the sacrifices they made. By resisting attacks against themselves, each contributed to another American legacy—the heritage of free expression. We are grateful to all of them for that and for the cooperation and friendliness they extended to us. We were saddened to learn that, since we interviewed them, Scott Nearing, William Howard Melish, Sarah Cunningham, Edward Lamb, Jack Miller, Mike Myerson, Harvey O'Connor, and Min Yasui have passed away.

More than one hundred persons were interviewed. All told compelling and important stories that deserve a wide audience. The interviews included in this book were selected because we felt they best illustrated a particular repressive technique. Each interviewee was photographed for the portraits that accompany the stories, and each interview was tape-recorded. We were faced with the task of editing transcripts as long as one hundred pages or more, reducing them to a fraction of their original size. In editing, we tried to be true to each person's outlook and maintain his or her expression. Our edited versions were returned to the interviewees for their approval.

We appreciate the efforts of those who have helped us think about the topic and find persons to interview. We want especially to thank John Brittain, Anne Mari Buitrago, David Christiano, Richard Criley, David Flatley, Rabbi Robert Goldburg, Ernest Goodman, Curtis MacDougal, Ottilie Markholt, George Novack, Theresa Onda, Pat Richartz, Susan Sangree, and Flint Taylor for their assistance; Linda Backiel, Anne

Braden, and Karen Northcott for clarifying some legal or historical aspect of repression; Candy Hamilton for permission to use her interview of Roselyn Jumping Bull in the Leonard Peltier story; Margaret Randall for permission to include her poems "Immigration Law" and "Under Attack"; and Trinity College for the grant that carried us down the final stretch of our work. We are indebted to Frank Donner, Bruce Ellison, Morton Stavis, and William Preston for their careful and thoughtful reading of portions of this manuscript and to Mary Renaud of the University of California Press for her close attention to the manuscript and her suggestions that improved its accuracy and readability. Of course, we are responsible in the final analysis for what we have written here.

Most of all, we are grateful for the help given to us by Edith Tiger, Executive Director of the National Emergency Civil Liberties Committee. She made us think the crudest idea had potential; she boosted our morale; she was a helpful critic; and she opened doors that led to many interviews. Finally, Miriam Schultz listened to the readings of the draft of each interview and responded with only constructive suggestions. She made us feel at every turn that what we had done was more than worth the effort.

—Ruth and Bud Schultz
Hartford, Connecticut
June 1988

Foreword

Consider what presidential candidate Ronald Reagan said to Robert Scheer, crack reporter for the *Los Angeles Times,* in the spring of 1980: "There was no blacklist of Hollywood. The blacklist in Hollywood, if there was one, was provided by the communists."

I cite Reagan's comment because his Cold War obsession with communism allows him to deny the existence of an institution which he and everyone else in the industry and the political culture at the time knew to be a fact. Not only was there a Hollywood blacklist, but there was also a blacklist in the academic community, from elementary school on up to graduate school, in the trade union movement, the scientific community, and throughout the government. Conductors on the New York subway system were fired from their positions because of their politics.

The blacklist was a pervasive system, a part of the dark side of the American legacy that goes all the way back to the alien and sedition laws, reasserting itself with a vengeance during the Palmer raids, dominating the postwar decade under the misnomer of McCarthyism (since it started before McCarthy came on the scene in the early fifties), and is still with us, permeating the political culture of the eighties. It is against this thematic background, in such striking contrast to the democratic promises of our Bill of Rights, that much of the moving testimony in *It Did Happen Here* must be read.

The repression and resistance recorded here go back to the early part of the century, as in the powerful memory of Jack Miller, the IWW organizer; through our own World War II internment camps, vividly recreated by Minoru Yasui; to the moving story of the more recent attack on political activist Margaret Herring McSurely. However, the so-called McCarthy era, the domestic Cold War, provides a particularly useful perspective on the Great Fear which has periodically informed and captured our culture down through the years. It started even as World War II ended. President Truman's executive order gave the FBI the power and duty to investigate the political backgrounds of every employee of the federal government. One can get a glimpse of the great red hunt from such victims as Arthur Drayton, dismissed after twenty-five years as a postal clerk. The House Un-American Activities Committee came into the headlines in the postwar years when it began hearings alleging subversion in the entertainment industry. The Hollywood Ten refused to answer the "Are you now or have you ever been" questions on grounds of conscience. Like playwright Arthur Miller later on, they were indicted and prosecuted for contempt of Congress. But unlike Arthur Miller, in the climate of their time Ring Lardner and the others of the Hollywood Ten spent up to ten months in prison.

The Cold War heated up: the Hiss case, the Smith Act prosecutions, the Rosenberg case. China had, in the phrase of the time, gone communist. The Russians had gotten the so-called secret of the atomic bomb and exploded one of their own. We were at war in Korea. In 1951, the Un-American Activities Committee recommenced its hearings on the day Alger Hiss went to prison, and people were called up to name names. Little un-American activities committees flourished throughout the country on state and local levels, not to mention the red squads of local police departments. Collectively, they contributed to a climate of fear and political hysteria unknown before or since.

In addition to violating people's rights and in every way doing the things that the civil libertarians of today accuse them of doing, there was something else going on. It turned out that when HUAC came to Hollywood, the committee already had all the names it pretended to be seeking. An undercover Los Angeles police agent had turned in many thousands of names he had accumulated. The LAPD shared those with the FBI, which, in turn, shared them with the congressional investigating committee.

So the whole search for names was not a search for names. It was a process by which those named were stigmatized and punished for their beliefs. But more than that, it was a way of requiring submission by those who named them. Larry Parks, who played Al Jolson in *The Jolson Story,* said to the committee, "Look, I'll tell you about myself. I was a member of the Communist Party. I joined because I thought it was the most liberal thing around. But don't make me crawl through the mud like an informer. What kind of heritage is that to leave my children?" The committee insisted on it, and he did so. It was a form of what I think of as a degradation ceremony.

Nor were individuals the only ones compromised. Officers of protective organizations like the American Civil Liberties Union turn out to have been cooperating behind the scenes with the agents of this Cold War repression. There were rumors of an arrangement between the ACLU and the Un-American Activities Committee. The ACLU general counsel, Morris Ernst, met privately with FBI Director J. Edgar Hoover. The Americans for Democratic Action, organized to protect liberal humanist values, ended up spending much of its time attacking and disassociating itself from those to the left of it. Even though they simultaneously attacked the McCarthy phenomenon, by their other actions they strengthened the ability of those committees to do their work and legitimized them. The unstated message in "Hey, you've got the wrong guy" was that there is a right guy to get.

The reverberations of the domestic Cold War are still with us. The Foreign Service purge of dissenters from our China policy left no one around to dissent from our Vietnam policy. The ritualistic congressional investigations of the forties and fifties simultaneously stigmatized dissenters, wounded the left, and fueled the fantasy of an international communist monolith bent on world conquest, which eventually led to the investment of billions of dollars in a nuclear arsenal with risks that boggle the minds even of those who specialize in thinking about the unthinkable. The ideological exclusion clauses of the 1950s' McCarran-Walter Immigration Act have resulted in the denial of visas to more than eleven thousand foreigners since 1980.

Eventually the investigating committees of the Cold War era so lost their ability to punish people through accusations and exposure that they were virtually laughed out of business. This was symbolized to me when Abbie Hoffman and others mocked the committee: They screamed at the committee members; they dressed as witches and swept up and down the aisles with brooms. With their outlandish costumes and behavior, they attacked the committee's legitimacy. The committees had sullied their reputations to such an extent that the two biggest—

HUAC and SIC—first changed their names in the sixties and then were abolished in the seventies.

But when civil libertarians hailed the demise of HUAC they were celebrating a pyrrhic victory, for, in fact, the FBI under J. Edgar Hoover had already undertaken its most shameful undercover operation, COINTELPRO. The bureau was visiting direct, violent, illegal punishment on its ideological enemies—where the congressional committees had done it indirectly and, as it were, nonviolently. The FBI sent the infamous note to Martin Luther King, Jr., suggesting that he consider suicide. It infiltrated organizations on the left, with agent provocateurs who may have been responsible for the most violent acts carried out in that period. Vietnam Veterans Against the War was, as Scott Camil reveals, especially preyed upon by government agents who sought to provoke the vets into violence.

Those activities were thought to be so illegitimate and so fundamentally un-American that even the FBI denied them at the time. We found out what the FBI was doing only through the Freedom of Information Act, the Senate Select Committee that investigated intelligence agencies, and some of the political cases brought by victims of COINTELPRO, like the Socialist Workers Party and Frank Wilkinson, who tells his story below. We still don't know its full dimensions. But now it appears we are well into a phase that involves the attempt to make legitimate that which was previously illegitimate, to do overground that which the FBI used to do only underground, to use the state not so much to stigmatize as to legitimize, to make respectable that which is shameful.

One of President Reagan's first acts on assuming office was to pardon the two former FBI officials who had been convicted of authorizing break-ins without warrants and probable cause. These convictions bore a symbolic importance because they stood for the principle that the intelligence agencies must obey the law and are bound by the Constitution. Yet the president chose to view these men as heroes who were acting on what he called in his pardon statement "high principle."

By his legislative initiatives and executive orders, Reagan has restricted the free flow of information that is vital to the uninhibited exchange of ideas in a democracy. The Freedom of Information Act was a ray of sunshine, although from the outset its implementation left much to be desired. The administration, attempting to roll back the FOIA, instructed its agencies to reverse the presumption that the people have the right to know.

The 1981 Agents Identification Act, called by Professor Phil Kurland of the University of Chicago Law School "the clearest violation of the First Amendment in our history," makes it a crime to reveal the identity of any intelligence agent, even if that identity is already a matter of public record.

The Export Administration Act has been interpreted by the Department of Commerce to permit governmental interference into *un*classified university research by restricting the exchange of scientific information.

The Foreign Agents Registration Act has been interpreted to require documentary films made by the National Film Board of Canada, including the Academy Award-winning *If You Love This Planet,* to be preceded by a statement saying the films are "political propaganda." Efforts were even made by the Department of Justice to learn which groups and individuals asked to see the films.

The McCarran-Walter Act has been used to bar a wide range of individuals from our shores: Hortensia Allende, the widow of Salvadore Allende; the Reverend Ian Paisley and Owen Carron, spokesmen of radical Protestant and Catholic groups in Northern Ireland; and members of the Japanese peace movement, among many others.

It's a depressing list, and there's more: the executive order increasing the ease of classification of government documents; the institution of lie detector tests for government employees; the attempts of the president, the State Department, and others to smear the nuclear freeze movement. Potentially most ominous of all, the Reagan administration, by executive order, expanded law-enforcement authority to do political surveillance at home and unleashed the CIA for the first time to conduct operations on American soil.

I fear that in its next phase the repression may consist of scapegoating, of placing blame on those responsible for the progressive agenda of the sixties—affirmative action, gay rights, feminism, the antiwar movement—if the Reagan/Bush economic program fails, or if scandals like the Iran/Contra arms deal put the ability of the administration to govern in jeopardy, or if escalating debts and deficits hasten the decline of the United States as a world power. The danger, then, is that the search for scapegoats will take us farther down the road to a police state.

One of the lessons from the stories in this book is that to successfully resist repression we have to take the protective freedoms, most notably the First Amendment to the Constitution, seriously. Consider the man who, explaining why he named names as a HUAC witness in the fifties, said, "I'd be willing to jump off the cliff for something I believed in, but I had quit the Communist Party ten years earlier. I had a wife, two kids, and a mother to support. Why should I go to a concentration camp for something I didn't believe in?" What this man didn't understand is that the principle at stake wasn't the credo of the Communist Party. The principle was the First Amendment, the right of people not to be punished for dissenting beliefs. That is an important and fundamental element of a democratic society.

There are times when personal resistance becomes identical with public morality. If every single witness who had been called before the committee had refused to cooperate, the repressive fifties couldn't have happened the way they did. If the civil liberties organizations had stood true to their values, repression couldn't have happened the way it did. In Hollywood, if one major studio had been willing to break the blacklist and make films, people would have come to see them, and it couldn't have happened the way it did. If the talent guild, the directors' guild, the writers' guild, the screen actors' guild, if one of them had said, "If you blacklist one of our members, none of us will ever work for you," it couldn't have happened the way it did.

I hope it's not sentimentality to suggest that the examples of those who resisted and prevailed have not been lost on history. I'm thinking of people like Lillian Hellman, who told the committee she would talk about herself but not others "because I cannot and will not cut my conscience to fit this year's fashions"; or Pete Seeger, who said he would sing his songs for the committee but would not tell them what political groups he sang for and invoked the First Amendment; or the trade union organizer Tom Quinn, who said he was not hiding behind the Constitution, he was standing before it, defending it; or the character actor Lionel Stander, who told the committee he was prepared to name names, to reveal a group of conspiratorial fanatics out to undermine everything the country stood for, and started to name the members of the committee that called him. I like to believe that by their example people like these, and the many others whose voices sing out in the pages that follow, taught us how to behave—and that makes it more difficult for it to happen again.

—Victor Navasky

Part I
The Commandments of Repression

Introduction to Part I

Across this century the commandments of repression have been invoked against those who dared to think thoughts of dissent and then had the audacity to act on their thoughts. Legislatures, courts, investigating committees, loyalty programs, the FBI—all tried to silence rebellion, whether it took the form of speeches protesting child labor, songs condemning war, or sermons preaching coexistence. Education in the service of freedom and petitions for the right of Blacks to vote became targets for suppression. Nevertheless, rooted in the tradition of protest, Scott Nearing, Pete Seeger, Myles Horton, William Howard Melish, and Chuck McDew—each in his own way, time, and place—rose to stir the American conscience.

In each of their cases, cross-fertilization between government agencies and the press, employers, and vigilantes rendered the dissidents unemployable or incited racist or Cold War passions as a complement to and context for the denial of constitutional rights. But there was more to such experiences than the hardship and turmoil created. In reaction to the repression, these five and others resisted. As a result, the response to the firing of Scott Nearing established academic freedom as an honored principle; the blacklisting of Pete Seeger became symbolic of intolerable capitulation to injustice; the many-sided and sometimes life-threatening assaults on Myles Horton's school only strengthened his resolve to promote grassroots participation in the union and civil rights movements; the denial of the pulpit to Reverend Melish on transparent political grounds made similar denials less likely; and the violence of vigilantes against young Blacks like Chuck McDew betrayed the moral bankruptcy of brutal southern racism to the nation at large.

We begin with the recollections of these five because they epitomize the kinds of persons who have been under attack. Their stories, stretching from 1915 to 1969, show what repression was intended to repress, as well as the extraordinary stamina of its targets. All were prepared to accomplish their purposes against the force of established power. Scott Nearing, for example, viewed his trial under the Espionage Act as an opportunity to popularize the causes of peace and socialism. Chuck McDew said of his work in the South, "I felt that we were doing what we were doing because our fathers had not done it. The fact that the system had been in place for three hundred years was not all that impressive to us. We had the feeling that now is the time to change it and we will."

Thou Shall Not Speak

Scott Nearing

*Outside the fieldstone house he and Helen Nearing had built them-
selves, Scott Nearing, ninety-nine years old, loaded wood into a wheel-
barrow. He pushed the load toward the kitchen door, summertime
work against his last Maine winter. An assurance in the rightness of his
beliefs and a fierce self-sufficiency of thought and living had held him on
his radical course for nearly a century, as debater of Clarence Darrow,
author of fifty books, grower of his own food, brewer of maple syrup,
and guru to a later age then taken by homesteading. He began to talk
about his life in 1906 and the first case testing the principle of academic
freedom in America. It was his speeches on behalf of child labor legislation that cost him his job at the University of Pennsylvania and his writing against the First World War that led to his indictment and publicized
trial under the Espionage Act of 1917.*

At the beginning of the 1880s there was a profoundly religious
Quaker named Joseph Wharton. He came from a well-to-do family and
he was president of Bethlehem Steel Corporation. Bethlehem Steel was
very closely interwoven with the arms trust group in Pennsylvania. That

SCOTT NEARING

whole area in there, including du Pont to the south, was an arms-producing, dynamite-manufacturing area.

Joseph Wharton didn't wear a collar button, nor a cuff button nor a watch chain. He was an austere Quaker. He was also rich enough to give three-quarters of a million dollars to the University of Pennsylvania to found the Wharton School of Finance and Economy. He was the patron saint of that department of the university.

When Mr. Wharton gave this gift to the university, he also gave a statement upholding and supporting protection, as against free trade. He made speeches to the students again and again publicizing Bethlehem Steel and protection and these other elements for which he was one of the most vocal champions. And when I got to teach at the Wharton School in 1906, from 1906 to 1915, it was already an accepted thing that you were for protection, that you were for big business.

I was from a coal and lumber county in northeastern Pennsylvania. I had been born and brought up in a company town in which the Morris Run Coal Company owned the roads, the schools, the churches, the shops, the houses. My grandfather was the superintendent of the Morris Run Coal Company, and he ran the town and all its activities. He was known as Czar Nearing. I didn't follow along in this aspect of my grandfather's footsteps.

In the country where I grew up lay a number of important coal veins. And in this country stood some of the finest timber that you ever saw. It was a land of rich natural resources. One of the first memories that I have was getting an opportunity to talk as a youngster in favor of the conservation of natural resources. I remember this very distinctly. I didn't know very much and I couldn't say very much, but I was, what shall I say, ready to talk against the family interests.

I started to teach at the Wharton School when I was twenty-three. From that time forward, I found myself in a little group, a little complex of young men who held what you would then call the liberal progressive point of view of Bob La Follette and Theodore Roosevelt. We were a rising generation of progressive thinkers, young people who had more or less the same background. We were beginning to recognize domination by big business over not only the pocketbook of the country but the mind of the country.

I don't know why I was the one in our group who eventually got fired. I suppose it was because I was rather vocal. As a youth I was exceedingly shy. I had difficulty expressing myself in public. I couldn't teach and I couldn't speak. So I went to Temple University and took courses in public speaking—public presentation, they called it. It was a four-year program, which I finished in three years at the same time I was finishing my work at the University of Pennsylvania. That's why I had a little advantage over the rest of these young fellows.

The employment of children in industry for wages had become a controversial issue. There was a labor department of the state government, but comparatively little regulatory legislation. And nobody paid any attention to the factory laws we had. They weren't intended to be enforced. The employers and manufacturers did about as they pleased.

Pennsylvania child labor became notorious in the textile mills, in the glass factories, in the nut and bolt shops, and other shops producing small things children could easily handle. And it was notorious in the mines. All through the mine there were wooden partitions that sealed up each section so it was more or less poison-proof. When they shot off blasts in one section, the partition was closed so the other side continued to have fresh air. Children stayed by the doors to open and close them at the proper times.

The breaker boy worked on the outside of the mine. Coal was hauled out in cars by mule or by hand and then dumped over a rather steep place where it slid down an incline. As it went down, breaker boys picked out the stone and the slate and the other so-called impure matters and left the coal to slide on down the hill. Any smart youngster at four or five or six or ten who could separate stone and slate from coal might make a good breaker boy or girl. They worked as long as the mine worked. Sometimes it would start up and work for two hours, sometimes eight or nine hours.

A friend of mine, Sally Cleghorn, said of that time: "The golf links lie so near the mill / that almost any day / the working children can look out / and see the men at play." It was true. The golf course was here and the mill or mine tipple was just over yonder. They were both operating at the same time.

I became interested in the conditions surrounding the employment of children in factories, mines, and other workplaces in my native state. Child labor had become so notorious that the Pennsylvania Child Labor Committee was set up to oppose it. I joined that group, and after two years I was made the secretary. I gave many speeches throughout the state condemning the exploitation of children. I went to women's clubs and other organizations where people had no idea there was such a thing as child labor. But the university authorities thought I should confine my activities to the classroom and should not speak in public.

I taught at the Wharton School for nine years, and until the last year I was only an instructor. Now, usually after the first three or five years, if you didn't get promoted you were dropped from the teaching staff. Generally speaking, if you did your job, and unless there was some extreme reason like a divorce or a scandal or something of that kind, you were promoted. Either you did your job and got promoted, or you didn't do your job and were dropped. I did my job, but I didn't get promoted.

When promotion time came around and they passed me up, the *North American,* a Philadelphia businessman's paper with an editor who was more or less of our way of thinking, became concerned. It raised the question, Why is this particular teacher passed over? I had taught as well as I could. My classes were well attended. The boys and the girls in the classes were, what shall we say, well satisfied. They thought they were learning something. I began to get more speaking engagements outside the university. Macmillan had published six of my books. Two of them were textbooks which were selling very well. Nevertheless, year after year I was kept on as a teacher but not promoted academically.

I didn't think I was going to be able to make a living teaching for more than a few years. I'd probably get kicked out. You see, a teacher has an ethical problem: Shall he keep his job, period, and do whatever he must do to hold it? Or should he risk the livelihood of his family by telling the truth, whatever it happens to be, and perhaps find himself out on the street? In that case you have a profession and you can't practice it anymore. I knew in advance what I was going to do.

I was dismissed on the sixteenth of June, 1915, in a curt letter from the provost of the university, Edgar F. Smith. He wrote, "Dear Mr. Nearing: Your services at the university will not be continued after this year." In other words, you're fired. They never talked to me. They didn't even bother to explain except to say, you'll not be hired another year. And they waited until the faculty left the university, until the whole place was on vacation—then they pulled this thing off.

A *North American* reporter went to see J. Levering Jones, who was one of the most influential of the trustees. There were twenty-three trustees representing twenty-three points of view of business. The reporter said, "Why have you dismissed this man?" Mr. Levering Jones answered, "When I dismiss a stenographer, do I have to give a public reason?" So that was our status. Like any stenographer, if you didn't do your job, out you went. And that was the extent of academic freedom in 1915 and throughout that period. There was no tenure, no such thing.

Professor Leightner Witmer was head of the Psychology Department of the University of Pennsylvania. Witmer and I were at swords' points on the war, which was on then. Professor P. H. Shelling, head of the English Department, was extremely pro-British and extremely pro-military in his outlook. However, these professors supported me. Witmer wrote a book about my dismissal, *The Nearing Case*. "If they can do that to you," he said, "they can do that to me. They don't have to give you a reason. They don't have to even give you any notice. You're fired!" One hundred percent of our faculty at the Wharton School were for me and against this dismissal. But it was already done. I was one of the army of unemployed.

Of course my activities contributed to my dismissal. The Pennsylvania State Manufacturers Association was opposed to child labor legislation. They wanted freedom to do as they pleased, and they didn't want the state to step in and interfere in any way. They didn't just *try* to influence the state legislature, they *influenced* it. The university had been getting about a million dollars a year from the legislature. The story is that when the university came in 1915 to ask for money, legislators said, "How about that fellow Nearing on the Child Labor Committee? What is he doing? Does he have to stay?" That undoubtedly was related to my dismissal.

I was invited to go to the University of Toledo, which was a municipal university, owned and operated by the city through a board of nine trustees. I had a friend on the board of trustees, Dr. John S. Pyle, a surgeon with liberal leanings. As a matter of fact, he was a socialist at the time. All together, there were enough trustees representing the trade union movement and the La Follette forces who were in favor of academic freedom and worked to secure my appointment.

By the time the war was two years gone, things were different from what they had been in 1915, when I was first hired at the University of Toledo. You were now told: "Sit down. You're rocking the boat." The boat was on the way to war. Every day, every day, every day, the rah-rah boys in various positions, preachers and teachers and newspapermen, were saying, "Whatever you do, don't rock the boat."

The war hysteria mounted. The right to conduct meetings was canceled. Canceled? There weren't any meetings. When people like us tried to hold meetings against the war, we were called traitors. People who opposed the war were fired without it disturbing anybody. They lost their jobs widely and freely. I was fired from Toledo in 1917. But if I had "sat down and not rocked the boat," there would have been no further question about my job.

A meeting of the board of trustees was held to vote for my dismissal or retention at the university. One of the trustees who supported me was Ben Johnson, a liberal lawyer. In some way or other he was persuaded not to go to the trustees' meeting. When the vote came up, nobody could find him. That gave them a majority of one. The most crucial people on the board were liberals, and they could stand just so much pressure. I wasn't surprised that they did what they did. Why not? After all, it was their bread and butter. And the pressure of the times and the pressure of Toledo and big business were too great.

I left Toledo to teach at Chautauqua Summer School. My house was empty except for my secretary, who was staying there. Federal agents came with a search warrant and took all my opened and unopened letters, everything they could lay their hands on, including research notes for a book I was preparing.

Sometime later, I wrote a pamphlet that was published before the end of the war. It was a simple little thirty-two-page pamphlet called *The Great Madness*. President Wilson had said in one of his speeches at the time, "Madness has entered everything," describing the war situation. I took that idea as the title for the pamphlet. I analyzed the causes of the war: the political causes, the economic causes, and so on, showing that it was not a war of patriotism or a war for democracy, but a definite businessman's war. The war was making the machine go. You've got to recollect that in 1913 we were in a very bad depression, and in order for the machine to start again, you had to have orders. The war served that purpose.

The Espionage Act that was enacted ostensibly to cope with the German spy system was used against people like me who opposed the war. Why not? What's a "spy act" really for, except to prevent people of a certain point of view from influencing policy? An indictment against me under the Espionage Act was handed down in New York after the end of the war. That was in the fall of 1918.

I was charged with writing *The Great Madness,* a pamphlet that would interfere with recruitment and enlistment in the armed forces of the United States. The "evidence" was that any young man reading it might or would refuse to go into the armed forces, to enlist or be conscripted. Therefore it was treasonable, and therefore I should be punished. It carried up to a twenty-year sentence in the penitentiary.

We had a meeting of interested people in New York about the indictment. We said, now here's a chance to publicize our views about the war. Because the pamphlet was part of the indictment, we used it in presenting our case. When I was on the stand, my attorney, Seymour Stedman, said, "Mr. Nearing, turn to page three of this pamphlet. Would you read paragraph two?" And so I read that. Then he said to the jury, "My client will now defend this paragraph." We spent eight days going through the pamphlet, paragraph by paragraph, and I gave a detailed explanation each time. The newspapers and magazines were full of it. We said we didn't care if we were to be found guilty or not. We were interested in furthering the cause of peace and socialism in America. It was the obvious thing to do.

In the end, the jury acquitted me for writing the pamphlet and convicted the Rand School for publishing it.

Toledo was the last teaching job I held. After that, nobody would hire me. I had intended to make teaching my life job. I prepared myself to teach, and I went on teaching until I was fired. Since then I've been homesteading in the hills of Vermont and then in the hills of Maine. I've been writing all the time, writing as much as I could or should, and speaking up on every possible occasion.

Thou Shall Not Sing

Pete Seeger

Pete throws his head back, his voice reaches above the audience's, his banjo rings out. He and his audience sing as one: "Wimoweh," "Which Side Are You On?" "If I Had a Hammer," "Big Muddy."

For more than four decades, Pete Seeger's songs have given inspiration to protest. He has sung with Woody Guthrie in a union hall ringed by company thugs; from the flatbed truck made into a stage at Peekskill, New York; on the civil rights march from Selma to Montgomery; at a New England benefit for demonstrators arrested at a nuclear power plant; and to 750,000 peace marchers packed into Central Park. He has found audiences in hobo jungles, on picket lines, in school auditoriums, on the deck of the Hudson River sloop the Clearwater, *and in Carnegie Hall.*

Because he sang for unpopular causes, he was investigated for sedition, picketed by superpatriots, harassed by the FBI, and called before the House Un-American Activities Committee (HUAC). He was blacklisted with the other members of the Weavers at the height of their popularity, when their songs were on the Hit Parade. He was shut out of radio, recordings, clubs, television, but he could not be kept from

PETE SEEGER

singing or profoundly affecting a new generation of musicians who, with him, gave voice to the protest movements of the sixties.

The Peekskill riot was in September 1949. From the conversations I've had with various people, it now seems pretty clear it was organized by the Ku Klux Klan, which had members in the local police departments. When Paul Robeson made the statement in Paris that American Blacks would not fight against the Soviet Union, the one country that had outlawed race discrimination,* they were outraged. He touched America's Achilles' heel, and when he was going to give a concert in Peekskill, they said, "Let's get him."

The mob came to the site of the concert, overturned the stage, beat up the people who were setting up the public address system, and the police didn't do a thing to stop it. The police just stood there and made sure that the Ku Kluxers did what they wanted to do. But then they were surprised because Robeson got on the radio and said, "I've got a right to sing anywhere I want to. I'm going to sing in Peekskill next week."

The next week ten thousand people came to hear him. The field was surrounded by a thousand or more union members, shoulder to shoulder, to see that no mob would get in to disrupt the concert. There were people with eagle eyes standing next to Robeson.

There was an opposition crowd of maybe one hundred to one hundred fifty at the gate. They were hollering things like "Go back to Russia! Kikes! Nigger lovers!" There were about three or four policemen, though, who kept the gate open. The ten thousand or more people drove their cars in, parked them, and then sat down and enjoyed a wonderful concert. I was among the singers in the first half. Robeson did me

---

* Internationally acclaimed Black singer and actor Paul Robeson was a powerful spokesman for civil rights as early as the 1930s. Advocating independence for the colonial peoples of Africa, allying himself with the left, and praising the Soviet Union for its treatment of Black people, at the height of the Cold War hysteria he was denied access to the concert stage in the United States, denied a passport and cut off from his international audiences, subpoenaed before congressional investigating committees, and blacklisted from radio and television. Robeson's extraordinary stature is conveyed by the comments of a friend: "Paul was a man and a half," wrote actor Ossie Davis, "and we have no category, even now, to hold the size of him. Something about him escapes our wildest, most comprehensive embrace, and we've never been able to put our finger on exactly what it is. Athletic champion, yes; Phi Beta Kappa scholar, singer, actor, spokesman, activist, leader—yes! Africanist, socialist, Black nationalist—all that too, but something more, something new, something different" (Philip S. Foner, ed., *Paul Robeson Speaks* [New York: Brunner/Mazel, 1978], p. 23).

the honor. I was very unknown and very unskilled, but I sang three or four songs, including the song "If I Had a Hammer." Then Robeson took over the second half. At the end of the concert, the crowd moved very slowly out the gate. It must have been an hour and a half at least before my family and I finally got our car through.

I wanted to turn left because my home was north of Peekskill. A policeman said, "No, all cars go here." He pointed south, along the road which is ironically called Division Street. We hadn't gone but a hundred yards when I saw glass on the road. My wife and two baby children, my father-in-law, and two friends were all in a little jeep station wagon. I said, "Oh-oh, I see glass. You better be prepared to duck. Somebody may want to throw a stone."

Ha! What an understatement. There were young men with piles of stones waist high waiting around each bend. Each stone was about as big as a baseball. Wham! Into every car that passed they would throw a stone at close range with all their strength. There must have been at least fifteen or twenty of these piles.

We ran a gauntlet. Every window but the rear window was broken. Two stones came through completely, and I later cemented them into the fireplace in my house so I would never forget them. At one point there was a policeman standing not more than a hundred feet from a man throwing stones. I stopped, and I said, "Officer, aren't you going to do something?" He said, "Move on, move on." I looked around. The man in back of me couldn't move because I was in front of him, and he was getting stone after stone after stone. He was a sitting duck. So I moved on.

When we got back home, we put our children in the shower and washed the broken glass out of their hair. No one in our car was hurt, but others were. One person at the concert lost his eyesight. Robeson himself was saved by people who put their bodies on top of his.

In Peekskill there were signs in many windows, bumper stickers on many cars, and more signs in barrooms saying, "Wake up, America! Peekskill did." They were quite frankly calling for the rest of the country to start a wave of terror against anybody who could be suspected of being a Communist or a Communist sympathizer.

Following Peekskill, there were many people who said this was the beginning of fascism in America. This was the way Hitler started in Germany. The police were going to stand by and watch the fascists lynch and murder and kill. However, I was not convinced. And I remember not being convinced. I knew some relatively well-to-do people who were leaving the country, going to Mexico or England or Canada. I knew some people who were burning their books. I did participate in a project to microfilm our song library, which is a priceless collection of labor songs. But I wasn't convinced that things were going to be as bad as some of my friends said they were going to be.

About a month or six weeks after the Peekskill affair, many of those "Wake up, America" signs disappeared. Although I don't have any proof, I'm personally convinced that in many a family there was an argument. It might have been a grandmother who said, "You mean you threw stones at women and children? Well, I don't like these people either, but still you don't throw stones at women and children." There is a strain of decency in America. I bet there were people saying, "Well, is this what Thomas Jefferson was talking about? Is this what Abe Lincoln was talking about? I mean, we've heard of lynchings down South. Do we really like them?" And so while there was terror in many places and disaster in many places during the 1950s, Peekskill actually wasn't repeated.

The McCarthy period was perhaps an extreme case in American history. But it's been known throughout American life, in one form or another, for three hundred years. It's been known throughout the world for as long as recorded history that if you have unpopular opinions you're going to be persecuted. This happened in the religious wars. It happens in any tense period, especially when there is a fear of war.

During the Cold War anybody could be persecuted who was called a Communist or a Communist sympathizer or a fellow traveler or who associated with fellow travelers. The list grew longer and longer, and the net was thrown wider and wider. People lost their jobs. Friends said, "I'm sorry. It's not personal. But I just can't speak to you anymore. Please don't telephone me again. Please don't write me a letter. Please don't visit me." So, for many people who had never been through this, it was very frightening.

I was much better off than most people in the 1950s. I didn't have any job I could be fired from. I'd always been broke, making five dollars here and ten dollars there. And my family all stuck very closely together. My mother-in-law and father-in-law, as well as my own father, supported me going out and singing songs about unpopular opinions in "strange" places. I did feel that I should sing them.

I moved up to Beacon, New York, in 1949–1950. I wanted to become a member of the Beacon community. I really wanted to settle down there for the rest of my life, in spite of whatever difficulties there might be. I also wanted to sing as widely as I could. My audiences were not big in the 1950s. But we sang pretty good just the same. And the funny thing was, because of a fluke, the Weavers got some of their songs well known in 1950 and 1951. We were singing "Wimoweh" and "Saints Go Marching In."

During the 1950s I sang songs like:

> Last night I had the strangest dream
> I never dreamed before.
> I dreamed the world had all agreed
> To put an end to war. *

I sang that to audiences in schools and camps and colleges. And before "We Shall Overcome" was so well known in the 1960s, I was singing it throughout the 1950s. I learned it in the forties from a woman in Tennessee. She learned it from Black people in North Carolina. A man I taught it to took the song south in 1960 and taught it to students sitting at a lunch counter in Greensboro, North Carolina. They added new verses and gave it a better rhythm than I had. Six months later, it was known throughout the freedom movement.

The 1950s had a lot of good songs. They weren't as widely known as they are now, but Woody Guthrie's "This Land Is Your Land" got started then. Robert De Cormier's Jewish Young People's Chorus adopted it as their theme song. They loved it. I learned it from them, actually. I never heard Woody sing it much. I heard it on Woody's record, I guess, put out by Folkways. It sold, maybe, all of a thousand copies.

In 1953, when the Weavers were blacklisted out of work, I started teaching. Then, some of the kids I sang to in summer camp asked me to come to their colleges. They'd grown up, and I suddenly realized that I could make a living singing for college students. I went from Oberlin to Antioch and then widened my list of friends till I was singing at more "respectable" colleges. By the end of the 1950s, I was even singing at some state colleges. Of course, I was picketed from time to time by the American Legion or John Birch type of people, but this only sold tickets. It was funny. My manager and I used to laugh. He'd say, "Now, if this

---

* "Last Night I Had the Strangest Dream," words and music by Ed McCurdy. TRO—© copyright 1950 (renewed 1978), 1951 (renewed 1979), and 1955 (renewed 1983) Almanac Music, Inc., New York, N.Y. Used by permission.

concert doesn't look like it's going to sell out, we'll just have to arrange for you to be picketed."

So when people look upon me as having had a hard time, I have to dissuade them of this. Some people had their lives ruined by the blacklist. Some people committed suicide. But I was a moving target. I called it cultural guerrilla tactics. I not only managed to survive the 1950s, but I enlarged my audience and learned. Some of the best songs I ever wrote in my life were made up during that period, like "Where Have All the Flowers Gone?"

In 1955, I was hauled up before the House Committee on Un-American Activities along with about thirty other people who were actors and musicians of one sort or another in New York City. The committee claimed that it was investigating the Communist conspiracy in the entertainment business. Of course, they were just investigating heresy, their own definition of heresy. They came to New York at that particular time because some of the liberal entertainment unions like the American Federation of Television and Radio Artists were resisting McCarthyism. "Now hold on," they said. "Why do we have to join the witch-hunt?" And these HUAC hearings were supposed to slap down that kind of liberalism.

When they hauled me up, I felt I was in a much stronger position than the average person. There was no job I could be fired from. So I didn't have to bother using the Fifth Amendment, which says, in effect, you have no right to ask *me* this question. Instead, I relied on the First Amendment. I simply said, "These are questions I don't think *any* American should be forced to answer, especially under the threat of reprisal." So I just clammed up. I didn't feel like cooperating with them one little bit. But I was urged to be polite: "Answer your name and address. When they start asking you questions you feel you shouldn't answer, at that point, don't." I'm only sorry I hadn't done what Robeson did. He stood up and shouted at them. He pointed his finger and said, "You are the un-Americans. This whole hearing is a disgrace. *You* are the un-Americans."

The committee asked me, "Did you ever sing a song called 'Wasn't That a Time' at such and such a place?" I sang that song from time to time, and I still do. It was written by Lee Hays and Walter Lowenfels in 1948. It had a verse for Valley Forge, a verse for Gettysburg, a verse for World War II, and it had a verse for the McCarthyite days, the Cold War. But it ended on an optimistic note. Lee Hays said: "We dare to reach out our hands . . . our faith cries out. Isn't this a time, a time to free the soul of man."

When the committee asked me about that song, I said, "Well, that's a good song, and I know it. I'll sing it for you."

"No. We don't want to hear it. We want to know, did you sing it on such and such a place and date?" I said, "I would be glad to sing any song I ever sang. But as to where I've sung them, I think that's no business of this committee. I've got a right to sing these songs. I've got a right to sing them anywhere."

Finally the committee dismissed me. A year later, I was cited for contempt of Congress because I had refused to answer the committee's questions. A year after that, I was indicted by the Justice Department and, in 1961, tried and convicted. When I went before the judge, I wanted to sing the song again. He said, "No, you may not sing it." He sentenced me to a year in jail. And I remarked, "Well, maybe you'll hear it some other time. It's still a good song."

Historically, I believe I was correct in refusing to answer their questions. Down through the centuries, this trick has been tried by various establishments throughout the world. They force people to get involved in the kind of examination that has only one aim and that is to stamp out dissent.

One of the things I'm most proud of about my country is the fact that we did lick McCarthyism back in the fifties on this issue. Many Americans knew their lives and their souls were being struggled for, and they fought it. And I felt I should carry on. I didn't feel myself being particularly heroic. I was doing what came naturally. My family and friends stood behind me. And all around the world people sent in dimes and dollars to help pay the legal expenses.

A year later, when the appeals court unanimously acquitted me, I felt vindicated, although all through the sixties I still had to occasionally face picket lines and bomb threats. But I simply went ahead, doing my thing, throughout that whole period. I fought for peace in the fifties. And in the sixties, during the Vietnam war, when anarchists and pacifists and socialists, Democrats and Republicans, decent-hearted Americans, all recoiled with horror at the bloodbath, we came together. I sang for the biggest audience I ever sang for in Washington, D.C., in November 1969. I sang "Give Peace a Chance" for half a million people, it looked like.

We've got to fight like hell so people don't get persecuted now when they speak out. People have a right to hold an unpopular opinion. You can attack them if you want, attack them with words, but you don't fire them or put them in jail because you disagree with their opinions, no matter if they're spoken or sung.

MYLES HORTON

Thou Shall Not Teach

Myles Horton

Myles Horton is plain, engaging, and warm, an Appalachian institution, an American educator who "teaches" people to trust themselves and change their world. Underneath his wry mountain wit is a devotion to grassroots democracy, inspiring and indestructible. Highlander, the integrated school he set up in the mountains of Tennessee more than fifty years ago, has counted among its supporters Reinhold Niebuhr, Harry Golden, Eleanor Roosevelt, and Martin Luther King, Jr. Used in the thirties to train organizers for the CIO (Congress of Industrial Organizations) and in the sixties to train civil rights activists and to teach the literacy skills that qualified Blacks to vote, Highlander has always single-mindedly pursued the goal of human empowerment. "Highlander showed me a different direction in which to project my thoughts and actions," said Rosa Parks, whose refusal to move to the back of the bus inspired the Montgomery bus boycott.[1] Subjected to vigilante attacks, trumped-up arrests, and congressional witch-hunts, Highlander survived them all.

I grew up in a religious background, like most people in the South. And poor. We were living in the country, sharecropping. I had to start work away from home when I was fifteen. I wanted to do something in the way of education, and I assumed I could get a job in the mountains in some kind of college or high school. I wanted my teaching to have to do with helping people live a more creative life. I also wanted to help people deal with economic problems, because it was such a poor area.

There were no examples or models of the education I had in mind. After I spent about five years trying to find them, including visiting schools in this country and other countries, I decided that the best thing to do was to think through the principles I believed in, set up a school that would enable me to teach that way, and then get a job teaching in it. That's how the Highlander Folk School came about, in 1932.

Highlander was located in Grundy County, one of the eleven poorest counties in the United States. We used education as a way of organizing. We made it clear that we weren't bringing people together to tell them what to do. We had confidence in their ability to share their experiences and learn from each other and learn to trust their own judgment. That's pretty much what Highlander has always done. And we did organize. We had eighty percent of the adult population in that county in unions of one kind or another—women, men, everybody.

Most of the district directors of the WPA * tried to discourage union organization. WPA workers were getting nineteen dollars and twenty cents a month, practically nothing. We got pretty desperate. A friend of mine got me the WPA manual that was sent to the regional directors. The manual made clear that you could have a union. That became the textbook in the county. We passed it around and studied it. People sat under trees and would read it. Those people really got to know the law. Then, armed with that information, they were emboldened to organize a union and make demands.

But after that we had trouble. Colonel Berry, who was the state administrator of the WPA, made a statement that was carried in all the papers. He said that Highlander was feeding mountain people "Moscowitz hops," teaching them communism. He hated Highlander. He hated unions, hated Black people, hated minorities. He was just a real autocrat. So we feuded with him.

At that time, there was no welfare or food stamp program. So we started a co-op in our neighborhood. Some government officials came down to visit and got all excited about it. One of them, Camille Ross,

* The Works Progress Administration (WPA) was a New Deal work relief program launched in 1935 to offset the effects of the Great Depression by providing federally supported jobs to five million unemployed.

helped us write up a proposal for a grant. When the money came, it was announced in the paper. The local politicians got hold of it and said, "Here's government money going to that bunch of Communists up there." They demanded that the agency that gave the grant to us withdraw the money. And they withdrew it.

Then they brought in Billy Sunday, the famous evangelist, to rant and rave about the Communists taking over. In his later days Billy Sunday had kind of lost his appeal and was being hired by coal companies to preach the old scripture stuff against unions. Now he preached that Highlander was the devil, a mark of the beast, a terrible blight that was going to wipe out civilization. He got himself all worked up and did a great sermon, and that afternoon he keeled over and died of a stroke. It was the last sermon he preached.

We had an old patriarch in the community, Uncle Billy Thomas. He was a great, great man, a local lay minister, a coffin maker, a chair maker, a patriarch. And he said, "That preacher, he's not preachin' God's word. The Bible is the history of the rich trying to oppress the poor, and God's always on the side of the poor. So when he was preachin' against Highlander, which was for the poor, he didn't have the Bible on his side. That's why the Lord struck him dead."

Sunday said he was on the Lord's side and we were on the devil's side, but after what happened we weren't quite sure.

From the beginning there was opposition to Highlander. After we got involved with the Wilder strike in 1932, the coal company actually hired somebody to kill some of the Highlander students and staff. Two or three people were targeted. We had to guard the place night and day for two weeks.

The Southern Manufacturers Association financed a statewide program to get rid of Highlander. The Southern Association was organized because some manufacturers thought the National Association of Manufacturers was communistic. They spent two years organizing what was called the Grundy County Crusaders. Finally, the Crusaders supposedly got an impressive list of people, the head of the Girl Scouts and the heads of other organizations, to sponsor a newspaper advertisement stating that Highlander was subversive, communistic, and un-American.

At that time, the state director of the CIO, Paul Christopher, taught at Highlander. He had a lot of influence in Tennessee. I called Paul about one o'clock in the morning and told him what happened. He got on the phone and woke up the officials of the listed organizations and asked them if they had signed the ad. Most said no, they hadn't, and their organizations hadn't sponsored it. Those people called the *Nashville Tennessean,* and the paper canceled the ad for the next day.

The Crusaders were put on the spot, since they hadn't been able to deliver. In desperation, they decided to use violence. They planned to burn down the school. They made big announcements and tried to rouse the people in Grundy County. After a rally, several hundred Crusaders started marching from Tracy City. They were four miles away, and they were really mad. They were drinking and they had guns.

Our neighbors came over. They all wanted to know how they could help. Highlander meant a lot to them. It was their community center. The kids came and took shower baths there. They played there. We had a nursery school, a youth program, a camp for children, and recreation facilities.

The neighbors decided to get Uncle Billy Thomas. The old preacher was sick. They put a mattress in the back of the station wagon and went over to where he lived, about a mile away. They got him out of bed, wrapped him up, and brought him over here. He came in and said, "You didn't need to bother me."

"But Uncle Billy, the Crusaders are just two miles away, and they are getting closer. They're yelling, 'We're going to burn this place down!'"

Uncle Billy said, "I been preaching to you all these years, and I been telling you that the Bible is the story of the rich people oppressing the poor and God is on the side of the poor. Now, this is a poor people's school. You are all poor people. And if you believe me, you'd know they ain't going to bother this place. God won't let them bother this place."

They said, "But Uncle Billy, some of them are right out in front. Some of them just came by."

"They'll turn back," he said. "God will turn them back. Now take me home." They took him home. In about ten minutes, our lookouts said the Crusaders had turned back. The people swore it was exactly the time Uncle Billy said they would. They said Uncle Billy just came and laid the Lord on the drunken rabble and they turned around and went back.

The next morning, I ran into some mountain people in town. I said, "Hey, I missed you last night."

They said, "We were out there. Nobody seen us, but we were there. Now, Myles, we love you, and we're not going to let anything happen to you. They would never have got anyone near Highlander." I found out that about twenty people had been out in the woods with high-powered rifles. They were waiting for the Crusaders where they had to turn off the main road to come to Highlander. When the Crusaders realized they were there, they turned around and left. They knew they would never have gotten a block down that narrow road. Uncle Billy was working one end of the line and these mountain neighbors were working the other. Those Crusaders didn't have a chance.

By the time the CIO was formed, Highlander had more contacts in the South than anybody else. They asked us for organizers, and we recommended people for most of their key jobs. When the CIO organized unions, they sent their members to Highlander for training, because that's where they got their ideas and they liked our way of working. Pretty soon Highlander became the educational center of the CIO in the South.

In the early days, the policy was to welcome anybody who could help build the CIO. They didn't care whether you were Communist or reactionary or Catholic or the AFL. This policy was very sound because it involved a tremendous number of people. Anybody who had any interest in building a labor movement had a chance to work. The Communist Party had more trained people who were used to working and organizing than any other political group in America at that time. John L. Lewis, the head of the CIO, had no problem using Communists because he wanted to get the unions organized and they were good organizers. He was glad to have them.

Later, the time came when the unions got fairly strong. They were strong enough to start fighting among themselves for power. Phil Murray, who by then was head of the CIO, tried to promote a program of labor-management sharing. The opposition to Murray wasn't just from the Communists. Many of us were against that, because the program would be dominated by management. John L. Lewis was opposed to that idea. I was absolutely against it. I believed it would do away with union militancy.

There was a priest from Pittsburgh who went all out for the Cold War. His whole religion was fighting communism. Murray was influenced by him and kicked out all of the known Communists. In the process, they kicked out some people who had never been Communists, simply because they were opposed to Murray. They just made them "Communists" and threw them out because that was a good way to get rid of the opposition. I know a lot of people who were never Communists, who were actually anti-communist, and were thrown out because they were against the Murray administration of the CIO.

Highlander was an official CIO school, really, from their point of view and, they assumed, from ours, because we were heart and soul with them. We really believed organizing industrial unions was the biggest, most important thing we could do. We were organizing integrated unions. A Highlander staff member organized the first integrated CIO textile union in the South. And we got some real democratic participation in the unions. We had a free hand to do things like that. So we liked to work with the CIO.

But they told us that we'd have to stop working with unions that wouldn't bar Communists from holding office, like the Mine, Mill and Smelter Workers. The CIO educational director, George Guernsey, was a wonderful guy who worked with Highlander a lot. He came down and said, "Now, Myles, I know this is a very touchy thing with you 'cause I know how stubborn you are, and how much you value your independence. But if you're going to be the CIO's official school, you're going to have to change."

I said, "The CIO can do whatever it wants to do, but we're going to have the Mine, Mill and Smelter Workers here next week. They're going to come. Now, George, let me tell you what the problem is. The ore miners who come from Alabama are Black preachers. They are Baptists, Methodists, fundamentalists. They preach the gospel right out of the Book."

I asked him, "Did you ever pray before a class?" He said, "No." I said, "They pray before everything. They're the prayingest damn bunch we've ever had. I'm going to have a hard time telling these people they're Communists and they can't come here again. And that's just half the problem. The other half of the people who will be here are from Michie, Tennessee. They work in the lime hill mines over there. And the union president is probably a member of the Klan."

He said, "What!"

"Yeah. And he's a good leader. And other people there are Klansmen. Now I gotta tell a bunch of preachers they're Communists, and I gotta turn around and tell a bunch of Klansmen they're Communists. You go back and tell the people in Washington what kind of problem I've got. And just tell them I ain't going to do it."

During the McCarthy period, the Senate Internal Security Subcommittee, which was run by Senator James Eastland, was investigating those of us who were working with Blacks. They were trying to harass us and make charges of communism to scare Black people away so they wouldn't associate with us. When I was called before the committee in

1954, they wanted me to name names of people who had been at Highlander and who had been associated with me in various activities. I refused to do that. I told them I'd be glad to answer any questions about myself, because I never had any problem talking about what I believe. In fact, I spent my life talking about what I believe. But I wouldn't talk about anybody else.

I'd learned from my good friend Alexander Meiklejohn that when this country was born, all power was vested in the people. They had taken power away from the British and had it in their hands. The people had to decide what to do with that power. So they decided to delegate some of it to a federal government and some to state governments. But there was one power that they never delegated to the state or federal government. That was the power of freedom of speech and of petition. They said, "We'll keep that to ourselves. That's something we're not going to let anybody handle."

So I said to the Eastland Committee, "I still have that. I have that power that was never delegated to you or to anybody else, and I am going to exercise it. If the freedom to speak means anything, it means the freedom not to speak. Because if you can make me speak, if you can tell me what to say, then I have no freedom. That's the power over which your committee has no jurisdiction. It's just up to me and my conscience."

Eastland got furious: "I'm going to cite you for contempt if you don't answer the questions." And I said, "I don't see that that will be much of a problem, senator. I'm willing to testify that I'm in contempt of this committee. I'm in contempt of you and everything you stand for." And he said, "Throw him out!" I was picked up by a couple of federal marshals and thrown down on the marble steps of the court of justice.

We had come to the conclusion that we couldn't make much headway working toward democracy without dealing with the problem of racism. Out of that kind of thinking another Highlander program grew. Most of the people who became leaders of the Student Nonviolent Coordinating Committee attended Highlander workshops. We also developed the Citizenship School Program, which spread all over the South. It finally became the official program of the Southern Christian Leadership Conference.

We had the same experience with the civil rights movement we had with the CIO. People who had already been to Highlander became leaders of the civil rights movement, so Highlander was kind of on the inside. Rosa Parks started things off in Montgomery by refusing to get off her seat on the bus. That wasn't just one of those fluke things. For a Black person to violate the law and custom, to carry out an act of civil disobedience, takes a lot of thinking and courage. It isn't just something somebody does incidentally.

A Black labor organizer in Montgomery, E. D. Nixon, a pullman porter, immediately took that situation and organized it. It took what Rosa Parks and E. D. Nixon did to lay the basis for the great bus boycott in Montgomery. Then Martin Luther King, Jr., joined in and became the leader everyone knows about.

Fortunately, the Communist issue was never a big issue in the civil rights movement. It was an issue for some northern supporters, liberals, but not in the South, not with SNCC, and not with the Southern Christian Leadership Conference. King would just not allow it. He knew it could be the most divisive thing that could happen to the movement.

But the opposition tried. The governor of Georgia appropriated money to send an undercover photographer, a man named Ed Friend, to take pictures of Highlander's twenty-fifth anniversary in 1957. He took a whole lot of them. There were pictures of Blacks and whites swimming together, Blacks and whites dancing together, eating together, meeting together, and so on. They put one of those pictures on billboards all over the South, captioned "Highlander, A Communist Training School." The John Birch Society and the Governor's Committee of the State of Georgia put them out. They claimed that they spent over a million dollars on billboards. The picture had Martin Luther King, Jr., Rosa Parks, Aubrey Williams, and Septima Clark and me and other people in the front row. And Pete Seeger's elbow. Pete said he came within an elbow's distance of being in the famous picture.

That picture was used all over the South to discredit King and the civil rights movement. FBI Director J. Edgar Hoover said that King was connected to Highlander, and Highlander was Communist, therefore King was Communist. When the local FBI office in Atlanta told him Highlander wasn't Communist, Hoover said, "Well, King is Communist, and that proves Highlander is Communist." You could have it either way.

In Tennessee, the opposition tried to close Highlander down at a committee hearing of the state legislature in Nashville. Ed Friend, the Georgia governor's undercover photographer, was at the hearing. He made some interesting statements. He said that integration is communism and it's against our way of life. He said that he could prove it, and he showed all those pictures he took at our twenty-fifth anniversary. I said, "They are good pictures, and we're very proud of them." I offered to buy them from him.

At the same hearing, they tried to prove that Highlander was Communist through guilt by association. They said such and such a person was accused of being a Communist, and they wrote his name on the blackboard. Somebody else was accused, and they put that name up. All the names of the people who were activists in the South and trying to bring about racial equality and organize labor unions were put on the blackboard. Then they wrote Highlander in the middle, and they drew lines from Highlander to all these people. They'd ask me these questions: "Do you know these people? Did you speak at this place? Did you take part in this conference? Did you help organize this?" I answered yes to all their questions. Highlander was involved with everybody on that list, one way or another.

"Now," they said, "we have proof that some of these people are Communists. Look at this drawing. Doesn't it prove that Highlander is Communist?" And I said, "Well, it only proves that you can write names on a blackboard and draw lines between them." They were fit to be tied.

Later on, they used more sophisticated ways of trying to do Highlander in. It started with a raid on Highlander while I was at a conference in Europe, but that didn't keep them from charging me with walking around the lake at Highlander that night with my one arm around a Black woman and a bottle of beer in my hand. The fact that I had a passport showing that I was out of the country at that time didn't cut any ice with the court. Well, if you think that's being framed, I was arrested once for drunken driving when I wasn't drunk and I wasn't driving.

The night of the raid in July 1959 was the night that one of the verses of "We Shall Overcome" was born. A group of young people, a youth choir from Reverend Seay's church in Montgomery, was at Highlander. He thought it would be good for them to know there were white people that they could deal with as equals. They were looking at a movie called *Face of the South*. It was dark. Suddenly, raiders came in with flashlights. They must have been vigilantes and some police officers, but they weren't in uniform. They demanded the lights be turned on, but they couldn't get anybody at Highlander to do it. They were furious, you know, running around with flashlights. In the meantime, the kids started to sing "We Shall Overcome." It made them feel good. The raiders yelled, "Shut up and turn on the lights!" Then some kid said,

"We're not afraid." Then they started singing, "We are not afraid. We are not afraid." That's when that verse was born, the night of the raid.

Recently, we had some visitors at Highlander from Ireland. They said the Irish were singing "We Shall Overcome" there. The verse "We are not afraid" was used more than any other because the Irish were trying to say they were not afraid of the British army. And that came out of those kids at Highlander the night of the raid. So there was both civil disobedience history and music history made that night.

Three staff members at Highlander were arrested and charged with serving liquor and drinking. It was a church group. Mrs. Septima Clark, who was arrested, is a great Methodist leader who doesn't drink. And Guy Carawan is a folk singer who doesn't drink. The other guy who was arrested didn't drink either. They arrested three people who didn't drink on the charge of serving liquor. The raid was to set up the legal situation so they could void our charter and confiscate our property. The people who opposed us had to have a technical way of getting a case against us into the courts.

It took two years to get the prosecution witnesses to memorize their stories, and even then they got mixed up at the trial. They didn't have a single witness, not one witness, who wasn't forced to testify because their sons were in prison or they were facing charges themselves or their husbands were up on charges. They promised these people to let their kids out of reform school, to drop charges against them, and to pay them if they testified. And even though a lot of them got their testimony mixed up, the judge and jury didn't object.

Finally, through a series of clever plans that were evidently agreed on in advance by the state supreme court and the district judges, they were able to get a conviction on technicalities with which they could void our charter and confiscate our property. Which they did. Highlander was found guilty of selling beer without a license.

The judge said that if there are three people in a room and one goes out and gets three bottles of beer and brings them back, and the other two give him a quarter apiece, legally he's selling beer and he has to have a license. He used that as an example. He said that Highlander did that. People at Highlander did do that when union workshops were in session. They did it because they didn't want to go in town to a white-only bar and leave the Blacks behind. Well, that was one of the technicalities on which we were charged and convicted.

The other technicality was that I had set up Highlander so I could use it for personal gain. The jury agreed that I hadn't used it for personal gain yet, but I was going to and had set it up in such a way that "when the melon got big," I was "going to cut the melon." So I was convicted of going to cut the melon when the melon got big—that I was *going* to do something, not that I *did* anything.

What really bothered them was that Highlander was integrated. Integration was against the Tennessee law until just a few years ago. We violated that law for forty-six years. That was the basis for confiscating the property, the basis for lawsuits, for everything else. But we just kept on violating it as an act of civil disobedience. We had no intention of stopping. After they confiscated our property, we reorganized, set up a new school, and kept violating the same law. We violated it until the state repealed it.

WILLIAM HOWARD MELISH

Thou Shall Not Preach

William Howard Melish

In 1986, the Reverend William Howard Melish returned to the Church of the Holy Trinity to preach on the occasion of the fiftieth anniversary of his ordination. It was the same Brooklyn Heights church to which his father had come as rector in 1904 and where, in 1939, he had become his father's assistant. Both were driven out by the hysteria of the 1950s that closed the church itself for a decade because the congregation would accept no other preacher. Arthur Miller wrote of Melish in Father and Son *more than thirty years ago: "A sensitive man is not built to buck the press and the jingo warwhoop. Bill Melish that night was only the scholarly young man, the thin, tall minister most of whose life had been spent at his books. There was nothing a man could study that could tell him how to laugh when black headlines were calling him a traitor to his country, when lifelong friends were whitening with fear at his approach. He had only now begun to sense the bottomless, endlessly ingenious ways in which decent-seeming newspapermen could write entire lies. Under the lamplight he was a man who seemed breathless, not knowing where or how to begin to get to his feet after being knocked down."* [1]

But the Reverend William Howard Melish regained his footing. He returned at last, proudly, to the pulpit he would not be kept from.

My father was the rector of the Brooklyn Heights Holy Trinity Church, one of the most active Episcopal parishes in the city of New York. We had always had monthly forums on contemporary subjects, where we tried to apply the Christian gospel to the general social, economic, and political scene. We were unusual in that respect. Nearby, a conservative pastor used to say of his congregation, with pride: "We are the pullman car on the Episcopal train." But father was considered a distinguished person in the Episcopal church, so his social activism had been accepted during his years, in spite of tensions.

Because of father's poor health and need for an associate, the vestry unanimously invited me to join him in the parish and ultimately, upon his retirement, to succeed him. This had the approval of the then bishop of the diocese of Long Island. Of course, I had grown up in this beautiful church, so I looked forward to being here with my father. In October 1939, my wife and I—we had just gotten married—found ourselves beginning a community ministry, which already had a long parish history of social action.

World War II was soon upon us, and many of us in New York worked together to support the war effort. One day, Thomas Harris, a predecessor of mine at Jesus College in Cambridge, England, came to my office. "The great issue now," he said, "is the war effort with the Soviet Union." I agreed with that. Our fate hung, in large measure, on what happened to them. The whole strength of the Hitler armies had hit the Soviet Union, and ultimately the German Panzers went as far as the Volga River; the Russians were in absolutely desperate circumstances.

I helped to form many Russian war relief chapters and participated in the great rallies at Madison Square Garden. Out of this was born the National Council of American-Soviet Friendship in January 1943. There was a meeting in New York, a great meeting under Ambassador Davies's leadership, at which the vice-president of the United States spoke. We had been encouraged in all of our work by the Roosevelt administration. I made hundreds of speeches around the country with the support of Washington. I remember one army camp where I spoke to four thousand troops at the invitation of the War Department. I could call the White House. I could call the secretary of state at the Waldorf-Astoria.

Now, I tell you all this because within a very short time after the atomic bombs were dropped on Japan, you sensed that something was taking place, very fundamentally, through the whole postwar world. I felt its full effects in the fall of 1947, over a very touchy issue. The Nazis, being shrewd, had set up three Roman Catholic independent states in Central Europe, including one in Yugoslavia, in Croatia. There, Archbishop Stepinac was the power, the religious authority, and he collaborated with the Nazis. You know, the fascists killed seventy thousand Jews, and Stepinac had blessed the Croatian fascists and their banners. He was tried after the war under the laws of Yugoslavia and imprisoned.

The Catholic church feared social change and the possibility of revolution in Western Europe also. They attacked Yugoslavia, charging there was no religious freedom. The Yugoslav ambassador asked Dr. Shipler, of *The Churchman,* if he could get a group of clergymen to go to Yugoslavia. "All we want is for you to tell the truth about religious conditions in our country."

Ten prominent American Protestant editors and clergymen were invited to go. When the Methodist bishop, G. Bromley Oxnam, turned down an invitation, Shipler asked me to take his place. I jumped at the opportunity. We spent two weeks in Yugoslavia, saw the churches, and interviewed people. One day we rode in an open jeep along dusty dirt roads to Lepoglava prison. Stepinac was there in jail, all right. He hadn't been martyred, and he wasn't on the rock pile. Those were just plain lies. He had two cells together, with a typewriter and books, and he was visited regularly by the U.S. ambassador. He had a chapel where he could celebrate Mass. We photographed him. One year later, *Time* and *Life* published pictures of Stepinac in the same prison.

Shipler and I wrote the report that went out over all of our names. We had two lectures at our church, where I showed slides of Stepinac and told the story of our visit. Each time five hundred people came. I did the same thing in Manhattan Center with a huge audience. And thousands of Protestant ministers rallied behind the publication of our report.

But we soon discovered that when the Vatican goes after you, beware! When it turned its public relations steamroller on us, it hit, and hit hard. It seemed as if every parish newspaper in the United States, Australia, and England carried denunciations of us. The results were quite cataclysmic. We found ourselves catapulted into the limelight.

In Brooklyn, where the criticism was directed at my father as well as myself, we had to contend with the most reactionary elements in the Roman church, the Catholic Truth Society and Father Curran of the

Brooklyn Tablet. These groups, plus the *Brooklyn Eagle,* now defunct, gathered together to attack us. My father wrote Mr. Schroth, who was the editor of the *Eagle:* "Why are you doing this to us?" Schroth answered, "We're going to drive the Melishes out of Brooklyn."

In the midst of this kind of assault all across the country, the attorney general of the United States, Tom Clark, issued arbitrarily and without hearings the first list of so-called subversive organizations. And there, number one on it, was the National Council of American-Soviet Friendship, of which I was then the national chairman. I had succeeded Dr. Corliss Lamont when he returned to teaching at Columbia University.

A few days after the listing, I was to appear on the radio program "Town Hall of the Air" to debate U.S. foreign policy. I was really defending Roosevelt's policy of coexistence. This time, everything was different from my previous appearance on the program. Instead of courtesy and secretaries and typewriters being available to me, I was greeted by dead silence.

"Wild Bill" Donovan, the head of the OSS, the predecessor of the CIA, did the axe work on me before five or six million people. Knowing our organization had just been listed by the attorney general, he read a telegram from a leading anti-Soviet paper on the air even though it had no relevance to the topic of the debate: "Will you ask Mr. Melish how he can be chairman of the National Council of American-Soviet Friendship unless he's a member of the Communist Party?" That was exactly the same tactic used by the House Un-American Activities Committee— guilt by association.

After that, the telephone would ring at four o'clock in the morning when we were asleep. Sometimes you could hear the sound of a bar in the background, and a voice that was unidentifiable would say, "You goddamn bastard. Go to Russia where you belong." Night after night, this kind of thing would happen.

Almost immediately after we were listed, we found ourselves in legal struggles, both for the council and at the church. Five of us who were injured in spirit and rights by this listing felt it our duty to bring suit against the attorney general. We carried it to the Supreme Court of the United States and obtained a five-to-four decision in our favor, declaring we had been improperly listed because we had been denied due process. The Court sent the government back to a lower court to support its allegations with evidence. The government, however, never did that, but neither would they take us off the list, in spite of the Supreme Court decision.

In the meantime, the bishop who had been friendly to us died, and the diocese elected another man who was an Anglo-Catholic—what we called a High Churchman, as opposed to Low Churchmen, which we were. He was against my father and me on ecclesiastical as well as political grounds. He began to work with the vestry to get us both out. First, they demanded that my father fire his assistant, me, which he refused to do. He said courageously, "My son is doing precisely what I would do if I were thirty years younger." Then, they moved against him in an ecclesiastical hearing. The bishop charged that a division in the parish had been caused by my associations with Corliss Lamont, Vito Marcantonio, W. E. B. Du Bois, Paul Robeson, and others. The hearing ended with father's removal from the parish after forty-five years of honorable service. This is shocking now when you look back on it, but in 1949 we were just going into the McCarthy period.

Father's closest friends, business, legal, and other professional people whom he had known his whole lifetime, couldn't deal with the government suddenly branding me as subversive. The headmaster of the Polytechnic Preparatory School, where I had gone as a boy, was the secretary of the parish. A number of "Poly Boys" were in the FBI, and they were deliberately sent to call on the headmaster about me. They tried to persuade him that he should do something about getting rid of me. He told me that himself. Almost every member of the vestry at one point or another was pressured by the FBI.

The parishioners, of course, loved my father. He'd been their minister since 1904. Arthur Miller, whose wife at that point was a member of the congregation, wrote the most striking defense of my father and myself, called *Father and Son*. It was a beautiful thing. The parishioners formed a "Committee to Retain Our Rector" that collected signatures from seventy percent of the church membership to oppose the vestry's actions. But the vestry, with only two exceptions, conspired with the bishop to ultimately get my father removed.

A parish meeting was called, and there the congregation voted two hundred sixty-one against twenty-seven to remove the vestrymen who forced my father's dismissal. Shortly afterward, a special election was planned to select their replacements. But the old vestry went to court. They got a judge to issue an injunction against their own parishioners, forbidding the special election until a court could consider the dispute.

At the trial, the bishop and the vestry were on one side and my father, the congregation, and I were on the other. The vestry held that father's refusal to discharge me led to a division the parish could not possibly survive. We argued that we could not be removed just because the bishop or vestry disagreed with my political views—something they made clear they did—but only on grounds of heresy or immorality. The bishop could bring no such ecclesiastical charges against us. When he was on the witness stand, our lawyer asked: "You concede that there is no doctrinal question, or question of heresy?" "That has not been considered, no, sir," said the bishop. Our lawyer continued: "And there is no question of immorality, or anything of that sort?" "Oh, absolutely not," the bishop responded. "That I put in my statement: I have every confidence in the moral integrity of these men."

In other words, this thing was political, purely political. But the judge supported the bishop and vestry. The court upheld the removal of my father and declared the parishioners' meeting that removed the old vestrymen illegal. Then the judge enjoined me from taking the services.

My father said of those proceedings, "We believe it compromises the basic principles of democracy within the church, the rights of the congregation, the freedom of the pulpit, and the freedom of conscience and speech. Unless these rights are sustained, no minister is free." Many religious leaders agreed. Our appeal to the Supreme Court was supported by more than twenty-five hundred Protestant clergymen from across the country, including many bishops, faculty members of divinity schools, and prominent writers and editors, in a friend of the court brief. But in the hysteria of that moment, it was to no avail. The Supreme Court refused without comment to review it.

Father was out, period. But I was in the unique position of being left in charge of a parish in which I was forbidden to preach. So for the next year and a half I ran the parish, while fifty-five Episcopal clergymen, voluntarily and at their own expense, came in Sunday after Sunday to take the services. When the terms of some of the vestrymen expired, the parish voted overwhelmingly to replace them with others more sympathetic to my father and myself. The new vestry applied to the bishop for me to be instituted as rector. The bishop refused, and the vestry would not appoint anyone else in my place. So for five more years I continued the work at Holy Trinity as acting rector.

The pressures of this period broke every one of the social action groups in the major Protestant denominations, with one exception: the Methodist Federation for Social Action, into which some of the rest of us were drawn. Our own Episcopal group was destroyed, in spite of some wonderful people in it.

By 1954, the National Council of American-Soviet Friendship had to go before hearings of the Subversive Activities Control Board * to defend itself again against the charge of being a "Communist front." That responsibility fell largely upon me. I was the chief witness, appearing before the board for some twenty-four hours over five days. Under oath, I was subjected to one of the most terrifying experiences I ever had.

Each morning the prosecuting attorney came in with a briefcase full of documents and questioned me about some aspect of my life. They had a file on just about everything that I had ever been interested in. I'd been associated with a lot of liberal and progressive organizations. In this red-baiting period, all the prosecutor had to do was connect you with them to give you the appearance of guilt. Then that was immediately in the headlines the next day. You were ruined by association, you see.

I had sworn I was not a member of the Communist Party. But the government brought in paid witnesses from their stable to say that I was. Obviously, they were setting me up for a perjury indictment, which could mean five years in prison. One of the informers was Louis Budenz. Another was Harvey Matusow. I can tell you now, years afterward, that Matusow went to prison for perjury and Budenz's testimony was discredited. But at that time, the risk of perjury was very frightening, particularly after what had just happened to Alger Hiss.[†] Our appeal of the board's action dragged on ten years, until 1964, when the Supreme Court finally upheld us.

Ever since the death of Roosevelt, when Truman took over, J. Edgar Hoover had said quite explicitly in his directives that war with the Soviet Union was inevitable. He was just as blunt as that. Because he went under that assumption, anybody who worked for peaceful coexistence or détente was subversive to him. Perfectly innocent people fighting for peace—you suddenly become a menace.

---

* The Subversive Activities Control Board was established by the Internal Security Act of 1950, which was passed over President Truman's veto. The board could hold hearings at the request of the attorney general to require organizations to register as "Communist action," "Communist front," or "subversive." Once so designated, organizations were subject to sanctions.

† Alger Hiss, a New Dealer and a ranking official in the State Department, was convicted of perjury in 1950 for denying the accusation by Whittaker Chambers that he had passed classified documents to Chambers. The notoriety generated by the case helped launch the McCarthy era and propelled Richard Nixon into national prominence. Controversy surrounding the verdict has continued to the present; after four years of imprisonment, and now after four decades, Hiss maintains his innocence and seeks vindication.

As far as I could tell, the FBI kept two lists of "subversives." One was for people to be kept under surveillance. The other one, apparently the more serious of the two, simply had the code name DET COM. I suspect it designated those people to be detained in the event of war or a "national emergency," just the way the Japanese were taken into detention. I later found that I had been placed on both lists.

We knew there were some FBI informers in the parish. It's very clear that they were keeping close watch on my activities. One of my sermons at Holy Trinity, in which I accused the FBI of invading religious freedom, was sent to J. Edgar Hoover. Hoover was stunned by the thing and had it sent to all his bureaus. He personally thanked the informant and said he would appreciate any additional information that could be sent to him.

The FBI called on the new men who had been elected to the vestry, just as they had on those who removed my father. Even some of your closest friends and supporters change once the pressure is applied. One of the leaders of the movement for the rights of the parishioners wrote to the Internal Revenue people without my knowledge, accusing me of giving money to the Communist Party. That, of course, was nonsense. Everything we gave was to a social or religious philanthropy, and the record was absolutely clear. After the auditor looked at our papers, he shrugged his shoulders and said, "This obviously has been done in spite." He showed me the letter he had received. It was on stationery I instantly recognized, that of Lewis Reynolds, the warden of our church.

Leroy Peterson, another vestryman who was originally very excited about our struggle, turned against us when we began to lose. He became the spokesman for the opposition and ended up as a real scoundrel. The diocese paid him off by giving him our apartment in the rectory to live in after we were forced out.

Those things, of course, are pretty shattering to you. It shows how people who had supported us, my father for forty-five years and myself for eighteen years, couldn't stand up to the government's denunciation of us as un-American. The head of the Brooklyn Navy Yard, who later was given the rank of commodore because he'd been a hero in World War II, belonged to the parish. He was a sweet, absolutely honest guy. But they were bothering him because he and his wife came to the church. Once he asked me, "Why couldn't you give in?" I said to him, "When you were under fire by the Japanese, you didn't run. You stood up to it." Well, bless his heart, he remained very friendly to me, but he had to drop out of the parish.

Finally, the bishop was able to get his rump vestry to elect a series of men to be rector in my place. When the first two of these chaps saw what they were walking into, they had both the wisdom and the decency to pull out. But the third time, the bishop got one of his classmates, Dr. Sidener, who was on his payroll, really, and had him elected as the rector.

The bishop took possession of the church and announced that Canon Thomas, one of his assistants, would conduct the services. He ordered me not to take any services that Sunday. If I disobeyed, I would be confronting the bishop's representative in the services. That would have been the basis for an ecclesiastical trial and defrocking. But my lawyers said to me, "If you don't carry through that service, it's all over. You've got to have possession of that church."

Our problem was that Peterson had the locks changed and we no longer had entry to the church. That Saturday was a very desperate day. I actually considered getting locked inside the church overnight so I could conduct services in the morning. I was already in the church when I heard one of the vestrymen shout, not knowing I was in there, "The Pinkertons are going to be here at four o'clock." So I knew that this wasn't the solution and I got out.

Very early Sunday morning, a parishioner slender enough to squeeze through the ventilator in one of the stained-glass windows entered the church. Fortunately, the guard, with his weapons, was sleeping in my father's study. In a matter of minutes all the doors were open. A young clergyman over in Jersey City, Paul Moore, now the Bishop of New York, loaned me some communion vessels.

When Canon Thomas came to conduct the early service, there were fifty people already in the church attending my service. As we were finishing, Thomas deliberately held a second service, in competition with us, with a handful of people. But we stayed there in possession of the church. More than five hundred people came later for our main morning service.

We went to court because the vestry didn't have a quorum when they elected Sidener. Here the bishop did a thing that laid him open to very serious moral and ethical questions. Instead of waiting for the court decision, he proceeded to institute Sidener.

We stood our ground once more against the bishop. The result was an episode almost without equal in American church history. At the Lenten service we were to conduct on the day Sidener was to be instituted, the Special Services Department of the New York police surrounded our church with a choreographed display of police authority, policemen standing every ten feet, Black and white officers alternating, each with a notebook in hand and a pointed pencil. They weren't taking names actually, but the parishioners of our church who tried to go into that noonday service had to run a gauntlet of policemen, police cars, and radio trucks.

Inside the church, a Dutch Reformed minister, a friend of ours, preached. His name, of all names, was Martin Paul Luther. He just went up to the pulpit and described the trial of Jesus. Not another thing. It was hair-raising.

Armed Pinkertons were at the head of each aisle during the service, with caps on their heads, revolvers at their sides, and cigarettes dangling from their mouths. They were there to intimidate and to keep possession of the church. They did more that day to horrify some of our wavering older people, convincing them of the rightness and justification of our position. It certainly had the appearance of Nazism. And, as this whole business was going ahead, my father was having a mild heart attack up in the rectory.

Sidener was instituted later that afternoon. For the occasion, the bishop brought in busloads of parishioners from all over Long Island to create a congregation. The bishop used this religious service to compel a political consequence. Then the court decision came down that week: Sidener had not been legally elected, because the vestry did not have a quorum. There was no legal basis for the bishop to change the locks and take over the building. I was back in the pulpit the next Sunday.

The court of appeals in Albany heard the final case. The bishop had one of the shrewdest corporation lawyers, Jackson Dykman, who was head of the New York Bar Association and everything else in New York. He sold all the judges on the court of appeals a bill of goods. The judges, we learned afterward, privately had decided that this case had gone on too long and was an embarrassment to everybody. So they ended it summarily, unanimously, and in such a way that it denied us any appeal to the federal courts.

Sidener was finally given possession of the building. For three Sundays he tried to conduct services, but most parishioners would not support him. They notified the bishop that he was unwelcome. On the third Sunday, to everybody's horror and shock, Sidener got up in the pulpit and said, "You cannot make a good omelet out of rotten eggs." This is the congregation he's talking to! Then he read a letter from the bishop saying, "Because of the strife in this church, which is now unresolvable,

I declare that the church is permanently closed." Then he closed the doors and locked us all out.

No further appeal was possible. And just to make it complete, Jackson Dykman and the diocese went to the state legislature. There they had the church liquidated, the corporation of the church declared nonexistent. They did it by the pure legal fiction that there were no longer the twenty-five adult communicants in the church that were necessary for its existence. In 1959, we were forced out and the church was closed. And for ten years one of the most beautiful churches in the United States lay there deteriorating, simply because of the hostility around the peace issue of that period.

We, of course, had to improvise for a while. After all, I had a wife and three kids. About that time, I won an International Peace Prize, awarded by the World Council of Peace, which kept us alive for two years. We bought a home with the help of the prize money. There we held services for some of the congregation in our big living room once a month. That helped keep us together. Then, the oldest integrationist movement in the South, the Southern Conference Educational Fund, asked me to work as its eastern representative. I did that for ten years.

During that time, I never left the Episcopal church. It was rather difficult, but I went to conventions and all the rest, maintaining my presence. I was screamed out of one of the conventions. It's hard to believe the absolute hysteria that can seize a body. I tried to speak. I tried to get up and speak, and they just screamed me down. I never had an emotional experience like that. But I stuck it out.

I used to substitute on Sundays for a friend who had a little parish over in Corona and preach on occasion when he went on vacation. That kept me in touch with things and sort of kept my ego alive. When my friend had a heart attack and had to retire, the senior warden asked if I would be interested in coming. A new bishop who was friendly to my father and myself gave his approval, and the vestry elected me.

It was very touching. My father was now ninety-five years of age, a complete invalid, living at home in the old rectory. He had just two desires. He wanted to see the old church open. And he wanted to see me back in a parish. I had the privilege of coming in beside his wheelchair and telling him that both of these things were going to happen.

Father's last appearance in public was the day I was instituted at Grace Church in Corona. He was wheeled up the aisle in his chair. And the first service that reopened Holy Trinity was his funeral. Several hundred of our old friends were there.

Tomorrow I will be back in my old place, in what is now the Church of St. Ann and the Holy Trinity.* It was vacant all those years, but we're there now. The church is open, and it is doing precisely the same thing around the nuclear freeze that we did all the years before, for a peaceful world. A fine young rector is in charge who understands the history of that church and is willing to stand up.

* In 1982, Reverend Melish was invited to return to St. Ann and the Holy Trinity Church as assisting priest.

Thou Shall Not Resist

Chuck McDew

The 1960 sit-ins in Greensboro, North Carolina, inspired young Black men and women to a level of political activity unheard of since Reconstruction. The youths who formed the Student Nonviolent Coordinating Committee withstood terror from officials and Klansmen alike in their work to change the political face of the South. Above all they sought human dignity, and their bravery gave hope that it might be regained. Into Albany, Georgia; Philadelphia, Mississippi; and Selma, Alabama they went: marching, registering voters, and risking their lives. Chuck McDew was the second national chairman of SNCC. He was beaten, jailed, and charged with criminal anarchy for encouraging Black citizens to exercise their franchise.

I was raised in Massillon, Ohio, a town of about thirty-five thousand, where they produced steel and football players. Initially I had planned to go to Oberlin College. But it was my father's feeling that we should all—myself, my sister, and my brothers—spend at least one year of school in a Black institution, where we would see Black professors, lawyers, and other professionals as role models.

I had no great desire to go down South. I had never been there. I

CHUCK McDEW

had never been in a totally Black environment in my life. But in 1960 I was sent to South Carolina State College, in Orangeburg, to do my year of "penitence." * I very quickly ran into a racism that had not been a problem when I was growing up. I had gone to a party in Sumter, South Carolina, with one of my roommates. He had been drinking, so I drove home. The police pulled us over. I got out and asked, "What's the problem, officer?"

He said, "Where you from, boy?"

"Ohio, why?"

He said, "They never teach you how to say 'yes sir' and 'no sir' up there?" I was completely naive. I said, "Oh, you've got to be kidding, man." At that point, he struck me. I hit him back and ended up in jail for the first time in my life. My father sent some money to a friend's mother, who then posted bond. He told her to put me on the train and send me right back to school.

The "Black" car on the train was full, but there were seats in the other cars. The conductor told me, "Get on back to the baggage car." My response was, "Look, I didn't pay eight bucks to ride with dog crates and caskets. This train has seats and I'm sitting in them." So I went into the "white" car and was sent to jail for violating the segregation laws, less than five hours after I'd gotten out. When I finally got back to school, my experimental learning had cost my father an extra three hundred dollars. He gave me instructions: "Stay on campus until you get ready to come home."

At Christmas time another student bought my ticket for me because I was not going to go to the segregated bus counter, where there were Black waiting rooms and white waiting rooms. You couldn't go and sit in the restaurant at the bus stop. Instead, you'd get your food from the kitchen. So I packed my little lunch and was determined to get on the bus and not mess with the stations.

When we stopped at Columbia, South Carolina, I met this white guy I had been raised with, who was down there playing professional baseball. He had lived a couple of houses from me, and we'd gone from first grade through high school together. I had three hours till the next bus, so Mike said, "Why don't we play some handball?" From the time we were sophomores in high school, we'd gone to the Y every Saturday to play. Looking back, I guess I just refused to believe or accept the rigid

* South Carolina State College at Orangeburg is also the site of the Orangeburg Massacre, which occurred in 1968 and is described later in this volume by Cleveland Sellers (Part III).

segregation that existed in the South. I thought that since I had my little international YMCA card, I could present it anywhere in the world. That's what they told me when I paid my hundred dollars in Massillon.

When we presented our cards now, we were told that Mike could stay but "this nigra here got to leave." We got into an argument, and I was back in jail. By the time I made it home, having been at school less than a semester, I had cost my father about five hundred dollars above the tuition. He said, "Okay, we can hang this up. My little experiment has backfired." We decided that since we had already paid for the semester, I would finish up in February and that would be it.

Well, things happened then that changed the course of my life. On the first of February, they had the sit-in at Greensboro. I was approached a few days later by a group of students: "We should do something like this." My response was, "*You* should do something about this. These white people here are crazy. And besides, in a few days I'm leaving. It's not my struggle. It's not my battle."

Well, I happened to be reading the Talmud just then. There was a section in it that said: "If I am not for myself, who'll be for me? If I'm for myself alone, who am I? If not now, when?" I spent a long time thinking about that statement and what it meant. I realized that it wasn't just their fight, but it was mine, too.

I knew the first thing that would happen if we went to the lunch counters and the segregated library was that I would be kicked out of school. That was a given. So I called my parents. They were wonderful: "Look, Chuckie, you were raised to be able to make responsible decisions on your own. We love you and we'll always support you in whatever action you choose to take." Well, with that feeling of goodness, I joined the movement.

I was not just a participant, but the spokesman and leader of our Orangeburg organization, which we dubbed the Orangeburg Movement for Civic Improvement. We would go to a restaurant, at Woolworth's or Kress's, sit down, and ask to be served. They'd say, "We don't serve Negroes in here. You are invading our property." When we didn't go, the police would come. It was just "You either leave or you're going to be arrested."

Even before we were arrested, the whites would often try to beat us up. Since we were practicing nonviolence, we did not strike back. But we were the ones who were charged with breach of the peace, not the white people who beat us up. The theory was if we hadn't been there, they wouldn't be beating us. So by our presence we caused their violence. A weird sort of logic.

Then we'd try to go to the library. When we walked in, we'd be arrested for trespassing on *private* property. The *public* library! They would say, "There's a Black public library too."

We had a great belief in the Constitution, that we had the right to petition to redress our grievances if things were being done wrong. So we'd have demonstrations to protest the arrests. But when we did that, there'd be more arrests. We had one large march to city hall with about a thousand students. We were stopped: "Okay, Charles. That's far enough. Tell your people to go back. If you don't, we're going to arrest you."

I turned around and said, "I've just been asked by the chief of police to tell you to return to campus. I don't know what you're going to do, but me, I'm going to city hall." And, of course, we were stopped and arrested.

Mass arrests were common in demonstrations where we'd be exercising our First Amendment rights. I remember water hoses turned on us. One time, in Orangeburg, several hundred students were herded together and put in a parking lot compound because there were no jails large enough to hold everybody.

Then SNCC, the Student Nonviolent Coordinating Committee, was formed. We were at the cutting edge of the civil rights movement, and everybody wanted to capture our dynamics, the dramatic sorts of things we were doing. Dr. King and his people were very anxious that we become the youth arm of the Southern Christian Leadership Conference. We probably would have, except that they had a policy of nonviolence as a way of life.

We said we'd use nonviolence as a tactic, but only as a tactic. We didn't think it could work at all times. Part of the theory of nonviolence is based on the concept that if a person starts hitting me and I don't respond violently, he'll eventually stop because he will recognize my humanity. Well, some of us argued that it succeeded with Gandhi because he was dealing with the British, who had at least some sense of moral history. When Gandhi and his people lay down in front of a train, they could assume that the British engineer's sense of humanness would respond to their humanness and he'd stop the train.

But in the United States there never was a code of ethics or morals that included Black people. We were not seen as human beings. If we were to lie down in front of a train in Georgia or Mississippi, those white folks would run over us and then back up to make certain that they'd done the job right.

Down South they referred to the sheriff as the high sheriff, like the high sheriff of Nottingham, because it was such a powerful position. They had their own little fiefdoms and ruled the lives of the Blacks who lived down there. They certainly weren't happy about SNCC's plan to register Black voters. I can remember once in Liberty, Mississippi, a man had gone down to register to vote and the sheriff pistol-whipped him. There was discussion afterward: "Let's make a citizen's arrest on the sheriff, since he violated this man's rights."

I argued, "Look, you guys, this is ridiculous. That man has a gun and an attitude about us anyhow. How are we going to arrest him and put him in his jail?" Well, once we approached consensus, that's what we did. The sheriff was quite startled when we said, "Hand over your weapons and your handcuffs. You're going to jail." And, of course, he arrested us instead.

Down in McComb, Mississippi, we worked on both a voter registration drive and direct action. The high school youngsters had a march, and we went with them: Bob Moses, Bob Zellner, and myself. Bob Zellner was the only white person on the march. When we got to the courthouse steps, they started beating and kicking him. We covered Bob with our bodies, Bob Moses and I, to keep him from getting his face kicked in. Then we were all arrested.

It was one of those really scary times. I'd been arrested before, but McComb was such a rural community and things were so tense and reactions by the whites were so violent. In fact, we used to talk about going up north to Jackson, Mississippi, to get out from under the pressure of McComb.

We were jailed in the basement of city hall. The police would come and take us away, one by one. And those they took didn't come back. So when your name was called, you'd say good-by to the others because you really felt that you were about to be killed. My turn came at two in the morning. I was taken upstairs. A couple hundred white men were there, just private citizens, and I had to run a gauntlet between them to get to the end of the hall. They were kicking and punching and spitting at me and calling me names. Then I went and sat down on a bench. I thought: It's all over. I'm about to die.

In times like that you go through all sorts of emotions: What am I doing here? Why are they doing this? I'm not a bad person. I don't want to die. I was so deep in thought it took me a minute to realize that a man was hitting me across the face with a rope. He was saying, "You son of a bitch, you son of a bitch, you'll never marry my daughter."

I thought, "These white folks are truly crazy. Here I'm sitting, thinking about dying, and this fool is talking about a daughter I don't know, never met, and probably would never see in my life. And he's about to kill me because of some nonsense about my marrying her." I snapped out of my shock and said, "I don't even know your ugly-assed daughter." He struck me some more. But I was not about to meet my maker that night. We were taken to another jail and once again charged with breach of peace and inciting to riot.

We all knew of the strange justice they had down South. There were laws on the books against "reckless eyeballing." That's what it was called in North Carolina. They even had laws like rape and molestation by sight. You could be sent to jail for raping a woman with your eyes. We weren't that far from where Emmett Till had been brutally murdered for looking at a white woman.* And we knew that the sheriff had a hand in it. We knew that it was more common for police officials to be involved in lynchings than not, that most lynchings took place with the sanction of the police. So it was very frightening, because there was absolutely no place you could turn to.

It's very difficult to be in that environment, until you deal with the emotions brought about by the realization that you're going to be killed. I can remember when I first accepted my mortality. I was eighteen or nineteen years old. I was sitting and looking in the Pearl River, down in Natchez. This was after Schwerner, Goodman, and Chaney had been missing for a few days.† The FBI was looking for their bodies, and when they were dragging the Pearl River, they pulled out nine or ten bodies of Black men. These were people who had been decapitated and their hands tied behind them with barbed wire. They finally stopped the

---

*The kidnapping and lynching of fourteen-year-old Emmett Till in 1955 and the exoneration of his killers symbolized the impunity with which Black people could be murdered in the South. Widely publicized in the Black press, the murder aroused the indignation of the Black community and moved some to activism. Ben Chavis (Part II) and Cleveland Sellers (Part III) both refer to Till.

†Three civil rights workers, Andrew Goodman, Michael Schwerner, and James Chaney, two whites and one Black, were murdered in Philadelphia, Mississippi, during the Freedom Summer project of 1964. The desperate search for the three missing activists is described by Cleveland Sellers (p. 253). Twenty-one whites, including a deputy sheriff, were arrested in the case. State charges against all twenty-one were dropped; six were eventually convicted on federal charges of violating civil rights laws.

dragging because, they said, "if we keep doing this, we'll just be dredging up bodies for months."

In lynchings down South they always took time to mutilate the bodies in some way. It used to be a tradition for people to take souvenirs from the lynchings. There were white people who kept a hand in a bottle of formaldehyde on display in their front room. That tradition of mutilation had been with them since they'd been children. They grew up playing hopscotch and going to lynchings.

I remember sitting by the Pearl, looking in the river, and thinking once again about some of these strange people. I had just read *Life Plus 99 Years*, which was the story of Leopold and Loeb. They were both believers in Nietzsche and the superman. They felt they should experience all sorts of things and wanted the experience of killing somebody. So they killed a kid in Chicago and went to jail for life. I was thinking, though they were geniuses, Leopold and Loeb were sort of dumb. If they wanted the experience of killing somebody, all they had to do was come South. You could kill a Black person just like that, and nothing would happen. Absolutely nothing. There had never in the history of the republic been a white man who had been tried and convicted for killing a Black person, up to that point.

And I thought: You're in a place where if somebody wants to kill you, all they have to do is walk up to you and kill you. Doing the things that we were doing, you knew that you had, at best, ten years left, that during that time you'd probably meet a violent death. After I stopped shaking with that realization, it was over. It was a sort of catharsis. I was nineteen years old and had accepted not only the inevitability of my death, but that it might happen very soon.

Of course, you could leave and not deal with it. But that was not an option for me. I felt that we were doing what we were doing because our fathers had not done it. The fact that the system had been in place for three hundred years was not all that impressive to us. We had the feeling that now is the time to change it and we will.

People had never voted in the areas we were working. In Amite County, Mississippi, eighty-five percent of the people were Black, and yet no Black person had voted there since Reconstruction. When we tried to register them, we understood why. Herbert Lee attempted to register one Tuesday. By Saturday he had been murdered. I was asked to come and identify the body. Lee was freshly dead. I turned his face over, and I can remember his brains sort of running through my hands.

Then later on at the funeral the wife of Herbert Lee got hysterical. She was slapping me and saying, "You murdered my husband. You murdered my husband."

And I was thinking, "In a way she's right. If we had never come here, he would have never tried to vote and he'd be alive today." It was a very difficult time for us because we had to deal with that emotion and the question, Should we stay? If we keep doing this, there will be other people who will be killed. Do we have the right to do this? We talked about it and concluded that if we hadn't put ourselves in the same danger, then we would not have the right to ask others to do this. But since we were just as subject to being killed as any of them—even more so— then we can, *shall* continue asking people to register.

Herbert Lee was killed by a Mississippi state representative. There were three Black men who witnessed the killing. They said they'd be willing to talk about what happened if they could be protected. I can remember having a conversation with the attorney general, Bobby Kennedy. He said, "They should testify. It's their duty as Americans." But he wouldn't protect them. I remember cussing him out.

We were very turned off by the Kennedy administration because when we talked to Bobby or the president about federal protection, they would go into their song and dance: "Well, the FBI is an investigative unit. They aren't there to protect you." So the FBI would watch us being whipped and beaten, but do nothing about it.

The argument the FBI put forth for not helping us was, "We have to deal with car thieves and people crossing state lines, so we need a good relationship with the local police. If we support you, that damages our relationship with them." There wasn't much help we got from the feds, and we really looked on the FBI as our enemy.

I must have been arrested thirty-six times, from breach of the peace and inciting to riot, to criminal anarchy in Louisiana, which was the last big one I had to deal with. It started when we sent Dion Diamond, one of our field secretaries, to Baton Rouge to organize the Black students at Southern University. He never had a chance. Right after he got there, he was arrested and charged with trespassing. Bob Zellner and I went to Baton Rouge to get him out. But when we went to post the five-thousand-dollar bail for Dion, they brought another charge against him and raised his bail to ten thousand dollars. It was evident that we were being priced out of our ability to get him out.

But we wanted to reassure Dion, because it often happened that when SNCC people were put in jail they wouldn't know if anyone else knew about it. So we went to jail and asked to see him. They told us we couldn't visit until "colored" day, which was the following Tuesday. We asked them if we could bring him some books and fruit. They said we could, and we went out and bought the stuff in a little store a couple blocks from the jail.

When we came back, it was evident that something was amiss. Earlier, when we left, just a few redneck cops had been around. Now a lot of Baton Rouge's legal heavyweights were there. The state attorney general was there, the lawyer for the city of Baton Rouge, and all those guys in suits. They questioned Bob and me separately.

"Where are you from?"

"Atlanta."

"What is your business in Baton Rouge?"

"We're passing through and stopped to see Dion Diamond."

"Do you have check stubs to prove your employment?" We usually did carry check stubs for that purpose, but we didn't have any then. I told them it didn't matter because I had a plane ticket from New Orleans to Atlanta and five thousand dollars. You could hardly be considered a vagrant with all that money. Finally I said, "This chat has been interesting, gentlemen, but I have to go. I have a plane to catch."

One of the attorneys said, "You ain't going nowhere tonight. We're arresting you for possible vagrancy." I said, "You can't arrest me for suspicion of being a vagrant. You either have to bring a charge of vagrancy against me or forget it." Well, he was right, and I didn't go anywhere. It was a long time before I saw the light of day, because by morning the charge had been changed from possible vagrancy to criminal anarchy.

It went something like this: Because Charles McDew is chairman of the Student Nonviolent Coordinating Committee, and because the Student Nonviolent Coordinating Committee has as one of its avowed purposes to overthrow the government of Louisiana, he is now charged with criminal anarchy and high treason against the sovereign state of Louisiana. You must admit it's certainly frightening. All I knew of criminal anarchy was that Sacco and Vanzetti had been executed for being criminal anarchists.

I had just been to Massillon, Ohio, to see my folks. Nobody there knew me as the chairman of SNCC. In Massillon I was just Chuckie McDew, not the spokesman for the Black students of the country. It was, "Hi, Chuckie, where you been?" And it was always sort of a gentle resting place. Two days ago I had been in Massillon, sitting and talking with Mrs. Pendolino and having spaghetti, talking with Rosemarie Pendolino, whom I'd known all my life. Two days ago I was there, in this integrated situation at home. I'd been in Louisiana less than a day, and now I was in prison. It was all very surreal.

Anyway, Bob Zellner was put with the white prisoners. They were told: "There's this white boy down here with some nigger. You take care of him and we'll take care of you." Bob was very badly beaten. I was put in solitary for my entire stay. It was a small cell, about eight feet by five feet, maybe even smaller. It had an iron cot and a toilet. There was no mattress. There was no sink. And they'd do things like turn the lights on for three days and then turn them off for three days. Then they'd turn them on for two and off for three. You became so disoriented, you started feeling like you were losing your mind.

It was summer, and they used to keep the heat on. It came out of the vents in the ceiling. I'd just lie there and roast. It was like being put in a steel box and put out in the sun. Remember, there was no sink in my cell, so I didn't get any water. I'd get coffee with my meal twice a day and that was it.

I could look out of my cell and see the water cooler. Every day at three-thirty a Black trusty put ice cubes in it. One day he was filling it when our eyes met. He asked, "Do you want an ice cube?" I stretched my hand out as far as I could. He put an ice cube in it. It was a grand gesture because he could have lost his freedom. I never knew his name and we never talked, but he did this every day. My life revolved around getting that ice cube.

The prison had tours for all sorts of groups, like the Lions Club and Christians United in Christ Against Communism. And to this day I can remember the spiel that the guard would give as he'd show them around. It went, "In this cell here is our nigger anarchist. Do you know what an anarchist is? An anarchist is one who endeavors to overthrow the state by force and violence. That's what we charged him with. In his book *The Enemy Within,* J. Edgar Hoover says that there are a hundred thousand known Communists in the United States. This is one of the biggest of them."

Once, they brought in a high school civics class. They had already been to the fire department, the hospital, and to the city hall to see "democracy" in action. I was lying in bed, waiting for my daily ice cube, when I heard someone say, "Psst, hey, mister." I looked over and there were these two little white girls about fifteen or sixteen. They said, "Say something Communist." They had just gotten the whole spiel about this "nigger anarchist," "J. Edgar Hoover's hundred thousand Communists," and "he's one of the biggest," et cetera.

I said, "Go away, will you?"

They repeated, "Say something Communist. Say something Communist."

So I said, *"Kish mir in tuchus."* Now they were thrilled. And it made my day because I was imagining: Those sweet little schmucks will go home and say, "Mommy, mommy, I was at the jail today and I heard one of those Communists speak in their international language." And they would teach it to their mother, who would tell it to her friends—all those people who didn't run in circles where they'd hear Yiddish. My mind just wandered into a thousand scenes. After I got out of jail, whenever that would be, I'd find these white folks all over Baton Rouge, walking around and greeting each other, *"Kish mir in tuchus"*—kiss my ass.

I'd been roasting in that metal cage for weeks. Finally a deal was struck: If SNCC did not operate in Louisiana, they wouldn't bring the case to trial. It was an effective sort of deterrent. I'm not a terribly religious man, but I remember the one promise I made to God: I will never again in this life go back to the state of Louisiana. When I got out of that jail, I said, "Give me a ticket, get me my passport. I want out, not just of Louisiana, I want out of the United States." I had been sufficiently shaken by that experience that I considered leaving the United States forever.

Recently I was talking to a young guy in a bar in St. Paul. He was a construction worker. And before that he had been a policeman in McComb, Mississippi.

I asked, "How did you get to be a policeman in McComb, Mississippi?"

"I got out of high school," he said, "took the test, and became a cop." A Black cop in McComb! I remember thinking it was one of the most gratifying things I had ever heard. On the other hand, it was sad that he was unaware of how much pain and blood it took for a Black to be able to be a policeman in McComb, Mississippi.

Part II
The Method to the Madness

Introduction to Part II

Each branch of government, the judicial, the legislative, and the executive, has contributed to the selective denial of rights to persons it considers a threat. The pursuit of presumed heretics in the courts, which at times became relentless, is predicated on laws that compromise free expression. Pete Muselin's advocacy of unions was heresy in the 1920s in a tightly controlled company town. He was charged with sedition. Gil Green's advocacy of socialism was heresy in the late 1940s in a country wracked by fear of the Soviet Union. He was charged with teaching the forcible overthrow of the government. Benjamin Spock's advocacy of ending the Vietnam war was heresy in the 1960s to an administration bent on extending that war. He, like Scott Nearing fifty years earlier, was charged with interfering with the draft. In fact, all were put on trial for nothing more than their public utterances. All were convicted, and two served prison terms before their final vindication. "What's a 'spy act' really for," Scott Nearing asked concerning his own indictment under the federal Espionage Act, "except to prevent people of a certain point of view from influencing policy?" Such heresy trials make dissent risky and divert movements for change into costly legal defenses.

The longevity of statutes prohibiting heresy is considerable: their origins stretch back to the Alien and Sedition Act of the late eighteenth century. Some of these laws have been overturned; some have been reincarnated, assuming new form in a latter-day law. Others remain dormant, lying in wait, as it were, for the next assault. At times of great national hysteria, like the red scare following World War I and the McCarthy era of the 1950s, the proliferation of the passage and use of such laws has been complemented by the repressive activities of other government agencies.

Congressional committees have led the most widely publicized attacks on dissidents. Those subpoenaed to testify before these committees were denied even the assurances due process afforded in the courtroom, and many were publicly "exposed" in stage-managed performances. Reluctant witnesses had virtually no means of escape that allowed both reputation and conscience to remain intact.

The congressional inquisition began in earnest after World War II, with the heralded Hollywood Ten case—the glamour of the film industry promised an irresistible send-off—and it found its heyday in the early fifties. The stories of these congressional hearings are presented in chronological order, tracing the committees' shifting attention to different targets. Ring Lardner, Jr., and Frances Chaney Lardner recall the hearings that initiated the inquisition and the blacklisting that complemented it. Later, congressional committees entered partisan battles within the labor movement. Their attacks on left-wing unions like the United Electrical Workers and unionists like Tom Quinn were devastating and were usually timed to interfere with internal or jurisdictional disputes. In education, the committees' purpose was little more than to purge the academy of radical thought—scholar Barrows Dunham, for example, was banished from its ranks. The communications and entertainment industries were likewise purified. John Randolph was one of a contingent of Broadway artists with the effrontery to challenge the blacklist, and he paid for that with a summons to testify before the House Un-American Activities Committee.* Author Harvey O'Connor was hauled before McCarthy's committee after the senator's lieutenants Roy Cohn and G. David Schine, in a madcap junket to Europe, found copies of his books in the suspect State Department's overseas libraries; O'Connor, a civil libertarian, received a HUAC subpoena as he was about to address a meeting of New Jersey teachers who were being investigated by the committee.

---

*The House Un-American Activities Committee (HUAC) has also been known at various times in its history as the House Committee on Un-American Activities (HCUA) and, after 1969, as the House Internal Security Committee (HISC). We have used the more common designation HUAC throughout.

Administrative agencies of the executive branch—the Immigration and Naturalization Service (INS) and departmental loyalty boards—have also played formidable roles in repressive activities as they attempted to ensure the ideological purity of immigrants and persons in government employ. The wide-ranging work of these agencies was largely unencumbered by any consideration of the constitutional rights of their victims. Sonia Kaross, like many immigrants caught up by the INS in the early years of the century, was interrogated about her political beliefs and associations without benefit of counsel and without protection against self-incrimination. Unlike many, she was spared deportation. Arthur Drayton and Jim Kutcher held positions that posed no conceivable threat to the nation's security; both were forced out of government employment during the Truman loyalty purges that initiated the McCarthy era. Organizations they belonged to, their associations, were labeled subversive in a procedure that allowed no challenge to the Justice Department's unilateral conclusions. The government was so intent on dismissing Arthur Drayton that he was twice fired, with no regard for the double jeopardy involved. Although Jim Kutcher's loyalty had been emphatically established on the battlefield, the government's relentless pursuit of him extended beyond his dismissal to attempts to evict his parents from their home and withdraw his veteran's benefits. More recently, the Immigration and Naturalization Service was doggedly intent on deporting Margaret Randall, solely because of the ideas expressed in her writings, a case that demonstrates the longevity of the reincarnated turn-of-the-century immigration laws that ensnared Sonia Kaross.

Finally, to return full circle to the courts, the criminalization of dissent occurs when the government uses serious criminal charges such as murder, arson, and kidnapping to silence dissent. The cases of Joe Hill and Tom Mooney, labor radicals early in the century, are famous examples.* The telltale signs of a frame-up are that the activist is singled out for prosecution and is denied due process by government misconduct that precludes the possibility of a fair trial. Often the sentencing is

---

* Joe Hill, the Wobbly balladeer, was convicted of the murder of a Salt Lake City grocer and his son in 1914. Labor radical Tom Mooney was convicted of charges arising from the bombing of a World War I parade in San Francisco in 1916. Both Hill and Mooney were tried in highly charged political climates and under dubious proceedings. Their convictions provoked outcries, in the United States and abroad, that their trials were political frame-ups. Crucial government witnesses against Mooney later admitted they had perjured themselves, as similar witnesses did in the trials of Ben Chavis and Leonard Peltier. Joe Hill was executed by a firing squad; Tom Mooney's death sentence was commuted by President Woodrow Wilson, and in 1939 he was fully pardoned.

out of proportion to the alleged crime, reflecting the political bias of the judge or the times.

The Reverend Ben Chavis was arrested more than thirty times, for offenses that ranged from obscure traffic violations to arson, before the arrest that led to the Wilmington Ten case. A Justice Department memorandum is reported to have called for hounding American Indian Movement leaders, such as Leonard Peltier, on any possible charge until the movement no longer had funds for bail. Leonard Peltier and three other Native Americans were charged with the murder of two FBI agents. After two of Peltier's co-defendants were acquitted, the FBI revealed that the government had dropped charges against the third "so that the full prosecutive weight of the Federal Government could be directed against Leonard Peltier."[1] In both the Chavis and Peltier trials, government misconduct was substantial and was acknowledged by higher courts. In both cases, the activists' organizing work was disrupted as attention shifted to the overwhelming problems of legal defense.

This form of repression is especially insidious. Once charged with heinous crimes like arson or murder, political activists find their reputations tarnished and their integrity questioned; even evidence of substantial government misconduct or support from recognized human rights organizations such as Amnesty International does not dispel these doubts easily. And, more significantly, the movements led by these activists are tainted or, worse, left in disarray.

Outlawing Dissent: Trials of Heresy

The Steel Fist in a Pennsylvania Company Town

Pete Muselin

State sedition laws had their own victims who rarely received national attention. Between 1917 and 1921, two-thirds of the states enacted sedition laws that made criminal those utterances, writings, and associations that were presumed to advance violence as a way of effecting political or social change. In fact, these statutes were vaguely written, loosely construed, and used to chill expression of radical ideas and inhibit the organization of unions and, much later, the civil rights movement. In 1926, the attorney for Jones and Laughlin Steel Corporation, which owned the town of Aliquippa lock, stock, and barrel, prosecuted Pete Muselin under the Pennsylvania sedition law.

Used against radicals in the fifties, state sedition laws were revived again as the civil rights movement gained strength. Chuck McDew was held in a Louisiana prison under that state's archaic criminal anarchy law (see Part I). Margaret Herring McSurely was indicted for sedition in Kentucky because of membership in SNCC (see Part IV). The judge in her case could have been speaking about all sedition laws when he ruled that the Kentucky statute "contravenes the First Amendment to the Constitution of the United States because it unduly prohibits freedom of speech, freedom of press and the right of assembly."[1] His and similar court decisions effectively laid state sedition laws to rest—too late,

PETE MUSELIN

however, for Pete Muselin and many others who had served time in prison for constitutionally protected activities.

I arrived in this country in 1912 with my brother. He was fourteen and I was twelve. Our parents had come here earlier and settled in Pittsburgh, where my dad worked in the steel mills. We lived in Pittsburgh until Jones and Laughlin Steel Corporation broke ground for their Aliquippa mills, right on the site of the old Aliquippa amusement park. My dad was offered a job up there, so the family moved to what was then known as Woodlawn. The Jones and Laughlin Steel Corporation was its one industry.

We lived in the Logstown section, a typical settlement of foreign-born mill workers. It was populated mainly by Croatians and Serbs. Everyone in Logstown spoke our languages. In mom's home, if you tried to speak English, she'd chastise you: "This is not an English family. I don't know what you're saying. Speak Croatian." Would you believe that the Jewish storekeeper learned to speak Croatian? That's how deeply imbedded the Slav culture was. If you were to analyze Logstown, our life there, our habits, and our mannerisms, you could liken that to a village in Croatia. Definitely.

Many of the foreign-born in Aliquippa came to this country illegally. I remember as a child still in Europe they used to talk about how steamship agents would ship people here without a passport or credentials of any kind. These agents worked very closely with employers in this country because the whole purpose was to send labor here. My grandparents told me that they would herd people from villages into boxcars. Do you know, even the engineers were in cahoots with those agents? When they got near a border, like the Swiss or the French border, they'd stop the train so the immigrants could get out of the boxcars and hide in the fields until the immigration authorities would disembark.

Here in the U.S.A., industry was in its infancy. They needed labor, and they didn't care how they got it. People in Europe were made to believe that in America the sidewalks were made of gold. All you had to do was get yourself a pick and a shovel and just dig. Most of them came here with one purpose in mind: work for a while, make some money, and go back. All their lives, my parents planned on going back to Europe: "We'll earn enough to buy some land over there. Then we'll buy some horses or oxen. And we'll work that land and live nicely upon our retirement."

Well, none of that ever materialized. There was no such thing as going back with the wages Jones and Laughlin paid. You know where my parents ended up? In the Woodlawn cemetery here, with so many others who had the same dream.

The economic situation was such that we foreigners wouldn't dare think of going any higher than public school. It was unheard of. Many children left school in sixth or seventh grade to work in Jones and Laughlin as manifest boys. Public school didn't do me any good. The teacher, Miss McMurray, was a very nice person, a typical schoolmarm. I liked her, but I didn't understand English except a few choice dirty words I learned from other kids. So my brother said, "What's the use of going there?" He had a barber shop up in Logstown. "I'll make a barber out of you." I never wanted to be a barber, but I got in the barber business when I was thirteen.

In Europe, before I came here, I was very good in school. I've always been an avid reader, and I liked history. That prompted me to want to read more and learn more about this new land I came to. Somehow, I hit upon the idea of taking excursions through the dictionary. I would just open it at random and memorize at least one or two words a day. Then I would ask some of the fellows who did know a little English what the words meant. That's how I built my vocabulary.

In 1917, I joined the army and went to France for twenty-two months. The war and everything about it overwhelmed me. I began to ask myself very seriously: What am I doing in France? After all, I don't know a single person in the enemy lines. They haven't harmed me in any way whatsoever. No doubt they were just like myself, young and exuberant with life. They wanted to get out of that man's army, just as I did.

So, I began to ponder over the whole thing: What could be the reason we were killing each other? I couldn't conceive of anything more stupid than a war, human beings killing other human beings without any apparent reason. But the more I thought about it, the more I understood the underlying cause: War is predicated on profit. After I got back in 1919, I saw the fallacy of this war ending all wars and making the world safe for democracy. To me, it was clear that all of these slogans were false. I became involved in the socialist movement. My dad had always been a progressive mill worker. Mom was especially progressive. All their adult lives they were endowed with revolutionary ideas, dating back to Europe.

In the town of Woodlawn, I don't believe there were as many as a dozen registered Democrats. At that time, to be a Democrat, you had to be either brave or nuts. The postmaster, a fellow by the name of Chris Henderson, was appointed by Woodrow Wilson, so naturally he was a Democrat. Then there was myself, and a few others. When they would have balloting, Jones and Laughlin used to bring people from the mills in trucks to the voting place. They weren't even naturalized citizens, but they'd all vote the straight Republican ticket. Out of maybe several thousand votes, there would just be a half a dozen of us Democrats. J&L couldn't lose.

Jones and Laughlin controlled everything: the churches, the schools, the whole system. They domineered the town of Woodlawn through their private coal and iron police and the police captain, Harry G. Mauk. The J&L police carried their guns openly wherever they went. Their purpose was to intimidate people throughout the town, not only within the limits of the corporation. Harry Mauk—he was the main cheese, and he was cruel. He had a lieutenant by the name of Harris, who was his henchman. I remember them well because they questioned me and threatened me dozens of times.

The coal and iron police were domiciled right next to the J&L main office there in Aliquippa. The upper part of their place was the original dance floor of the old amusement park. They had all their machine guns, all their paraphernalia and tear gas and what have you, in there. And they had a shooting range right next door. Every day we could see them off of mom's dining room window, practicing with pistols, rifles, and so on.

This Harry G. Mauk, he was the power. Definitely! For instance, if there was a vacancy on the police force in town, it was always filled with a Jones and Laughlin coal and iron policeman. Or if there was a vacancy for chief of police, it was always filled with a cossack well trained by Captain Harry G. Mauk. Mauk was the fellow behind the political scene for J&L. The borough council was composed of strictly Jones and Laughlin people and the town's professionals. Mauk would direct Dr. Stevens, the physician, and Bud Scott, the dentist, and others. The reason I know is that Bud Scott was my dentist. A long time afterward, he told me, "Pete, I've been sympathetic with you all the time you were being persecuted by J&L. I hated that Mauk. He ordered me to be a councilman and told me, 'You will do at these council meetings what I tell you to do, and you will vote the way I tell you.'"

The council made the ordinances to suit J&L. If you had any kind of a gathering, you had to go down to the borough building to get a permit. If they felt you were leaning to the left or might be talking union, you did not get the permit. And those people didn't mince their words: "If you dare to have a meeting, Pete, we will blow your head off." They were told by J&L to make sure I didn't hold any meetings and that I didn't preach unions.

Well, I had the meetings anyway. So they'd arrest me. I was arrested so often I could have put my name tag on that cell down in the borough lock-up. Mom, naturally, was behind me one hundred percent. Every time they arrested me, she'd bring down the usual blankets and pillows.

The council would pass these ordinances, and I would defy them on the grounds that they were unconstitutional. They would tell me, and be very emphatic about it, "We make the rules. This is not the United States. This is Woodlawn, and we're going to do what we please because J&L gives bread and butter to all these people." I said, "No, wait. J&L gets bread and butter from the toil of these people. Their machinery wouldn't be worth a damn, wouldn't produce a thing if there was no labor injected into it."

Once I went down there and I started reading the Declaration of Independence: "When in the course of human events, it becomes necessary. . ." A cop said, "That's communistic stuff you're reading." When I got to the part where "all men are created equal," he wanted to put me in jail. And he did arrest me. But Charlie Laughlin, the chief of police, just happened to walk in. He said to that cop, "You dumb so-and-so, he's reading the Declaration of Independence."

Every once in a while the cops came to my home and just raided the place—no warrant, no nothing. They would take every book, every periodical, every bulletin; they'd just dump them in a pile and throw them in the police cruiser and they would never return them. They were looking for books on Marxism, but they could not distinguish one book from another. In order to make sure, they cleaned out the house.

When Mike Kane became chief of police, I'll tell you what he used to do. He'd ride up Baker Street in Logstown on his motorcycle and go between those company houses, go around back, and ride right into a boarding-house kitchen. With a *motorcycle* he'd go into the kitchen, dispersing the men who were there, and shout, "Break it up, you Hunkies!" And do you know what the men had been doing? They were either playing Ferbel, a card game, or they had a glass of wine in front of them, or maybe they were singing a little bit. Harmless, you know. Just having a little fun, relaxing. And they had very little of that in general because in those days they worked twelve-hour shifts, seven days a week, most of them.

When you left the mill at the end of your shift, you were pretty tired, really fatigued. And naturally an average person of middle age would be almost groggy from overwork. Do you know they used to arrest workers on their way home from the mill on a charge of intoxication? A cop would pick them up—"You're drunk, Hunky"—and then run them down to Squire Miller, who was right across from the police station. Miller was a big, fat guy who worked with the police so close and slick. Miller would levy the usual fine: "Eleven sixty-five, Joe." Everyone was "Joe." The story was he retired in California with a bundle of half a million dollars from dispensing J&L justice and civil order. That was Woodlawn.

Woodlawn was your typical coal and iron town, only probably one of the worst in the country. According to law, it takes three or more to "incite to riot." In Woodlawn that was not the rule. When two people met peacefully, and might have been talking about who knows what, according to the Woodlawn police they were inciting to riot: "Break it up, Hunkies." They assumed they were talking unionism.

See, they feared unions. They feared any talk of unionism, so they watched the workers in the mill for any sign of union literature and made sure they broke up any meeting. Do you know that a policeman used to attend our Croatian fraternal lodge meetings? He stood in the back there, big guns strapped to his side, his arms crossed, with a club dangling down. He didn't know what we were saying because he was not Croatian. He just wanted to make sure that he didn't hear the word "union" or something like that. He had no business there, but what could you do? Woodlawn in those days was a typical cossack town.

I was arrested during a raid, in 1926, at our lodge meeting. There were thirty or more people arrested that evening. Most of them were released except for five of us. That was myself, Tom Zima, Milan Resetar, Steve Bratich, and Philip Vidovich. We were indicted on a charge of sedition. They said we wanted to overthrow the government of the United States. Judge Frank Reader threw that indictment out, and we thought we were in the clear. But Frank Reader was being shrewd. He knew he'd never get a conviction in a federal court in Pittsburgh because there was no evidence. So he personally drew up a new indictment against us for violating the Pennsylvania state sedition law. According to him, we just hurt Pennsylvania. Not Ohio. Not West Virginia. We were only bastards in Pennsylvania.

The district attorney was a fellow by the name of McGowan. He wouldn't touch the case. He said there was no evidence to convict us, because we didn't do a damn thing. So Dave W. Craig had himself appointed special prosecutor for our case. Craig had been the solicitor for Jones and Laughlin for years and years. Dave Craig was also an archreactionary and the chairman of the Republican Party of Beaver County. He was the undisputed boss at that time.

Would you believe that when Craig was a state senator, in 1917, he voted against this same sedition law? He thought it was too drastic. Why arrest anybody for their ideas? Yet he used that very same act that he voted against. According to our attorney, the state sedition law should have terminated when the war was over. But, hell, nobody in Harrisburg saw fit to enter that motion to wipe it off the books. It just stayed. It was the same law that was used during the McCarthy period in the 1950s. And now Craig was using it effectively against us.

Craig entered the indictment in the court. At the next session of the grand jury, they found a true bill against us. And we were reindicted for violating the state sedition act. We were tried in 1927 and found guilty. Henry Wilson, the only Democrat in the Beaver County Bar Association, took our case. He was a brilliant lawyer. But Dave Craig had everything. The judge was his, the witnesses were his, everything was his.

Judge William McConnell sentenced us to five years in the Allegheny County workhouse in Blawnox. The workhouse was known as one of the dirtiest, the toughest jails in Pennsylvania. The food was repulsive. The treatment was so bad on the part of the administration there that for any minor infraction of the rules, they'd put you in the hole. You'd get one or two slices of bread and one cup of water per day. With that one cup of water, you had the option of drinking it if you were thirsty, brushing your teeth, or washing yourself. And you slept on the floor, on a couple of boards nailed together. You had no bunk or anything. That was cruel and unusual punishment. That's why Judge McConnell sentenced us to Blawnox workhouse.

Of course, we appealed our case. When we exhausted all of our appeals in the lower courts, we went to the Supreme Court of the United States. They wouldn't review it, so we were committed to jail in 1929. We were in there two years and a couple of months. At one point, they wanted to give us parole, but we wouldn't accept that. We wanted an outright release, no conditions, because we knew we were not guilty of anything.

The American Civil Liberties Union finally took up our case. It was very active in our behalf and got Cornelia Pinchot, the wife of Governor Pinchot, interested. Cornelia was very good that way, and she was able to influence members of the pardon board. There were five of them, I think: the lieutenant governor, the secretary of the state, the attorney general, and a couple more. They commuted our sentences, fully realizing we had been framed.

In February of 1932, we were released. Resetar died about two or three months before. He had been committed to the prison hospital. They had a very well equipped hospital, by the way, but that didn't help Resetar. All of a sudden I was told in my cell, "Your buddy passed away."

Dr. Mitchell was the prison doctor, a big-time legionnaire, and a major in the army reserves. He detested anybody who was progressive. I remember when I was taken to the same hospital, Dr. Mitchell didn't do anything to help me. One of the orderlies said, "Pete is running a high fever." Mitchell said, "I don't give a damn. If he croaks, don't disturb me at home. I'll be back here in the morning." Well, I pulled through, but poor Resetar didn't. I believe they actually killed him.

After we were released in 1932, I resumed my activities. There had been efforts to unionize the steel mills. There were picket lines at National Metal Moulding and H. H. Robinson in Ambridge, across the river from Aliquippa. Then John L. Lewis sent old Joe Timko from the United Mine Workers down to Ambridge as an organizer. He had an office on Merchant Street. We started a political organization together; he was chairman and I was vice-chairman. Wimber was our first candidate for burgess of Ambridge. Of course, we didn't stand a chance because the companies controlled the ballot box. We just wanted to show that there should be opposition to the entrenched powers.

In 1933, there was the strike at what is now known as American Rolling Mill, at Twenty-fourth and Duss. The workers there were making very low wages and didn't have any fringe benefits, not even holidays. Philip Caul was the burgess at that time. He was the former captain of the Ambridge police. He really didn't know what side he was on half the time. During that strike he flipped over to the other side, against us. Caul rode up and down Duss Avenue with a big shotgun in the crook of his arm: "I'm going to shoot every goddamn communist I run across."

I was one of the leaders of that strike, with Jimmy Egan from Pittsburgh and Patsy Moore, Bill Heinz, and Joe Potts. The strike was broken up when deputies and thugs came from Aliquippa to brutally attack the strikers. They were deputized at the American Legion Post there by none other than Dave W. Craig, whose nephew ran that post. The legionnaires had been deputized so quickly, they needed some form of identification so they wouldn't shoot and club each other instead of the strikers. They all wore white handkerchiefs around their arms. They came across the bridge in buses carrying rifles loaded with ammunition. They were throwing tear gas bombs and shooting. They killed Adam Pietrowsky.

It was probably meant for me. See, my brother Tony was standing right next to Adam when he was shot. Tony and I looked almost like twins. They must have taken aim at Tony but hit Adam, right beside him. I petitioned Governor Pinchot for a public hearing on the killing. The hearing took place in the high school auditorium. Craig was there, and he made it seem like it was accidental: "Things like that just happen." But some deputies were there who testified that they were gunning for me.

The brutal attack of the deputies upon the Ambridge strikers and the murder of an innocent man were whitewashed by the corrupt political machine of boss David W. Craig of Beaver County. Much, much more could be said about the iniquities perpetrated upon the workers and residents of Aliquippa by the henchmen of the Jones and Laughlin Steel Corporation.

Forbidden Books on Trial

Gil Green

It's difficult today to imagine the intensity and scope of the U.S. govern-
ment's attack on the Communist Party during the Cold War. Commu-
nists were fired from government jobs, forbidden to hold elected posi-
tions in unions, denied old-age benefits, deported, trailed day and night
by the FBI, and barred from appearing on the ballot in twenty-five
states. In nearly as many states, the Communist Party itself was out-
lawed. Ten internment camps were prepared for American Communists
in the event of a "national emergency."

In 1949, Gil Green and ten other leaders of the Communist Party
were convicted under the Smith Act. Modeled after the New York state
sedition law, the act prohibited teaching or advocating the duty or de-
sirability of overthrowing the government by force and violence. The
proof of the government's claim against Gil Green and the other ten
was sought in passages from books the defendants had studied and
taught, as interpreted by government witnesses.

Inevitably, it became a trial of written and spoken ideas, which
placed the First Amendment in serious jeopardy. "I repeat that we deal
here with speech alone," Justice William O. Douglas wrote, "not with
speech plus acts of sabotage or unlawful conduct. Not a single seditious
act is charged in the indictment."[1] But the dominant opinion of the
Court at that moment was that Communists, by teaching the doctrines

GIL GREEN

of Marxism, were a great enough evil to justify this invasion of First Amendment rights.

More than one hundred prosecutions of Communists followed, using virtually identical charges and evidence. Then, six years later, the Supreme Court considered a case against California Communist leaders. This time, the Court ruled in favor of five of them, stating that "so far as this record shows, none of them has engaged in or been associated with any but what appear to have been wholly lawful activities."[2] A new trial was ordered for the others, but, faced with having to produce direct evidence of the advocacy of action by each defendant, the government's Smith Act cases collapsed. The wave of Smith Act prosecutions was brought to an end, but it had already contributed to a climate hostile to the expression of dissent.

The red scare was on. Supposedly, Russians had infiltrated everywhere and there were spies everywhere. Alger Hiss, a top adviser in the State Department, was suddenly accused of being a Soviet spy. The Rosenberg case aroused the country and inflamed public opinion; the Rosenbergs finally paid with their lives. The hysteria grew to immense proportions. It swept over from one area of life to another. The top leadership of the CIO, which had worked with Communists up to that point, expelled eleven of the most progressive unions from its ranks. The House Un-American Committee caused thousands of people to lose their jobs because they were accused of being Communists or sympathetic to Communists. Only the courageous spoke up. People were so frightened that when a reporter for the *St. Louis Post-Dispatch* went out into the streets with the Preamble to the U.S. Constitution, they refused to sign even that.

As part of all this, the government claimed there was an organized conspiracy of considerable influence and strength in this country—the Communist Party itself. A grand jury had been set up to investigate espionage and spying. There had been articles in the press that something was being cooked up, but they couldn't come up with anything against the party or its leaders. Then, just before the grand jury disbanded, on July 20, 1948, the Justice Department produced the first Smith Act indictments against the Communist Party, the twelve members of the national board. I was one of them and at that time the chairperson of the Communist Party of Illinois.

We were not charged with acts of force and violence or even conspiring to practice force and violence. We were charged with conspiring to *teach* and *advocate* the duty to overthrow the government by force and violence at some future time. The only "acts" of the conspiracy were that there was a Communist Party, that we were elected leaders of it, and that we believed in and taught from the classics of Marxism-Leninism. Clearly, what was going to be on trial was our beliefs.

The trial began in January 1949. The whole area was roped off. Police were everywhere. They were mobilized as if there was going to be a major encounter or a civil war of some kind. The purpose of it all was to frighten the nation with the specter of a revolutionary plot. The *New York Times* reported it was the largest armed contingent for a court case in police history.

The government's "evidence" consisted mainly of excerpts from books and ludicrous stories told by informers. A man by the name of Nicodemus testified he had attended a Communist Party school where somebody said, "The revolution wouldn't be successful in this country without the help of the Red Army." When someone asked, "How can the Soviets invade the United States without a navy?" the answer supposedly was, "They can cross the Bering Strait to Alaska, and then come across Canada and destroy Detroit."

Now, no one could seriously believe the country was threatened by revolution, but many feared that war with the Soviet Union was inevitable, if not imminent. The government used Nicodemus to link the two together. It made us laugh because it seemed so ridiculous. Judge Medina rebuked us for "smiling broadly." He said, "It may seem funny to the defendants, but I don't think it is." Then, giving credence to what Nicodemus said, he asked, "They could even destroy Detroit, as I understand it? Did you say that?" And Nicodemus answered, "That is what I said."

The government used selections from the writings of Marx, Engels, Lenin, Stalin as evidence of the conspiracy. These books are in most libraries and used in college and university courses. Some of them, like the *Communist Manifesto*, were a hundred years old. Our attorneys objected strongly to the introduction of books into the record: "It is not proper in a court of law to try men upon the fact that they recommended a book for study." My own lawyer said, "Putting books into the record was like putting them on trial." The judge overruled their objections: "Yes, but these are the tools of their conspiracy," as if we were thieves and the books were our weapons.

We studied the books for their general principles, not as dogmas. Although in earlier years we had talked glibly about revolutionary overthrow like the Russians, in time our position changed fundamentally. Obviously, what happened there didn't apply directly to the United States. But the government said our use of Marxist classics was proof that we advocated force and violence.

The prosecution did it by the clever use of one witness, a man by the name of Louis Budenz. Budenz had been an associate editor of the *Daily Worker*. When the Cold War started, he turned tail, ran in the opposite direction, and then became the professional "expert" on communism for the inquisition. He was the star witness against us. Budenz was shown the constitution of the Communist Party, which said that the party based itself upon the principles of scientific socialism, Marxism-Leninism. He said those were code words for the violent overthrow of the government. It was "Aesopian language" and those "on the in" knew that the paragraph in the constitution that decries force and violence means the opposite of what it says.

Well, I'll tell you, I was stunned when I heard that. The fact that we had not advocated violent overthrow was used as evidence that we had. We were being found guilty because of what we did not say. How could anyone defend themselves against that? The only way we could imagine was to make clear what it was we did advocate. Certainly we would have been justified by the First Amendment to say, "We have the right to advocate what we want." But in those days it would have been interpreted as "These bastards *are* guilty of plotting the overthrow of the government by force and violence." So we had to combine the use of the First Amendment with an explanation of our beliefs and activities.

We described what our party classes were like, the schools we taught, other things. The point of our struggles was to help people win more democracy. We organized workers into industrial unions, for Black freedom, against the poll tax. We fought for social security and unemployment compensation. Yet when we tried to show what we actually did, the judge said, "That isn't an issue here."

I had written an article in 1938 called "A Note in Defense of American Democracy," together with Eugene Dennis, the general secretary of the Communist Party. We said there was a time before fascism when the party felt its objective was to expose the limitations of our democracy, the hypocrisy involved. You don't have democracy when Black people are disenfranchised, when lynchings are common. You don't really have democracy when a few people own such immense wealth and so many are poor and have nothing. You can't separate political from economic democracy. But with the rise of fascism in the world, we felt it was important to defend those democratic rights that had already been won by the people. It was wrong to think that there's no difference between capitalism under fascism and capitalism under a democratic rule. We said Communists had to come forward as champions in the struggle for increased democracy.

Now, here was an article written by two defendants long before the trial that showed we advocated democracy, not force and violence. But when my lawyer introduced this as evidence while I was on the stand, the prosecutor jumped up and said, "I object, your honor. This isn't relevant." The judge said, "Objection sustained."

Well, I turned to the judge and said, "Your honor, I thought we were going to be given a chance to prove our case. This article is germane to the very heart of the issue." Whereupon he took his gavel, banged it down, and said, "I'm going to charge you right now with contempt of court." So in the midst of the trial my bail was withdrawn and I was incarcerated. For the last four and a half months I was taken handcuffed from the prison every morning to the courtroom.

You should know that this ability of a judge to cite and jail a defendant for contempt right on the spot had been used only against Communists. It was first used against John Gates, the defendant who testified before me. A veteran of the Spanish civil war and World War II, he had been a member of the veterans' commission of the party. He was asked to name the other members of the commission. In that period, to name names meant you were only adding people to be called by the House Un-American Committee, people who would be fired from their jobs and blacklisted. So Gates refused; Judge Harold Medina insisted, and Gates was remanded to prison for thirty days. There was turmoil in the courtroom. Gus Hall and Henry Winston rose up to protest. The judge remanded them back to prison, too.

This judge was biased even before the trial began. William Z. Foster, chairman of the Communist Party, had a heart attack, and his case was severed. We wanted to postpone the trial for ninety days to give him a chance to recover enough so he could take part in the preparation of the defense. Our lawyer went to the federal court in New York and asked for a three-month extension. The prosecutor objected: "Your honor, if you give them a three-month postponement, it will be three more months in which they can continue to carry on their unlawful activities." The judge agreed: "If we let them do that sort of thing, they'll destroy the government." He had already found us guilty of acting to overthrow the government, something that went far beyond the indictment. This was the same Harold Medina who, with all his bias, was chosen to be the judge in our trial.

I was the second defense witness to testify. I talked about my past and what led me to the movement. There was an incident that seems small, but it stayed with me all these years. When I was ten or eleven, there was only one Black child in my class; her name was Mary. During recess she sat alone on the curb. She was ostracized and kept to herself. Every Friday for ten minutes the teacher let us play "tag." We'd all put our heads in our hands, and the person who was "it" went around the room and poked somebody. He or she would have to get up and try to beat the other person to their seat. Mary was never tapped by anybody, over weeks and months, never. I felt a growing sense of shame and decided the next time I got to be "it," I would tap her. That day came, and I did. But she just sat there. I thought maybe she hadn't felt my tap. I went around and tapped her again, and this time she burst into tears.

That had a profound effect on me. Maybe it had something to do with my own experience as a Jew. When my father became gravely ill with diabetes, my parents opened up a little cleaning and dyeing store on Archer Avenue, a Polish-Irish community. Between them they were able to eke out a living. We lived in back of the store behind a wooden partition. My brother Harry and I were the only Jewish children in the school. As soon as that became known, the kids would shout, "Sheenies, Christ-killers!" And we would periodically have to run all the way home with a gang of kids chasing after us. So we tasted something of anti-Semitism as children.

Generally, it was a rebellion on my part, what I saw with my own eyes and experienced as a young person, that made me a radical. My father died when I was nine years of age and he was only thirty-three. We moved to the Jewish ghetto in Chicago, on the west side. My mother had to go to work to feed the family. I was the oldest of three boys, and as soon as I could I sold newspapers or whatever to earn a little bit. I wrapped packages after school at a mail-order house, washed dishes on weekends, and worked as a millwright's helper over the summer. Wages and conditions were miserable. I was struck by the fact that in the richest country in the world such poverty existed. I couldn't explain it to myself.

Some answers I heard from a blind soapbox orator who talked about socialism. I was influenced by my uncle, who gave me socialist literature to read once in a while. As I grew a little older, I began to read about the Russian Revolution, and I was taken with what they were trying to do there. Then a friend of mine took me to his piano teacher, who had a library of socialist books. I became friends with this old man, and from him I was brought more and more to what was then the socialist-communist movement. About the same time I graduated high school I joined the Young Workers League, which later became the Young Communist League.

After three months of looking for full-time work, I was finally hired by the Sinclair Refining Company. My job was to type bills of lading and help with the physical work of getting the drums ready for shipment. This job reinforced what I had been reading about the pyramidal structure of society. The few bosses were up on the top floor. On the middle floor where I was, you had mainly white-collar workers. In the basement, where oil was refined in huge vats, most of the workers, mainly Polish-born, did the heavy, dirty work.

One of the objectives of the Young Workers League was to help organize the unorganized. There was certainly plenty to find fault with on the job, but the workers were afraid to talk about unions. We worked a fifty-four-hour week, with no time and a half for overtime. One week there was a rumor we would have to work on Sunday, too. The workers resented very much giving up a day when many went to church and spent time with their families. They swore they'd say no if asked. But when the superintendent, Barlow, announced it, nobody said anything. I waited. He started to leave, and I spoke up. I told him it wasn't fair to make us work Sunday, our one day off. Barlow was angry: "The man that doesn't show up tomorrow morning needn't show up on Monday." He turned to me. "As for you, you better keep your mouth shut. You're not old enough to know what's right and what's wrong." That was it. When he left, there was no talk amongst us. We knew we would be there the next morning.

I was a kid then, but somehow I'd grown up in their eyes because I had the gumption to say something. Two weeks later I was called into Barlow's office. "You're a good worker," he said, "but I know you've been discussing unionism at Communist meetings. Go there one more time and you're through." I wondered how he knew about my Friday night meetings. I stayed away for a while and then attended the next meeting, being careful I wasn't followed. But when Monday came, I was fired. I never found out who the stool pigeon was, but my experience bore out what I'd read and heard about the use of company spies to keep unions out.

After trying to get jobs and being turned down at a number of places, even where I knew others had been hired, I drew the conclusion that there was a blacklist at work. I finally did get a job in the McCormick Reaper plant, but under the assumed name of George Gilberts. I worked at the same building where, in 1886, May Day was born. We had a small Communist Party group that discussed working conditions, how to have unity among the many nationalities there, and how to start an industrial union. We put out a paper regularly that I helped edit to keep alive the traditions of 1886 and the goal of socialism.

In the 1930s, I was the national chairman of the Young Communist League. The YCL then was affiliated with the Young Communist International, which had its headquarters in Moscow. So I made a number of trips to the Soviet Union. When I was on the stand, the prosecutor tried to paint them in conspiratorial colors: "When did you leave on this visit? What boat did you take?" He wanted the exact times after all those years. I only knew that I always left from the port of New York and came back to the port of New York and went with my own passport. When I said I couldn't remember, he made it appear to the jury that I was trying to hide something. But there was nothing to hide; all the records were open.

I did tell the jury, however, that I violated an administrative decree when I went to Spain during its civil war. Franco, the fascist general, was engaged in overthrowing the democratically elected government of Spain. The Western countries imposed an arms embargo in the name of "neutrality," while Hitler and Mussolini shipped Franco huge quantities of weapons and bombed Spanish cities like Guernica. It was the first time in warfare that a civilian population was made the enemy.

The United States had forbidden travel to Spain. I got word there was to be a joint meeting of representatives of the Young Communist International and the Young Socialist International, to work together in defense of the Spanish Republic. I had been chosen as one of the three to represent the Young Communist International. So I had to face this question: Was I going to go there in order to help bring about this unity, or was I going to stay at home because there was a legal edict against it? I made up my mind I would go.

The prosecutor told the jury that this proved that here is somebody who has not lived up to the letter of the law, who set himself above the State Department. And in the eyes of those who were seeking conspiracy, that seemed to be some evidence.

The trial lasted from January to October 1949. The verdict against us didn't come as a surprise, that's for sure. Our case went quickly from the lower court to the court of appeals to the Supreme Court. With the outbreak of the Korean war the hysteria only grew greater, and the pressure was on the Court to act rapidly. The Supreme Court did not rule on the sufficiency of evidence, but they upheld the constitutionality of the Smith Act under which we were indicted. In June 1951 we were ordered to prison.

It was a shocking thing for my family, but the one who had the greatest difficulty of all was my mother. She was a simple woman who worked well into her seventies in the needle trades industry of Chicago. She never really learned to read and followed everything by listening to the radio. She believed in her boys, that they were doing only what was right, but she couldn't understand what this all meant. The fact that I had to serve a prison sentence was a terrible shock. My mother suffered immensely during that period.

When the Supreme Court upheld our conviction, we were determined not to give up the fight. We considered whether some of us should go underground. But we knew people could point to us: See, obviously they're conspirators. The national board itself was divided. Some thought nobody should go underground. Others felt everybody should go. At the very time we were discussing the matter, twenty-one leaders of the New York party were indicted under the Smith Act. And it was openly said that this was just the beginning of indictments all over the country. A headline in the New York paper the *Journal American* read, "FBI Ready To Move on 20,000 New York Reds." What if they had fifty other trials? A law was introduced in Congress to declare the party illegal. Concentration camps were being set up.

We remembered how devastating the raids against the IWW, the Wobblies, had been after World War I. The entire leadership, over one hundred, went to jail. J. Edgar Hoover had orchestrated those raids. We've since learned from FBI files that our fears were well founded. The FBI was very critical of Truman when his administration indicted only twelve of us. They wanted a John Doe indictment that could be used against anybody all over the country, in the same way it was done against the IWW.

An FBI document I have shows this:

> It had been hoped that the Grand Jury investigation would be carried out in much the same manner as the investigation of the Industrial Workers of the World (IWW) in 1917 during World

War I. The IWW case was inaugurated by a simultaneous national move against every IWW headquarters throughout the United States. All national and local leaders of the IWW were indicted for conspiracy by the Federal Grand Jury in Chicago, were convicted and over one hundred sentenced to long prison terms. As a result of this joint national action the IWW as a subversive menace was crushed and has never revived. Similar action at this time would have been as effective against the Communist Party and its subsidiary organizations.[3]

We preferred to be out in the open. Look, we tried to be out in the open. But if we could exist only by going underground, then that's how it would be. Once it was decided upon, a small committee was made responsible to choose who would go. Four of us were chosen: Gus Hall, Henry Winston, Robert Thompson, and myself. I didn't know I was one of them until a couple of days before I had to surrender to do my time.

I had come into New York from Chicago with my family. We took nearly a week, slowly making our way, so we could have time together. My wife and I had made arrangements for the two oldest children to spend a month in a left-wing camp in New Jersey. That way they would at least be removed from the adverse publicity of my going to jail. Maybe things would calm down by the time they got back. The day we got into New York, a Friday, there was a party given for the eleven. We were supposed to surrender on Monday. At that party, I was taken aside and told, "You're one of those we believe should go underground." I must confess I didn't like the idea. I wasn't sure whether part of it was a fear of living a hunted life or the responsibility for something I had never undertaken before. Maybe I was afraid. But I thought, "Like it or not, I've got to do it." I agreed.

As soon as the FBI found out I had not turned myself in, they demanded that the management of the camp exclude my children and send them back home. And they finally gave in. That was a terrible blow to the children. I was very angry when I heard it. How could progressive people do something like that? But they argued—and I've talked to some of them since—that the FBI threatened that the camp would be surrounded by agents, the community would be alerted, and the camp would be in danger. Previously, when Paul Robeson had come to sing, there had been threats to burn the camp down.

What reason could the FBI have for forcing my kids out of camp except to take it out on them? That began their psychological warfare against my family. The FBI tried to get my mother to cooperate, on the assumption that she knew where I was. She had no idea, but when she refused they kept after her. They came to her place of work in order to intimidate her: "Look, we don't know under what conditions we may find your son and whether we will have to use force. We know you'd rather have him alive than dead." Soon, in her own mind this was transformed into something else—that they had found me and I had been killed. And she lived haunted by the fear that actually I was dead. That was a terrible, terrible thing.

The FBI confronted my wife in the same way in front of the children. They said that sooner or later they were going to find me and that it would be better if she cooperated: "You don't want to see your husband dead, do you?" FBI cars were posted outside day and night where my wife was living and where my brother was living. My children were followed every day, to and from school. It had a traumatic effect on my daughter. At ten years of age all she knew was that we were in trouble, that I was away from home, that I was underground and sentenced to go to prison. It's a lucky thing I had my brother Ben in Chicago. He was a wonderful human being, and he helped my wife a great deal and he helped the children. He was able to turn the constant FBI surveillance into games with the kids, taking the edge off some of their fears.

Shortly after I went underground, I received word telling me to make arrangements to go to Mexico as soon as I could. I assumed it came from Gus Hall or Henry Winston. I wrote back, telling them I was unalterably opposed to it, that I never would have agreed to go underground if it meant leaving the country. I didn't think there was the kind of repression that necessitated going across the borders, and if I was to function well, it would have to be here. I never received a reply, but sometime after that I heard on the twelve o'clock news that Gus Hall was picked up in Mexico.

It was then that the other three of us got together. We chose a Brooklyn home, although I was in Chicago and Bob Thompson was elsewhere. Henry Winston, who was Black, lived there, and we knew it would be more difficult for him to travel than for us. We decided that going to Mexico was wrong, that we should stay here and find some way to maintain our relationship with those in the open leadership. We had to find a way to do the things they couldn't do, because they had tremendous problems. There was one trial after another. Huge sums of money had to be raised, and they had a hell of a time finding lawyers.

In our trial, for the first time, lawyers for the defendants were sent to prison for contempt along with their clients. My own lawyer, Abe Isserman, a prominent labor attorney and national board member of the American Civil Liberties Union, served a four-month sentence and then was disbarred from practicing law. It was not until eleven years later that he was permitted to go back to the bar. The same thing happened to Harry Sacher. It was a warning to stay away from Communist cases.

Throughout that period, I wrote articles under an assumed name. Then Bob Thompson was picked up in California, in the mountains there. Now only Henry Winston and I were left. By that time, the McCarthy period had ebbed. Some of the first group of defendants were about to be released from prison and would be able to function. We suggested that the underground be done away with. We wanted to turn ourselves in and end this business. But our co-defendants argued that they were still under parole jurisdiction and could be sent back. That meant another year.

I used that time to write a book called *The Enemy Forgotten.* I tried to answer how this could happen to our country. My explanation was that Americans had forgotten their real enemy for a fictitious one. The United States, the most powerful capitalist country, faced no threat of revolution, whether peaceful or violent. And it was not menaced from abroad. Other capitalist countries, much smaller and weaker, much closer to the Soviet Union, with powerful socialist and communist movements, were not as hysterical as we were. Why then the hysteria here? I said the red scare led Americans to lose sight of what progressive forces historically saw as the real foe, the vested interests: whether it was the British Crown, the propertied class, the slaveholders, the robber barons, or, now, the multinationals. As a result, gains won by labor and progressive forces in the New Deal era were lost, labor militancy and radicalism were snuffed out, and the nation was intimidated into accepting a staggering armament burden.

When the year was up, Winston and I surrendered. Knowing J. Edgar Hoover was racist, we were fearful that Winston would be treated harshly. So we decided I would go first, to establish a precedent as to how he should be handled. Ten days before I was to surrender, I wrote a letter to the press signed with my own handwriting: I would be at Foley Square Courthouse at twelve o'clock noon on Monday. I sent a separate letter to my wife. Once the story broke, many friends and comrades gathered on the steps of the courthouse square, awaiting me.

Well, I knew the FBI would be watching that square from all sides to grab me beforehand. I wanted the satisfaction of turning myself in. I had been living for the last few weeks with some friends across the river in New Jersey. I was driven to the Hudson River tubes, took them across to New York, and got off at a station in Greenwich Village with the manuscript of the book under my arm. I immediately dropped the manuscript into a mailbox.

This was about eleven-forty. I hailed a cab and asked the driver to drive around. I told him who I was, that I'd been underground, and why I was turning myself in. I said, "Look, I want you to drop me at the Foley Square Courthouse punctually at twelve o'clock, not on the street side, but on the entrance side by the steps." And he did exactly that. The cab stopped. I got out right into a crowd of friends. It was a very emotional moment. First I embraced the family. Then, of course, the press crowded in. They wanted to know where I'd been. I said, "Well, I lived on the corner of Bill of Rights Avenue and Constitution Street."

I was put in a cell, and my lawyer got permission for my family to spend a half hour or so with me. I had a chance to talk to them for the first time in nearly five years. Then I was brought before a judge, charged with jumping bail, and sentenced to three additional years. The five-year sentence became eight years.

To me, prison was a very important forward movement. To become free again, I had to do my time. And while in the underground I could not have any personal contact with my family, at least in prison I could. I used to see a kid on the street and say, "My God, that looks like Danny." Then it suddenly struck me that I didn't know what Danny looked like because years had passed. So to be in touch with the family again, to be in touch with my wife meant to be alive again as a human being, as terrible as it was to be in prison.

Prison wasn't an unknown quantity. I had spent four and a half months there during the trial. Once you know something, you can cope with it, so to speak. But Leavenworth is a very tough place, and it was hard to be locked up in a cell by yourself; or to be with other inmates convicted of all crimes, people who are completely different from you; to live with the doors clanged shut behind you; to have to carry through orders; not to be referred to by name as much as you were by number.

After the Supreme Court decision, there were thirteen additional trials of Communist leaders across the country for violating the Smith Act. Every one of the defendants whose name was submitted to a jury was found guilty. The California defendants, like the others, were convicted on the same charge with the same kind of evidence as we were. In 1957, their case reached the Supreme Court. By that time, the war in

Korea was over and the hysteria that it could lead to war with China or the Soviet Union was not there. And there was a change in composition of the Supreme Court. As against Vinson, a reactionary, Earl Warren became chief justice. This time the Supreme Court looked into the sufficiency of evidence and decided there was no evidence the Communist Party conspired to teach and advocate a violent overthrow. Six years after the Supreme Court had found us guilty, they, in effect, found us innocent.

There were a number of other trials pending before the courts. All those cases collapsed, and the Smith Act was never used again. I was in prison then and wrote my attorney, John Abt, "Look, John. This is the opportunity to spring me." He wrote back, "Too bad, Gil, but court decisions are not retroactive." I had to do my time anyway. I did some five and a half years in Leavenworth. Add to that the four and a half months when Medina sentenced me for contempt, and all together I spent almost six years in prison. By then Danny had married. When I came out I was a grandfather of two grandchildren.

You pay a price for fighting, and I paid a lesser one than others. At least I came out of prison healthy. Look at Henry Winston. He was blinded in prison. Bob Thompson was hit on the head with an iron bar and died a few years after. Innumerable young friends of mine paid with their lives in the struggle. Joe York and Joe Bissell were shot down in cold blood on a hunger march in Detroit. Harry Simms was shot on a railroad trestle down in Kentucky, working with the miners during a strike. There were so many incidents of that kind. In Chicago, fifty thousand workers, poor people, marched behind coffins of unemployed workers who were shot. And think of the men and women who died to put an end to slavery or in the American Revolution. In other words, I can't just take what happened to me personally, not that I didn't feel it deeply.

And I always figured I was well off compared with those who sold their souls to save their skins. Remember, that was when so many people went before the House Un-American Committee and said anything they were told to say in order to get exoneration for themselves. I was in prison, but I felt both anger and sorrow about them. I didn't know how they could continue to live with themselves. At least I didn't have to face that problem.

BENJAMIN SPOCK

The Conspiracy to Oppose
the Vietnam War

Benjamin Spock

The Selective Service Act of 1948 made it a criminal offense for a person to knowingly counsel, aid, or abet someone in refusing or evading registration in the armed forces. In 1968, Dr. Benjamin Spock and four others were indicted for conspiring to violate this act. Evidence of the conspiracy was to be found in the public expressions of the defendants: hours of selectively edited newsreel footage of press conferences, demonstrations, and public addresses they had made in opposition to government policy in Vietnam. What could better symbolize the damage such prosecutions inflict on the free marketplace of ideas!

Why were they charged with conspiracy *to counsel, aid, and abet rather than with the commission of those acts themselves? Conspiracy, Judge Learned Hand said, is "the darling of the modern prosecutor's nursery."* [1] *It relaxes ordinary rules of evidence, frequently results in higher penalties than the substantive crime, may extend the statute of limitations, and holds all conspirators responsible for the acts of each. The conspirators may have acted entirely in the open; they may never have met; they may have agreed only implicitly; they may never have acted illegally. It's enough that they were of a like mind to do so.*

When applied to political activity, writing, and speech, a conspiracy charge has virtually no limits. Government attorneys could have included as co-conspirators the publishers of Dr. Spock's books on the war, the booksellers, and even members of his audiences who applauded in support of him. Yale Law School's Professor Thomas Emerson warns: "It thus becomes dangerous for any individual to participate in a campaign or demonstration that in the course of its unfolding may give rise to some violation of the law. It is hard to conceive of a more chilling effect upon the system of free expression." [2]

"If I were Attorney General now," said Ramsey Clark, the attorney general who initiated the prosecution of Benjamin Spock, "I would be inclined to prohibit the use of conspiracy charges altogether." [3]

I was a New Deal Democrat. I was always interested in politics, but I wasn't active until I joined the National Committee for a Sane Nuclear Policy in 1962. They had asked me to join them two times previously, in the late 1950s, but I told them, "I don't know anything about radiation. Besides, I reassure parents; I don't scare them."

The issue at the time was the need for a test ban treaty. When SANE came back a third time, in 1962, they got through to my conscience. I have to give them credit for persistence. They convinced me it was a pediatric issue. I realized that if we didn't have a test ban treaty, if all nations kept inventing arms, more and more children would be born with mental and physical defects and would die of cancer and leukemia.

Then I was asked, in 1964, by Lyndon Johnson's campaign committee to support him on radio and television. His Republican opponent was Barry Goldwater, who had said: Let's erase Vietnam if it's in our way. But Lyndon Johnson promised he would not send American boys to fight in an Asian war. So I said, "Sure. I'll support him as a citizen, as a pediatrician, and as a spokesman for the disarmament movement."

And I did enough so that he called me two days after the election to thank me. "Dr. Spock," he said, "I hope I prove worthy of your trust." Then he betrayed all those who voted for him as a nonwar candidate. He waited only three months to do the exact opposite of what he had promised. I was outraged and horrified. And I quadrupled my antiwar activities.

When I retired as a professor in 1967, I became a full-time opponent of the war in Vietnam. I visited a different university every day of the week at the invitation of undergraduates. There would be a press conference at the airport, lunch with students, teaching a class after lunch, television interviews, a radio interview or two, supper with students, say a few words, speech from eight to nine, answer questions from nine to ten, repair to the student lounge for more questions from ten to eleven. At eleven they'd say, "Now we're going to Professor Jenkins's house where we can really relax."

But there was no relaxing. As I sat on the professor's sofa, the discussion with students about the war and what they ought to do about it went on, intensely. I thought the young people who were opposing the war were wonderful. I had the greatest admiration for them, and I learned a lot from them.

I supported the Call to Resist Illegitimate Authority that twenty-five thousand people eventually signed, many of them leading academicians. We said that the war was totally unconstitutional, illegal, a crime against humanity, and full of war crimes. We said that the U.S. combat troops in Vietnam destroyed rice crops and livestock, burned entire villages, put villagers in concentration camps, and slaughtered peasants. The Call also made this statement, this bold statement drawn from the Nuremberg Principle: ". . . every free man has a legal right and moral duty to exert every effort to end this war, to avoid collusion with it, and to encourage others to do the same." Then it said that we would give moral and financial support to those who resisted the draft.

I had participated in a demonstration at the Whitehall Street induction center in New York City. At five A.M., the center was surrounded by five thousand police, with the street lights glinting on their badges, and two thousand demonstrators. Dave McReynolds was in charge. He asked me to lead the main body of people up to the police barriers in front of the building and wait for a signal from him to crawl under the barriers. I waited for half an hour, with the press asking me every few minutes what we were going to do. Finally, without a signal, I dropped to my knees in the crush of people and press and tried to crawl under the barrier. But the police closed ranks, and I couldn't get through their shins. I had to stand up again and face the press, who demanded to know what I'd been trying to do. I pushed my way down the line of barriers and tried twice more to get under. Then I tried to climb over. But the police pushed me back and laughed at me.

Then I found an opening in their ranks, and there stood Chief Inspector Garelick. In a voice like that of a small child who's been denied a lollypop, I whined, "Inspector Garelick, I want to commit civil disobedience." He pointed to the end of the block where there was just enough space between two barriers for one person at a time to squeeze through. As I did so, a police captain demanded, in a loud, ceremonial voice, "Do you have business at the induction center?" I didn't know the counter-sign, so I answered loudly, "Yes, I do," walked past him, sat on the steps, and was arrested. My first civil disobedience.

In jail, I met Ginsberg, the poet; Peck, the pacifist; and Susan Sontag, the writer—good company to be in. In the afternoon, we were taken to court, where I pled guilty and put up bail of twenty-five dollars. In subsequent arrests I learned that it's best to plead not guilty, if it's convenient to return for trial, because in half the cases you can win on one technicality or another.

In January 1968, I found myself indicted by the Johnson administration for conspiracy to counsel, aid, and abet resistance to the military draft. I was supposed to have conspired with four other people, including William Sloane Coffin, the chaplain of Yale University; Michael Ferber, a Harvard graduate student; Mitchell Goodman, a novelist and professor; and Marcus Raskin, an author and former White House disarmament adviser.

The lawyers explained to us that the conspiracy indictment makes the prosecutors' job easier. They don't have to prove that there *was* counseling, aiding, or abetting. They only have to show that there was an "agreement" to do that. And, it turned out, the agreement didn't have to be among people who planned anything together or even knew each other. It didn't have to be secret or include illegal acts. As the judge made it clear the first day of the trial, conspiracy only means going on a parallel course. He said conspiring was simply breathing together. That's it, breathing together: Con—together, spiring—breathing; con-spiring.

Although some of us had never met one another, we were all working toward the same objective: to end the war in Vietnam. We were doing that very publicly. Yet that was enough for the government to assume that there was a conspiracy. Our lawyers thought this was a serious issue of First Amendment rights.

The indictment included more than the five of us. In the late 1960s, many people were "breathing together." Lots of others, "diverse other persons, some known and others unknown," the indictment said, the thousands of people who were in those demonstrations, were presumed by the government to be co-conspirators and just as liable to prosecution as we were. Certainly the purpose of the trial was not so much to punish us as to intimidate the others.

The judge, Francis Ford, had been a classmate of Franklin Roosevelt at Harvard. They said he was very proud of that. If so, it certainly didn't seem to be a factor that worked in our favor. On the first day of the trial, a friend of ours was going down the stairwell and heard the judge say, "They brought a bunch of slick New York lawyers to try to interfere with justice here, but they're not going to do it." And, from the first day, he referred to "the conspiracy," though it was a trial to see whether there had been one.

The jury selection was absurd. The official who made up the jury pool said he stood in front of the list of names, closed his eyes, and ran his finger down it. Then he opened his eyes and took that name. Well, it was extraordinary for him to come up with a pool of jurors that had eighty-three men and only five women that way. The probability is pretty small. Needless to say, our lawyers took exception to that. The jury turned out to be made up entirely of white men. I do remember that our lawyers were trying to squeeze on at least one woman, thinking she would be sympathetic to me. But the government threw her out. Ironically, we found out afterward that she believed we were very guilty, long before the trial began.

The government charged us with several overt acts. Our basic "crime" was circulating the Call to Resist Illegitimate Authority. The indictment also charged us with holding a press conference in which some of us denounced the government for its war. Then there was a meeting at the Arlington Street Church in Boston where draft cards were turned in. There was the civil disobedience demonstration at the Whitehall Street induction center. And we were charged with turning in a couple of hundred draft cards to the attorney general in Washington.

There was a ludicrous aspect to that. The man who met with us there was low on the totem pole in the attorney general's office. We took turns denouncing the government and the war to this poor guy who never asked for the job. When we finally got up to leave, the briefcase full of draft cards was still on the table. He saw that he was conspiring in a way by letting us leave it there. So he asked, looking down at it, "Are you tendering me something?"

Bill Coffin, who was the main spokesman, said, "Yes."

"I'm not authorized to accept it." And he tried to give it back. But Coffin wouldn't take it and we left.

For the most part, the trial itself really was dull. I could go to sleep after lunch every day. Most of the evidence they showed was simply television news footage of us addressing an audience. But first they'd interrogate the cameraman: "What's your name?" "What's your profession?"

"Cameraman."

"What is your age?" "What is your address?" "Were you present at the induction center in New York on the early morning of so-and-so?" "Yes, I was."

"And did you take the film that we are about to watch?" You know this took forever, and it didn't prove very much except that he was the cameraman who took the pictures.

The government's case relied heavily on this news footage of *public speeches,* and certainly its use suggested a threat to First Amendment rights and to dissent.

The government also had two FBI agents testify about a conversation they had with me at my apartment. I was completely frank with them about my antiwar activities. I had nothing to hide, but I had no idea then that they were there to try to get evidence to support the coming indictment. Two-thirds of their testimony about the conversation was true. But then they needed something more criminal than that, so they just invented the other third. They said I told them my main purpose was to interfere with the levying of troops. I didn't know the word "levy" had been used for troops since George Washington's time.

I never thought of myself as trying to interfere with the levying of troops or the recruitment or the drafting. I was trying to stop the war in Vietnam. When I stood on the steps of the Whitehall Street induction center, they said I was trying to block the recruitment of troops. But I was not in anyone's way. It was symbolic. I was there to express my opposition to the war.

I was indignant to find that the FBI will lie to get a conviction. But they left their raw notes on the table overnight. We studied them and brought out the next day that the FBI had invented a lot. I enjoyed being able to say in all my subsequent speeches, "Never believe the FBI! I know that they are unscrupulous from my own experience."

I felt our defense at the trial should be based on the Nuremberg Principles mentioned in the Call. The United States put German war criminals to death, tried them and put them to death, for the kind of crimes we were committing in Vietnam. When the Germans said, "I was only obeying the orders of my superiors," our judges ruled that that was no excuse; they were obligated to refuse to obey the orders. If we could put Germans in prison and put them to death for obeying orders to commit war crimes, certainly that means American young men should be able to refuse to participate in similar crimes. And we should be able to talk about their refusal to participate. But our judge said the Nuremberg defense was "not justiciable."

Judge Ford was not going to listen to any arguments that the government was wrong about the war. Early in the trial he made another crucial ruling: The legality of the war was not a relevant issue. That meant we could not challenge the legality of a war that had never been declared by Congress, as we hoped to do. Instead, we were left to defend ourselves within the narrow limits the judge used to frame the issue.

The judge's bias influenced the jury, there's no question about it. All through the trial he was playing footsie with them, telling them little funny stories and making little side remarks. He was wooing the jury all the time. But when one of our lawyers smiled at something someone whispered to him, the judge became absolutely furious: "If you laugh again, I'll throw you out of the courtroom."

The judge treated our witnesses brusquely. He wanted to hurry them through. "That's enough. That's enough!" he'd say. Mayor John Lindsay came up to testify that our demonstration at the steps of the Whitehall Street induction center was a symbolic, not a bona fide, interference. And, he testified, it was all worked out with the police department and him when he was the mayor. Well, the judge hustled him along.

I had some classy character witnesses. I had the provost of M.I.T., and a professor of pediatrics and psychiatry at the Yale Medical School, and a senator from Ohio. It seemed like the judge was scared to death the jury would be impressed by these people. So he clamped right down on them, demanding one-word answers: Was my reputation "good, bad, or indifferent?" Nothing more.

Toward the end of the trial, some people in the antiwar movement were disappointed that we had been so docile. They felt we should have loudly declared our position, more like the Chicago Eight.* Not that we would have gotten rowdy, but we could have been more insistent. When we were shushed up in court, at least we could have held a press conference at the end of the day. To me, it seemed perfectly clear that this was

---

*The 1969 conspiracy trial of antiwar and New Left leaders stemming from their participation in demonstrations at the 1968 Democratic National Convention in Chicago. The defendants—Bobby Seale (whose case was severed from the others), Rennie Davis, David Dellinger, John Froines, Tom Hayden, Abbie Hoffman, Jerry Rubin, and Lee Weiner—dramatically challenged the legitimacy of the proceedings against them. With their irreverent dress, behavior, and testimony, they attempted to portray the trial as a mockery of justice. "When decorum becomes repression," Abbie Hoffman commented, "the only dignity free men have is to speak out." Their convictions were reversed on appeal.

a political trial. We had been doing the things we had been charged with for political reasons. Then why not use the trial politically, as far as we could? I didn't feel like being docile.

I was the last one on the witness stand. When it came to my turn, I was ready to be bolder and more positive in my statements than the others. And my lawyer, Leonard Boudin, got the judge to allow me to make political statements as long as I prefaced them with the words "I believed." Well, I believed that the government was wrong in pursuing the war in Vietnam. The government was blindly stumbling down this path because we had a macho president, advised by some macho assistants, to put it crudely. It was very clear to me that we in the peace movement were trying to save the country. No question about it. We were trying to persuade the American people to stop them. I was able to say these things firmly and positively. And I wasn't the least bit evasive.

I always knew that if two out of three people who were drafted resisted the draft, the war would be over. If somehow or other the less educated men who were most likely to be drafted could see that they had it within their power, if not within their right, to resist, it would be over. I said at the trial I *hoped* young men would conclude that the war was illegal and would refuse induction, refuse to obey orders. But, I added, that isn't the same as *urging* them to.

I couldn't do that. My psychiatric training says: Never counsel anybody about anything important. You'll only louse up the situation. Never say, "You should get married," or "You should get divorced," or "You should have a child," or "You shouldn't have a child." If a person can't make up his mind whether to get married or to get divorced, he's not ready to get married or get divorced. And if you stick your nose in, you'll only cloud him up further.

At the end, the judge repeated in his charge to the jury many of the same things the prosecutor had said about us in his closing statement. Then the judge gave them a series of questions they had to answer: Are the defendants guilty of conspiracy to counsel? Are the defendants guilty of conspiracy to aid? Are the defendants guilty of conspiracy to abet? These instructions were later found by the court of appeals to be prejudicial.

Four of us were found guilty of conspiracy. Marcus Raskin was the only one acquitted of all charges. It was, I would say, because he was shorter and quieter and, in the scenes of demonstrations shown to the jury, he wasn't as visible. He was ashen pale after the verdict. When he stepped out of the elevator into a hundred members of the press, he was weeping. They couldn't figure it out. The ones who were convicted smiled, and the one who was acquitted wept. He felt very guilty. He was a main author of the Call to Resist Illegitimate Authority. And that was the keystone of our "crime."

I made an angry statement to the media right after the verdict, shouting that the government was behaving criminally in Vietnam, was trying to silence its critics, and that citizens must wake up and demand an end to the war.

The *Boston Globe* got to three of the jurors afterward. They said they thought we were pretty good guys but that the judge persuaded them that it was their patriotic duty to convict. One juror said the way the judge charged them, there was no choice. Another said he was in full agreement with us until they were charged by the judge, which was the kiss of death. Well, anybody who knows anything about the law knows that the point of a jury trial is how it looks to the jurors, not what it looks like to the judge.

We were sentenced to two years in prison. The judge said in sentencing us, "Rebellion against the law is in the nature of treason." My conscience told me that trying to save the country from an endless, brutal war was not treason at all. I was absolutely sure I was right. It was not just by studying the war in Vietnam that I knew I was right, but morally I knew I was right. I was brought up by a fiercely moralistic mother. And everything in the rest of my life has been decided on a moral basis. I knew exactly the steps I'd taken and what they meant to me. And when I know I'm right, I don't worry about anything.

I was in this to end the war in Vietnam and prove the government wrong. If I were freed, that would be a victory. If I went to jail, that would outrage a whole lot of people. Even in England, Vanessa Redgrave was leading a long parade of moms from Trafalgar Square to the American embassy with big signs saying "Hands Off Spock!" In this country, having been tried gave me tremendous appeal to undergraduates. I spoke at eight hundred colleges and universities all over the United States. That's a tremendous number. And the reason I was such a popular speaker was because I had been convicted for my opposition to the war.

We appealed. A year later the court of appeals reversed the convictions. Ferber and I were acquitted because they said there was insufficient evidence. Coffin and Goodman were supposed to get a new trial because of Judge Ford's biased instructions to the jury. But one of the three judges on the court of appeals felt we were all innocent because the conspiracy laws were never invented to go after political dissidents. If one other judge had joined him, this would have been a very significant case. It would have meant that you couldn't use the conspiracy law to go after people for their political activities. Unfortunately, the decision was reversed on a technicality.

The trial radicalized me. I became convinced that the United States truly is an imperialist country. I had never given a thought to that accusation before. And I realized that as surely as the government represents industry on the international scene, it also represents industry on the domestic scene. I became a socialist.

I used to be a very cautious person and considered very carefully anything I said. But when the federal government tried to throw me in jail and I beat them at their own game, that did a lot of good for me. I became much bolder. I don't mean that I'm terribly bold, but I'm a lot bolder than I used to be. At one point, one of my sisters who hadn't seen me for a couple years said to another of my sisters, "Say, what's come over Ben?"

Nowadays, I'm frustrated that even though a majority of the American people are for disarmament, a majority are against intervention in foreign countries, a majority believe that Reagan is taking it out of the hides of the poor and other disadvantaged people, nevertheless they say that he's a wonderful leader. It's as if he's a great leader of the lemmings. He's leading the people to their destruction. So again, I have to demonstrate and commit civil disobedience, and keep at it until I keel over.

The Congressional Inquisition

The Beginning:
The Hollywood Ten

Ring Lardner, Jr., and
Frances Chaney Lardner

The House Un-American Activities Committee ushered in the silent generation. In 1947, after its wartime hiatus, HUAC resurrected itself amid the glamour of Hollywood stars. Ring Lardner, Jr., and others of the Hollywood Ten unsuccessfully challenged the committee's license to require witnesses to reveal their political affiliations under threat of imprisonment. HUAC then launched its career of hounding left-wing union members, teachers and professors, journalists, members of the clergy, and government employees. Without the assurances of a court of law—the right to face and cross-examine one's accusers, for example— witnesses were convicted by mere accusation in the sensational headlines that followed the committee's proceedings.

Persons named at a Flint, Michigan, hearing were physically attacked by local vigilantes. A woman named at a Pittsburgh hearing, a mother of two children, was cut off from relief benefits. A Stanford University research scientist committed suicide after being served the committee's subpoena. Three days later, his wife was refused permission to present her statement in his place: "Is it a crime for a young man in his twenties to dream of a bright new world? Must the children of our country leave their idealism in the cradle so that their future careers will not be blighted by the Un-American Activities Committee?"[1]

A screenwriter with one Academy Award to his credit in 1942 for

FRANCES CHANEY LARDNER

RING LARDNER, JR.

Woman of the Year, *and another to come for* M*A*S*H *in 1970, Ring
Lardner, Jr., found himself unable to work under his own name during
the McCarthy era. Frances Chaney Lardner's career was cut down just
as she had established herself as an actress. The blacklist began with the
Hollywood Ten; it swelled to include others until, Frankenstein-like, it
lurched out of control, destroying its victims' lives and careers.*

RING: We had begun to hear rumors in the latter part of 1946 that
there was some kind of investigation coming up. The Republicans had
won a majority in Congress. In January of 1947, a vote was put through
the new Congress to make the temporary Un-American Activities Committee a permanent committee of the House. A Republican, J. Parnell
Thomas of New Jersey, became chairman. They announced that one of
the first places to investigate would be the motion picture business.

In May, they held hearings in Los Angeles, which met in executive
session. They summoned only witnesses who were to testify to the "red
menace" in Hollywood. There were just secondhand reports about
what went on. The committee said it would hold open hearings later on.
In September, nineteen of us who would characterize ourselves as "unfriendly" witnesses received subpoenas. About ten of the nineteen had
specific days they were supposed to appear in Washington, and the rest
of us did not. But we flew to Washington together, stopping first in
Chicago.

FRANCES: That was when we had supper with Larry Parks, swear-
ing endless loyalty to each other. It was a lovely, lovely occasion. There
were Larry and Dalton and Ring and I, and it was just one for all and all
for one. And someone was saying that Larry, as an actor, would be the
one who had the toughest job. If anything ever happened to him, by
God, we would see to it that he would get work.

RING: We got to Washington when the hearings opened. We sat
through a whole week of testimony by Adolphe Menjou and Robert
Taylor, Gary Cooper, Louis B. Mayer and Jack Warner, Ronald Reagan
and Robert Montgomery. And we listened to this picture they presented
of a terrible menace posed by the people they thought might be Communists. Some of them said there was subversive propaganda in the pictures. Ayn Rand testified about a picture, *Song of Russia,* that showed
Russian children smiling. She said that had never happened in her experience and she had lived in Russia until she was thirty years old. Ginger

Rogers's mother said that Dalton Trumbo had put into a picture a line which Ginger had to say: "Share and share alike, that's democracy." Lela Rogers pointed out, "That's not democracy. That's socialism."

There was contrary testimony from people like Mayer and Warner who said: No such thing. Nobody got any subversive content in the pictures because they oversaw everything and would cut anything that was "dangerous." Reagan testified about what went on in the actors' guild and said that there were some people who always behaved in a way that made him think they were Communists. It was very virtuous testimony, kind of straight, corny patriotism.

The second week began with the appearance of the unfriendly witnesses, starting with John Howard Lawson. He had the toughest time because, as the first witness, he had no idea what it was going to be like. He was a very good speaker, and he talked about what this committee meant and the parallels to Nazi Germany. He and a couple of others, such as Herbert Biberman, were quite forceful. Others were fairly gentle and restrained. I don't think it made any difference at all how we spoke.

The committee ran two or three a day, and I still didn't have a day assigned to me. On the third afternoon, Frances and I were listening to the hearings in our hotel room, and suddenly I heard them call me to the stand.

FRANCES: It was such a strange feeling. I remember thinking: Oh my God, Ring, you're not there! You're supposed to be.

RING: It was arranged by the lawyers that I would appear after lunch. But I wasn't called until the next morning. I went up and sat between our two lawyers. We had Bob Kenny, who had been attorney general in California and was also a former judge. He was very cautious. The other attorney, Ben Margolis, was very militant. Somebody described it as Ben Margolis on one side saying, "Give it to them," and Bob Kenny on the other saying, "Take it easy."

The lawyers thought we shouldn't say, "I decline to answer those questions." We might have a better case in a contempt trial if we said, in effect, "Sure, I'll answer the question, but I want to answer it in my own way." We would then go into all the reasons why the question was offensive and intruded on private rights. We all did some of that, but probably it didn't achieve anything.

There were two basic questions they asked: Are you now or have you ever been a member of the Screen Writers Guild? And are you now or have you ever been a member of the Communist Party? We didn't answer either of them directly. We said that the guild had had a tough fight for recognition and that trouble could still come up again, that membership rolls were actually private. It was not any of the committee's business to inquire into membership of a union.

When they asked me the "sixty-four-dollar question," I infuriated Thomas by saying, "I could answer that question, but I'd hate myself in the morning." He started to scream: "You've been coached like all the others!" He was a small, heavy man, who was sitting on a couple of telephone books in order to be on the same level as the other members of the committee and look better for the pictures. He got very red in the face and finally said, "Remove the witness." I still tried to say something, but a couple of marshals took my arms. I managed, "I'm being removed by force," and that was all.

I was one of the very last; I testified, then Lester Cole, and then Bertolt Brecht. They quite quickly called off the hearings after that, probably because the committee was not getting very good publicity. That week we had been joined in Washington by members of the Committee for the First Amendment, including people from Hollywood like John Huston, Bogart and Bacall, John Garfield, and William Wyler. And because a few stars were there, they got more attention in the papers than the hearing did.

FRANCES: I remember when we left Washington and came to New York, there was an enormous rally in support of the people who had testified. I'd never experienced anything like it. Suddenly we were recognizable, all because there had been so much press and so many photographs and so many flashbulbs going off. There was a terrific amount of notoriety about it. I'm positive that's why they started with Hollywood first.

There seemed to be strong support for us from the community, from the producers, and from the people who were big in Hollywood. I don't think anybody felt that it would collapse as quickly as it did.

RING: Eric Johnston, who was the president of the Motion Picture Producers' Association, told our attorneys in a private meeting, "I will never be party to such a thing as a blacklist." That was in October 1947. By November, all the producers, the heads of the companies, had met in New York. They said they would discharge the Ten and anybody who subsequently was accused of being a Communist and didn't deny it, or who took the same attitude toward the committee as we did. It was really the boards of directors of the various movie companies, mostly New York bankers, who dictated that policy.

I had just finished one script for Twentieth Century-Fox and had recently signed a contract with them. I was given a new assignment after the hearings, working with Otto Preminger. Darryl Zanuck, who was in charge of Twentieth Century-Fox on the West Coast, said that I was the only employee there who was involved and he would not fire me unless specifically ordered to by his board of directors. And they obliged him.

Subsequently, when we had suits against the studio for breach of contract, I won a jury verdict on the basis that they had waived their right to discharge me by giving me a new assignment after the fact. But the appellate court ordered a retrial, and at the beginning of the retrial we made an out-of-court settlement.

In the meantime, the committee reported to the full House of Representatives, which voted affirmatively for a citation for contempt. It went to a federal grand jury, which indicted us for contempt of Congress. That meant we had to stand trial. Because the trials were going to be expensive, we agreed to have just two, John Howard Lawson and Dalton Trumbo, and we would abide by all the points of law that were decided in those trials. Lawson and Trumbo were found guilty. Their cases had gone up to the Supreme Court. But two of the most liberal justices of the Supreme Court, Wiley Rutledge and Frank Murphy, had died in the summer of 1949. Without them, we didn't have the necessary votes. The court refused to hear it.

After that, Trumbo and Lawson had just a couple of weeks to clean up their affairs and go off to prison for a year. About three weeks after that, the rest of us went to jail. This was in June of 1950. We were distributed to four federal prisons around the country. We could only assume that they considered it too dangerous to have all of us at the same place. They ended up sending Lester Cole and me to the prison in Danbury, Connecticut.

FRANCES: They were able to meet their old "buddy," Parnell Thomas.

RING: Thomas had been charged with padding the government payroll. After he had pleaded nolo contendere, he was sentenced to Danbury, too, and put in charge of the chicken yard. Lester went by there, and they looked at each other. And Lester spoke to Thomas. He said something about still handling the chicken shit.

FRANCES: Lester's exact quote was, "Still pushing the shit around?"

RING: I actually felt kind of sorry for Parnell Thomas. He had lost about fifty pounds. Somehow, losing all that weight made him look, as it often does, more haggard. The lines show up in your face a lot more.

He was very worried, I was told, because my job was in the office of classification and parole. He was afraid that somehow I would manage to sabotage his parole. But actually the civilian clerk handled his case. I did know about a day ahead who was going to get paroled and who wasn't. We were never supposed to tell anybody, but I always told every inmate. I didn't tell Thomas.

The general consensus among the prisoners was quite favorable toward us. What got around was that we didn't talk to the cops. We didn't cooperate with the authorities. We weren't stool pigeons. But some of them did find it difficult to understand us. Before we got there, several people were sent to prison from the Joint Anti-Fascist Refugee Committee. Howard Fast was one of them, along with Doctor Jacob Auslander. They had been convicted for refusing to give records to the Un-American Activities Committee. The records were really lists of names of Spanish loyalist prisoners whom they were helping. They were afraid members of this committee would give the names to Franco's fascist government. So they refused.

A few months after Auslander left, I was sitting at the lunch table with a couple of prisoners. One of them said to the other, "When I came in, there was this inmate doctor who examined you. He did a very thorough examination, was a good man." The other prisoner, newly arrived, asked, "A doctor? What was he in for?" The first guy replied, "Drugs, I guess."

I felt obliged to interrupt, and I said, "It wasn't that." I explained about the Joint Anti-Fascist Refugee Committee and why he had refused to turn over those records. They listened very patiently. The inmate who had first mentioned this added, "Well, I guess it was some of that. And drugs, too."

I was the only one of the Ten who got not only sixty days off for good behavior, but fifteen extra days off for meritorious good behavior. My kind of prison term isn't too much to adjust to. It's a short enough time, less than ten months, so that you live through it and you know it will eventually be over. It's not like two or three years or more.

FRANCES: When Ring went to jail, we had to sell the house. In order to get rid of it, Ring put an ad in the paper, the *Hollywood Reporter,* that said, "House for sale. Owner going to jail."

RING: In those trade papers, they frequently had something like "Owner going to New York for six months." *Time* picked up our caption as a news item. A Beverly Hills doctor saw it in *Time* when he was at the gaming tables in Las Vegas and came that very night to buy the house.

FRANCES: At a great loss to us, of course. But we did get our hands on a bit of cash to live on while Ring was in jail. We certainly couldn't count on my income being enough to sustain three children and me. So we sold this house and got a tiny house in Hollywood.

The hard part was the separation and the fact that daddy wasn't home. That's tough when you have a little baby who doesn't know what's going on around him. But for the most part it was toughest on the older children. They were from my marriage to Ring's brother, David, who was killed in the war.

RING: When I went to jail, Katie was seven and Joey was six.

FRANCES: There were so many questions that they had to cope with. "Where's your dad?"

"My daddy's gone to jail."

"Why's your daddy in jail?" That's tough for a kid of six: "Because some fellow in Washington asked him something he didn't have any right to ask him. And my daddy told him he didn't have any right to ask him that. And that's why he went to jail."

Our kids managed. But it was very hard on all the children of the blacklisted people, and certainly the children of the Hollywood Ten. The wives supported each other. There was a sense of community, a sense that you weren't totally alone. On the other hand, you began to feel like a pariah because a lot of people dropped off. I mean, a large mass of them dropped away. It was hard on a lot of people. Some didn't survive. Some died in the process.

RING: Like Phil Loeb of the theater. And J. Edward Bromberg died of a heart attack, which might very well have been due to this.

FRANCES: John Garfield had a heart attack.

RING: There were people whose careers were completely destroyed among the two hundred fifty to three hundred who were blacklisted. Fewer than half of them ever did get back into the motion picture business. Some who did get back in some way or other never really got re-established. People would say, "What about your credits in the last few years?" Certainly actors who were in their prime at the time, and Frances was one, had the most important part of their careers taken away from them. It was the blacklist, really, that turned our lives around.

FRANCES: I was an actress, and I had had a decent career in New York. But after the hearings in 1947, I couldn't get any real work. From

1947 till 1963 I was able to play only one part on nighttime television. That was in 1952, when Ring and I came back East. We were completely broke at that time. We really were. So we went to live with his mother. I said I was going to get a job. I was determined to do it.

Somehow or other—to this day I don't know how it happened—an agency sent me for a big part on a nighttime television show, the "Philco Playhouse." Whether they were stuck or they couldn't find anybody else or they weren't able to catch up with me or what, I don't know. But they cast me in a script written by Paddy Chayevsky, and I did it and it was very good and very successful. I thought: See, by God, I've sneaked through. They don't know. I did this show, got this fine notice, and a good salary. It was wonderful.

That spring, I was called by the same agent, and he said that they had a part for me in *Marty*. Chayevsky had written it with me in mind, and all they wanted from me was script approval. Script approval! I'd have crawled on my hands and knees to do it. I went into New York the next day, and then the process started: Call us back in an hour. We can't get hold of Mr. Coe. Would you call again? We have to get him in East Hampton.

It wasn't until the end of the day that they finally said they were very sorry. They'd made a terrible mistake. Somebody else had been cast in the part. And I wasn't sure. I wasn't sure that it might, indeed, have been a terrible mistake—until the following summer. Then they repeated the first Paddy Chayevsky program I had been in.

RING: It was called "Holiday Song," and it was about Yom Kippur and Rosh Hashanah. They did it again at the Jewish holidays. And everybody was cast in the same roles except Frances.

FRANCES: I was cast out. I really did feel awful. I met with Fred Coe, and he was very forthright. He admitted that the other people in the cast had said they would quit if I wasn't on the show. He told them he was with them and understood how they felt, but that their protest wouldn't do any good. All that would happen is that they wouldn't have a job, either.

I felt awful for years. The thing that was particularly bad was that I never was able to talk about it. When I'd go for a job, they would ask: If I were so good, why hadn't they seen me? Where had I been? I would just talk fast about raising my children. But never in all that time could I come out and say, "I'm blacklisted."

I think that had I been able to speak openly about it, I would have felt a lot better. I wasn't able to be right up front until Carmen Capalbo, a very nice man, called me to read for him for a play on Broadway. He said, "I know you were in *Three Sisters,* I know you were in a play called *Winkleberg.* What else have you done?" And I suddenly heard myself say, "Well, I did those and I did a lot of radio many years ago, and then the shit hit the fan." That was the first time, and it was a very good feeling. I had that good feeling again at a conference in Chicago about seven or eight years ago. It was the first time I said anything in public about it.

RING: We both appeared in a forum in Chicago with Studs Terkel and John Henry Faulk.

FRANCES: I was asked to participate in it, and I've felt much better since then. It took a long time to begin feeling all right about all this stuff.

RING: The blacklist started immediately after the producers' meeting in November of 1947, when we were discharged. From 1947 to 1951, it just applied to the ten of us. We were able to get some kind of work for greatly reduced fees. But by the time we got out of prison, it was much tougher. There was a whole new atmosphere. You couldn't find any people who were willing to stick their necks out. The Trumbos and the Maltzes and our friends the Ian Hunters and Hugo Butlers and Gordon Kahns were all blacklisted. They moved to Mexico City because it was cheaper to live there. We did, for six months.

Trumbo started an involved operation of selling original stories through a front. During the war, Dalton had gone to the Pacific as a guest of the War Department and met a young newspaperman named Murphy. Afterward, they continued to correspond. When the blacklist began, Dalton persuaded Murphy to put his name on stories Dalton wrote. He needed a real live person who could discuss it with the studios. Dalton sent his story to this young man and then didn't get any response. Later, he read either Hedda Hopper's or Louella Parsons's column: "Too bad about poor Dick Murphy dying right after selling his story to Paramount."

I was able to work during all those years. I wrote a novel first, and then my friend Ian McLellan Hunter and I got together and started doing television films for Hannah Weinstein. She knew and deliberately hired blacklisted writers. We wrote kids' programs: "Robin Hood" and "Sir Lancelot" and "The Buccaneers." We must have done forty "Robin Hood" episodes. She was able to sell them to the networks.

FRANCES: That was pretty weird, with our kids watching these pictures and knowing that their daddy wrote them and that they had to keep their mouths shut about it.

RING: Katie and Joe, the two older ones, knew that I was writing these things, but they weren't allowed to tell Jimmy, who was only six then. It really was a secret. We had a bank account under an assumed name and got checks in that name. It all went through a company in New York, called Official Films, which put up the money for the series and then sold them to the networks. Even they didn't know. NBC and CBS were quite capable of canceling the shows.

In 1959, Carlo Ponti and another Italian, Marcello Gerosi, had brought Sophia Loren to Hollywood and were producing pictures with her at Paramount. An agent friend of mine, Otto Preminger's brother, Ingo, sold them the idea that I could write a script for them. I went to Hollywood and had to register at a motel under another name, Rick Spencer, so that if we talked on the Paramount switchboard, they wouldn't get my name.

The film was shot in Vienna and Rome and then got in very bad trouble. The director, who also directed *Casablanca,* was really dying and had nothing left of his old spark. At a meeting in the Rome office of Paramount, we were trying to decide what to do with what was turning out to be a terrible picture. The head of the Rome office was on the phone with Y. Frank Freeman, the head of Paramount and one of the most militant executives in Hollywood in promoting the blacklist. I heard him say to Freeman, "Ring thinks . . ." Suddenly I realized their secrecy on the Paramount switchboard was just so no people on a minor level would hear about this and spread it. Ponti and Gerosi would never have dared hire me without getting the approval on top to begin with. Freeman knew all the time. It was okay as long as it was kept quiet.

A number of people on the blacklist went through the procedure of trying to "purify" themselves. In most cases, they were told they had to appear voluntarily before the Un-American Activities Committee, which obliged by having special hearings with one or two members present, thereby constituting a subcommittee.

FRANCES: When a person had already been named, those who named names felt it was all right to do it again. They thought: Well, what the hell, they've been named anyhow, so I'll name them once more.

RING: The committee knew that anybody who cooperated to that extent, even though they hadn't named any new names, was making a gesture of submission. It was an indication that the person would be no more trouble. There was at no time any necessity for the committee to find out any of these names. It became apparent that there had been FBI agents in the Communist Party and all the left-liberal organizations in Hollywood and elsewhere. They already had all the information they were asking people about. So it was just a question of getting up and making the submissive gesture, just like in animal packs there are ways in which the younger males show their submission to authority.

There were others on the blacklist who were cleared by a group called the Motion Picture Alliance for the Preservation of American Ideals. Ronald Reagan had become one of the main people involved in that process. If you were named before a committee or you found you weren't getting a job, you could go to clear yourself by making a statement to the Alliance for the Preservation of American Ideals. One actor-director named Phil Brown went to the alliance because he had been told he was blacklisted. They said, "All you have to do is tell us when you joined the Communist Party, what it was like, and who was there." He said, "I never did. I never had anything to do with the Communist Party." And they said, "Well, then, there's nothing much we can do for you." They had this regular clearance procedure, but if he couldn't take the first step, he couldn't take the second. He moved to London, and I think he's there still.

Sometimes they arranged for blacklisted people to get in touch with the local office of the FBI, which had been feeding the committee all of its information anyway. They would check on whether what these people were saying indicated genuine atonement. It didn't necessarily have to be truthful. A lot of people got cleared that way.

There were people like Robert Rossen, the director, who was one of the original nineteen, one of those who didn't have a date. He got a few years of grace. In 1951, he was called before the committee. There was no point in anybody using the First Amendment after we lost the case. Rossen took the "diminished" Fifth. He said, "I am not now a member of the Communist Party." But when they asked him, "Were you a member of the Communist Party last week?" he said, "I refuse to answer."

So Rossen was blacklisted. He had just started to be a director during that period of grace after 1947. He directed his first movie, which was *Body and Soul*, with John Garfield. His second film, *All the King's Men*, was a very successful picture based on Huey Long. It won the Academy Award as best picture in 1949. Rossen joined us in Mexico after he first appeared before the committee and was still in a very defiant mood. But he was very ambitious. Six months later, he asked to go back before the committee and told them everything they wanted to hear. He directed a few more pictures and then died of a heart attack quite young.

I don't know whether it was a coincidence that, of the people who weren't directly involved in the original hearing, Edward G. Robinson, Melvyn Douglas, and John Garfield were particularly attacked. It happens they were the only three prominent Jewish stars in Hollywood. There was a congressman named Rankin from Mississippi on that Un-American Activities Committee who was one of the most notorious, open anti-Semites. He used words like "kikes" in speeches in Congress.

Edward G. Robinson was picked on severely. He had lent money to Dalton Trumbo after we were jailed, and that was held against him. He got very frightened and did all sorts of things to clear himself. Robinson was finally able to get back, although never to the same kind of stardom he'd had.

John Garfield did go before the committee. They asked him if he thought the Communist Party should be made illegal. And he said: Yeah, it would help slobs like me if we knew what was legal and what wasn't. We wouldn't be contributing to causes that would get us into trouble. He tried to appease the committee, but I don't think he quite satisfied them. And he wasn't able to get back into Hollywood. He had started a company of his own, which had produced a couple of successful pictures. But Bob Roberts, the president of the company, got named and blacklisted. *Body and Soul* was directed and written by two guys who were then blacklisted. *He Ran All the Way* was directed and written by Hugo Butler and John Berry, who both got blacklisted. Garfield drank a lot and was very unhappy. He was only forty-one years old when he had a fatal heart attack. You could say that his ordeal contributed to it.

Most of my friends had a policy of not speaking to people who had cooperated with the committee. I was always kind of curious about how they felt about what they did, though I've never renewed friendships. One of the cooperative witnesses, Budd Schulberg, had been my closest friend. I've talked to him a few times.

It turns out, in the long run, that most of us who were on the black-list are rather favorably regarded by younger people today, including people in the motion picture industry. And those who cooperated with the committee, like Elia Kazan and Budd Schulberg, find that there are people who won't talk to them. They get reproached for their behavior. So, in a sense, I think Dalton Trumbo was right when he said that everybody was a victim of the period.

FRANCES: I really felt passionately about not speaking to those people. I don't feel that anymore. But I do feel far greater sympathy and sorrow for a man like Larry Parks than for someone like Kazan. Kazan was a top director. He could have continued being a top director in the theater. He had all sorts of gifts and talents and lots of money. It wasn't that he was struggling for a living. Whereas a poor wretch like Larry just couldn't hold out. He didn't have the guts or whatever it took. It was truly sad.

RING: Larry cried and pleaded with the committee, saying, "Don't make me name names. I don't want to do this."

FRANCES: Betsy Blair, who had been married to Gene Kelly and was living in France at the time, was very sympathetic to the cause of the Hollywood Ten. After people started naming names, I remember Betsy telling us her French friends would ask, "What did they do? Did they torture them?"

No, nobody was tortured, I mean physically tortured. It wasn't that. It was just that some people fall under pressure, and some people are able to say, "No, damn it, I won't do that because that's rotten and dirty and no good."

I think the main thing that offended me was the big lie. Whether people agreed with Communists or didn't agree with Communists or were Communists or weren't Communists, there certainly never—at least not from anything I ever knew—was an "international conspiracy" to destroy the government. I never saw anything that in any way represented a menace to the Constitution of the United States.

Maybe there were misguided ideas. And I certainly have changed my views about many things since I was a young woman. I feel now that I never again in my life want anybody to say, "This is *the* answer." If they say, "This is *the* answer," I'm going to run a mile because there are many answers in the world. Nobody has *the* answer. But I never witnessed anything in those years except a kind of decency and a brotherhood. Everybody started out in the late thirties wanting to do good. You know, "Let's have more wages for the worker," "Black and white unite and fight." Those ideals had nothing of the menace or evil that these people who named names ascribed to them. That's the *big lie*. And that was terrible.

You know, if they'd said, "Oh, God. I can't work. I can't support my wife unless I name some people." Okay! Poor son of a bitch can't support his family, and he's going to do it for that. But to say that it's because this is an "international conspiracy" and "I was duped"—that was a lot of baloney. Nobody was duped. It's as if some of that mass of humanity that gathered in protest on June 12, 1982, in Central Park in New York City, were to say afterward, "Well, I was duped into demonstrating against the possibility of an atomic holocaust." Duped, my foot!

There was such terror of being blacklisted or of being tainted or of being named or of losing jobs. During that period when Ring was in jail, when there was fear that it was going to get worse, people got very, very frightened. People started going through their books and hiding them or throwing them out because there were stories going around Hollywood that anybody who ever belonged to anything was going to be incarcerated. They were going to be in concentration camps. People remembered when the Japanese were interned. And if the Hollywood Ten could go to jail, anything could happen.

RING: It did seem at that time that there was a serious danger of it going further, that this seemed to be a kind of pre-fascist atmosphere. But they went too far, and the American sense of fair play turned against them. Basically, I think it was the recognition that the blacklist itself was kind of ridiculous that brought about the return to sanity in Hollywood.

It was mostly one individual, Dalton Trumbo, who was the main force in a campaign to show how ridiculous the blacklist was. He took every opportunity to appear on radio or television. After a series of incidents in which Academy Awards were given to blacklisted writers, it began to appear ridiculous to other people. It finally took just one act— that was Otto Preminger's decision to put Dalton's name on the picture *Exodus*. This was followed by Kirk Douglas deciding to put Dalton's name on *Spartacus*. Then, in one city—Indianapolis, I think—the Americanism Committee of the American Legion sent out some pickets, but people just walked through the pickets and into the theater. Then it was over.

It actually wasn't over just like that. It was still hard to get jobs and renew contacts. It was two years after that before I was able to get a job with Otto Preminger. The first picture I had my name on was called *The Cincinnati Kid*, with Steve McQueen in 1965.

FRANCES: The terrible thing about the whole business, really, is what it does to people. It makes the victims of the blacklist suspicious and fearful. I remember so well, I got my first important job in a Broadway play in 1962. There was a lovely woman who understudied me. We were in the dressing room we shared in Boston, and I suddenly felt, "What if she's from the FBI?" I had nothing to conceal whatsoever. There were no secrets that everybody in the world didn't know, and yet I had this sense that maybe she was put there. Maybe I was being neurotic, but I don't think so. You're worried or you're fearful because there are things that have to be protected. Children have to be protected, your livelihood has to be protected. I went from being an open, free, healthy, outgoing person to suddenly having these walls around me. I think it does that to you. I think it is terrible and very un-American and unhealthy.

To Swing a Union Election

Tom Quinn

For the first twenty-five years of its history, the House Un-American Activities Committee amassed, it admitted, "three hundred thousand card references to the activities and affiliations of individuals," printed and distributed six and a half million copies of its own publications, spent almost eight million dollars on other committee expenses, and subpoenaed five thousand persons—all to produce only one major piece of legislation: the Internal Security Act of 1950.[1] Parts of that act, fortunately, were declared unconstitutional; other sections were repealed or fell into disuse.

The purpose of investigative committees is to seek information pursuant to Congress's legislative function. HUAC's abuse of its investigative powers was openly described by its chairmen. The chief function of HUAC's forays into all aspects of American life, J. Parnell Thomas declared, "has always been the exposure of un-American individuals and their un-American activities."[2] Francis Walter, his successor, hoped out loud that "loyal Americans who work with [these individuals] will do the rest of the job."[3] In short, punitive exposure of individuals who otherwise could not be found guilty of violating any law became an end in itself. When court decisions like the one in Tom Quinn's case tried to limit the purview of the rampaging committee to some legislative purpose, HUAC easily devised evasive tactics. It cast its net as broadly

TOM QUINN

when he was called before it in 1959, because of his progressive leader-
ship in the United Electrical Workers (UE), as it had ten years earlier
when he was first subpoenaed for the same reason.

I was fortunate I worked for Local 601 of the United Electrical Workers. That union tolerated, in fact encouraged, people to speak out on views that were contrary to the prevailing wisdom. It represented workers at the Westinghouse Electric Corporation in East Pittsburgh, one of the largest plants in the nation during World War II.

In 1946, workers in electrical, steel, auto, and all the major industries in the country walked out. During the course of the strike at Westinghouse, I took an active role in the local. After the strike, I was elected to a major office in the union. In 1947, I became the district representative of UE for an area that covered western Pennsylvania and West Virginia.

The UE represented six hundred thousand people. It was the second or third largest union in the CIO, the Congress of Industrial Organizations. It came under attack by the CIO, beginning in 1948 and more intensely after Truman got elected. You go back and look at things: Why was this attack leveled at a union like UE? I believe the main reason is that the UE supported the Progressive Party, while the CIO demanded that all affiliates endorse and support Truman. The Cold War psychology that began to grip the country influenced the CIO. There was a concerted policy against the UE, dictated by CIO President Philip Murray and the top leadership. At the 1949 convention of the CIO, we were expelled. Other unions that hadn't supported Truman were also expelled. "Communist domination" was used as the excuse.

The CIO was originally intended to provide an opportunity for rank-and-file democratic unions and for diversity of political opinion. It may not have encouraged radical opinions, but it tolerated them and permitted them within the organization, while the AFL, the American Federation of Labor, didn't. Now we saw the CIO going down the same road as the AFL.

Pittsburgh was a backwoods place in terms of political freedom, and it was just terrible when all the red-baiting began in 1948. I was a Progressive Party candidate for the state legislature. Progressive Party candidates, Henry Wallace and others like myself, needed signatures of registered voters to get on the ballot. The Pittsburgh papers actually published on their front pages the names and addresses of all the people who signed those petitions. There was no news value in that; its sole purpose was to intimidate people. It provided the information bigots needed to threaten and abuse you on the phone. Rabid anti-communists, encouraged in many cases by the Catholic church, gave some people, some very fine people, an extremely difficult time.

A series of so-called FBI undercover agents emerged. The most notable one in Pittsburgh, in the beginning, was a guy named Matt Cvetic. He went to Washington and started feeding names to the Un-American Committee. Well, again, these names appeared on the front pages of the papers. These people then became objects of ridicule or worse. People would throw stones at their windows. They faced harassment on their jobs. Many were frightened. It was so bad that some people just had to pack up and leave the community because of what was occurring to them, to their jobs, and to their families.

I was called before the House Un-American Activities Committee in 1949. That was all part of the effort by a group inside the UE to take control of the union before our expulsion from the CIO. They called themselves the anti-communist faction and were part of a national group led by Jim Carey, who had once been a president of UE before he was ousted in 1941.

Our Westinghouse local became a major target for the Carey faction. They used Father Rice, a labor priest who organized the Association of Catholic Trade Unionists. Father Rice and some of the Carey people from East Pittsburgh went to Washington and met with the staff of the House Un-American Activities Committee. The committee scheduled hearings for two or three days before the union elections. Then they subpoenaed people who were prominent in Local 601 and who were candidates for offices in the upcoming election. The newspapers ran headlines about "UE Reds" for a week or so. Then the papers repeated this guy Cvetic's stuff that we were Communists. I was never a Communist Party member, but he made me the chairman of the party in East Pittsburgh. That was an effort to discredit me before our membership.

When we were called to appear before the committee, I was a district council delegate and a candidate for reelection. Two of the others were also up for reelection: Tom Fitzpatrick was president of the district and of the Westinghouse local, and another fellow, Frank Panzino, was business agent and an important leader of the local.

We went to Washington with nothing to hide. We knew they were going to ask: Are you a member of the Communist Party? If you said you were, they would ask you to name names of other people you thought were. And if you said you weren't, then they would say, "Well, this witness said you were." Now you faced the possibility of perjury, because your testimony wasn't protected and the other person's was. So you had difficult choices.

This was still new ground for everybody. Our attorneys told us what had happened when the Hollywood Ten used only the First Amendment as a reason for not answering questions. They were on their way to jail by then. We agreed among ourselves that whoever was called first would make a statement about the position all of us would take. It happened that Fitzpatrick was the one. He indicated that we were going to rely on the First and Fifth Amendments, refusing to answer questions about our political associations. The committee grilled Fitzpatrick. They asked him to give them names, and he simply referred them to his statement. Then they called Panzino. Panzino did pretty much the same thing.

I was the last one called. I was on and off in about five minutes. I was so mad at this point because we knew this whole deal was a frame-up. We knew they selected us because they felt an attack on us would have the greatest impact on the union elections. So I challenged the committee about the reasons for calling us and for interfering in our union. I told the committee they had no business doing this, that it was unconstitutional.

Then they asked me some questions I wouldn't answer. They implied that I was hiding behind the Fifth Amendment. "I'm not hiding behind the Constitution," I said. "I'm standing before it, defending it." In the course of the questioning, I never did use the actual words "First and Fifth Amendments." But I did refer to Fitzpatrick's statement, saying I associated myself with it. I was cited for contempt of Congress along with Fitzpatrick and Panzino.

That year, 1949, Congress cited sixty-four people from unions and other organizations for contempt on the recommendation of HUAC. Thirty-nine of them were from the Longshoremen's Union in Hawaii, Harry Bridges's union. Then they went ahead with the trials. The thirty-nine cases in the Longshoremen's Union were thrown out along with almost all the other cases. Fitzpatrick and Panzino were acquitted. But I was convicted of contempt of Congress because I didn't utter the words "First and Fifth Amendments." Contempt of Congress is a misdemeanor, like spitting on the street, but it's subject to a jail term of up to one year and a fine of not more than five thousand dollars.

When the judge sentenced me in 1951, he read a prepared statement. It was all about our dead servicemen in Korea, and he associated me with that. Then he sentenced me to four to twelve months in prison and a thousand-dollar fine. The union appealed my case to the Supreme Court. The vote there was six to three for acquittal. It was a landmark decision, really, that placed some limits on the congressional committees' investigations. The Supreme Court asserted that a congressional committee could not question people except when it had a valid legislative purpose. What the committee had been doing with us was just for the purpose of exposure.

In the meantime, the raids against the UE were on. Carey and the CIO had formed a rival union called the International Union of Electrical Workers. Elections were held in 1950 between UE and IUE in all the plants. They really put the pressure on those Catholic workers. Father Rice would have the parish priest call in the wife of a UE leader or an active supporter and tell her that her children might not be able to continue in parochial school.

A county judge named Musmanno got into the act, too. The weekend before the election, Musmanno came out to East Pittsburgh. He was a reserve officer in the Navy, so he wore his naval uniform. He had uniformed soldiers with him in military jeeps. And, of course, the flag. He made this big speech urging all of the workers to vote for the IUE.

The churches, the politicians, and the press made it seem that if you voted for the UE in 1950 it was almost like voting for Stalin. Really! That's how they framed the issue. You were voting against God and country if you voted for the UE. But even so we almost won the election. It was so close they had to have a run-off, and we lost that by just a couple hundred votes.

I went back to work at Westinghouse in 1951, as a welder. They fired me at the end of 1953. One day they just came down and said, "Pack up your tools and get your coat and hat." The business agent of the IUE local there, Charles Copeland, had been calling on the company to fire me. He had been one of the "friendly" witnesses who testified against us before HUAC. And now he would tell people, "Tom Quinn doesn't do anything but weld better relations with the Soviet Union," that kind of crazy stuff.

Copeland was one of those guys who could get up and make great speeches; he'd scream and holler. When you first listened to him, you thought: This guy's really impressive. He's telling workers what the company's doing to them. But what the workers wanted to hear was what he was going to do about it. Charlie never had any answers. If they wanted answers, they had to find guys like Fitzpatrick and Panzino.

The company fired Fitzpatrick and Panzino a year after they fired me, even though they had signed non-Communist affidavits and joined the IUE. And it wasn't just the few of us. They fired other people, too. The atmosphere then was against anyone who was called a red. Since our whole union was accused of being a bunch of reds, Westinghouse could get away with it.

In 1955, the day before McCarthy was to lose control of his Senate investigating committee, he subpoenaed a whole lot of people, including about eight or nine from the East Pittsburgh Westinghouse Plant. The company fired them all. They fired them just because they were subpoenaed, not because of what they said at the hearing. One woman had more than twenty-five years' service with the company. Physically, she just couldn't take the stress. She ended up in the hospital, unable to even appear before the committee. She got a call anyhow, saying she was fired.

Another guy had been prominent in the American Slav Congress. His son called me: "Dad got a subpoena for ten P.M." I said, "It must be a mistake." Everybody else was subpoenaed for ten A.M. on that day. So I told him to take his dad to Washington and be at the Senate Office Building at ten P.M. And that's what they did. They showed the subpoena to the guard at the desk. One of the staffers from the committee came down and said, "Gee, that's a mistake. We'll have to call Westinghouse right away." This is actually what he said: "We'll have to call *Westinghouse*." His dad never testified, but he got fired along with everybody else, and he stayed fired.

Bill Heiston committed suicide. He was the district representative of the UE before me. Bill had used up his three-year leave of absence while he was a union representative and had to go back in the plant. He went back in 1947. In 1955, they sent him a telegram saying, "You're fired!" Bill was a highly skilled electrician. He'd go to an interview with credentials that were impeccable in his field. He'd be hired. They'd tell him to report for work on Tuesday morning. Then they would call him Monday afternoon and tell him they were sorry. This happened enough times so there was no question that he was being blacklisted. He was single and didn't have a family to give him support. One day they found Bill. He couldn't take it any longer.

John Nelson was president of the UE in Erie, Pennsylvania. He was really a fine young leader of the union, an international executive board member, just an outstanding man. He was also a devout Catholic, the kind who went to Mass every morning. He was called before a 1954 Senate investigating committee. Then he was fired by General Electric. G.E. was very cute. They didn't fire him outright; they gave him ninety days to "clear" himself. That meant he would have to go before the committee and name names. He refused. He spent a couple years suffering from what they did. He died in his mid-forties, and I don't think there's any question that that contributed to his death.

I was called in 1954 by the same Senate investigating committee. It was a subcommittee, headed by Senator Butler from Maryland. Of course, there I pleaded the straight Fifth Amendment. I said I had a case pending before the Supreme Court and I would answer no questions. That's all there was to that.

They weren't really after us as individuals. It was all part of a continuing conspiracy between the politicians and the electrical manufacturing companies to destroy the UE. By 1959, the UE had been pretty well decimated. But they were going to put the crusher on us. They brought the Un-American Committee to Pittsburgh again and called leaders from the different local UE unions around western Pennsylvania.

By then, they had a collection of stool pigeons. It was like a circus here. It began with Matt Cvetic. He named a group of people. Then a couple of years later, some of the people he had named turned out to be FBI undercover agents. And then a couple years later, the people they named turned out to be FBI agents. It just kept going on and on. I can't even remember all the names. There were still more coming out of the woodwork by 1959, saying, "Oh, yes! We've been undercover agents for years." And they started naming names.

I finally told our guys, "How long do we keep playing this game with these people?" And my legal counsel said, "Well, you know, there's certain risks if you don't." I really hadn't made up my mind what to do this time until I got right up in front of the committee. When it was my turn, I challenged the whole thing and I kept citing the Supreme Court decision in my case. I asked, "What's the purpose of this?" They said they didn't have to tell me what the purpose of this was. All I was up there to do was to answer questions. I said, "I don't have to answer your questions." We went back and forth for quite a while.

Before I testified, another witness who had been named by Cvetic as a Communist and subsequently unveiled as an FBI undercover agent testified that he had known me for many years, that I was a Communist, and that he used to meet with me. I never saw him in my life before that day. Then the committee asked me about that. I said, "No, that's a lie. That guy who said I was a member of the Communist Party, he's a liar." That threw the whole place into turmoil. It really got them because I challenged the committee's right to ask questions, I challenged their witnesses, and then told them under oath I wasn't a Communist. They recessed for about twenty minutes. Then they came back and said they were going to cite me for contempt and for perjury.

What happened with that? I never found out until recently. Under the Freedom of Information Act, I got my FBI file. It was mostly garbage because a lot of stuff was censored out. But one thing was there, an exchange between people at the highest levels of the FBI. I found out that when the committee went back to Washington, they intended to pursue the charge of perjury against me. They sent for information from the FBI to support it. The correspondence back and forth showed they didn't have any other witnesses and they didn't have any evidence. There was some intimation in one of the communications that heads might roll in the Pittsburgh office of the FBI. Then they dropped it.

My FBI file was interesting because they had very close surveillance of me through the fifties and into the early sixties. Then it just tailed off. Every once in a while there would be a reference in there, as if someone were to ask, "Hey, what's Tom Quinn doing?" And then it sort of disappeared. There weren't many entries until the Vietnam war.

In Pittsburgh I was one of the outspoken critics of the Vietnam war. There were only a few of us then. By this time, Monsignor Rice had become an opponent of the war, and he and I appeared on platforms together. One day, there was a big rally in downtown Pittsburgh on Market Square. He introduced me, a very flowery introduction about what longtime friends we were. And I just looked up to the heavens. During that whole period, we were always bumping into each other. Things really turned around for him. Now he became a lightning rod for red-baiting in the Pittsburgh area. All the "antis" were really after him. He became the "Communist," the Pittsburgh Communist, during that period. He had a radio show, the same program he had had for many years. People would call in and heap abuse on him.

The committee and everything connected with it had had a serious effect on the labor movement. People didn't want to be associated with the leaders under attack, the very ones who would have provided militant, aggressive leadership in the unions. It took its toll on what the unions were able to achieve in benefits, because the most effective leaders were just wiped out. And those who took their places were, for the most part, a collection of inept, selfish leaders. They were all out for their own interests. It wasn't one for all and all for one, as it once had been.

We began, in the late fifties, to put the UE back together again. I was the international representative, and we had a staff in western Pennsylvania. We started winning elections in a small shop here and a small shop there. Of course, in some places we had to have an election at almost every contract because some union would come in to raid us. All those vultures from the IUE, the International Brotherhood of Electrical Workers, and the International Association of Machinists were there at the gates. It went on and on. It just tore the unity apart. Obviously, if you're divided all the time that has to have an effect on what you're able to do when you sit down to negotiate a contract with the company.

Look at the wages in the electrical industry compared to the steel industry. In 1948, the electrical workers were the highest paid in the CIO. But the actual hourly rate for a steel worker now averages around three dollars more than the electrical worker makes. That's what happened over that period. In UE, we had paid holidays before the auto workers and steel workers. Seniority and many of the other conditions that had been established in the electrical industry were far better than they were in the others. It was just reversed after the split. The workers paid the price, a tremendous price in wages and conditions.

After 1959, the committee ran into all kinds of opposition. The civil rights movement was under way. Young people were organizing. Then, somewhere along the line, the committee quietly folded up. I was finally able to go on several television shows to talk about what happened. Gosh, I'd hear from people I hadn't heard from in fifteen years. They'd call up and say, "It's about time somebody told the truth." But many of them weren't about to do it themselves. They just wanted it erased from their lives. It had been too painful.

To Smear a Professor

Barrows Dunham

In 1953, the House Un-American Activities Committee, under its new chairman Harold Velde, was vying with two Senate committees to investigate education. So politically attractive a venture was it that the Republican leadership tried to prevent the committees from colliding in their competition for "star witnesses." By the end of the season, Chairman Velde's hearings had cost the jobs of hundreds of teachers and professors. Twenty-nine persons were cited by the House for contempt that year. The first among them was Barrows Dunham, whose eventual acquittal by a federal district court helped reestablish the Fifth Amendment as a defense against the committee's intrusions.

Barrows Dunham, chairman of Temple University's Philosophy Department and author of the well-respected book Man Against Myth, *was dismissed by the university for his silence and frozen out of regular employment for fifteen years. The Association of American Universities held that merely asserting the privilege of the Fifth Amendment placed upon the offending professors the burden of proving their fitness to continue teaching. The American academy's commitment to academic freedom had all but collapsed. "Professor Dunham," wrote journalist I. F. Stone, "was one of a handful who came through the ordeal with honor in a period when few American intellectuals showed much in the way of*

127

BARROWS DUNHAM

*guts."[1] It wasn't until 1981, after the third request from its faculty sen-
ate, that Temple reinstated Barrows Dunham, as professor emeritus,
ending a "painful vestige of McCarthyism."[2]*

The point at which the attack on constitutional rights was leveled
was not at us lefties. We were unimportant except to be used as pawns.
The attack, I am quite sure, was aimed at breaking up the coalition Roosevelt had established between the liberals at the center and the socialist
left. There was a group of people you could call left-wing liberals, and
these were the chief victims, the spectacular victims. Alger Hiss was
one. Owen Lattimore was another. These guys, along with others, were
connected with developing our policy toward China during and after
the war. They argued for a coalition government between Chiang Kai-
shek and Mao Tse-tung, a coalition between the capitalist and communist forces. Those who held that view, Owen Lattimore and John Service
and Edmund Clubb, lost their jobs in the State Department.

I mention this because the victims show you where the attack was
aimed. The phrases of the period, like "fellow traveler," and the efforts
to prove guilt by association were aimed at splitting the center off from
the left. It was very effective. The liberals were scared of being called
reds, from Truman on down. They showed you, in those days, a clean
pair of heels. Most did. Of course, there were some who were quite stal-
wart, who really did believe in the doctrine of free speech.

In September of 1952, Alice and I were down at the shore, at Wild-
wood, New Jersey. College opened late in those days. And September
really was the best time, after the summer residents were gone. Down
there, I read in the *New York Times* one day about the attack by one of
the congressional investigating committees on professors in New York
City. I had been a member of the Communist Party of the United States
from 1938 to 1945. So I thought it was beginning to get pretty close.

We just said: Well, we'll see what happens. On the third of October,
I was called from class at Temple University. I was told there was somebody to see me. I had an idea who it was going to be. Sure enough, it
was a United States marshal with a subpoena from the House Committee on Un-American Activities. I was scheduled to appear in November
1952. It was the election year.

I received the subpoena when I returned to my office. I sort of sank
down in my chair. The marshal asked, "Do you want this to be public?"

I said, "No, I don't want this to be public." So he went to the telephone—I think it was a fake call—and pretended to call somebody. He said, "Kill that story." We used to wonder afterward what was the point of all this stuff. Then someone told me he wanted a tip, maybe five bucks, from me. I thought, anyone who wants five bucks from a professor, especially a philosopher, has to be more definite.

At any rate, the hearing was held in Philadelphia. It was held but my appearance was postponed. Eisenhower was elected. There was a whole new Congress, and my subpoena lapsed with the old Congress. During the month of January of 1953, I was free. I was unsubpoenaed. When the new Congress was organized, I began seeing things on TV. And Velde, who was chairman of HUAC that year, was saying that he was going to call various professors. So I thought, sooner or later . . .

Meanwhile, I thought I might evade it if I could get a leave of absence somehow. I applied for a Ford Foundation faculty fellowship. To do that, you had to have three people write on your behalf. Alice suggested that since Albert Einstein had written such a splendid blurb for my *Man Against Myth,* I could ask him. I was reluctant to do it, but one very rainy and cold January day we went to Princeton.

Einstein had told me that before he wrote such a letter he would like to see *Man Against Myth* again. He had sent his to Israel. So I brought a copy of it. I was received by his secretary at 112 Mercer Street, where he lived. He was upstairs on the second floor being sculpted by a lady sculptress. He came to the head of the stairs to greet me in an old brown sweater and baggy pants and that marvelous leonine hair. You would have thought we were old friends—the geniality, the absolute ease and graciousness with which he received this, to him, pretty much unknown person. And I was, of course, in awe of the greatest physicist of the twentieth century.

None of that. He threw all this kind of thing aside. I've known, I suppose, five or six great men in my life, and this is a trait they all had, regarding you as an equal. They see no distinction between themselves and you as far as regard is concerned.

I had wanted to tell him that I had one subpoena and expected another. But I couldn't tell him with that woman sculpting away there. We talked for about twenty minutes, I guess, and then I took my leave. The secretary, a middle-aged woman, led me downstairs. At the bottom of the stairs, I said to her, "You know there are going to be three investigating committees in the new Congress, and I may be called." She made a gesture and said quietly, "He doesn't care about that." And of course he didn't. He later became a kind of adviser to various victims, if you want to call them that. You could go to him and get support and advice for what you might do. People did, at any rate.

Einstein did write a letter on my behalf. And that ended in the Ford Foundation sending a field representative to see me. But it was too late. He came here to dinner on the night Alice and I got back from my appearance before HUAC on February 27, 1953.

Two weeks before that, the second subpoena had been served here in this house by two guys who came up the walk on Lincoln's birthday, February 12, 1953. When I saw them go by that window, I sort of knew what this was. Alice went to the door, and I had a momentary panic. I thought I'd duck into that coatroom there. But then I realized that, although they couldn't come in if you didn't let them in, I also couldn't go out, at least not without getting served. So we let them in.

They stood on either side of this fireplace. The one on this side was tall and fat and falsely jovial. The guy who stood on the other side was short and thin and what Freud would have called the anal type. He was very tight and very unsmiling.

Alice asked them, while we were sitting on the couch, "What does the committee want?" They both said, "Names. Names." It was the plainest confession of what they were after. They lived on names. The more names they had, the more hearings they could have, the more people they could drag to the pillory before the public to spread the terror. They lived on names until they ran out of names, and then they died of inanition toward the end of the 1960s.

To oppose them and to assist in defeating them, you had to withhold the food that they lived on, namely, names. And besides, you can't name friends. What the hell kind of person would that be? It's morally repugnant. But even without that, I had the sense that somewhere in my childhood I had learned that you don't tell tales on people, that you're not a tattle-tale. It felt to me as something laid way deep in my psychology. I couldn't do it no matter what, no matter what.

And that made the decision easy. I didn't have to ask shall I or shan't I. I suppose a lot of guys wavered. Some tried to make compromises. They named people who had already been named or they thought had been named or they were told that they had. They were lured into more talking.

What the committee did really was contrary to the American tradition, or at least to an important part of the American tradition. I think the tradition is composed of two opposites: the Bill of Rights versus the witch-hunt, and the court of justice versus the lynching bee. The Bill of Rights and the court of justice represent the truly legal kind of behavior in the history of the country, and these others are anarchist behaviors, extralegal, a kind of vigilante stuff.

The idea of the committee was originally that of John W. Davis, who ran for the presidency against Calvin Coolidge in 1924. He was a lawyer for Morgan and Company. And the way in which he bent the theory behind congressional committees tells the tale about this. You see, a congressional committee is set up to consider legislation which it then proposes to the House or the Senate to be voted on. And congressmen don't know everything, even if they seem to think they do. It's quite rational for a committee on taxation, let us say, to call in tax experts to tell them what they think is wrong with the tax situation and what kind of corrections it needs. So Davis apparently considered that if you had a committee that investigated radicals it could call people as "expert witnesses."

But that's where the pillory begins. Although in theory we were expert witnesses, none of us was ever allowed to describe what actually went on. They wouldn't let you say why you did what you did. You were absolutely confined to the narrow questions they would ask. Nor did the House Committee on Un-American Activities bother to propose legislation. They didn't make any pretense of that until later when the Supreme Court required them to.

I had a closed session when I appeared before the committee. February 26, 1953, was the day we first went down, Alice and I and my attorney. The committee had called a professor from Harvard named Wendell Furry to testify the same day. His sister-in-law happened to be married to Klaus Fuchs, who was supposedly a spy on atomic secrets. Fuchs did go to jail, I guess, in England.

I'll never forget how Furry looked when he came into the committee's offices. He had the look of black terror on his face. I'm sure that's how he felt. The Rosenbergs were doomed at that time, you know. They were executed in June of 1953. That was three or four months after that particular February morning. It was grisly stuff.

We had that atmosphere hanging around us at that time. The committee manufactured atmosphere, which they substituted for evidence. They gave Furry a big to-do in the hearing room. The witness sits in a chair on the floor at a table with his lawyer beside him. The committee members sit higher up on a set of benches, and they have desks in front of them so that they can give the impression of birds of prey about to swoop on carrion. That's the impression they gave me.

Well, I didn't want to see this, so we spent the morning in the committee's office. My attorney went up to watch things. Then he said, "I want you to go up and watch this afternoon." So I did. They stopped Furry after I heard him for about thirty minutes. Then they called Granville Hicks, the old renegade. Hicks had been a big shot in the Communist Party, their great literary light in the thirties. Very scholarly. His field was American literature. He wrote a book called *The Great Tradition*. It was rather good, written from a Marxist point of view. He broke with the party after the Soviet-German nonaggression pact in 1939. They must have quarreled bitterly, because he spent the rest of his life trying to do Communists in.

So they trotted him out after Furry. And I watched him naming names. They would say, "Was so-and-so a member of the Communist branch at Harvard University?" And he would say, "Yes." He identified twelve people, I think. I heard him do this, him with his little beady eyes. He had a little mustache. He made me think of a rat there. I think this is accurate. I felt him to be a rat as I watched it, at any rate. I think back and wonder, did he really have a mustache, or did I just think that he had? His little narrow face—a kind of eagerness to get in on this nipping and biting.

After I watched him, I saw for sure that's the thing you can't do. You just can't do that. I had never thought of doing it, but it was very strengthening to have it confirmed by the actual sight of it being done.

When they finished that day's hearing, they told me to come back the next day. It had been a Thursday. I came back on Friday, February 27. I sat in a quite comfortable armchair. My attorney had one also. We whispered back and forth in a fairly large room. I guess there were six or seven members of the committee plus the chairman, who was Mr. Harold Velde from southern Illinois. Velde was new to this chairmanship. He appeared in a cut-away coat and striped trousers. With his blond hair and a cleft in his chin, I thought, "God! He'd look just great in a storm trooper's outfit."

What I had to do was withhold names from them and keep out of jail at the same time. There's a clause in the Fifth Amendment that says you don't have to be a witness against yourself. That's an absolutely important clause that defines the difference between inquisition and no inquisition. The inquisitors would get some guy suspected of heresy, and they'd question him at length until he finally would say something that could be pronounced heretical and, bango, he was in for it. So the founders of the country said we will not have any of this in our country. That's what they said with the Fifth Amendment.

Now, there had been the case of a Mrs. Rogers, a year before, maybe, who testified that she had been a member of the Communist Party, because she wanted to be quite candid about it and not appear to be scared or conspiratorial. But she refused to say anything about anybody else. She was convicted of contempt of Congress, and the case went up to the Supreme Court, which upheld the conviction. The Court ruled that if you open up an area by answering a question, you have to answer all the questions that may be asked within that area. Every question, in fact, does open up an area. So then the defense tactic was not to open up any areas.

I began using the Fifth Amendment quite early. I answered my name and address because they are entitled to make sure that you are the person that they intended to call. Then they asked, "Where were you born and when?" Well, I said when, but at first I wouldn't tell them where. It was Mount Holly, New Jersey. Then my lawyer said, "You'd better answer that." So I did.

You understand, my awareness was constantly impeded by the tension that I felt myself to be under. Physically, it felt as if I had an iron bar running between my ears. I was conscious of being in peril all the time.

The next question was about my educational history. That opened up an area I had to close off. So I respectfully declined to answer that. You had to use this formula: "On the grounds that the answer might tend to incriminate me." Nasty language, but that was the legal language. "Incriminate" only meant that it might get you involved in a lawsuit, not that you had committed any crime. The question after that was, "Where are you presently employed?" Well, that would have been Temple University. I'd have been liable to questions about my colleagues and my students.

Now, this gives you a chance to see the kind of bind that a teacher was in. Suppose, in order to keep your job, you showed your willingness to name names. Your usefulness as a teacher would automatically cease. What kind of class would you have thereafter, where the students knew that under pressure you would tell what their opinions were? The classroom, I think, should be as sacrosanct as the confessional or the psychiatrist's couch. The same with your colleagues. What kind of relationship would you have with your colleagues if they knew that under pressure you would tell on them?

So that was absolutely out. I declined to answer that. It was by this time apparent that I wasn't going to "talk." They had never been stopped so short up to that time, at least so I was told. Then Congressman Walter jumped up from his chair and said, "D'ja wanna keep dis up all morning?" He talked like that. We'd been going about ten minutes, maybe. So they stopped.

Then I was outside sitting with Alice. After about twenty minutes, somebody came out and said the committee had no further need of me. I went over and filed my expense account, which was thirty bucks for four rides on the Pennsy. I got the thirty bucks but lost my income at the same time.

We got back home that Friday around three o'clock. It had been fairly tiring, so we were lying down on our beds. Around five o'clock, our son, who had been driving around in the car, came running in to say he'd heard on the radio the committee was thinking of citing me for contempt. If so, I was liable to a thousand-dollar fine and one year in prison.

It was about that time that the representative from the Ford Foundation arrived. He was very sympathetic, of course. He was an academic person, a very nice guy. We were sitting here in the living room. Alice was getting dinner. I made martinis. I had about three of them. And we were out of bread, so I went around the corner to the delicatessen to buy a loaf. When I got back, there was a reporter from the *Evening Bulletin* in the kitchen. The Ford Foundation guy was alone in the living room with his martini. By this time I was feeling kind of high, real strong, after all the sagging that had gone on during the day. So I stormed up and down in the kitchen. I told the reporter this was the old medieval inquisition, this was the thumbscrew and the rack, all of which he put in the paper the next day. I sounded as pugnacious as you could imagine. Well, it was true. It was sort of the thumbscrew and the rack.

Then the wire services began calling up. It was a kind of hectic dinner we had. And the Ford guy said, "Well, I'm just afraid this won't go through, because one of the requirements is that the college you come from has to agree to take you back at the end of the scholarship." I suppose that was to prevent colleges from dumping their unwanted faculty members on the Ford Foundation. It was a good enough rule. He said, "I don't believe your university is going to do that." And I didn't either. So that was that.

I was suspended immediately by the president of Temple University. I was in limbo. I couldn't go back to teach. I was even ordered not to show up on campus. The president said I had by my action raised some doubts about my loyalty status. Now, there was this Pechan Act in the state of Pennsylvania which required teachers to take a loyalty oath. College professors didn't have to do that. Their president certified once a year that he had no subversives on his faculty. I discovered shortly after this that we had all been cleared earlier by the FBI, including me.

On the seventh of May, I had a hearing before a committee down at Temple that had been set up to determine whether you were or were not subversive within the meaning of the Pechan Act. That committee made no finding whatever, for or against me. They couldn't, because under oath I gave the text of the Pennsylvania Loyalty Oath as expressing my own principles in the matter. After all, I wasn't going to overthrow the Constitution of the United States. It was all such nonsense.

They wanted to get me out, but I had pretty much deprived them of the grounds for doing that by endorsing the loyalty oath. In fact, my lawyer argued, "They can't fire you. There are just no grounds for it." I said, "Well, we'll wait and see." They didn't need any grounds. They create a whole fictitious universe in which they can make events justify what they want to do.

I was dismissed on September 23, 1953, on grounds they had never mentioned before. I was heard on one charge and fired on another. You really can't beat that. The trustees, in their statement of dismissal, accused me of intellectual arrogance, that is, setting my will up against that of the legal arm of the government. I thought it was nice that they called it intellectual, anyhow.

And then they said I had misused the Fifth Amendment. It would take, and in fact it did take, a regularly constituted court to decide whether I had misused it or not. And later, that court found that I hadn't. But at that time the trustees constituted themselves a rump tribunal and passed on the constitutionality of what I had done. They had bum advice from their lawyers, or advice that turned out to be bad, at any rate.

My father died a month after I was fired. He was eighty-three years old and he suffered from cancer of the lymphatic system. My father was originally a Presbyterian minister before he became dean of the college at Temple University, a position he held from 1915 to 1942. He was a man who helped me develop my mind. He encouraged that all the time, but he never directed it, never insisted that I think this or that.

When I left Temple after that morning of September 23, and I was told I was out, I phoned Alice. Then I drove to my parents' apartment to tell them. My mother was very vigorous about it. She stormed around the apartment denouncing them. My father was within a month of his death, but nobody could tell then. He sat in a chair and I sat on the sofa beside him. We locked our arms. I told him, "I'm glad you're taking it so well." Then he said to me, "I'm glad *you're* taking it so well." It was a lovely father-son moment. He was quite a fellow.

A year after my appearance before the House Un-American Activities Committee, in March of 1954, the House of Representatives voted to cite me for contempt for refusing to answer the committee's questions. The Washington grand jury indicted me in November of 1954. I came to trial in October of 1955. Leonard Boudin, who was my attorney, had put the government in a dilemma. He got the judge to require the government to show that the questions I had refused to answer were relevant to the inquiry. Now, you see, if they were not relevant, it didn't matter that I didn't answer them. If they were relevant, I was in danger and had the right to invoke the Fifth Amendment. That dilemma stood up.

It was a three-hour trial down there in the federal district court building. I must say that in recent years I've enjoyed watching all those bastards, all those Watergate characters, go in those doors and up the very steps I went up. The prosecutor was a guy named William Hitz. His main argument was that the committee needed the answers to those questions in order to identify me. He had to try to argue that there might be another Barrows Dunham. There are names you could do that with, but he was stuck with a unique name. I can remember the government attorney struggling with this argument. Along about three o'clock in the afternoon, Leonard asked the judge to give a judgment of acquittal, which he did. I remember his leaning over the bench to say it. They were awfully nice words.

I remember how tired the government attorney looked as he put his papers back in his briefcase and prepared to leave. I enjoyed that, all right, I can tell you. I got up from the table to go back and shake hands with Alice. I found she was so worried and the anxiety in her mind was so great the acquittal hadn't penetrated. I had to tell her I was a free man.

So there I was, acquitted, but my former bosses, whose arguments had just been overturned, kept to their conclusion. They were overruled, but they wouldn't take me back. There was an effort. The American Civil Liberties Union wrote to them and pointed out that I had been acquitted. They still wouldn't take me back. Not only that, they hounded me on further jobs. They would send copies of the trustees' statement of dismissal to prospective employers.

I appealed to the Temple chapter of the American Association of University Professors, and through them to the national office. At that time, the head of it had been there for a long while. He was one who couldn't produce any kind of work. The story was that after his death they went into his office and opened the closet door and a whole lot of cases he never handled came pouring down onto the floor. By 1956, he was gone, and they got in a professor of law from the University of Indiana named Ralph Fuchs. He was just a splendid fellow. He got some pretty active guys around him, and in 1956 they censured a whole bunch of colleges, including Temple.

The censure of Temple remained until 1961. They got Temple University to say that they would never do that kind of thing again; they would obey the rules of due process. But the AAUP censure didn't do anything for me. I didn't get my job back or even a monetary settlement.

There were a lot of friends who dropped away. Most did. This other chap in the Philosophy Department remained loyal to me. In fact, his wife, who teaches at the University of Pennsylvania School of Social Work, got me a visiting professorship there in 1970, the one year of full-time teaching I've had since 1953. But that was it. I've had a certain amount of part-time work, but I was completely out for fifteen years.

It was painful to be cut off from the students those fifteen years. I missed the youngsters. When I got back to them, I found their whole point of view was different. Perhaps I wouldn't have noticed it if I hadn't been away. In the 1950s, everyone felt, and the students too, that a social problem would require a social solution. I thought in terms of social solutions. When I got back to Beaver College in 1968, I found that they were concerned, all right, but they were concerned about how to be a decent person in a lousy world.

My best book, I think, came out in early 1964: *Heroes and Heretics.* It grew out of this experience, out of a specific moment in that experience. The day I was fired, September 23, 1953, was my son's birthday. They called me at nine o'clock to tell me of my dismissal. I knew by that time that the papers and the wire services would call up. My wife composed a short statement. At four o'clock the phone rang. It was a reporter from the *Philadelphia Daily News*. He had the text of the trustees' statement, and he chuckled and said to me, "They say you're intellectually arrogant." I thought he chuckled a little more than the thing required.

Being a scholar in the history of philosophy, that rang bells. This was essentially the charge against Socrates. I was being called something that had been used in the past, and I began studying that in the next years. And, sure enough, that was the usual charge in one form or another against dissenters. I wrote a political history of philosophy founded on this idea. It revealed philosophy as a struggle between those leaders and members of organizations who were trying to keep the organizations intact, and dissenters who were trying to correct mistakes. It was fun to write, and it was quite good, I think. It is my answer to HUAC.

JOHN RANDOLPH AND SARAH CUNNINGHAM

There's No Business Like Show Business

John Randolph and Sarah Cunningham

The choices facing those subpoenaed to testify before the House Un-American Activities Committee were not pleasant ones. Some, such as Albert Einstein, urged resistance based on the First Amendment: "Every intellectual who is called before one of the committees ought to refuse to testify, i.e., he must be prepared for jail and economic ruin, in short, for the sacrifice of his personal welfare in the interest of the cultural welfare of his country."[1]

But suppose, for whatever reason, that was not an acceptable alternative. What then? If you were or once had been a member of the Communist Party, why not tell the committee, but refuse to name anyone else? Your lawyer might warn you that by supplying the first answer, you waived your rights to refuse to answer subsequent questions about others and, accordingly, were liable for contempt and imprisonment. Suppose you had never been a Communist and had no scruples about telling that to the committee. Then, if government witnesses lied about you—as they did about Edward Lamb,* to cite just one example—you were liable to prosecution for perjury, a serious offense.

In either event, the Fifth Amendment's protection against self-incrimination offered the "unfriendly" witnesses their only recourse. De-

---

* Edward Lamb's story appears in Part IV.

signed to protect the innocent, the Fifth Amendment was soiled by congressional committees that established its use as an admission of "guilt." Invoking it would save you from jail—as it did Sarah Cunningham, an actress descended from signers of the Declaration of Independence— but not from economic ruin and social ostracism. In show business, its use ensured blacklisting. John Randolph's film credits reflect that blacklist in the lag between the 1950s and the 1960s: Naked City, *1948;* Fourteen Hours, *1951;* Partners in Production, *1952; then, after thirteen years,* Night Song, *1965;* Seconds, *1965;* Pretty Poison, *1967;* Gaily, Gaily, *1968; and so on.[2] Only after his blacklisting was lifted in 1963 did he appear in television episodes of "Mission Impossible," "Bonanza," "Hawaii Five-O," and, more recently, "All in the Family," "Columbo," "The Bob Newhart Show," "Trapper John, M.D.," and "Who's the Boss?"*

JOHN: When the House Un-American Activities Committee came to New York in 1955, it announced that Sarah and I had been subpoenaed. My picture appeared on the front pages of the *Herald Tribune* and the *New York Times* the day I testified. We were living at 107th Street then. The phone stopped ringing, except for the hate calls. At three or four in the morning, you'd hear: "Jew-Commie," "Kike-bastard," "Go back to Russia." Suddenly your best friends disappeared because they were too scared. Hysteria was all around us.

I knew an actor who was raised in the tradition of that wonderful Jewish socialism. I loved this guy. When he was a kid, he used to do stand-up comedy on the borscht circuit. After the war, we were in class together at the American Theater Wing. He had the great gift of doing many voices. You've heard him in a million commercials and cartoons. He wanted to be successful, and he did become very big in a series on NBC. By that time, I'd been blacklisted there.

After I testified, he showed up at our house at midnight. We invited him in, and he laid down a check of one hundred fifty dollars for the lawyer. "This is guilt money," he said. "I want to do something for you and Sarah, but I have to tell you the truth." He told us somebody on the show with him had pointed to my picture and asked, "You know this joker?" He heard himself say, "No, I never met him."

It even got to my mother. I'm not exaggerating. I was sitting in the kitchen with my own mother, who knows I am probably the most gentle person she ever met. I was never involved in a violent act, even in the army. But she said to me, "Listen, I'm your mother. You can tell me. Do you believe in the overthrow of the government by force and violence?" I said, "Ma, you know me. I'm too busy rehearsing to overthrow the government by force and violence." To think that your own mother would be sucked into this bullshit!

But there was another side to the coin. When I was subpoenaed, I was working in Cambridge. The week before, I had finished playing Sam Levine in *Guys and Dolls*. That's what I figured was my métier. Then I was hired to do a completely different character in *Much Ado About Nothing*, with a bunch of Shakespearean actors I considered very esthete. I felt I just didn't belong.

At the same time, I had signed for *Wooden Dish*, a new Broadway show that Louis Calhern directed and starred in. I thought I'd go right into it after *Much Ado About Nothing*. Then two items appeared in different sections of the *New York Times*. One said I had been subpoenaed by the House committee, the other that I had been hired to star opposite Louis Calhern. The producer was a Hollywood mogul who had blacklisted actors. I figured, "Well, I'm finished."

On the train from New York that night, I made up my mind to send out four thousand leaflets saying: I have a right to work. I was determined to fight this goddamn thing. I knew when I got into Cambridge, to the Brattle Theater, the stage manager was going to be standing there with a telegram nullifying my contract for *Wooden Dish*. I just knew that. And why, I asked myself, was I stuck with that shitty company of Shakespearean actors? I felt terrible, really depressed.

Sure enough, the stage manager was waiting outside the theater with a telegram. He watched as I read it: "I just want you to know I'm very glad to have you with us in the show. I know we'll have a splendid engagement together." Signed, "Louis Calhern." He didn't even know me! That he would send that telegram at that moment was a wonderful thing.

Then, as I walked into the dressing room, these Shakespearean actors began to sing "Which Side Are You On?" I'm looking at Mendy Wager and Pernell Roberts and the others. Then they sang "Solidarity Forever." Well, they had me on the floor. There they were in their Spanish period costumes, singing songs Pete Seeger had done. And they were all in sympathy with me. It turned out to be quite a wonderful, wonderful experience.

I did go into rehearsal with *Wooden Dish*. I did thank Louis Calhern for that wonderful telegram. But Americans United Against Communism, something like that, went to the backers of the show: "Do you know you're supporting a Communist, John Randolph?" Opening night, they were out there, led by Roy Cohn, picketing us. Charlie Chaplin's picture *Modern Times* had been picketed by the American Legion, but I was the first actor to be picketed in the flesh. Many times when we were sitting around before the curtain, Louis Calhern would ask, "Are those hoods still out there?" They were there every night.

The rash spread. They threatened to picket *Bus Stop*. Tennessee Williams was considered a red, and they were going to picket anything he wrote. But the League of New York Managers and Actors Equity put a leaflet in every program saying they had a right to produce whatever they wanted and those people didn't have to go into the theater. They had signs outside proclaiming their fight against censorship. Eli Wallach, Lee Grant, Sarah, and others in Actors Equity all worked with me on an anti-blacklist resolution. The union passed it and negotiated the first anti-blacklist clause in any union contract.

SARAH: Blacklisting began earlier than most people think. It started with the drive to make the Screen Writers Guild a union. Members of the governing body of the union, the Hollywood Ten, were blacklisted and jailed.

JOHN: In 1947, when the Hollywood writers got the shaft, I was in *Command Decision*, a big hit on Broadway. Those of us in *Command Decision, Streetcar Named Desire*—Marlon Brando, Jimmie Whitmore, and others—we all knew eventually it would come to the East Coast. I mean, we had that much wisdom. So a group of actors from the different Broadway shows went down to the hearings to give our support to the Hollywood Ten.

I remember we took a midnight train and arrived in Washington at five-thirty in the morning to get into the hearing. It was called a hearing, but it was a trial, a hangman's trial. You were dead before you began. The way they drove at those writers, like Ring Lardner, Jr., who took the First Amendment and were held in contempt. They were thrust in the public eye and accused of being disloyal. It was frightening to me before I ever went through it myself.

I must say I appreciated how difficult it was for those Hollywood actors who fought back. The stakes were high. Morris Carnovsky and Howard Da Silva and J. Edward Bromberg, all those wonderful actors had worked all their lives on Broadway and never made much money.

They were the great creators of the Group Theater.* They were a stimulus to those of us who were young and looked up to these actors who finally went to Hollywood and made it.

I remember Conrad Bromberg told us about the beautiful house his father built in Santa Monica, overlooking the ocean. They would have a party there every week. When the blacklisting hit, that stopped. Nobody came to the house. He said one of the most terrible sights was his father sitting by the telephone, waiting for it to ring.

Bromberg went to see his agent. This was a top-notch actor. When you're that big, the agent will see you right away. The secretary said, "Of course, he'll be right with you." Then he waited. Hours passed. People came in and went into the agent's office, and Bromberg sat there, paralyzed. Finally, the agent came out: "I didn't know you were here." J. started talking, but the agent cut in, "Oh, everything is going to be worked out. There are several parts that we're lining up"—all as if nothing had ever happened. Bromberg never heard from him. Well, that was shattering.

Phil Loeb was another tragic figure. Phil Loeb was Papa Goldberg on "The Goldbergs." He'd been in many Broadway shows, a distinguished actor. He was an officer of Actors Equity and one of the big fighters for every decent thing we ever had, like rehearsal pay. He was being fired. The network admitted they were giving in to outside pressure. And Phil Loeb was the scapegoat. I was on the American Federation of Television and Radio Artists committee to investigate his blacklisting. We came to an AFTRA meeting prepared to organize tremendous support for him. And at the meeting Phil Loeb started to cry. He had made a settlement; he would leave "The Goldbergs" for a certain amount of money a week. We never expected Phil Loeb to give in.

SARAH: They got him where he hurt. His son meant everything to him. He was a schizophrenic, living in a private sanitorium in Baltimore. It cost Phil fifteen hundred dollars a week. The only way he could keep up the payments was to make the settlement. But then he couldn't get work, and his son was put in a state institution. After that, Phil Loeb committed suicide.

JOHN: Our committee went on to investigate other areas of blacklisting. Rod Steiger testified about the CBS loyalty oath. Charles Dubin,

* A left-wing, New York ensemble of dramatists, actors, and directors during the Depression era.

who later won Emmies for directing "M*A*S*H," and David Pressman, another top director, had the courage to tell us about the graylist.

SARAH: The graylist was a hodgepodge of actors: some who couldn't remember their lines, some who were considered subversive, and others. Will A. Lee was on the graylist just because he had the same name as Will Lee who had been blacklisted. Children whose parents were suspect were on the graylist.

JOHN: The testimony given to our committee was supposed to be private so nobody would feel intimidated. But the AFTRA secretary gave the notes of what everyone said to the heads of the union. We didn't know how closely the union leadership was working with Aware * and how much they were in sympathy with blacklisting. David Pressman and Charles Dubin were blacklisted. Every one of us on the anti-blacklisting committee ended up being blacklisted.

I was co-starring on a television show with Anthony Quinn when suddenly I was told by the producer, "John, don't tell anyone I told you, but we were just called up to the vice-president of CBS. A man named Laurence Johnson said you were a Communist, and he was going to put signs up in his chain of supermarkets that our sponsor, Ammodent toothpaste, supports Communist actors." Talk about blackmail. CBS didn't know anything about me, but they said, "Get rid of Randolph." The director, Sidney Lumet, said, "We can't do it. We're going on the air tomorrow, a live show, and John has a big part in it."

They told Lumet, "All right. But if you hire John Randolph again, you're finished." I didn't work with Sidney Lumet until *Serpico,* twenty-nine years later. If it hadn't been for Broadway, I would not be able to work anywhere. The theater kept us alive, but from 1951 I was literally blacklisted from television.

SARAH: With no reason, no explanation. Usually you weren't told you were on the blacklist. You just began to not work. Then, after a while, you blame it on yourself. It eats at you. Even John was saying, "Listen, I'm not really that good an actor. I don't know why I'm in this business."

JOHN: It used to be when you got an offer on the telephone, it was a verbal contract. Let's say my agent called and said, "John, we have an offer from the Mary Tyler Moore show. Are you available?" If I said yes, that was the contract. Suddenly the term "available" came to mean

---

* A self-appointed watchdog group during the 1950s, Aware, Inc., passed on the loyalty of actors as a criterion for employment in the East Coast entertainment industry. See John Henry Faulk's account of his lawsuit against the group for blacklisting (Part IV).

something different. I'd get a call: "They're casting a show at NBC, and we think you'd be right for a part. They want to know whether you would be available." If I said yes, it no longer constituted a contract. First they had to check with Aware to see if I was politically acceptable. Aware was run by Vincent Hartnett, an ex-FBI guy, who terrorized the entire industry, with the help of Laurence Johnson.

If there were seven parts in a television show, they'd have ten people for each part. All of them would be called and asked if they were available. All of them would be checked by Vincent Hartnett. He charged seven dollars and fifty cents for each name. With seventy names, that's already five hundred bucks for only one show. And Hartnett was clearing all the shows for Broadway and television. He was the hatchet man who cut people down. We knew that. But for a long time we didn't know his "Aware Bulletin" with its list of "Communists" was being sent around to every advertising agency, every casting director.

Finally we saw a copy of Bulletin Number Thirty-Nine and got an idea of what made actors politically unacceptable. Today, you would consider it ridiculous. We sent out an enormous mailing of this "Aware Bulletin," with all the names removed, as an exhibit of what was going on. It really shocked everybody. The *Herald Tribune* had a wonderful column. John Crosby wrote articles against blacklisting. The *New York Post* ran a series on Phil Loeb and Jean Muir. Then we did a mailing of that. Kim Hunter and Pat Neal, who were doing *Children's Hour* on Broadway, both sponsored it. *They* ended up being blacklisted.

The House Un-American Activities Committee came in 1955, when the fight against blacklisting began to win in the unions. The committee was called to investigate the "red sweep" that was taking over Broadway and the networks. The next thing we knew, subpoenas were issued to those of us who worked against blacklisting. Then we were sent a telegram from AFTRA: You can be fined, suspended, or expelled if you don't cooperate with this legitimate committee of the United States government. The tie-in became apparent between all these groups: the AFTRA leadership, Aware, and HUAC.

SARAH: HUAC seemed to be getting husbands and wives that summer. They got Jack Guilford and Madeline Lee. They were after Ossie Davis and Ruby Dee with a subpoena while they were working in summer stock, but the cast hid them in the wardrobe department. They put Ruby Dee in the hamper for a while to get her past the subpoena server and then got them both out of the theater. And, of course, they subpoenaed John and me.

JOHN: The hearing was like a three-ring circus. There was press from all over the world: newspapers, television cameras, radio broadcasters. You were surrounded by this tremendous spotlight of publicity. And all the hate groups were there every day in the first three or four rows. You knew you were finished. If you hadn't been blacklisted by that time, you were definitely going to be for the rest of your life. It's one thing to see someone else go through it, but when you go through it . . . !

SARAH: I almost fainted when you were called by Chairman Walter, John. But when John got up there, he was grinning. I heard him say, "Hello, boys." And I thought, "Thank God, now I know John will be all right."

JOHN: I went in with this attitude: You have no right to ask me what my political opinions are. It's none of your business whether Joe Schlamps is a Communist or a Socialist or a Republican or a Democrat. That's his right. And I refused to answer questions of that sort.

They started with their whole rigmarole: "What's your name? Where did you go to school? What shows have you been in?" My record was an open history, like any other actor. They could go to the union and find out what shows I'd been in. But they really weren't interested in that. When they asked, "Are you working now?" I said, "With no intention to make any comment about this committee hearing, I'm in a play called *Much Ado About Nothing.*" That got the first and maybe the only laugh at the hearing.

There's nothing your lawyer can do except kick you under the table if you're getting into an area where you might end up in jail. Leonard Boudin told me, "John, you can say, 'I want a five-minute recess. I have to talk to my lawyer.'" Well, I needed that because as much as you plan, you may open up an area that would lead to other people being smeared by the committee.

SARAH: The pressure gets to you. You realize that they're shooting, but you don't know what they're aiming at. So you take time out. Like what I did. I said, "I need to breathe, Leonard." He said, "That's all right. Breathe awhile." We looked like we were conferring, but I just had to get the pressure off, so my brain could then say, "Okay, now, next question."

JOHN: I was concerned that just answering, "Yes, I was a member of the Ibsen Theater," would open up an area. "Who else was in there?" Suddenly you're mentioning eight other actors. What if they had some stoolie say that the Ibsen Theater was run by a bunch of commies?

SARAH: Very innocuously, you could say, "I was in the Hollywood

PTA Theater," or "I was in the 163rd Street Y Theater." They could ask, "Well, who ran this and who ran that?" Immediately, that person is suspect. When we came back from the hearing, one of my neighbors asked, "Why didn't you answer their questions?" I said to him, "What if I had mentioned I was working in a group with you? Your name would be in the paper and everybody would assume you were a Communist. I don't think you'd get another job."

You never knew who they had testifying against you. Suppose I had answered, "No, I'm not a Communist," and the government came up with a witness who said I was. I could be charged with perjury. Do you know what it takes to win a perjury case against the government? They did come up with a guy named George Hall. He was their only favorable witness. He gave all the names. I didn't know George Hall, but I knew of him.

JOHN: I did know George Hall. We'd both been in Shaw's *Too True To Be Good* at the Playhouse in the Park in Philadelphia. The actors stayed in a place called the Sheep's Pen. For fifteen bucks a week, you had a room with a shower and you shared the kitchen. Each night, one of the actors would cook his favorite dinner for the group. George and I talked a lot about everything in those days. I thought he was a good actor, very funny. And all that time he was going to the FBI. It's hard to imagine the kind of pressure that would cause people to give the names that ruined other people's lives.

SARAH: George Hall claimed that I was always collecting money and serving food at "Communist cause" parties. Well, I went to a lot of parties that were cause parties, and I was always collecting money and washing dishes and things of that sort. I remember I had gone to one for Willie McGee, who was about to be legally lynched.

JOHN: Willie McGee, a Black man, was railroaded for the supposed rape of a white woman. And "white womanhood" had to be defended. It took a jury in Laurel, Mississippi, one minute to convict him and sentence him to death.

SARAH: Talk about equal justice. A white man had never been executed for raping a Black woman. Never! Not even apprehended!

JOHN: We were very deeply concerned with this frame-up. On Broadway I helped organize thousands of telegrams. And Sarah went down to Mississippi.

SARAH: The Civil Rights Congress made a last-ditch attempt to get publicity to prevent the execution. They asked a group of white women to go to Jackson, Mississippi, and they wanted it led by a southern woman. In Jackson, we started walking toward the governor's mansion. The state police were waiting for us. We told them we had an appointment with the governor. They insisted on herding us into their cars; they would take us to the governor. They took us to jail instead. "Protective custody," they called it.

We weren't even allowed to make a phone call. They fingerprinted us. We asked why, and they said, "For the FBI." When they wanted to question me, I put on my best "Miss Lucy": "You tell Mr. Peacock if he wants to talk to me to come out here and sit down like a civilized man. I will not go in there." Well, they picked me up and carried me in. Then they took my picture with a number in front.

JOHN: There had been demonstrations all over the world to save Willie McGee. After a five-year fight for his life, he was to die the next day. And within earshot. We understand that Rosalie McGee heard Sarah and the others singing songs in support of Willie McGee from their cells.

SARAH: We sang that night.

JOHN: And he died the next day.

Before Sarah was called to HUAC, an FBI agent visited Greenville, South Carolina, and questioned her cousin. They showed her Sarah's picture with the numbers across the chest.

SARAH: My cousin called my mother, who was quite old by then. It could have killed her. This is a shocking thing for a small southern town. The government counts on that kind of pressure to bring you to your knees.

JOHN: I don't think the committee realized when they called Sarah that they had this courageous southern belle there or that she's a descendant of two presidents of the United States.

SARAH: They were probably two of the most innocuous presidents we ever had. William Henry Harrison died after two months with pneumonia. And Ben Harrison wasn't very good. But it is true that some of my relatives signed the Declaration of Independence. I am descended from people who helped form the Constitution of the United States. I told the committee that my relatives fought for the freedom of expression this country was founded on.

JOHN: The committee pulled out before they planned to. They didn't know what to do with these actors. I remember Lou Polan, a wonderful guy. He's dead now. He goes back to the Jessie Bonstell stock company, the Shakespearean actors and Lunt and Fontanne. Well, he kept insisting on reading his statement to the committee, and they kept gaveling him down. "You can't talk to me like that!" he shouted. "I'm Mr. Theater! You're not attacking me, you're attacking Mr. Theater." He was going on in this loud voice, and they kept banging and finally they got rid of him. In the confusion he took the First Amendment, but they never held him in contempt.

SARAH: Lou had that all planned. He was working in *Bus Stop,* for Whitehead. Whitehead had said, "I'll support you if you take the First Amendment, but don't come to work if you take the Fifth." He was very brave with Lou Polan's life. The First Amendment could have meant jail.

JOHN: Years later, I was in a show called *Case of Libel.* I was playing Quentin Reynolds, who had sued Westbrook Pegler for calling him a Communist in his column. Quentin Reynolds was a big sportswriter and war correspondent. Westbrook Pegler, who had been a pal of his, suddenly attacked his old friend. Reynolds asked Louis Nizer to take the case. Nizer refused at first. So Quentin Reynolds bawled the shit out of him: What happened to your principles? Eventually Nizer agreed.

When I was in that play, I was still being blacklisted on television. I couldn't even get on "The Defenders," although E. G. Marshall was a friend of mine. Then one time, I got a call from my agent: "Johnny, are you available? 'The Defenders' is shooting."

I said, "What do you mean, am I available?"

"Well, you know."

SARAH: She frankly asked, "Are you cleared, Johnny?" And he said, "I never went to anybody to get cleared."

JOHN: But I had just done "East Side, West Side" with George C. Scott on CBS. For some reason, this time they didn't use the blacklist against me. My agent asked, "Johnny, what network was 'East Side, West Side' on?" I told her. She said, "Good, because 'The Defenders' is on CBS, too. I'll call you right back."

I didn't hear anything for the rest of the day. Then all the old anger about "Are you available?" came back. All that crap began to seep in on me. That night when I went to do *Case of Libel,* I was just boiling. I had to walk on that stage and face Van Heflin, who was playing Louis Nizer. I had to accuse him of going against his principles, that he hadn't the guts to stand up for me. Poor Van Heflin. I must have really come down on him. At the end of the first act, he said, "Are you all right, kid?" But he understood my anger. His sister, Fran Heflin, had been blacklisted. His brother-in-law, Saul Kaplan, a musician, had been blacklisted.

At the end of the show, I went to Forty-second Street and picked up the *Times.* I read that "The Defenders" was going to air a program about an actor, played by Jack Klugman, who defied the House committee and was blacklisted for ten years. I got home, and there was a call that I was to report the next day for a part on "The Defenders." When I got there, I said, "I'm very glad to be here after being blacklisted myself for ten years."

I found out later that when my name came up, one of the vice-presidents said to the scriptwriter, Ernie Kinoy, "We can't use John. He's on the list." Ernie exploded. "On the one hand we do a script on black-listing and we're proud of it, and on the other hand we're doing the same thing here?!"

That was in 1963. In 1976, when Woody Allen did *The Front,* I was offered the part of Laurence Johnson, the guy who had me blacklisted. I had to turn it down, but I saw it in Westwood. I was thrilled when the audience applauded the credits of those who were blacklisted. There's a reservoir of good fighting spirit still left. If I have one virtue, it's that I've never given up my faith in people.

He Said No to Joe

Harvey O'Connor and Jessie O'Connor

"The House Un-American Activities Committee is the most un-American thing in America," said Harry Truman.[1] The Senate rivaled HUAC with its own subcommittees, one for internal security and the other the instrument of Joseph McCarthy's notorious investigations. It was before that latter body that Harvey O'Connor—a civil libertarian, journalist, and author of Empire of Oil, Steel Dictator, *and* The Astors—*was called. Harvey and Jessie O'Connor symbolize the strong-minded dissenting tradition among American intellectuals. Harvey challenged McCarthy, asserting his rights under the First Amendment, with the full realization of the fate of the Hollywood Ten. The courts failed to address the First Amendment issue in his case and in so many others. They turned instead to technicalities of one sort or another as the basis for their rulings.*

HARVEY: I am indebted to the Daughters of the American Revolution for starting me off on the radical line. When I was growing up, the DAR had an annual essay contest in the schools. One year the subject was the Bill of Rights. Preparing for that was my introduction to what the Bill of Rights really meant. And it's thanks to Tacoma High School

JESSIE O'CONNOR

HARVEY O'CONNOR

that I found out about socialism. In 1912, when Debs was running for president, one of my teachers decided to have a debate on socialism. I didn't know beans about it. I went to the library and got hold of a book called *The Elements of Socialism,* or something like that, by John Spargo. Pretty dull stuff, but it had a lot of material in it. The more I looked into it, the more impressed I was.

JESSIE: Greatly helped by his mother: "Young man, take that book back and never bring it in this house again."

HARVEY: Later, I edited union and socialist papers in Seattle and Centralia. Then I worked for the Federated Press, a labor news service for dailies and weeklies. That's when I met Jessie. She was a journalist and became our best human-interest reporter.

JESSIE: The Federated Press had news the regular papers didn't cover.

HARVEY: It was started around 1919, and it was quite successful while it was in existence. We had bureaus in New York, Washington, Chicago, and Detroit, with daily coverage of important strikes and happenings in Washington and elsewhere. It lasted until the 1950s. Then it became a victim of the anti-red hysteria, implemented in this case by the American Federation of Labor, which forbade their newspapers to print anything with guts. That pretty much ruined our operation.

It was during the anti-red hysteria that I was called before both the House and the Senate investigating committees. McCarthy was having a dispute with the secretary of state, Dean Acheson. He called him the "Red Dean," although the Red Dean was as anti-communist as anyone could ask for. I got caught up because the State Department had some of my books in their overseas libraries. This was found out by a couple of guys on the committee staff who roamed over Europe looking into libraries to see what American authors were there. And so I was subpoenaed.

McCarthy's attack was based on his assertion that I had received government money from the sale of my books and that I put the money into the "Communist coffers." That was the way he phrased it. I had been brought to Washington to explain all about it. One of the books was *The Guggenheims* and the other was *Steel Dictator.* It was all news to me to learn that my books were in the overseas libraries. As for all the money I received in royalties . . .

JESSIE: Both books had been sold out long before. The State Department must have had to buy them on the used book market. McCarthy made up this business of the Communist coffers, payments for books Harvey didn't get any money for to start with.

HARVEY: It was just a case of aggravated book-burning. It did cause a lot of concern. And there was the possibility of going to jail for a year. I didn't look with any pleasure on that prospect. On the other hand, what the hell, I wasn't going to knuckle under.

JESSIE: Because he wasn't going to answer them, you know. This was in the early fall of 1953. It started when we were sitting on the porch listening to one of our guests recite poetry. It was very nice. Then we had this phone call. I ran up the stairs to take it. The person on the other end said, "I'm Roy Cohn. We want your husband to appear before the committee."

Then he told Harvey that he had to appear in Washington the next morning. Harvey said, "Is that equivalent to a subpoena?" And Cohn said, "The committee has so ruled." Then Harvey called his lawyer. The lawyer said it couldn't be equivalent to a subpoena.

HARVEY: The next headline in the local paper was "O'Connor Goes Sailing." When I finally testified, McCarthy said I was the most contumacious witness ever to appear before his committee. That means "to have contempt for." I'd like to have that engraved on my tombstone.

Well, he asked me the same question nine times, but he kept on varying the wording between Communist Party and communist conspiracy. By the ninth question, I got tired, and I turned to my lawyer and asked, "How can I shut this guy up?" Then McCarthy directed me to answer his final question: Was I a member of the communist conspiracy? Stupid ass. I refused to answer, and he said, "You may step down. You'll be cited for contempt." That was his favorite phrase: "You're in contempt," to dozens of people—hundreds, I guess—"You're in contempt."

JESSIE: Harvey stood on the idea that the senator's opinions, or those of someone the people vote for to represent them, are the business of everybody. But the opinions of a private citizen are not the congressmen's or the senators' business.

HARVEY: It was none of McCarthy's damned business *what* my politics were. When the elected representatives turn around and begin asking you your politics, you've stood democracy on its head. Upside down.

JESSIE: Then Harvey went up to the clerk and said, "How about my witness expenses?" People had been going down at their own expense to get their reputations ruined. But Harvey insisted and finally got a check.

HARVEY: It had his signature, bold and bright: "Joe McCarthy." That was a wonderful check.

JESSIE: Harvey made it over to the American Civil Liberties Union.

HARVEY: Finally, I was convicted of contempt. But the judge apparently wasn't too keen about McCarthy, because he suspended the sentence. People congratulated me, but I said, "What the hell. I've been convicted. I want to appeal."

And so we appealed to the circuit court, which unanimously overturned the conviction, saying that there was no such thing on the statute books as a "communist conspiracy." And you can't be a member of something that didn't exist. Now, there was a law, the McCarran Act, that made it illegal to be a member of the Communist Party. If McCarthy had directed me to answer to the Communist Party, it would have been much different. There is a Communist Party, and you're either a member of it or you're not.

JESSIE: The court decision was based on the Sixth Amendment. In order for a person to be convicted of a crime, he has to be accused of a crime.

HARVEY: Thank God for the Bill of Rights. The founding fathers thought of everything. The Sixth Amendment was a catch-all for quite a few experiences they had had with the British. And this one, that you had to be accused of a crime to be convicted, was one of them. Apparently the British had been pretty loose about it.

JESSIE: The position Harvey took before McCarthy was based on the First Amendment, but the judges would never rule on it. For years, they would not support the First Amendment.

HARVEY: That's what we had fought for. The Hollywood Ten had taken the First Amendment and had gone to jail. After that, people began taking the Fifth Amendment. And I figured: To hell with the Fifth Amendment. I'm basing my objection on the First. I was happy to reestablish that precedent there. But we never did get a decision on it.

After the hearings, we went on a speaking tour. We decided that the thing to do with McCarthy was to enter into a counter-campaign, to arouse public opinion against him. I think it was the Emergency Civil Liberties Committee that set up the tour.

JESSIE: Your very first speech drew a crowd. That was after the hearing in Washington, wasn't it? The Liberal Citizens of Massachusetts hired a hotel room for Harvey to speak about his case. We got there about ten minutes to eight. It was so crowded, they had to move to a bigger room. That was the first open meeting against McCarthy, and people were just spoiling for a chance to get back at him, evidently.

HARVEY: Well, after that we headed west: Pittsburgh, Cleveland,

Chicago, Denver. In Denver, my successor on the Oil Workers' paper I once edited took charge of it. He had me working for a whole week on radio, TV, meetings, and all the rest of it. We also went to Salt Lake City and wound up in Los Angeles with a great meeting that started the National Committee Against HUAC. We got a beautiful response everywhere. Big meetings. This was right after the McCarthy hearings.

JESSIE: Later, the House Un-American Activities Committee wanted him. The House committee was having a field day in New Jersey, calling teachers to appear before their hearings. There was a protest meeting in support of the subpoenaed teachers, and Harvey was to address that meeting. As we stepped into the hall, someone came up to him and said, "I have something for you, Mr. O'Connor."

HARVEY: It was a marshal with a subpoena. I kind of smelled it because I'd been through this before. So I turned away from him. And the subpoena fell to the floor like a wounded bird.

I had some clever lawyers. They were appalled, of course, when I rejected the subpoena, because you're supposed to respond to subpoenas. No monkey business about it. To defend me, they came up with the idea of subpoenaing the House committee records about my connection with communism in New Jersey. That was supposed to be the basis for the inquiry the committee was making. Actually, I'd never lived in New Jersey. I knew nothing about communism in New Jersey. Even if I had been a cooperative witness, I couldn't have told them anything.

JESSIE: The lawyers wanted those minutes to prove definitely that his being called had nothing to do with the questions the committee was supposed to be investigating. It was simply punishment for daring to speak at a protest meeting against the committee's actions. It was just a personal punishment. And the lawyers said that the committee minutes would show that. Of course, the committee didn't want to reveal their minutes.

HARVEY: Well, what happened was that I was cited for contempt by the House by a vote of three to one. I guess everyone else was absent. I was told that there were six congressmen on the floor. Four of them were in the business of having me cited and the other two were reading funny papers. That appeared in the *Washington Post* in the morning.

But I was never tried for contempt of the House committee. Year after year, I was on the docket there, awaiting trial. Some of the nicest people you can think of were on the docket, too, people who were accused of selling dope to schoolchildren, and so on. But I was number one for a year or two.

The Compulsion of Loyalty

The Palmer Raids:
The Deportation Mania Begins

Sonia Kaross

Sustained by an anti-alien and anti-radical phobia, the red scare that followed World War I was coming to a head in 1919. It was fueled in February when tanks were called in to quell a peaceful general strike in Seattle. It was given impetus with bomb scares in April and beatings of demonstrators on May Day, followed by simultaneous explosions in eight cities. The tempo mounted. September: the Great Steel Strike, branded a revolutionary plot, brutally repressed, and aliens among the strikers held for deportation. November: roundup of aliens in twelve cities, many arrested without warrants, some badly beaten. December: two hundred forty-two people deported as radical aliens, including Emma Goldman; seventy-three branches of the Communist Party raided in New York City, one thousand arrested, twenty-five tons of documents seized.

Attorney General A. Mitchell Palmer had already created the General Intelligence Division of the Justice Department to serve as an antiradical agency. With the young J. Edgar Hoover in charge, the division began files on hundreds of thousands of "radicals," infiltrated lawful organizations, and fanned the red scare by supplying sensationalized charges to the press. By the end of the year, the agency was prepared to combine its force of federal detectives with the older deportation tactics of the Immigration and Naturalization Service (INS) to set a pattern for political repression that was to last the century.

SONIA KAROSS

The stage was set for January 2, 1920: the Palmer raids. In an operation directed by Hoover and Palmer, upwards of ten thousand persons in thirty cities were seized—most without warrants—in one simultaneous action. Citizens and aliens alike were caught in the massive roundup that hit meeting places, pool halls, bowling alleys, and cafés. Actors and dancers were arrested in the midst of performances. Late that night, agents burst into the home of Sonia Kaross and her husband and dragged them off. "Alien filth," Attorney General Palmer said of those captured in the raids. "Out of the sly and crafty eyes of many of them leap cupidity, cruelty, insanity, and crime; from their lopsided faces, sloping brows and misshappen features may be recognized the unmistakable criminal type." [1]

I was born in May 1901, in Lithuania. I came here at five years of age with my family. My father was a revolutionary from old Russia who ran away to this country. He couldn't speak English well, but he was a well-learned man. After he was here a few years, the boss wanted my father to vote—I think it was for the Wilson election—so he got him citizenship. That's what it was like in those days. The boss fixed it all up. But when father was in the voting booth, he voted for Eugene Debs. Anyway, by my father's right, all of us children became citizens.

I was raised here, but I only went to grammar school. I never got a chance for more education because I had to go to work. My father was sickly, and my mother kept boarders to make a living. We had a hard time, my two brothers and I. We were dressed very poorly. My mother made over clothes the boarders left behind.

We lived in ghettos, then, the foreigners. In each city there was one ghetto for Polish, one for Lithuanians, one for Russians. It seemed that there were more foreign-born among the working people than there were Americans. The people who came during those years, they're all dead now and their children are American. But during that period they were good neighbors. And although they may not have believed in everything you believed in, they were friends. Evenings, I remember, people would sing, and they had parties in the neighborhood and everybody went.

English wasn't spoken by many. My father used to make me read Lithuanian in the evenings for the boarders. My mother didn't speak English, but when she went to a store, she got what she wanted. Some of the women whose husbands got arrested for being drunk or fighting or something would come to my mother: "Please, could you let your daughter speak in court for me? He's going to have a trial tomorrow." Or when a woman went to the doctor—and they had no Lithuanian doctors—she'd ask my mother, "Please, would you let your daughter go with me?" Very early I was taught to help people.

I married in 1918. I was just seventeen years old. My husband came in 1914 or 1915 to this country. He ran away so he wouldn't have to go into the czar's army. After we got married, I was no longer a citizen. A woman lost her citizenship then if she married a noncitizen. That's the way it was. My husband got a job on the railroads. I was working as a bookkeeper for a socialist newspaper, a Lithuanian paper, that had maybe ten thousand readers. I belonged to the Socialist Party, and so did my husband. We had choruses, an acting group, and there was a literary society.

At the time, there was a rumor that all the foreigners were going to be deported. Previous to that they had deported Emma Goldman, an anarchist. A couple hundred were deported with her. We were not anarchists, but we were Socialists. Naturally, we had an intuition that something like that might happen to us. The way the newspapers carried on, there was a scare among the people. And everybody was told to be cautious: Don't have papers, don't have stuff in the house, because it might happen.

Then it did happen. The Palmer raids were conducted simultaneously all over the country. Thousands were arrested on one day, January 2, 1920. Philadelphia alone had three thousand. New York had five thousand. And Boston had a couple thousand. Russians, Lithuanians, Poles, Ukrainians, all these different nationalities and peoples were put in jail. The police went around picking them up wherever they were: at different clubs, at meetings, and in their homes. Women with babies in their arms were arrested. A big group was sent to Ellis Island.

My husband and I were probably among the last ones. We were living in Philadelphia and had been at a chorus rehearsal. We came home—it must have been eleven or twelve—and went to bed. One o'clock, there was banging on the doors. It woke up the whole building. There were police cars and all kinds of detectives all over the street. They came in and took all my books, all my letters, whatever they found. They took everything, every little paper they could get hold of. They threw it all into big bags like the post office has. They just threw everything in there and took them away, and I could never get anything back.

Then they took my husband and me away. I was almost seven months pregnant. The police threw me in the wagon. And I was locked up with five or six prostitutes. I got sick from all the excitement and the way the police handled me. Those prostitutes, I want to tell you, were the nicest people. I didn't fully understand what was going on. I thought: Well, I'm just getting sick. But they realized that I might lose the baby. They raised an awful rumpus. They were screaming, hollering, knocking on the door. They were yelling, "This woman is dying! Get her an ambulance!" But nobody responded. All night they banged the door while I lay there suffering. Well, my companions in jail saved my life, but they couldn't save the baby's. Before the ambulance came it was morning, and the baby was dead.

After the baby died, I was in the hospital for three or four days, and then they brought me back to jail. I was held there until somebody brought bail. My husband was in jail for about two weeks. A woman, a neighbor of ours, offered to put up bail for him. She never was in any of our organizations. She was just a nice person.

We were charged with being undesirable. I thought: If they deport me, it would be awful to have to leave my family here, my husband, my brothers, and my mother. They had hearings where they would question us one at a time. They asked me where I belonged and who I supported. They asked me why I was with the Lithuanian newspaper. I told them it was my bread and butter. Then they said, "You're a Socialist Party member." We were told that until they proved it, to say no. So I said, "No." But in September 1919, the Communist Party had been organized. And it wasn't a secret. The Socialists sent delegates to Chicago. I was elected a delegate from the Lithuanian Federation and also from the Young Socialist League, and they had found that out.

Of course, they had people working in our organizations. A man who worked with me on the newspaper was one of their agents. He knew I got letters from someone who was with the paper for a short while and then went back to Russia. I used to read those letters to the others. He made reports on all that. And he used to come to our home. He knew what kind of books I had, where I kept them, and where my letters and papers were. So when the police walked in, they knew where to look. They went right to my desk and pulled out all the letters I had, everything. But there was nothing that they could really try me for. They were letters from people I knew, friends of ours. It wasn't anything criminal.

It took about three months before the bail was released and they dropped our cases. I think the government itself was sort of scared afterward because they had arrested so many. Ellis Island was full. Also the island in the Boston Harbor was filled with those they arrested from New England. They had to feed them, and they didn't know how to process them. They couldn't send them to the Soviet Union because they had no working relationship with the new government. Finally, they released most of them, and everything was dropped.

The foreign-born were being persecuted. Ten thousand were arrested in the Palmer raids for no reason. But there was nobody to get outraged. What could we do? We had no rights. And we couldn't reach the others. There was such a wide gap between the native Americans and the foreign-born. We didn't know any people who would help us, or even any lawyers. Finally, we did get a lawyer who offered help to the whole bunch of us together. That's why my case was never brought out separately. If it were now, I would have tried to sue them because they took the life of my baby. But you didn't think of that in those days. You didn't know.

The Ordeal of the Loyalty Test

Arthur Drayton

Arthur Drayton was dismissed from government service under Truman's loyalty program after twenty-five years as a postal clerk, a position with little imaginable connection to national security concerns. His poems, plays, and associations were weighed against him by loyalty boards, the beginning of an ordeal that disrupted the life of this gentle and sensitive man for decades.

A product of the Cold War, Harry Truman's loyalty program of March 1947 marked the onset of McCarthyism. All government work-ers had to pass a test of their beliefs and associations. Grounds for dis-missal were "membership in, affiliation with or sympathetic association with any foreign or domestic organization, association, movement, group or combination of persons designated by the Attorney General as totalitarian, Fascist, Communist or subversive"[1]—a grand statement of guilt by association.

Loyalty boards screened millions of employees to determine whether at some future date they might commit a disloyal act, based on books they read, friends they had, or groups they belonged to. The inquisitors' sense of what constituted disloyalty can be gauged from some of the questions asked: "Have you ever had Negroes in your home?" "Are you in favor of the Marshall Plan?" "There is suspicion in the record that you are in sympathy with the underprivileged. Is this true?"[2]

ARTHUR DRAYTON

Few of the safeguards so fundamental to a fair trial were afforded the employees. Once accused, it was up to them to prove their innocence. There was no impartial judge. The board that made the charge conducted the inquiry and rendered the verdict. There was no chance to confront and cross-examine the accusers. There was no protection from double jeopardy. Someone cleared once could be fired a second time for the same charges. No one fired by loyalty boards was charged with committing an illegal act, but thousands of people had their lives ruined. Jobs were lost, marriages were broken, and many suffered extreme mental and emotional distress. And what of those not yet suspect? They learned to be careful.

———————————

It's been so long ago, but I can tell you about my encounter with the great fear back there in the 1950s. McCarthy was riding high, and most Americans were frightened into thinking that the Communists were going to take over.

At that time, I happened to have been a postal worker. When I started out, my parents had been so proud of me. It was a great thing to have a son working in the post office. Then, in 1949, I was dismissed under the government's loyalty proceedings after twenty-five years of service. I had been an active member of the union, the National Federation of Postal Clerks. In fact, I had been the first Black officer in the organization. But when I was discharged, they expelled me from the union, too.

I remember when it all started. In 1948, we were told to list the names of all the organizations we belonged to. So I listed the NAACP. I also listed the Philadelphia Bi-Partisan Fair Employment Practices Committee. This was a time when Blacks were fighting for fair employment.

Then I listed the International Workers Order. It was an organization of Blacks, Poles, Jews, and others. And each ethnic group had its own lodge. I joined it because the insurance policy was very attractive, certainly more attractive than the Metropolitan or any of the other big insurance companies. The most a Black person in those days could get was a five-hundred-dollar industrial policy. We were limited to those inferior policies, no matter what our income or social standing. The IWO gave us term insurance, at the same rates for everybody, white or Black, miner or farmer.

But what attracted me most was that the meetings were so interesting. We discussed current issues and had social hours. Those evenings were stimulating. Every year we celebrated Negro History Week, as we called it in those days. Langston Hughes came over and spoke once. As a matter of fact, he visited us in September 1948, the period of my first suspension from the post office.

I had been a struggling writer all those years. I wrote poems and plays, short plays about historical Black figures. And here, in the IWO, was an opportunity to try out some of my plays. We would sit around and read them aloud as if they were radio dramas.

One of the historical figures that interested me, and still does, was Frederick Douglass, the great abolitionist, who defended the rights of women way back in those days. I wrote a short play about him. Another was Denmark Vesey, who took as his model Toussaint L'Ouverture of Haiti. In Charleston, back in the 1820s, Vesey organized an insurrection, but it was aborted when one of the house servants turned him in. When he and his followers were caught, twenty-two of them were hanged. There is a tree in Charleston that Black people call the Twenty-Two Tree. They say it is the tree where these people were hanged. It seemed such a dramatic time that I just had to write about it. The plays about Douglass and Vesey were performed at our celebrations of Negro History Week in Philadelphia and later on were published by the New York office of the IWO. This was the organization they gave me so much trouble about.

One morning, I was sitting on our porch, reading the *Times* and drinking my coffee. We lived in a twin house with just a window separating our porch and our neighbors'. I noticed this white man going into their house. I kept on reading my paper. After a while the door opened, and Mrs. Carter came out with him. "There's Mr. Drayton," she said. "Why don't you ask him if he's a Communist?" She told him the Draytons were fine people, and who did he think he was? She bawled him out.

The white man went across the street to some friends who knew my wife when she was a child in South Carolina. Everyone on the street knew us. My wife joined me on the porch. We watched this man go from one house to another, Mrs. Carter, my wife, and I. He looked scared and foolish; he knew everybody was watching him. Later, my friends in New York, who were neighbors when we used to live there, told me the FBI had been asking them questions about me, too.

Some weeks later, I was called up to the postmaster's office. In those days the post office was rigidly segregated. When I stepped into the room, I was the only black face there. Apparently, they all knew why I had come. I had to pass down this long aisle of white people, who stopped typing to watch me. I think they were expecting a show. At the back of the room, the inspector in charge handed me this envelope. "That's for you, Mr. Drayton."

I took the envelope. I said, "Thank you." I knew it was my suspension notice. He said, "Aren't you going to open it?" And I said, "No. I don't have to open it." I didn't intend to give them the satisfaction. And I walked on out.

At the same time I was suspended, friends of mine were being dropped from the post office. It was a very disturbing time. Then one morning I received a notice to appear at a hearing before the local loyalty board. I knew now it was my turn to be on the carpet. Mr. Morris Chaffitz, the IWO lawyer, came with me. The board was made up of five or six people, all white, of course.

They asked why I joined the International Workers Order. I told them of the liberal insurance policy and no discrimination. Also that it provided an outlet for me to discuss social issues with Black people like myself and to present programs on Negro history and that sort of thing. I liked the organization, and I liked the people in it.

So they said, "Did you know this was a subversive organization?" I told them I didn't think it was. "If we're telling you it is, don't you think you should get out of it?" "No," I said. "I will not get out of it, because I don't believe it is a subversive organization."

At the end, they asked if there was anything I wished to say in summation. I remember I had this outraged feeling about having to testify in this manner in a free country. Was it because I was Black? Most people I knew who had been expelled from the post office were Blacks or Jews. I thought of Socrates having to testify. I told them that being called disloyal sickened my heart and weighed on my soul. Then I quoted these lines from *Othello*:

> Good name in man or woman, dear my lord,
> Is the immediate jewel of their souls;
> Who steals my purse steals trash; 'tis something, nothing;
> 'Twas mine, 'tis his; and has been slave to thousands;
> But he that filches from me my good name,
> Robs me of that which not enriches him,
> And makes me poor, indeed.

They all looked shocked. My lawyer certainly was. But he said nothing about it when we were outside.

There were two appeals I could make: one to the Office of the Postmaster General and the final one to the Loyalty Review Board. Some of the people who had to walk the plank, as I called it, didn't go to hearings at all. They left town or just gave up. I decided to appeal and applied for a second hearing at the Postmaster General's Office in Washington. And, in due time, they told us to come down.

The first thing I noticed about this hearing in the nation's capital was that it was in a big, beautiful room. There was a mahogany table with armchairs around it and three or four executives of the post office, sitting there waiting for me. On the walls were disgusting pictures of Black men with razors in their mouths, playing poker and threatening each other. Some were crooks with cards between their toes and cards up their sleeves. I had heard about it from other Blacks who had been in that room. They had told me about those racist paintings around the walls, Black people eating watermelons, and all the old stereotypes in this beautiful, dignified room. I've never forgotten that. I can't remember anything else at that hearing because of those pictures. They have stuck with me.

I "flunked" that hearing, too. And all the while, I was not working. I couldn't get work in Philadelphia. By now, I realized that old friends were avoiding me. They would pass me on the street and be afraid to speak to me. We no longer received invitations. Our phone did not ring anymore. My wife was becoming upset and nervous, and I was at my wits' end. So I decided to go to New York.

I had a hard time getting work there, too. They'd ask me where I last worked. If I told them I worked in the post office for twenty-five years, they'd want to know why I was without a job. You can see what a situation I was in. So I bought a newsstand for six hundred dollars at 134th Street and Seventh Avenue. A nephew of mine helped me run it. But I couldn't make any money. I found that the guys who ran it before me used to take numbers to make the thing work. And there were newsstands on practically every corner. I'd have to work from five o'clock in the morning to around midnight because I wanted to sell every paper I could. I was fast losing money, so after three months I sold it for three hundred dollars.

Then I went to the Urban League. They were on 136th Street and Seventh Avenue in those days. I told them my story, and they tried to place me in a position where I wouldn't be questioned too severely about my past. They found me a job in a mailing shop. The bosses were very progressive-minded. They distributed mail for like-minded organizations. The *Daily Compass* was one of them. I got to talking to my fellow workers about what happened to me in the post office. Somehow or other, it got back to the *Daily Compass*. That's when Mr. Dan Gillmor, a columnist for the paper, took down my story. It was printed as a series in three issues.

In June 1950, I was scheduled for my last appeal, the one before the Loyalty Review Board. It was held in the Customs House in Philadelphia. This was the president's own board. On that board were Mr. Seth Richardson, Senator Harry Cain, and a third gentleman whose name I can't recall. Mr. Richardson, a Republican and a corporation lawyer, in 1946 had been the chief counsel for the joint congressional committee investigating the Pearl Harbor attack. They came into the room laughing and joking. They must have read the article by Mr. Gillmor that had just been published. They commented on it and said: This is the gentleman who quoted Shakespeare to the loyalty board.

They asked me only one or two questions. They were very friendly. They certainly weren't scared out of their wits that I was going to destroy the United States government or that I was a bomb thrower or anything of the sort. That board cleared me.

I returned to work in September and received ten months' back pay. It was around the Jewish holiday, and I always thought it was a nice thing for me, Rosh Hashanah. I remember the year, 1950, because my father died that December. I have such warm memories of him.

Around this time, I started writing again. I wrote a play about Richard Allen. Bishop Richard Allen led the first organized Black protest, peaceful protest in America. This was after the Revolutionary War, in 1788 or 1789. In those days Blacks and whites worshipped in the same church there, in Philadelphia. One day, the Black people were told that they would have to sit upstairs in the balcony. The next Sunday, Bishop Allen and one of his friends sat at the front as they had been doing all along. The white deacons and elders pulled them up from their knees while they were saying their prayers and told them they couldn't sit downstairs. Allen and the Black elders then led their people out of the white Methodist church and formed their own, called the African Methodist Episcopal church. There was this revolutionary spirit then in the Black church, and there still is.

This play about Richard Allen was more ambitious than the others. I wrote it to be acted, rather than just to be read aloud. When Jasper

Deeter, who ran Hedgerow Theater, saw it on the stage, he said, "Arthur, you have one act, that first act is a really good one." It went to my head, you know. I felt pretty good.

By that time, the Republicans had come to power. They were not satisfied with the Truman Loyalty Order. According to them, too many had escaped the net. They planned to throw a wider net. The new catch-all was called the Eisenhower Security Risk Order, issued in 1953. And I was one of the first persons called. So there I was, in double jeopardy. I had already been cleared once by the loyalty board, but now I could be thrown out of the post office a second time.

My birthday falls on February 22, on the old George Washington's birthday. Each year, two friends and I would throw a party on three different nights. I'd have a party on my night, a Black friend of mine would have a party on his birthday, and a Jewish friend would have one on his. This particular year, one friend and I were planning a joint party at his house.

I worked all day that Saturday. I had gotten home and eaten and bathed and was dressing to go to the party, when my bell rang. There was a Western Union boy with a telegram. I opened it. It was a message from the post office, notifying me of my immediate suspension from duty on grounds of my being a "security risk." They would notify me when to come for a hearing. There would only be one hearing this time, from which there could be no appeal. I went to the party with that bad news. You can imagine what an awful time it was.

The charges, as usual, were that I belonged to this organization, the IWO, got members to join it, and that I wrote these plays and presented them. At each of my past hearings, I had been ordered to present to the board copies of every play or poem I had written as evidence to be used against me. They wanted it all again.

The hearing took place in May. The board members looked to me like people who hated Blacks and Jews. They gave me the creeps. After they listened to my testimony, they told me I'd hear from them soon. I didn't hear from them for about four or five months. I knew that I was through then. I was through, apparently, forever.

I moved to New York, as I'd done before. I worked in a mailing basement for a firm right opposite the Waldorf-Astoria. It paid forty dollars a week, much less than my old job. It was hard for me to live on that, I can tell you. But on the whole, it was a pleasant environment, and they didn't mind my being thrown out of the post office.

In 1956, I read about the decision the Supreme Court had made on the Eisenhower Security Risk Order. It said that civilian employees could not be charged with being security risks, or something to that effect. Finally I was cleared under that decision. After my lawyer wrote to the post office, they told me I was now eligible to return. But they also advised me that if I had a job I should stay on it because the administration would be sure to pass another law that would be applicable to me. My lawyer said, "No, we're not going to take that advice. We're going to get you back into the post office." I had been out about sixteen months.

When I got back in 1956, I decided that I'd had enough of the post office. As soon as I reached the earliest retirement age, at fifty-five, I would retire. I did that. I worked from 1956 to 1959. On my birthday, I put in my retirement, that same day.

But the harassment continued all through the sixties and seventies. I lived down in the East Village. I can remember coming home and finding a manuscript I had typed, gone. Once my suitcase was ransacked. All my personal papers were missing. Every scrap. Then, my retirement checks, which were to go to the bank, would be delayed. It was a time when the IRS began hounding me on my income tax forms. My canceled checks would be held in the bank. And I'd get some checks back marked "Red Squad." I had no idea what it meant. I know now what it means. They were really intimidating me. I think they continued to punish me because of what I said in the article by Gillmor. Mr. Hoover was a vengeful man, you know.

They did frighten the hell out of me. They were hounding me so. And I'd complain to my friends and relatives. Nobody believed what I was telling them in those days. That drove me to despair. Nobody believed it until things came out later about what was happening to people all over the country, how government agencies were harassing people, isolating them, and then getting them into all sorts of trouble.

I decided that I had to live with this thing. I decided I wasn't going to be afraid anymore. What's more, the common use of these dirty tricks had become public knowledge by that time. I found more people were beginning to be understanding. I got over the fear because now I learned that this harassment was directed against people who, having something to say, said it.

Yes, my life had been disrupted—but not destroyed. And I somehow feel like a survivor. Maybe it was because of my stubbornness.

I remember back to my first hearing. They told me, "Well, if you got out, you wouldn't be in this trouble," which I took to mean that if I quit the IWO, they'd just let this thing go by. But later on I found out that if I had done that, if I hadn't kept to my principles, I'd still be on the outside. So my "stubbornness" saved me. Although I was weak at times, I had the necessary strength to survive, thank God.

A Purple Heart Was
Not Enough

Jim Kutcher

Sorting out the "loyal" from the "disloyal" always poses a danger for the First Amendment. To enter or remain in the country, to hold government jobs, people had to demonstrate that they were ideologically safe. The administrative procedures the government set up to conduct that test violated constitutional assurances of due process.

Near the end of 1947, the attorney general issued a list of "subversive" organizations, which was to guide those who administered the Truman loyalty program. Government employees were considered disloyal if they belonged to or were suspected of having sympathetic association with any listed group. The attorney general could designate any organizations as subversive without notifying them or affording them a chance to refute the charges.

When the Socialist Workers Party found out it was listed, the party contacted the American Civil Liberties Union. The ACLU, in turn, went to Attorney General Tom Clark. He had promised to hold a hearing for any group that protested its listing, but when the SWP asked for a hearing, he refused. James Kutcher, seriously wounded in World War II, was fired from his job at the Veterans Administration because he belonged to the Socialist Workers Party.

JIM KUTCHER

I never had any steady jobs before I entered the army in World War II. The longest job I had was working in a paint store, but that only lasted about six months. I sold paint over the counter. And my boss, in order to keep the business going, had to go out and do contract jobs on people's apartments. So I usually was left in charge of the store. He paid me a dollar a day.

During the war I was wounded. When I came back, I worked for the Veterans Administration in New Jersey. It was about a year and a half later when the attorney general, Tom Clark, issued a list of organizations that were supposed to be "subversive." These were organizations that, according to him, advocated the overthrow of the government by unconstitutional, violent means. I don't know how many organizations it had listed on it, but the Socialist Workers Party was one of them.

When this list came out, they took fingerprints of everybody in the place. Everybody. Only in my case, for some reason or other, they fingerprinted me a number of times. I also signed the loyalty oath when they sent the thing around. Everybody had to sign, saying that they were not members of a violent organization.

Then, in 1949, I received a letter from the Veterans Administration saying that because of my membership in the Socialist Workers Party, my employment was to be terminated. The notice that I was to be fired stunned me more than anything I experienced during the war. As jobs go, I guess mine was nothing to brag about, routine, even dull. But not to me. I had a real job, a sense of security. And, more than anything else, it meant that I could be socially useful, after all.

At first, I worked in the Loan Guarantee Division. I had to process claims for veterans who wanted to take out G.I. loans to buy homes or businesses. Then I was shifted to a vocational unit. That's where I was fired from. The thing that made it ridiculous was that I had no access to any kind of confidential information that could in any way benefit the enemies of this country.

I talked it all over with people in the party. They said there were three things I could do. I could resign my job, and the record would just show that I resigned while under investigation. Or I could deny membership and let them prove that I was a member. Or I could fight them on principled grounds and say that they had no right to fire me because of membership. After thinking that over, I decided to fight. I wouldn't just give up.

What I had to do was prove I was not disloyal. This reversed the normal judicial procedure. Many years ago, in the town of Salem, Massachusetts, there were a number of people who were tried and executed for the crime of witchcraft. If you got yourself accused of being a witch, you had to prove to them that you were not a witch. It was not a very easy thing to do. That was the same technique they used on me, only they didn't execute me. They just took my job away.

The issue, as I saw it, was whether or not the attorney general had the right to place any organization on a blacklist on his own say-so without a hearing, without a chance to see evidence against it, without a chance to rebut the evidence. I had not concealed my membership in the Socialist Workers Party, but I denied that the party was subversive. It was a legal political party that ran candidates for public office. I contended that the attorney general had never proved it was subversive and before I could be fired he had to do that.

But discussion of that was ruled out of order when we had the first hearing before the branch loyalty board in Philadelphia. The only issue was whether I belonged to an organization listed by the attorney general. The government attorney did question me about my beliefs. But he didn't present any evidence I ever did anything illegal. He couldn't do that. It was only that I belonged to the Socialist Workers Party. According to them, that was enough.

George Novack, who had so much experience on the Civil Rights Defense Committee, helped me plan to fight against this loyalty program. I went around to various cities organizing local committees to support my case. I appeared before labor unions; I was a guest of the Connecticut State CIO Convention. I spoke at Harvard and Yale and to other student bodies and to a veterans' organization in Los Angeles. And many of these people contributed money to pay for legal expenses. John Dewey, Barrows Dunham, C. Wright Mills, and Linus Pauling were part of the national nonpartisan committee set up to help me keep my job.

Mrs. Roosevelt wrote a letter to Tom Clark, the attorney general, about what had happened to me. Because of her intervention, I got to have the interview with Mr. Clark, although it didn't do much good. He apparently did not like the idea of my touring the country, talking about my case. He told me, "I don't see why you go around on a campaign like this. We're trying to protect you. Why do you have to have all this publicity?"

So I said, "I consider that the more publicity I have, the more protection I have." Then I made a personal appeal to him. I asked him if he would grant the party a public hearing on the subversion charges. He said that the Department of Justice does not conduct hearings under klieg lights and amid great fanfare. I asked him if he could restore me to my job. He said, "No."

I also wrote a letter to President Truman. At one time he made a speech when he visited a veterans' hospital, and he said, "Nothing is too good for these men." So I wrote him and told him about my own situation and asked him if he would use his influence to get my job back. "Mr. President," I asked, "is that the democratic way? Would you like to be charged with a crime, and not told exactly what the crime is, or even when you committed it, or where, and not be permitted to face your accuser, or examine the evidence, or have a lawyer or a trial—and then be told you are guilty?" I got no answer from him.

After an adverse decision before the branch loyalty board, we went to the VA loyalty board of appeals in Washington; then we appealed to the VA administrator, Carl Gray, Jr.; then to the top Loyalty Review Board of the U.S. Civil Service Commission. That exhausted all of the administrative procedures.

In 1950, we went to the federal district court in Washington. My suit asked that my discharge be set aside as illegal and that the executive order to list organizations as subversive be declared unconstitutional. The district court ruled against me, but the three-judge court of appeals handed down a unanimous decision in my favor. They didn't rule on the constitutionality of the loyalty program or anything like that, but they said that on technical grounds the government had no right to fire me.

That didn't mean I got my job back. Far from it. I was put on the VA rolls as a suspended employee, with the prospect of going through the same rigmarole as before, going all the way back to the beginning and then through all the appeals. We did that. And the second time we came to the court of appeals, it was a two-to-one decision in my favor. The Veterans Administration had to give me back my job. Altogether, this took about eight years. It took another two years, until 1958, to get some of my back pay.

Ever since I was discharged from the army, my parents and I had been living in a federal low-rent housing project in Newark, New Jersey. A few days before Christmas, in 1952, my father got a letter from the Newark Housing Authority directing him to sign a so-called loyalty oath within three days as a condition for living there. Congress had just passed an amendment that required all persons in federal low-rent housing to sign an oath that no one living in their apartment belonged to any of the organizations on the attorney general's "subversive" list. Failure to sign would mean eviction.

My father felt terrible. He didn't belong to any of those groups, and he was perfectly willing to sign the oath. But he could not do that without perjuring himself because of my membership in the Socialist Workers Party. The price for keeping the apartment would be to break up the family. The American Civil Liberties Union filed suit in the New Jersey courts to have the loyalty oath amendment declared unconstitutional and to stop the eviction of my parents and me. Three years later, the New Jersey Supreme Court stopped them from evicting us. But again the courts refused to rule on the constitutionality of the amendment.

Just about that time, in 1955, the government decided to cut off the disability pension which was my sole income. Again, it was said that there were reasonable doubts about my loyalty. Now I was faced with the difficult task of disproving statements attributed to me by persons I couldn't cross-examine. The government refused to produce them.

This hearing was the first time the press was allowed to attend a loyalty proceeding. The *Washington Post* reported on December 31, 1955: "The press saw a type of proceeding unlike anything that has come into public view. In this hearing there were no rules of procedure, no witnesses (except for the accused, Kutcher), nor any facts to back up the charges against him except the charges themselves." Early in 1956, the committee decided in my favor, but not in such a way as to clear me completely.

Through all this, the government never produced any evidence that I ever did anything unconstitutional. But my loyalty was constantly questioned. At the hearings before the loyalty board, they asked me, "Did you ever use force and violence at any time in your life?"

I said, "Yes."

"Where?"

And I said, "In the United States Army."

I was in combat a year and a day, and they never questioned my loyalty then. I landed in North Africa and went to Sicily and then to Italy, to a place called Mount Rotunda, in 1943. Mount Rotunda, I remember, was a mountain with a high peak. The Germans were on the top of that, and we were on the bottom trying to get up there and dislodge them. That took a while.

On November 9, I was wounded. I remember I'd been dozing next to another soldier. I woke up, I think, about the time to eat. I got up to perform one of the functions of nature, and in the middle of that we were hit. He was killed. It just knocked me off my feet. I found myself sitting on the ground surrounded by a ball of smoke. And that was the end of combat for me.

That night, I had two doctors working on me, and both legs came off about the same time. After that, they shipped me from one hospital to another, back to North Africa, and then back to the United States. They took me to Walter Reed Hospital in Washington, D.C., where I stayed until the time of my discharge in 1945. When I came home, I got the job at the Veterans Administration. And that's where I was fired from.

MARGARET RANDALL

Forbidden Utterances: Reason Enough for Exclusion

Margaret Randall

Several months after Sonia Kaross was arrested, the chairman of the immigration committee of the House of Representatives spoke about alien radicals: "Free press is ours, not theirs; free speech is ours, not theirs." [1] *And Congress acted accordingly. The Immigration Act of 1920 punished aliens for the mere possession of radical literature or contributing to radical causes.*

A later chairman of the House's immigration committee, Francis Walter, distinguished himself as much for the Immigration and Nationality Act of 1952, the McCarran-Walter Act, as he did for his chairmanship of HUAC. Arthur Miller called that act "one of the pieces of garbage left behind by the sinking of the great scow of McCarthyism." [2] *Today, aliens may be deported if they "write or publish, or cause to be written or published, or knowingly circulate, distribute, print or display" any printed matter that advocates "the economic, international, and governmental doctrines of world communism."* [3] *It was under that vague and sweeping language that an immigration judge ruled on August 28, 1986, that Margaret Randall, the feminist author, poet, and photographer, must be deported. He did it for no reason other than her writings.*

To enforce the ideological exclusionary provisions of the McCarran-Walter Act, the State Department maintains a blacklist of some forty to fifty thousand people who are to be denied visas. When British authors, South African poets, Colombian journalists, Nobel laureates, and peace activists are excluded, we, the "protected," are the injured.

IMMIGRATION LAW

When I ask the experts
"how much time do I have"
I don't want an answer in years
or arguments.

I must know if there are hours enough
to mend this relationship,
see a book all the way to its birthing,
stand beside my father
on his journey.

I want to know how many seasons of chamisa
will be yellow and then grey-green
and yellow
    /light/
        again,
how many red cactus flowers
will bloom beside my door.

I do not want to follow language
like a dog with its tail between its legs.

I need time equated with music,
hours rising in bread,
years deep from connections.

The present always holds a tremor of the past.
Give me a handful of future
to rub against my lips.[4]

I'm a woman, almost fifty, who was born in this country, who grew up in New York and New Mexico, and in 1961 moved to Mexico with my son. I married Sergio Mondragón, a Mexican poet, and together we edited a bilingual literary journal, *El Corno Emplumado*. In 1966, I decided to take out Mexican citizenship as a way of getting better work. We had three small children, and my husband didn't have a steady job.

After the breakup of my marriage, I moved to Cuba with my children. I spent ten years in Cuba, four years in Nicaragua, and came back to this country at the beginning of 1984.

I have a strong desire to live in the United States again. It may have something to do with my age and that I'm a little tired now. My children are grown, and I have a need to be physically close to my parents. I want to bring the parts of my life together—the years I spent in Latin America and my roots here—and see what that all adds up to.

I didn't really expect it would be particularly difficult when I applied for residency. It generally takes about sixty to ninety days. And I usually had a very easy time getting temporary visas. I'd been on lecture tours to Harvard, M.I.T., Yale, the University of California, the University of Kansas, Washington University. So I assumed that I would have no trouble now.

I was called in by the Immigration and Naturalization Service on two occasions. The first was rather perfunctory. But my second interview was quite long, and the questions surprised me. They were clearly taken from my writings. The INS was especially interested in a book I wrote on Christians in the Nicaraguan revolution, a book I wrote on women in Cuba, a book on women in Vietnam, and a book of my poetry. They had taken a number of quotes out of context and asked me what I meant by them.

I wrote a poem about the Attica prison uprising in 1972. I had called the Attica prisoners "my brothers" and the police who went in to massacre them "pigs." The INS official asked me, "What did you mean by that?" I said, "I meant I felt a kinship with those men, and I believed that the people who tortured and murdered them were acting like pigs. In the sixties we used that kind of language. Is it a crime?" And he just smiled.

There have been a number of moments in which I've said, "This is the kind of language we used in the sixties. It was a rhetorical language and in some ways a dumb language. I wouldn't write like this today." And as I explained it, I realized the way it came out was, "I'm sorry." It's tricky to be put into that position. I've had it happen with newspeople, when you're trying to explain something very honestly and then the headlines come out the next day: "Margaret Randall Says She's Sorry." But I thought: Wait a minute. I'm not sorry, and I'm not going to apologize for what I said in whatever way I said it. I had a right to be critical then, and I have a right to be critical now.

The next question the INS inspector asked was what I meant by spelling Amerikkka with three Ks. I said, "Well, three Ks is generally a metaphor for the Ku Klux Klan, and I was using it to show that I'm against racism and the Ku Klux Klan and the part of America which is symbolized by that." His other questions revolved around my criticism of U.S. policy during the Vietnam war days, the bombing of Cambodia, the murder of the Kent State students and the Jackson State students.

Well, you can and should criticize something you love. There are many things about this country that I will continue to criticize. Certainly I'm as vehemently against U.S. policy in Central America today as I was against U.S. policy in Vietnam or Southeast Asia. And nobody is going to change my mind about that. It just didn't occur to me that I would be denied residency in my own country because I took a critical stand that hundreds of thousands of Americans, if not millions, have taken.

The interview ended. Time passed, and more time. Instead of taking sixty to ninety days, it took seventeen months. In October of 1985, the INS denied my request for residency under the McCarran-Walter Act, the immigration law passed over Truman's veto at the height of the McCarthy period. The INS said, "Her writings go far beyond mere dissent, disagreement with, or criticism of the United States or its policies." What does it mean to go "beyond mere dissent"? Harold Fruchtbaum, a historian at Columbia University, challenged that concept in his affirmation to the immigration judge:

> To imply that there is an articulable boundary to dissent, disagreement or criticism which the writer must respect is antithetical to the history and ideals of American literature and political theory. . . . Margaret Randall's activities and writings, like those of Susan Sontag, Mary McCarthy, Father Daniel Berrigan and many others who criticize and disagree with the United States or its policies, are well within the distinguished tradition of the American dissent. . . . Her work clearly reflects that commitment to freedom, human rights, and international cooperation which has characterized dissent in this country since the founding of the republic.[5]

My application for adjustment of status was denied in a seven-and-a-half-page statement filled with my writings. Everything pointed to them and a loose category they called associations. They didn't actually claim I had been a member of a communist or socialist or anarchist party, but they did say that since I lived in Cuba I obviously associated with Cuban Communists, since I lived in Nicaragua I obviously associated with members of the FSLN, the Sandinistas, and those were associations that were unacceptable.

The INS ordered me to leave the country in twenty-eight days. I was supposed to be out by October 30, but instead I asked the Center for Constitutional Rights to defend me. As soon as I got over the first shock of "Why me?" I realized it was extremely important to fight the McCarran-Walter Act. It had been used to keep people out of this country for what they think, what they say, and what they write: people like Pablo Neruda, Gabriel García Márquez, Graham Greene, writers from around the world, several of them Nobel Prize winners. The list is very long. And I realized that I was fighting not just for myself but for cases much more serious than mine, for the thousands of refugees who are considered nobodies by Immigration and are just tossed around and often tossed back to their death.

The INS had certain people who took up its banner. Accuracy in Academia dedicated six pages in their national publication to my case. There was a huge picture of me and a coupon you could send in to support the INS position in deporting this "commie threat." A small group of college Republicans staged a flamboyant press conference at the federal building in Albuquerque, before a huge American flag. Once, I was physically attacked in my office. Then I had to change my telephone because of obscene phone calls. I also received a few negative letters, usually written in a deranged way. Some of them just told me to go back where I came from, which is kind of funny because it was Manhattan.

In November, they opened deportation proceedings against me. At the same time, I filed a suit against the government in the federal district court in Washington, D.C. My co-plaintiffs include Norman Mailer, Arthur Miller, Alice Walker, Grace Paley, Toni Morrison, Kurt Vonnegut, and William Styron. We are suing the district director of the INS in El Paso, the commissioner of the INS, and Edwin Meese, the attorney general, for a reversal of the decision in my case and also to challenge the ideological restriction clause of the McCarran-Walter Act. We are saying that the ideological exclusion clause under which I've been attacked is unconstitutional. My First Amendment and Fifth Amendment rights are being violated because I'm being kept out based on my writing and because my own writings are being used against me.

The deportation proceedings took place in immigration court in El Paso, Texas. The trial went on for four days. The first day, the judge was to rule whether or not he believed I was a citizen. We had a long affidavit from Ramsey Clark, who was attorney general of the United States when I took out my Mexican citizenship. He stated that I did not really lose my U.S. citizenship. But in spite of that, the judge ruled against me. The next few days were given over to whether I should be allowed to stay.

Residency depends on the ties to your family, community, and country, and on stipulations listed in the McCarran-Walter Act, such as having been a member of a communist, socialist, or anarchist party. I never was a member of any party except the time I registered as a Democrat to vote for John F. Kennedy. We brought out the facts that I had been born in this country; that my husband, two of my kids, my father, my mother, my brother and sister all are American citizens; that I live next door to my parents; and that my father is eighty years old. My contributions to the community were described by people like Anne Noggle, with my photography, and Adrienne Rich, who was my literary witness.

When Adrienne Rich was asked why the academic community would be injured if I were deported, she said:

> Because through her speak a great many others who have been silenced, who have been silent. And I feel also that the diversity of viewpoints that her work brings to us is something without which the academic community cannot thrive. I certainly can affirm that within my field of feminist studies, women's studies. And I can also affirm it as a poet who needs to know the work of other writers and poets in other parts of the world, even and particularly in cultures where there is a tendency to forbid or discourage American citizens from having cultural contact.[6]

When Adrienne Rich was being introduced as an expert witness, our lawyer asked a few questions to establish her credentials. Adrienne was winner of the National Book Award, distinguished scholar at Stanford, and writer of I don't know how many books. Then my lawyer said to the judge, "I move to qualify Professor Rich as an expert on writing, poetry, and literary interpretation." Guadalupe Gonzales jumped to her feet: "Your honor, I don't think there are any experts in that area."

Guadalupe Gonzales was the central attorney for the government. People have said, "Oh, it looks like they got her for you." That wasn't true at all. Guadalupe Gonzales was gotten for the undocumented workers who were being sent across the border at the rate of thirty or forty a day in El Paso. She was very clearly a token woman, a token Chicano. She relished what she was doing and did it with tremendous zeal. It was tragic to see someone like her playing that role.

Guadalupe Gonzales was terribly anti-communist, terribly blinded in terms of all of her conceptions, and she consistently exploited my womanness. Look at the kinds of questions she asked me: "How did you feel about publishing in a magazine that also published communists?" "Fine, fine." I mean, what are you supposed to say to that kind of a question? And: Did I pose nude for art classes? Is it true that I waitressed in a gay bar in the fifties? How did I fall in love with my husband? Was it some kind of spontaneous combustion? My lawyers jumped to their feet every time she asked a question like that, but in most cases the judge overruled their objections. Well, let her answer the question, for what it's worth, he'd say.

Those kinds of questions are offensive. To be asked them for four days, eight hours a day, could be tremendously humiliating. But I personally was not humiliated. I'm very sure about who I am. I know what my life is. And to be sitting before someone who found it necessary to ask those kinds of questions gave me a sense of immense strength.

But when my mother and father were on the stand, I was anxious and upset and really enraged that they were put through that. My father is eighty and had had a heart attack almost a year before. He spent a lot of time in the weeks preceding the hearing coming over to my house and asking, "What if they ask me this?" And I'd say, "Well, daddy, you just have to tell the truth." And he would ask the same question of the lawyers. It was clear he was very concerned about whether he could do a good job.

When newspeople across the country asked the INS to comment, they kept saying, "It's not a First Amendment case. It has nothing to do with her writing." Yet in the hearing itself, the only thing on trial was my writings. The government had no witnesses. They had pages and pages and pages of my books, magazine articles, and poems. I had written a poem to Che Guevara when he died. That proved I was a "Communist." I had spelled America with three Ks. That proved I was "ill disposed to the good order and happiness of the United States." Without a shadow of a doubt, the hearing in El Paso was a First Amendment case.

American writers raised their voices against my deportation. Norman Mailer, president of PEN,* wrote the judge:

> On behalf of the 2,000 writers of the American Center of International PEN, I am writing to request that you grant the writer Margaret Randall permanent residency status. . . . Ms. Randall is the accomplished writer of more than forty published books with well-known consistent views on social justice. She has been instrumental in having translated Allen Ginsberg, Michael McClure, Kurt Vonnegut, and many other prominent American poets and writers into Spanish for the first time, introducing them to Latin audiences by means of the journal she edited for eight years during the 1960s, *El Corno Emplumado.* . . . We American writers are not afraid of divergent views among us and believe our country grows stronger precisely because of diversity and vitality of expression.[7]

And Alice Walker wrote the judge:

> It is important for me, and I believe also for the community of women writers across America, that Margaret Randall not be deported. She provides a continuing, vital contribution to the national academic and literary community, which will be significantly diminished by her inability to live and work in this country. Her books are an important part of that contribution, but so too are her readings, lectures and literary appearances, and so too is her everyday availability to myself, my students, and other writers who rely on her input and views in our own work.[8]

There was a moment after a particularly long and intense line of questioning by the prosecution when my lawyers said to me, "You've heard a lot of allusions to yourself. Would you like to tell the judge how you see yourself?" So I began to talk about my role as a poet, a photographer, an oral historian, a teacher, mother, woman, and what those roles mean to me.

What I've wanted to express in my work are my ideas about life. I've wanted to show how women see the world. I wanted to translate the

---

*The International Association of Poets, Playwrights, Editors, Essayists, and Novelists.

voices of these women, voices that have been unheard and not only ignored but distorted for so many centuries. By listening to them, by living with them, participating in experiences in which they are attempting to change their world, I was able to do that. First, I transcribed their words in oral history. Then I found that their words entered my poetry and changed it.

> Dominga brings her memory down
> from the needle trade, Don Pedro,
> her own babies
> dead from hunger.
> "I want to tell you my story, leave it
> to the young ones
> so they'll know."
> We are rocking. We are laughing.
> This woman who rescued the flag at Ponce
> Puerto Rico, 1937.
> Known by that act alone.
> Until a book
> carries her words. Her voice.

Dominga de la Cruz was a Black woman, a member of the Nationalist Party in Puerto Rico. A peaceful demonstration that the Nationalists held on Palm Sunday 1937 was fired upon by the National Guard. Dominga was the one who picked up the flag at that Ponce massacre when the woman carrying it was killed. I wrote a book about her because she had been defined by that act alone: the woman who picked up the flag. I was interested in knowing about her life before and after that moment. She was a very poor woman who worked in tobacco factories, in cigar factories, and doing needlework in Puerto Rico. Her two daughters both died of hunger as infants. She was living in exile in Cuba when I met her.

These women, seeking a new life for themselves, simply do not fit the distorted image that's presented to the American public. Their real image is a threat to the current administration. And the attack on me is an attack on these people, their voices, and their lives, on what they mean.

> I bring you these women.
> Listen.
> They speak, but their lives
> are under attack.

> They too are denied adjustment of status
> in the land of the free. In the home of the brave.[9]

The people who supported me in the courtroom were absolutely wonderful. But when it was all over, we fell apart. Right after the hearing, I had to fly to Chicago. When I got there, I couldn't stand up. I was just so worn out I had to sit down all the time. Seven or eight of the people who had been at El Paso with me were having the same kinds of problems.

It takes a lot out of you. And you have to keep a balance between the enormous amount of damage and uncentering that something like this does to your daily life and the enormous amount that it gives to your overall life, to the central meaning of your existence. There are times when that balance is broken. This past winter there have been moments when I really felt the threads breaking in me. But with the tremendous amount of support that I had from my family and friends, I regained my perspective.

Once you understand that there's a historical continuity and you fit into it, you don't feel alone. What I've been feeling recently is a deep connection with the people in the fifties, those who suffered much more than I have and risked much more. They paid a price for us. Their risks really made the support around my case possible. People now are not going to take this in the way that it was taken then, with that kind of isolation and that kind of fear.

The governor of New Mexico has come out in my favor. So has the president of my university. I've had a lot of support from the student senate and the faculty senate, from my colleagues at the university, from my students. More than twenty committees sprang up around the country to support me. There's the Northern California Friends of Margaret Randall, the Feminists in Solidarity with the Peoples of Central America from Philadelphia, the Boston Committee. Someone in Wisconsin I'd never met got several hundred signatures from university professors and presented them to the governor of Wisconsin. It's been incredibly moving. Women from Las Cruces and Albuquerque came to the courtroom. My therapist closed her office for a week just to be there. I got a letter from a fifth grader in an Albuquerque school. He said, "I know just how you feel. I'm a Sikh, and I feel alone a lot of the time. People don't like me. But hang in there, because you have a right to be who you are."

After I had been on "Nightwatch" and "Nightline" and "Larry

King Live," dozens and dozens of people came up to me in the post office, the copy center, and on the street in Albuquerque. "You don't know me, but I know who you are, and I want to wish you luck." "I don't agree with you politically, but you have a right to be here and a right to your opinions. That's what this country is all about." Somebody shouted out to me in an airport, "I don't know why the hell they let Marcos in and they're making such a fuss over you." A guy walked up to me in Berkeley and pressed a twenty-dollar bill in my hand: "This isn't for your case. It's for something you may want to buy, because we need roses as well as bread." He walked away before I could even get his name.

On August 28, 1986, the judge issued his ruling. He used the clause in the McCarran-Walter Act that forbids advocating the doctrines of world communism to deny my application. He gave examples like my opposition to U.S. policy in Vietnam and that I said women in Cuba are better off now than they were under Batista. Conceivably, there are aspects of Cuban life that are more favorable for the people today. Saying that doesn't mean that you advocate the doctrines of world communism. But what if you had? The Constitution supports your right to advocate your ideas. The judge's decision once again, and more forcefully, situates the case in its First Amendment dimension.

If you just see my case as someone who's written books about women of Central America, whose books have been published by small presses and in not very large editions, this all seems crazy to you. If you just see mine as an isolated case, you wonder why the INS is doing this to someone who, if she were left alone, would probably be much less known. My books are selling three times better than they've ever sold. I'm receiving more invitations from universities than I ever received. Before my hearing, I felt, well, they're going to pull back at some point. But what I realized in El Paso is no, they're not going to pull back. They're very serious about making a scapegoat of me, and they feel very committed.

"The President of the United States has spoken clearly and unequivocally on the political character of the Sandinista government of Nicaragua," the prosecutors in my case wrote the judge. "In the exercise of his constitutional powers, he has decided the political 'facts' that the Sandinista Party (FSLN) is a Communist Party. These 'facts' as voiced by the President are directly at odds with those represented by Respondent." [10] This administration wants quashed any kind of thinking that questions its view of how things are. They want it censored. By the example of my case, by the example of the Sanctuary case* and other cases, the message the administration is giving people is: We will use the law or invent new laws or do whatever we have to do to prevent people from presenting a variety of views, to prevent people from acting, to prevent change.

---

*The Sanctuary movement, an ecumenical religious movement patterned after the Underground Railroad, provides refuge in the United States for Central Americans fleeing political persecution in their own countries. In 1986, eight Sanctuary workers were prosecuted by the Reagan administration for conspiracy to smuggle and harbor illegal aliens and were found guilty.

Criminalization of Dissent: The Frame-Up

The Wilmington Ten: Prisoners of Conscience

Ben Chavis

When Wobblies organized in lumber camps or copper-mining towns, they were hounded by local authorities on any pretext. More serious criminal frame-ups have become celebrated cases in American history: Sacco and Vanzetti, Joe Hill, and Tom Mooney.* The civil rights move-ment, in its early years, met with police dogs, fire hoses, and arrests for demonstrations. But by the late 1960s, criminal charges for serious fel-ony offenses were being brought against movement activists. "In North Carolina," southern civil rights organizer Anne Braden noted, "at one point, there were forty black activists in jail on a variety of criminal charges. One of those cases, the Wilmington Ten, sparked a decade-long fight-back that generated a new social movement. But most victims of repression languished long in jail, and by the time they emerged, local movements they had organized had long ago been destroyed."[1]

In March 1972, the Reverend Ben Chavis and nine other leaders of the civil rights movement in Wilmington, North Carolina, were indicted and later convicted of arson and other felonies. Declared a prisoner of conscience by Amnesty International, Ben Chavis spent four and a half

---

* See note on page 63 for information on the Hill and Mooney cases.

BEN CHAVIS

years in prison before he was released and his conviction overturned by a federal appeals court.

My family, the Chavis family, has been involved in the struggle for Black freedom in this country a long time. I am a direct descendant of the Reverend John Chavis, a free man who set up an underground school in Hillsboro when the law banned Blacks from teaching. He was born around the 1750s, the son of a slave in Granville County, North Carolina. That was the county I was born in a couple centuries later, in 1948.

I grew up in Oxford, North Carolina. Most everybody worked on tobacco plantations, but my mother and father were schoolteachers. I was brought up in a totally segregated environment. The movies were segregated; the public accommodations were segregated; the buses were segregated. Everything was segregated. I never sat in a classroom with a white person until my junior year in college.

I was eleven or twelve years old when I attempted to integrate the new public library. There was a library annex for colored people, a little wooden building where we got our books. I wanted to read a book with the covers on and all the pages. On the way home from school one day, I just went in. It kind of startled the librarian. She asked me, "What are you doing here?" I said, "I'd like to check out a book."

"You have to have a library card."

"Well, I would like to get a library card."

She called in this man, who proceeded to tell me that it was wrong for me to be there, that I was out of place, and if I wanted to get a book, to go to the colored library. I told him I wasn't going anywhere and that I wanted a book. A lot of my friends were looking through the window, and a big crowd was beginning to gather. The man gave in. "Okay, here, here. Fill out this form and you can have a card. Just get out of the library." That taught me at an early age that sometimes the structures of racism wait for someone to challenge them.

I must have been seven or eight years old when Emmett Till was killed down in Mississippi. I'll never forget it. Emmett Till was a young boy from Chicago who went down South for the summer. He made the mistake of whistling at a white woman. Later that night he was dragged out of his house, beaten to death, and thrown into the river.

I didn't know Emmett Till, but I felt like that could have happened to me. It could have happened to any one of us. And years later it did. I had come back to Oxford to teach chemistry in the same high school I had gone to. On May 11, 1970—I can remember this so vividly—some of my students rushed in to tell me that there was a shooting in Browntown, a Black community in the northwestern part of Oxford.

There were a lot of eyewitnesses to what happened. A group of young men—my cousin Jimmy was among them—bought something from Teel's convenience store, and they were walking away. One of them whistled at Mrs. Teel. Supposedly. Some remarks were exchanged between them. And Mrs. Teel went into the store. Mr. Teel came out with two of his sons. All three of them were armed.

Of course, when Jimmy and the others saw them, they began to run. Teel fired into the crowd. Shotgun pellets. Some of them hit my cousin Jimmy, who crawled off into the tall grass and hid. Most of the pellets hit Henry Marrow. Henry could not crawl, but he was still alive. Teel and his two sons beat him with the butts of their rifles. And all the time Henry was begging, "Please. Please don't kill me."

Then Robert Teel ordered his son, "Shoot the nigger son of a bitch." And one of them put his rifle to Henry's head and blew his head off. They left him lying there.

I knew Henry all my life. He and I were classmates in high school. Then I went to college and he was drafted in the army, like so many of my friends during the Vietnam war. Now he had come home.

Henry lay there for a while before anybody came to look at him. Everybody was a little afraid. It was known that Teel was the leader of the local Klan chapter. He was feared, not only by the Blacks, but by the whites. The police had refused to serve a warrant on him for an assault on a Black teacher just two weeks before. I went to the local police station to find out why Teel wasn't arrested. I couldn't get an answer. They just said, "Well, we don't know what happened." I said, "There were witnesses. You can go right up and find out." "You're not a police officer," they told me. "We'll handle it."

By the time I got back home, the lot behind the Soul Kitchen—the restaurant that had been in my family for years—was filled with hundreds of people. We had a meeting about what happened. We went back to the police station again and asked why Teel wasn't arrested. We still couldn't get an answer. So I called the governor in Raleigh. It was not until the state police came from forty-five miles away that he was arrested with his two sons.

The funeral for Henry Marrow was at the largest Baptist church one week later. Black people take funerals very seriously, particularly when one is a victim of racial injustice. The emotion and the anger and the reflection about what to do reach a peak. Sitting there in that congregation, you know that you could be in that box but for the grace of God. And it makes one buy into the struggle who normally would not.

The following Thursday, we marched from the church where the funeral was, through downtown. It was a march for justice. We wanted justice for Henry Marrow. We wanted an end to the racist violence perpetrated on the Black community. Since I organized and led the march, people began to call my house, threatening to blow it up, threatening to blow up the Soul Kitchen. The principal got threats about me.

The students in my school came to the hearing for Teel. They received an education that day in the courtroom, one that the classroom would never give them. They watched people from the banks and the chamber of commerce getting on the stand and saying what a good man Teel was and that the judge ought to give him bail. They could not believe it was happening, given the brutal murder that this man and his sons had just committed.

The judge was Robert Martin, the same judge who later sentenced the Wilmington Ten to two hundred eighty-two years in prison. Teel got out on bail. When that happened, we decided to boycott the city. Nobody went to any of the stores. It wasn't just what Teel represented, it was the collusion of the businesses that supported him.

Later, Teel and his sons were found by an all-white jury to be innocent. When these murderers were found innocent, with all the evidence in the world against them, I knew there was no justice to be found in the system. I made up my mind then to leave teaching and work full time for civil rights. I joined the staff of the United Church of Christ, Commission for Racial Justice, as a southern organizer.

During the boycott, there were Klan rallies every other day in Browntown, right there in *Browntown*. Weapons were openly displayed. Oxford became racially polarized. One night, a warehouse loaded with tobacco burned down. The whole sky lit up. A state of emergency was declared by the governor. State police were sent in to enforce a curfew that was really imposed only on the Black community. Whites in the suburbs went around doing whatever they wanted, and some of them came by and started shooting. They fired at my house. I had called for another march to dramatize the continuing victimization of the Black community.

It was during this period that Al Hood and David Washington

showed up in a brand-new station wagon. They said they came to help out. Well, I knew Hood and Washington were bad news. I told them, "I appreciate your interest, but everything is under control." They met some young ladies, and the last I saw of them they were going to take them home. I found out later they deliberately drove into a highway patrol roadblock. They were arrested and charged with possession of dynamite.

We kept the boycott on until we got tangible concessions. We got Blacks in decision-making positions on the police force for the first time. We got Blacks working in the water department and the tax department, the banks, and in the department stores.

In Henderson, ten miles away, they heard what happened in Oxford and asked the Commission for Racial Justice for help with their problems over school desegregation. The local authorities got police from Oxford and Warren and Henderson to stop us from entering the city when we organized a march. They even blocked the highway with fire trucks. We started out with a couple hundred people, but by the time we got to Henderson, we had more than a thousand. They couldn't stop us now. We just marched peacefully into the city and to the church for a service.

Another time, on our way back from a march to the school board, we saw a line of police with gas masks on. They teargassed us for no reason. We all ran to the church, where we thought we'd be safe, and began to sing. The police followed and shot tear gas canisters into the church. They had a new pepper-fog machine that blew out clouds of white smoke—fumes so thick they would choke you. An elderly Black woman died from the gas that day.

We went back to the school board in Henderson with hundreds of parents and children, enough to surround the building. We went back many times. Finally, the school board gave in to our demands. Then we marched back to Davis Chapel—where we had been gassed—to celebrate our victory.

After Henderson came Warren County. More school desegregation problems. I mean, I was really getting some good experience quick. I was getting arrested a lot, too. I was locked up in Henderson because my signal light didn't work. They put me in jail, and I had to go to trial for it. That was something I came to expect.

I've been arrested at least thirty-three times. It started off with various harassment charges. The first time was in 1967 or 1968, just because I made a speech against police brutality at a high school. The police came in, scooped me off the stage, and arrested me for trespassing. That charge was later dropped, but not until I spent a couple days in jail. Soon after I was released, Stanley Noel, a special agent of the Bureau of Alcohol, Tobacco, and Firearms, burst into my room, armed with a shotgun. He was "looking for suspects," he said. It was the first of my encounters with Stanley Noel.

Those experiences were frightening, at first. But I knew I was being arrested and harassed for trying to do justice, trying to speak out for freedom's sake. Once I came to grips with that reality, it became less frightening and it made me more determined. The more they harassed me, the more determined I became.

On February 1, 1971, the Commission for Racial Justice sent me to Wilmington. Fifteen days before I got there, Black students had attempted to have a memorial service for Martin Luther King, Jr. They wanted to have an assembly program, but the principal wouldn't let them. When they held a silent vigil around the U.S. flagpole, they were attacked. Barbara Baldwin was knocked unconscious. The principal expelled her, the victim of the violence.

Black students were being harassed and beaten as they attempted to go to the newly desegregated schools. The Black community had nowhere else to go but to the church, as a place to organize to seek redress for their grievances. When Reverend Templeton allowed the students to meet in the Gregory Congregational Church, he began to receive threats from the Ku Klux Klan and from the Rights of White People, a paramilitary racist group. He called the Commission for Racial Justice for help. I was sent in. It was the first time I had ever been in Wilmington.

I met with the students and suggested that we put down their grievances on paper. They wanted Black history courses. They couldn't be cheerleaders or majorettes. Some teachers made them sit in the back of the classroom. They were told Blacks couldn't type on IBM typewriters because "their fingers were too big and they would ruin the new machines." Real racist stuff. The students set a deadline: If the school board did not reply to their grievances by twelve noon that Wednesday, they would boycott.

At noon on Wednesday, the Black students just walked out of the schools. They even came from the elementary schools, two by two, holding hands. We had a big celebration that day at the church. Later, I led a march of more than a thousand students to the school board. And the next day, too. For three days in a row we marched, Wednesday, Thursday, and Friday. This was the first time a lot of these students and adults had marched or demonstrated about anything. To them, this was a major happening in their lives—marching on the system that was doing them in. And they were vocal marches, with lots of singing. There was a sense of jubilation, just being able to protest, even with the threat of violence all around them.

I had been giving daily reports to my national headquarters about the imminence of racial violence. The school board turned a completely deaf ear to what was happening. And people were calling in and threatening to blow up the church. I received orders Wednesday from the United Church of Christ to come on out of Wilmington. So I left for Oxford that evening.

Early Thursday morning, my director got a call from the governor's office asking me to return. Then I got a call from Preston Hill, of the governor's Good Neighbor Council, saying the governor wanted me back in Wilmington because I was the only one who could keep the peace in the Black community. I felt that was not the issue. The issue was who was going to keep the white community peaceful. I was assured that the State Bureau of Investigation would monitor Klan activity.

But Thursday night, whites in pickup trucks shot into the church and the community nearby. Two people were wounded. Nixon and Spiro Agnew were running all over the country talking about law and order. Well, we wanted law and order. So on Friday we marched downtown and told the local chief of police, "Look, we're in our own church, in our own community. We want some protection around here." And the chief said, "No." What happened? The violence escalated. All hell broke loose—a full-scale riot Friday night and all day Saturday. A lot of bullets. It was like racial warfare going on.

The Black community did not want to give in to intimidation from the KKK or others like them. We felt we had to stay in the church to defend our right to assemble. We barricaded ourselves in because we could not get the police to protect us. We barricaded the intersections around the church. We got lawn chairs, porch chairs, anything to keep those armed vigilantes from driving through with their pickup trucks, shooting up the community.

The Rights of White People, some of them Marines and some of them ex-Marines, were shooting military weapons at us that they got from Camp Lejeune, the Marine base forty miles from Wilmington. A lot of children and elderly people were in the church. Obviously, there was no way we could defend ourselves against Marines trained in Vietnam. But when Black soldiers at Fort Bragg—forty miles in the other direction—

heard that those racist Marines were shooting up this Black church, they grabbed weapons and came to Wilmington to defend it. That's how we survived. It was like being in a war. In some sense, the immoral war that we were engaged in in southeast Asia was coming home.

On Saturday, a fire broke out. I remember I was in Reverend Templeton's house at the time. Somebody rushed in and said, "Mike's Grocery Store is on fire." Steve Mitchell ran out to pull a fire alarm. We never saw him alive after that. We didn't know what happened to him till it came on the news an hour later. Steve Mitchell had been killed by the Wilmington police. Chief Williamson said, "I hope this teaches Blacks a lesson." When he said that, the whole county just erupted. Racial warfare continued all that night. Reverend Templeton and some of the students and I literally lay on the floor, and the bullets were just flying everywhere. That Sunday morning there was a low ebb; the violence subsided to just a few sporadic shots.

At about ten or eleven in the morning, Harvey Cumber drove a pickup truck up to the barricade outside the church. He got out of his truck with a gun and began to shoot. Then somebody shot him. All hell broke loose when it got on the news that a white had been killed. And that's the way they said it: A *white* has been killed. Now the governor imposed a state of emergency. When we had asked for a curfew on Thursday, the police chief said it cost too much. By Friday, when we asked for a curfew, he said he couldn't enforce it. He didn't have the manpower. Even after Steven Mitchell was killed on Saturday night, still no curfew. The curfew only happened after Harvey Cumber, a white, was killed on Sunday.

Sunday night, the governor sent in the artillery division of the North Carolina National Guard. The artillery division! They brought in tanks, helicopters, and armored personnel carriers. But they didn't advance on the church that night. Instead, they waited until Monday, when the national press corps got there. They had invited CBS, ABC, NBC, *Time, Newsweek,* all of them, and even provided them with a special National Guard bus. It was to be a publicity show for the state.

About six A.M. that Monday morning, they surrounded the Gregory Church with tanks, M-16s, a helicopter hovering overhead with a spotlight that lit up the whole block. High drama. They ordered everyone to come out with their hands up. When nobody came out, they assaulted the church. It was empty.

We knew they were not coming to protect us, so we left the church. We left the record player on with the song Steve Mitchell liked, "Get

Involved, Get Involved," playing over and over again in homage to him. As we crossed the bridge to leave Wilmington late Sunday night, we passed the National Guard coming in. On Monday, we held our own press conference in Raleigh to tell what had happened.

The state had, for all practical purposes, repressed our access to Gregory Church. So we opened up a storefront church, painted the building black with a red, black, and green cross on the top. We had church there every day, not just Sunday. It was a place for people to come to get revitalized. We set up a G.E.D. program, so students could get a high school diploma. We set up a voter education program. We taught Black history. And we started attending all the city council meetings, all the school board meetings.

During this time, the Rights of White People set up a "command post" two blocks from us, right in the middle of the Black community. They raised their Confederate flag and openly displayed weapons. But it was our church that was raided by the local police. I was arrested a couple of times myself. One time they said my car wasn't registered, and I spent two or three nights in jail for that.

By the end of 1971 and the beginning of 1972, I was arrested every month for something. At first these were harassment charges by local powers that be, but by 1972 they were charging me with major felonies and federal crimes. It's one thing to be accused of a misdemeanor; it's another to be charged with a felony. That's when they try to put you away for the rest of your life.

In December 1971, the federal government indicted Jim Grant, another civil rights worker, and me on the absolutely incredible charge of aiding federal fugitives. Al Hood and David Washington had left the country for Canada on the day of their trial for possession of dynamite. Then they voluntarily returned to surrender in Charlotte. The government dropped all charges against them for possession of dynamite and for fleeing the country. Then they indicted Jim and me for conspiracy to possess the dynamite that Hood and Washington actually had and for aiding and abetting them to leave the country. Classic. And who testified against us at our trial? Hood and Washington.

Hood had been convicted of auto theft and assault. Washington had been discharged from the Marines for being dangerously schizophrenic and had his own criminal record. After their testimony, all pending charges against them were dropped and years of prior sentences were wiped out. From then on, they seemed immune from prosecution. A year later, Hood was charged with narcotics possession and murder, but he was never brought to trial. At the very time Washington was under investigation for armed robbery and murder, Judge Robert Martin ruled that his probation restrictions from an earlier conviction were no longer warranted.

They each received four thousand dollars from the government for their testimony. Stanley Noel got them thirteen thousand more from the Treasury Department. And Stanley Noel, the BATF agent, put together the prosecution's case against us.

The jury acquitted me and somehow convicted Jim Grant. The same day I was freed, the New Hanover County Grand Jury indicted me and nine others from Wilmington: eight student leaders and Mrs. Ann Sheppard, one of the few whites who supported the movement down there. We were charged with burning down Mike's Grocery Store, two blocks from Gregory Church, and conspiracy to assault emergency personnel. They took me back to jail in shackles and chains.

When we wound up with a jury of our peers, ten Blacks and two whites, the state refused to go forward with the trial. Jay Stroud, the prosecutor, stood up and said, "Your honor, the state asks for a mistrial. The prosecutor cannot continue due to ill health." When Judge Robert Martin asked what was wrong with him, Stroud said he had a stomachache. And that was it. *The judge granted a mistrial because the prosecutor said he had an upset stomach.*

In the meantime, I got out on bail. On August 31, 1972, I drove to our Commission for Racial Justice office in Raleigh. I was there for about an hour. When I came back downstairs, I noticed my car was unlocked. I looked under the hood, in the trunk, I looked everywhere but under the front seat. When I cranked the car up and everything seemed all right, I drove off. All of a sudden a blue flame ejected from under my front seat, like an acetylene torch. I could hear the hissing. I immediately put the car in park and got out. I bent over and reached my right arm under the front seat. The whole car blew up in flames. Luckily, the impact pushed me back from the car, so only my right arm was burned. I was hospitalized that night with first-, second-, and third-degree burns. The car was totally destroyed.

The attempt on my life was initially investigated by the Raleigh police. The case was turned over to the county police, then to the state police, and then to the FBI. The FBI ultimately turned it over to the Alcohol, Tobacco, and Firearms Division of the Treasury Department. There, Stanley Noel, of all people, was put in charge of the investigation. To this day I have never seen a report on what happened, on the cause, on what kind of incendiary device it was. Definitely, no legal action was taken against anybody who attempted to burn me up in the car. But I went back to Wilmington the next day, with my arm in a sling, to be tried for arson.

This time, the state was determined to get a jury more to their liking. They had four peremptory challenges for each of the ten defendants. There weren't but forty-two Black people in the jury pool. Every time a Black person got up to answer questions, the state dismissed that juror. They used thirty-nine of their forty challenges on Blacks.

But when our lawyer challenged an admitted member of the KKK for cause, the judge said, "No." Robert Martin, the same judge who presided over the trial of the Klan leader who killed Henry Marrow, said, "This man has a constitutional right to be a member of any organization he wants to be a member of." Then the judge turned to the juror: "Can't you look at these ten defendants and disabuse from your mind any prejudice that you might have against them?" And of course he said yes. This time the jury composition was just the opposite: two Blacks and ten whites, not a jury of our peers. And that's the jury that convicted us.

Little did we know that during the year of 1971, the Alcohol, Tobacco, and Firearms Division of the Treasury Department had sent agents to Wilmington. If the government wants to really go after somebody, they use those treasury agents, because they have maximum flexibility. No oversight. No committee in Congress is watching them. And one of their agents, Stanley Noel, was present at our North Carolina trial. Just as he helped federal prosecutors prepare their case against Jim Grant and me, now he helped the state prosecutor, Jay Stroud, to convict us.

There were three witnesses who testified against us. They were Allen Hall, eighteen years old; Jerome Mitchell, seventeen; and Eric Junious, who was only thirteen. All three were in trouble with the law at the time of their testimony. Eric Junious had committed armed robbery when he was eleven. He was in a reformatory. Allen Hall and Jerome Mitchell were facing more serious charges. Mitchell had committed armed robbery and murder. He could have been in prison for the rest of his life. Hall was in prison on assault charges, serving a twelve-year sentence.

Hall testified that I told a crowd inside the church that it was time "to show the crackers we mean business." He claimed I joined him and others in burning down the grocery and shooting at the firemen. Jerome

Mitchell and Eric Junious claimed they also heard me say that at the church.

At the end of the trial, Stroud told the jury we were "dangerous animals who should be put away for the rest of their lives." We were convicted and sentenced to a combined total of two hundred eighty-two years in prison. Mrs. Sheppard got ten years, the other eight got twenty-two to twenty-six years each. I had a thirty-four-year sentence. No one has ever been charged with shooting at the Gregory Congregational Church. Check out what happened to Stroud: After we were sent to prison, President Nixon appointed this local assistant state prosecutor to be the U.S. Attorney for North Carolina. So he got his reward.

While I was in Central Prison, two inmates were burned alive. In late November 1972, John Cuttino, a leader of the Black inmates, caught on fire in his cell on the same tier I was on. Another inmate, Charles Richardson, had also been murdered in a similar fashion about three weeks earlier—burned alive. Some white inmates were let out of their cells and threw a five-gallon can of paint thinner on him, lit a broom, and stuck it in the cell. They just let him burn.

When Cuttino was burned alive, they had to clear all the inmates from the west side because the fumes were so bad. They put us in the cafeteria. We decided we were not going back to the cell block till we saw the head warden. We drew up a list of grievances, one of which was simply to install fire extinguishers.

We were ordered to go back to our cell block. Nobody moved. Black and white. Then there was an announcement over the loudspeaker that the warden wanted to see me outside in the yard. Me alone. If I would have gone out of that building and into that yard, they would have shot me. Some of the Black prison guards told me later that they had been ordered to shoot anybody who came out of the building. But I didn't go out.

When I refused, the assistant warden came into that crowd in the cafeteria. He leaned over and told me that if I didn't ask the inmates to go back to their cells, he was going to mop the floor with my blood. I suggested to him that he wasn't in a position to mop the floor with anybody's blood right then.

They wanted to do me in, but they couldn't. If you hold on to your personality, if you hold on to your humanity, they can't do you in. And I never felt isolated in prison. I got mail every day: from Germany, from France, from the Soviet Union, from Cuba. I held on to my ties to the

United Church of Christ and other organizations and to my family. They stuck with me through this thing. And that's really how I survived.

After we were in prison a number of years, the state's case began to fall apart. In May 1976, I was on a hunger strike that lasted one hundred thirty-one days. The press was reporting regularly that Chavis has so many days to live. I think Allen Hall's conscience got to him. He wrote a letter to the press and to my lawyer, saying he wanted to tell the truth. I have to give him credit for that. My lawyer got an independent investigator to interview him and a notary to get his sworn statement.

Hall said his testimony at our trial was not true. He said he lied because they offered him favors and the promise of a quick release. And he said that they told him I had threatened to attack his mother and that the only way he could get back at me was to testify against us at our trial. He was coached by Bill Walden, another agent of the Bureau of Alcohol, Tobacco, and Firearms: "And, ah, he asked me had I seen it, and I said, no, I hadn't seen no dynamite in the basement of no church. He said, well then, that's the dynamite that came out from under the church. You supposed to say you saw the dynamite in the basement of the church. And so, I said, well o.k. then." [2]

Several months later, Jerome Mitchell recanted, too. He told how Stroud and others, including Walden, convinced him to sign the statements they had prepared: "Stroud was straight out telling me that he wanted me to lie." And then he said, "All the details I gave about Chavis and the other defendants was false. I was not there at the church those nights and I did not participate in the burning of Mike's Grocery nor do I personally know who did. I testified to these matters only because Jay Stroud promised me I would get out of prison in six or seven months if I did." [3]

Then Mitchell told how he and Hall were kept in a Carolina Beach home that we later learned was owned by Tex Gross, the Grand Cyclops of the Knights of the Ku Klux Klan. Gross visited them there and told them that if they needed money or protection, he would help them. They stayed there before the trial and during the trial to rehearse their statements, and after the verdict they celebrated—grilling steaks and drinking whiskey.

This was not Jerome Mitchell's first recantation, although we didn't know it then. In 1974, he had written to the North Carolina Parole Board: "I can no longer go on with myself about it. Because of the fact that I committed perjure [sic] against every person in that case. I have done wrong enough. Please let me have my chance to help free those I lied upon." He added, "Ben Chavis and the others have their appeal in now. I hope I'm in time."[4] That letter, which obviously would have strengthened our case just then when it was in appeal, was never given to our lawyers. We had to wait three years to learn about it in the press.

Then Eric Junious recanted. He said he was coached, too, and trained to match our names with our pictures. He was promised a mini-bike and a job from Stroud for his testimony, both of which he got.

There was a growing awareness internationally about the Wilmington Ten. Angela Davis, who founded the National Alliance Against Racism and Political Repression along with Charlene Mitchell and me, talked about the Wilmington Ten in all her travels. People in Germany first found out about our case through Angela. The same thing in France; I remember in 1978 a group of French students chained themselves to the U.S. embassy in Paris.

The U.S. press was trying to ignore the Wilmington Ten, but they really couldn't. Our story appeared in the *London Times* and in *Le Monde*. It was appearing everywhere. James Baldwin wrote an open letter to Carter about us. The *New York Times* had to start covering it.

By this time, Jimmy Carter was using human rights as a foreign policy weapon. Carter wrote Sakharov, a Soviet dissident: "You may rest assured that the American people and our government will continue our firm commitment to promote respect for human rights—We shall use our good offices to seek the release of prisoners of conscience."[5]

Soon afterward, in April 1977, Amnesty International adopted us as political prisoners of conscience. So I wrote Carter from prison: "As only one of many American citizens who have been unjustly imprisoned not because of criminal conduct but as a direct result of participation in the human and civil rights movement in the United States, I appeal to you, President Carter, to first set a national priority of freeing all U.S. political prisoners." He never answered.

Sixty members of Congress sent Griffin Bell, then Carter's attorney general, a letter asking for redress for the Wilmington Ten. The NAACP, the Urban League, the National Council of Churches, and AFL-CIO unions appealed to Carter to use his authority to do justice in our case. City councils in Los Angeles, Detroit, Baltimore, and other cities urged Carter and Bell to intervene.

Carter, at a press conference, said we'd have to let the courts handle it. And then he said Attorney General Bell was "concerned" about the matter. Bell gave the impression he was shocked when the information about our case came out. He called a special federal grand jury to investigate the prosecutor's handling of the case. Obviously, they had enough to indict the state officials, but no bill of indictment was ever written.

Then, in May 1977, we had a post-conviction hearing for a new trial before a North Carolina judge, George Fountain. Reverend and Mrs. Templeton came back to testify that I had been with them at the time the grocery burned down. Jerome Mitchell, Eric Junious, Allen Hall all swore again that they had lied at the original trial. And when our lawyer questioned Stroud about the illegal coercion of Hall, Mitchell, and Junious, he repeatedly answered, "I do not remember." After seven weeks of hearings, it took the judge only five minutes to decide against a new trial. The *New York Times* said the judge's refusal was "more astonishing than the facts elicited at [this] hearing."[6]

All this time we were in prison. And it was rough. In 1978, in McCain State Prison, I got appendicitis. By that time, I had made minimum custody, so I should have been able to go to the local hospital, only ten miles away. But they called the governor's office, and he said, "No. Bring him to Raleigh." That was over a hundred miles away. They put me in the back of a station wagon with all the windows up. It was summer, and there was no air conditioning. My appendix burst on the way to Raleigh. Even after I got to Central Prison Hospital, they didn't operate until twelve hours later. I almost died.

In January of 1978, the governor reduced our sentences. We felt we should have a full pardon of innocence, as Amnesty International proposed. But Governor James B. Hunt refused. He went on statewide TV and said he believed that we were guilty and wouldn't pardon us. But because he was under pressure, he shortened our sentences.

I spent four and a half years in prison. The month I got out on parole, in December of 1979, the Justice Department filed an amicus curiae brief in support of the Wilmington Ten in our appeal before the federal court, a highly unusual procedure. But that made you think: What had the Justice Department been doing all these years we were in prison?

The Fourth Circuit Court of Appeals, on December 4, 1980, overturned our convictions in a unanimous decision. They cited prosecutor Stroud's misconduct in getting Hall, Mitchell, and Junious to testify against us and his refusal to give our lawyers access to earlier statements Hall had made that would have cast doubt on his credibility as a witness. We were convicted in violation of the Sixth Amendment, they said.

And Hall had been the "crucial witness," yet he "perjured himself in his repeated, unfounded testimony."

That's what the judges cited as the reasons why our convictions were overturned. But I believe the real reason was the same reason we were convicted—politics. It was politics and racism that put us in prison. It was politics that got us out of prison. Public pressure. The power of the people is not just a slogan.

That's the reason I'm still optimistic. I believe in the power of the people, organized and mobilized. I'm committed to it, and I'm just thankful for it. I think one of the ways that I can show that I'm appreciative of all the support that we got is to continue to struggle to help others. I learned a long time ago, we have to work to make our dreams come true, to make our hopes become reality.

I believe that one day a transformation of this society will take place. I really believe that, because I think we'll soon reach the point where the majority of people in this country will realize that it is in their best interests to have a just nation rather than an unjust nation, to have a nation where you don't put corporate profits over human life. So, yes, I am hopeful. I don't think the bad guys will win.

LEONARD PELTIER

War Against the
American Nation

Leonard Peltier

The parallels between the Peltier and Chavis cases are striking. Both men had been targeted by law enforcement agencies; both were charged with violent crimes, Chavis with arson and Peltier with murder; both were tried in venues where racial prejudice was substantial and under judges whose bias was apparent; both were accused by teenage government witnesses who later admitted lying under government coercion; and both represented political causes—they were activists seeking to improve the lives of their people.

From childhood, Leonard Peltier had seen the poverty and misery of his people. As he grew older, he learned that the United States had broken treaties with the American Indians. The Fort Laramie Treaty of 1868 recognized Indian sovereignty and Indian lands that comprised great sections of what is now Nebraska, Wyoming, Montana, North Dakota, and South Dakota. The violations of that treaty over the next decades left the Sioux with only a fraction of their land. Many Oglala Sioux were relegated to a desolate piece of the South Dakota plains south of the Badlands, the Pine Ridge reservation.

Just as their land was expropriated, so their sovereignty was lost. Traditional Indian government was supplanted first by the direct control of the Bureau of Indian Affairs and then by elected tribal councils supervised by the BIA. By the 1970s, Pine Ridge was under the grip of

Tribal Council President Dick Wilson. Traditional Indians were frustrated by Wilson's fraudulent election, his rigged impeachment procedures, his self-serving allocation of federal monies and jobs, and the reign of terror instituted by his private police, the GOONs.* The subsequent occupation of Wounded Knee by traditionals and members of the American Indian Movement was designed to draw public attention to their plight. Three hundred Indians—approximately the number massacred at Wounded Knee in the winter of 1890 by federal forces— withstood a seventy-one-day siege through the winter of 1973 by the army, BIA police, FBI SWAT teams, and Wilson's GOONs.

The aftermath of Wounded Knee was more betrayal: The promised congressional investigation of the Wilson regime never took place, and the traditionals and AIM supporters in Pine Ridge became targets of GOON-inspired violence and murder. By 1975, traditionals again sought AIM help. Leonard Peltier and other AIM supporters established a camp in Oglala at the Jumping Bull ranch. On June 26 the ranch became the site of a firefight between massed federal forces and traditional Indians. Joe Stuntz, a Native American, was killed; his death was never investigated. Two FBI agents, Jack Coler and Ron Williams, also were killed. Four Indians were indicted for the deaths of the agents; two were acquitted, and the charges against the third dropped so the government's resources could be directed solely at Peltier. He was convicted in a trial whose improprieties aroused international attention.

Despite the magnitude of the prosecutorial and FBI misconduct, despite appeals from South African Archbishop Tutu, the Archbishop of Canterbury, Amnesty International, fifty-five members of Congress, and fifty-one members of the Canadian Parliament, Peltier's request for a new trial was turned down by the Eighth Circuit Court of Appeals, and the Supreme Court refused to review it. "In the first moments after getting word of the decision," Leonard Peltier wrote, "I knew exactly how Crazy Horse, Sitting Bull, and Chief Joseph (who sat in prison at this same site) felt when they were up against the U.S. government."[1]

LEONARD: My first encounter with non-Indian people was an act of violent racism. I was six years old. I was standing on the street corner,

---

* A heavily armed force organized by Wilson. They called themselves Guardians of the Oglala Nation, GOONs.

waiting for my uncle, who went to the drugstore. Some kids came walking by and said, "Hey, you dirty Indian, go home." I didn't know what was happening. I didn't even know there was a difference between Indians and whites. They started throwing rocks at me. An older kid came along and started throwing rocks, too. They stoned me in the street because I was an Indian.

I remember it terrified me. I finally started fighting back, and I hit one kid in the head with a marble-sized rock. I got scared and ran straight home. His mom came over later and said they'd put me in the reformatory. And they would have. In the middle of the night, my grandpa and grandma packed up our truck and said, "We'd better get out of here." So we split back to the reservation.

Over the years, I've seen a lot of discrimination against my people. I've witnessed some very gruesome things, a lot of poverty, a lot of illness. I've seen mothers with tears in their eyes because their children were slowly starving to death. I was watching. But I was too young to understand why. When I was a teenager, I heard an old Ojibwa woman, a relative of mine, get up and speak at an Indian meeting. She was pleading for food for her children. "Are there no more warriors among our men," she asked, "who will stand up and fight for their starving children?" That day, I vowed I would help my people the rest of my life.

Many people in the United States are sympathetic to Indians. They are first to state that we have gotten a raw deal. But they think that was all in the past. They don't realize it's still happening. Naturally, the government is going to deny it. But what's any different between a hundred years ago and today, when it comes to dealing with Indian land?

Billions of dollars of minerals have been discovered on reservations. There's a lot of uranium, oil, silver, and other minerals. Multinational corporations are getting this stuff for practically nothing. They are stealing it. That has a lot to do with the traditionals and the American Indian Movement. Our main goal is to get these mining companies fully removed from the reservations and bring back our sovereignty.

AIM was the most successful and the most responsible Indian organization to bring the plight of the Indian people to the world. We revived the interest among our people in Indian religion and traditional philosophies. We were growing and growing every year. We became targets of the FBI and the federal government. A number of us realized then that it was very possible we would end up in prison for the rest of our lives, if not dead.

After Wounded Knee, there was quite a reign of terror put on by the

Dick Wilson regime at the Pine Ridge reservation. There were killings going on, beatings, children were being assaulted, elders. Mostly they were traditionals and American Indian Movement members. Our chief Frank Foolscrow's home was burnt out. Members of the Little family were well-known American Indian Movement supporters. One of their sons was beaten nearly to death. He was dropped off on a hospital driveway at Pine Ridge, and he died later. Mary Little Bear was nine years old; she came from a family of traditionalists and AIM supporters. She was playing out in her yard. A car came by full of GOONs; they machine-gunned the house, hit the little girl, and she lost her eye. The people who got the license plate number turned it in to the police. There were no results.

There were over two hundred GOON-related assaults and deaths on the reservation prior to the June 26 shoot-out. To this day, we don't know if there was an investigation. We do know there were never any indictments put out, except for one. That was when some of our attorneys and legal workers flew into the airport on Pine Ridge. Dick Wilson, with around six or seven cars of armed GOONs, surrounded them, beat them up, and destroyed their car. He only paid a ten-dollar fine for attempted murder, assault, and destruction of personal property.

> KAREN NORTHCOTT, legal worker: There was an attempt to impeach Wilson a couple of days prior to Wounded Knee. But Wilson presided at his own impeachment and ruled in his own favor. He controlled the tribal council, a form of government set up by the Bureau of Indian Affairs that was originally housed within the War Department. The BIA controlled everything from birth until death for the Indian people on the reservation. You couldn't buy or sell cattle. You couldn't make an improvement on your home without the Bureau of Indian Affairs okaying it. It was like living in an occupied country.
>
> There was affidavit after affidavit after affidavit of people who had been harassed, threatened, and hurt by Wilson's private police force. He funded his GOON squad by illegally taking money out of tribal programs and buying GOONs or paying them off with alcohol and guns. They had virtual freedom to do whatever they wanted. I mean, they roamed the reservation with impunity, going after AIM or AIM supporters. Children were being hit, people's houses were being shot at.

When we were living on the reservation one summer, every night people would call: "The GOONs are at so-and-so's house. Come over." As outside legal workers, we offered some protection. They would be less likely to shoot if we were there. But later, we were more likely to arouse their anger. I was in a home in Porcupine when four carloads of people shot into the house for about thirty minutes. All of us in the house had to lie on the ground.[2]

LEONARD: Our chiefs of the Oglala nation had written to the State Department asking them to investigate the terrorism that was going on. They received no response whatsoever. On June first, they wrote a second letter to the State Department and said that because they did not receive any response, they were no longer recognizing the tribal election system under the Bureau of Indian Affairs. They were going back to the traditional tribal system, and they were going to declare themselves a sovereign nation. After the June first letter, people started noticing a large mobilization of military force. They were seeing army personnel carriers, a lot of police enforcement agents, people running around in fatigues that looked like SWAT teams. It was a real tense area.

On June 10, we were having our AIM convention in Farmington, New Mexico. The chiefs of the Oglala nation sent a delegation asking us to come to Pine Ridge and give them some kind of protection. So we made a decision right there that we would go in. I asked for volunteers to come with me and set up a camp. It would be a camp where we would bring back our spirituality, another one of the American Indian Movement's goals.

When we got to Oglala, we set up a sweat lodge. We had a spiritual camp on the Jumping Bull ranch. We planted large community gardens. We helped build a business, a grocery store, and a gas station. We were also there to protect the people, and that's precisely what we did. Our being there stopped some of the killings, the terrorism. And there were kids running wild, destroying houses, and burglarizing the elders' homes. We put a stop to that.

> ROSELYN JUMPING BULL: Our boys . . . can't even speak up for themselves because they're just so scared of Dick Wilson and his goons. . . . So finally, we really got tired of it. . . . We had a meeting wondering what we should do. So I said, "Oh, let's get

us some boys over here that could do something for us, that could help us." . . . So we asked 'em to come in. . . .

One time at my daughter's housing, somebody ripped off the whole living room, trophies, everything. . . . Pretty soon, someone was breaking windows next door, trying to steal off that next house. So they went out and chased them all over. . . . Leonard said, "If you don't return those things by tomorrow morning, I'm gonna come look for you again. You're gonna give them back 'cause they're not yours." Next morning, first thing somebody was knocking at my daughter's place. And here a little-bitty boy said, "Come on, I'll show you where they hid those things." . . .

Oh, I used to drink before they came. Every weekend I was drunk someplace. After they came, they took me to ceremonies. I went regularly then—every week. I forgot about my drinking. Now I look back. Now they're all in jail and they're gone.[3]

LEONARD: We thought of ourselves as warriors. In Indian society, a warrior is not just a person who goes out to fight. A warrior has many duties. It's something we learn as kids. He's a policeman. He's a referee. He's a hunter. He even babysits, which I've done many a time. I washed clothes, cooked, everything. A warrior sacrifices his own lifestyle in order to make things more comfortable for his people.

In the short time we were there, we became very popular. That's one of the reasons why the Oglala people have been so strongly behind me since my arrest. The government always said I was an outsider. That's not true. I was married on the reservation, and I'd been living there off and on. I'm part Sioux, and these are my people.

> HAZEL LITTLE HAWK: I lived in Pine Ridge all my life. It's just like other towns, but not like white people's towns. I'm raising Leonard's children. His boy is nine, walks like him. He's got his curls. His daughter has the color of his hair, black, but she's got straight long hair. His children miss him so bad.
>
> Leonard's a fine man, a really good-natured man. He loves everybody. He cares for everybody, especially the Oglala people. He really helped them out. That's why I want to do my best for him.
>
> No place is safe for us Indians, the Oglala Lakota Sioux. The

white man wants to get rid of us so bad. They want our land. Why? They have all this land that used to be ours. Why can't they be satisfied and leave us alone? Now they are trying to get our Black Hills. But no, we wouldn't give that up. It's our sacred place.[4]

LEONARD: The day before the shoot-out, June 25, 1975, Dick Wilson had been in Washington. He gave away a big piece of the reservation. No tribal member or elected official has the right to give away any tribal land, not one acre. By law, it has to be approved by the whole tribe. I think they realized there was going to be a hell of a controversy surrounding that. The majority of the people were behind the traditionalists and the American Indian Movement.

The morning of the twenty-sixth, I was lying down at camp. A creek runs right through the Jumping Bull ranch where we stayed. It's kind of in a hollow. Some of the women were making breakfast. I heard this shooting going on. It sounded loud, but I thought it was because of how sound traveled through the hollow. About a week before, we kept hearing automatic gunfire. It was one of Dick Wilson's GOONs. "I'm just shooting fish," he said. So this time when I heard shots, I didn't pay too much attention to it. Then it started sounding like more than one weapon firing.

Someone screamed that we were under attack. I picked up a weapon and ran up toward the ranch houses. A firefight was going on. Agents were fighting with the Indians about a quarter of a mile from our camp. I immediately asked one of the brothers, "What's happening?" He said, "Man, we're under attack. We got all kinds of cops all over the place." Everybody was hiding. I was ducking myself, because I could hear bullets zinging over my head.

By the government's own statistics, there were something like two hundred eighty police there. The FBI had some of their best SWAT teams from Los Angeles, Denver, Philadelphia, and New York. For them to come as quickly as they did, they had to be real close, on standby. They had planes and all kinds of military equipment. They were there to fight a war.

BRUCE ELLISON, attorney for Leonard Peltier: We've found through the Freedom of Information Act that rather than being involved in a criminal investigation, the FBI was acting as a domestic security force on the Pine Ridge reservation. We have documents that show that three weeks prior to this incident the FBI was discussing at the headquarters level the need for a military-type assault on the community of Oglala, the exact community that, in fact, was assaulted on June 26, 1975.[5]

LEONARD: People were afraid there was going to be another massacre. "Look," I said to my brothers, "you've got to hold them back. I'm going to get the women and children out of the houses." I'm creeping and crawling, and I get up to the houses. Some of the little children, one and two years old, are screaming. One little baby is under the bed with her mother. They all crowd around me: "Help us. I don't want my babies to die." I calm them down. "Come on, I'll help you get out of here." I have them run in front of me. The bullets are close enough to zing by my ear. So I turn around and start shooting. It's my responsibility.

I got them approximately a quarter of a mile away from the firefight. It was a wooded area, but they could see the open ground from there. "When you see us going over that area, then all the cops are going to come that way. That's when you guys get out." I got back to where my group was and said, "We will have to make a run for it to direct all the police after us." We sat down and prayed with the pipe. "This might be the end of this world for us." We got up and fought our way out of there. And the women and children got away. I don't know, I guess it was the Great Spirit upon us.

DINO BUTLER: I was in the tipi with my wife. We were just getting up. And I heard the firing, the firing up there. Norman Brown came down and said . . . there's women and children up there. . . . So I grabbed my gun and told my wife to take Jeanne and the other girls out of here. . . . We got up there and we received fire. . . . There were two cars out in the field, and there were two cars down in the gully, and there were cars all around us already by the time I got there. . . .

So we withdrew from there and went back down to our camp. We got ready to leave when another brother came back. He said that Joe Stuntz was dead. So we all knelt down and prayed there. . . . And then we left. On the way out we met my wife Nilak and Jeanne and Lynn. . . . Everywhere they went they said there was a roadblock. . . . I did not see it, but

Norman Brown told me there was an eagle.* He saw an eagle come down while we were praying. . . . They had us completely surrounded, yet somehow we got through all of those people.[6]

LEONARD: The firefight lasted from about ten that morning to eight or nine that night. One Indian brother and two agents were killed. The FBI went into the Jumping Bull ranch around six, seven o'clock and destroyed the Jumping Bull home. They just shot it all up. There were large bullet holes, one and a half to two inches round. They machine-gunned the whole inside of the house. They had done the same thing at Wounded Knee; they machine-gunned the church after everybody was gone.

The FBI continued to stay on the reservation for about two weeks. They went around terrorizing people. One blind man and his wife lived way out in the country. These people were about eighty years old. She was up cooking breakfast and looked out the window. She started telling him in Indian: "The cavalry is here. They're coming with guns. They're surrounding our house." They came and kicked in the door, and the old man died of a heart attack.

WILLIAM F. MULDREW, U.S. Civil Rights Commission: At about 1:00 P.M. on Thursday, June 26, two FBI agents were shot to death on the Pine Ridge reservation near the town of Oglala, South Dakota. The FBI immediately launched a large scale search for the suspected slayers which has involved 100 to 200 combat-clad FBI agents, BIA policemen, SWAT teams, armored cars, helicopters, fixed-wing aircraft, and tracking dogs. . . .

In the days immediately following the incident there were numerous accounts of persons being arrested without cause for questioning, and of houses being searched without warrants. One of these was the house of Wallace Little, Jr., next door neighbor to the Jumping Bulls. His house and farm were surrounded by 80–90 armed men. He protested and asked them to stay off his property. Elliot Daum, an attorney . . . who had been staying in the house with Little's family, informed the

---

* The eagle was considered an omen by some; Butler alludes here to the belief that its flight path signaled the escape route.

agents that they had no right to search without a warrant. They restrained him and prevented him from talking further with Little while two agents searched the house.[7]

LEONARD: The FBI went out with blank subpoenas on the reservation. The majority of the Indian people ripped them up right there. They said, "We're a sovereign nation. You have no jurisdiction on this reservation to issue us any kind of subpoenas." Then all the tribes met. It was the first time in over fifty years that all seven bands from the reservation got together. They demanded the FBI and all non-Indian police get off the reservation.

Four of us—Bob Robideau, Dino Butler, Jimmie Eagle, and myself—were indicted for the murders of the agents. It was late January when I heard about it. I'd been back and forth from Canada to Pine Ridge. Under the advice of my chiefs and some of the elders, I went back to Canada. I got arrested there on February 6. They tried to deport me as an illegal alien, but I fought extradition and asked for asylum there. I realized the possibility of getting a fair trial was very slim.

At my extradition hearing, they presented a so-called eyewitness, Myrtle Poor Bear. She claimed to have been my girlfriend, that I was the father of one of her children. I didn't know who this person was. All of those I associated with had never met her. She came up with the story that she saw me shoot the two agents. She jumped on my back and started beating me. She said Dino Butler and some others had thrown her down and raped her. She said somebody named Ricky Little Boy started beating hell out of her and she wrestled a thirty-thirty out of his hand, jumped on a horse, and took off. And Ricky Little Boy jumped on a horse and took off, chasing her. She was shooting over her shoulder. When I read it, I laughed. I had to laugh. What else could I do but cry?

Later, we found out the FBI had gotten two contradictory affidavits from Myrtle Poor Bear. The first said she hadn't actually seen the murders but I had confessed it all to her. They kept that one secret. Then they got her to say she was an eyewitness. That's the one they gave the Canadian authorities. Later, Evan Hultman, the special prosecutor, admitted that there was no truth whatsoever to Myrtle Poor Bear's story. But that's what got me extradited. They violated international law by knowingly giving the Canadian government false affidavits.

I spoke to Myrtle Poor Bear on the phone during my trial. I asked her, "Why did you do this? I don't know you. You know I don't know you." "Well," she said, "they threatened me. They told me if I didn't do this they would take away my children." Myrtle Poor Bear was a sick woman. They used her like they used so many Indian people. I have no bad thoughts for her.

Dino Butler and Bob Robideau went to trial first. The case against them was the same as the case against me. They were found innocent by reason of self-defense. The prosecutors dropped the charges against Jimmie Eagle, an FBI memorandum said, so that the "full prosecutive weight of the federal government could be directed against Leonard Peltier."

Judge McManus, who Bob and Dino had, was also appointed to be the judge over my trial, and he was prepared to try me. But he was re-cused—the legal term for removed—from my case. He didn't know how it happened. The government doesn't have the right to recuse a judge, but somehow they had McManus replaced. The FBI must have gone shopping for a judge who would work for them, and they got Paul Benson, a Nixon appointee. To put it bluntly, he thinks he's God when he's in that courtroom. He looks very dignified, what you would imagine a judge to look like, but he made a farce of the federal judgeship.

Benson had ordered a complete transcript of Bob and Dino's trial for his own use. He must have studied all the motions McManus granted them, because he denied them to us. He wouldn't let me properly question the jury about their prejudice against Indians. The same testimony that resulted in the acquittal of Dino Butler and Bob Robideau was barred in my trial. We couldn't show how the FBI terrorized the Pine Ridge community. We couldn't show how the FBI had singled me out, how they were out to get me long before the shoot-out. We couldn't even show how FBI agents' testimony contradicted their own reports at the time of the shoot-out. Benson would not allow us to argue FBI misconduct. That left us only a day and a half of defense.

In the middle of my trial, the government decided not to use Myrtle Poor Bear as a witness. They more or less told her: Okay, you're excused, good-by. She came to us immediately: "Hey, look, I want to tell you guys what happened." She told us about the ordeal she had been through. When she testified before the judge, we asked her:

> "Miss Poor Bear, will you please tell us whether Agent Price ever threatened you?"
> "Yes, he did."

"What did he say to you?"

"He told me that they were going to plan everything out and if I didn't do it, I was going to get hurt."

"Did anybody else ever say that to you from the FBI?"

"Bill Wood." [8]

LEONARD: The judge didn't let the jury hear that testimony. He said she wasn't a believable witness. If she were, he said, it "would shock the conscience of the court." But Benson was the one who decided what was to be believed, not the jury.

The government knew if they had used Myrtle Poor Bear as a witness, the jury would have found out all the lies the FBI told to extradite me from Canada. Since the government didn't have Myrtle Poor Bear, they had to find someone else to try to connect me with the killings. The FBI threatened three teenagers who had been with us at Oglala into testifying against me and suppressed evidence that would contradict what they said.

> BRUCE ELLISON: The government's case was that the two agents, Coler and Williams, followed a red and white van into the Jumping Bull ranch and that someone in that vehicle killed them. They claimed it was Leonard Peltier's van and that he did it. At trial, we tried to argue that other vehicles had gone onto and left the ranch. But they suppressed all of the evidence that would allow us to prove this, so that the government then argued: Look at this defense. They're trying to raise phantom vehicles that they claim carried out the people who really killed the agents.
>
> It turned out they weren't phantoms. The government suppressed reports that the agents actually followed a red pickup truck onto the ranch, not a van. And they suppressed reports from a number of agents who overheard the last transmissions of Coler and Williams, identifying an *open-backed* vehicle. We now know from FBI radio logs that within a few minutes after the agents were killed, a red pickup left the scene. Numerous other vehicles left the scene as well. Much of this information was kept from us at trial. [9]

LEONARD: They claimed that this red and white van was mine. That red and white van wasn't mine. They claimed that I was in it and the agents were chasing me. That wasn't true, either. And they almost blew it when their own lawyer asked his witness Mike Anderson:

> "And what if anything then happened?"
>
> "Well, I guess they seen the orange pickup going down that way and they followed it."
>
> "Now, when you say 'orange pickup,' is that the red and white van to which—"

The defense objected and the judge sustained it. Then:

> "Mr. Anderson, tell us what the car was."
>
> "The orange and white and red and white van that was going down the hill." [10]

Mike Anderson said he saw me by the cars where the agents were killed. But he admitted under cross-examination that he had been threatened by FBI agents.

> "And what happened at the end of that hour?"
>
> "Well, I was refusing to talk until Gary Adams said, 'If you don't talk, I will beat you up in the cell.'"
>
> "And did that make you afraid?"
>
> "Yes."
>
> "And did you understand that you would get beat up if you didn't give him the answers that he wanted?"
>
> "Yes."
>
> "And did you then give him the answers that you understood he wanted?"
>
> "Yes." [11]

Wishy Draper was another witness they coerced into testifying against me. They refused to let him call an attorney. He was tied to a chair for three hours while they interrogated him. We asked him if his testimony was something an agent told him happened, not what he actually saw or heard himself. And Wish said, "Yes, that's possible." He also admitted he lied to the grand jury.

Norman Brown was the third teenager who testified for the government. At the trial, Norman Brown admitted the FBI told him what to say.

"When you testified before the grand jury that you saw
   Leonard and Bob and Dino down by the agents' cars,
   where did you get that information?"
"FBI."
"Did you ever see that on June 26, 1975?"
"No." [12]

The FBI threatened Norman Brown's life. He was only fifteen years
old. Grown men can terrorize a kid. They can get him to say anything
they want.

> NORMAN BROWN, before the Minnesota Citizens' Review
> Commission: Two BIA policemen, they grabbed me. They put
> me against the wall, said what's your name. . . . I tried to get
> out, but they wouldn't let me out. Four FBI agents came walk-
> ing in, told me to sit down. . . . Then I gave him that paper and
> said this is my lawyer, you can call him. He said, "No, we can't
> do that." . . .
>
> We sat there a couple hours. . . . My mom, she didn't know
> what was going on. I tried to explain to her . . . but they told
> my mom they had one of the guns that I used that killed FBI
> agents. My mom said . . . "What do you do, you killed one of
> those two FBI agents?" She started crying and one of the FBI
> agents said, "Shut up." I said, "You shut up, you don't talk to
> my mom like that." They told my mom to shut up . . . that they
> were going to haul me in right now. My mom was crying. . . .
> They took handcuffs and handcuffed me.
>
> I was standing there and he said, "We'll do everything in our
> power that you rot to hell . . ." And they told my mom that she
> would never see me again, never see my family, I'd never walk
> the earth again. . . . So my mom was crying and I didn't know
> what to do there. She says, son, I don't want you put in jail.
> They kept saying Leonard Peltier. They kept saying he and
> Dino killed the agents. [13]

LEONARD: I was being railroaded. The government will never admit
that they do it, but they've done it against the Blacks. They've done it
against the labor unions. It's no fantasy. They were manipulating witnesses, suppressing evidence, and manufacturing evidence.

Dr. Robert Bloemendaal did the original autopsies. His findings indicated those agents were killed by two different weapons. That contradicted the government's argument that I killed them both. So they paid Dr. Thomas Noguchi, the flashy coroner from Los Angeles, forty thousand dollars just to come and testify at my trial. What could be worth forty thousand dollars? Noguchi testified that these agents were killed by the same high-caliber weapon. Bloemendaal didn't say anything about his original findings, that two different weapons killed the agents. And we didn't learn about his original report until after the trial.

They were claiming the weapon that killed the agents was an AR-15 rifle and that it was mine. But that rifle wasn't mine. No one even testified that it belonged to me. The government never showed that I used it. They just said it was mine, and they said it over and over.

The government said an empty shell case was found in one of the dead agent's cars. In court, Evan Hodge, the FBI ballistics specialist, claimed that the AR-15 was so severely damaged he couldn't do a firing-pin test on it to match it with that shell case. But he said he was able to take the bolt out of it, put it on another weapon, and test it that way. Evan Hodge said that was not a conclusive test. But he still told the jury the AR-15 probably killed the agents. According to the prosecutor, that was the most crucial evidence against me. The Eighth Circuit Court of Appeals said the same thing.

Well, when we were trying to cross-examine Hodge about the tests he made, the judge kept cutting us off. After the trial was over, we got the document that showed Hodge *did* do a firing-pin test on that AR-15 rifle—that is the conclusive test—and it came out *negative*. It totally discredited their "crucial" evidence, but it was too late for the jury to see.

In his summation, the prosecutor told the jury that Mike Anderson testified he saw me get out of the van and shoot the agents. Mike Anderson never said anything like that. But the judge wouldn't let our attorneys show the jury what was really in the transcript. During the trial, he wouldn't let them take notes and afterward, when they asked to see parts of the transcript, he refused.

I spent a couple of weeks preparing the statement I told Judge Benson before sentencing. I felt I had to express my feelings: "I stand before you as a proud man; I feel no guilt! I have done nothing to feel guilty about! I have no regrets of being a Native American activist—thousands of people in the United States, Canada, and around the world have and will continue to support me to expose the injustices that have occurred in this courtroom."

I still feel that way. If I ever get another chance to make a statement before him, I'll tell him again: "You decided what was to be believed and what was not to be believed—not the jury! Your conduct shocks the conscience of what the American system stands for!—*the search for truth!* by a jury of citizens. What was it that made you so afraid to let that testimony in? Your own guilt of being part of a corrupt pre-planned trial to get a conviction, no matter how your reputation would be tarnished? I strongly believe you will do the bidding of the FBI and give me two consecutive life terms." [14]

On June 1, 1977, I was sentenced to two consecutive life terms. I was dropped off right here that afternoon, at Leavenworth. I was immediately put in the hole for ten days. Then I was taken to Terre Haute and then straight to Marion and put in the hole there for about a week. I was sentenced indefinitely to the long-term behavior modification lock-up. My lawyers started filing motions. And I guess there was too much pressure, and they let me out in the prison population.

The suppression of exculpatory evidence is a constitutional violation, really. We've received about twelve thousand documents through the Freedom of Information Act that were kept from us at the trial. We selected nineteen hundred pages with the strongest incriminating evidence against the government and filed them in a brief for a new trial. If we would have had those documents in court, we'd have destroyed their whole case. By rights, by constitutional law, I should have the charges, everything dismissed. But that's not what I'm asking for. I'm asking for a new and fair trial. I'm hoping for that. I dream about it. It's the only way I can prove my innocence. It's now up to the Eighth Circuit Court of Appeals.*

I've been in jail over ten years, but I'm optimistic. The support keeps me going, you know. Now that fifty-five congressmen have filed an amicus brief in my behalf, I have some political power behind me. I still have my ups and downs. The whole case is horrifying. But I feel good that it has brought the Indian struggle in the United States to the attention of the world. I'm very proud of that, and I feel that my sacrifice has been paying off in a sense.

---

* The Eighth Circuit Court of Appeals denied Peltier's motion for a new trial shortly after this interview was conducted.

Postscript from William Kunstler,
Attorney for Leonard Peltier

On April 18, 1977, Leonard Peltier was convicted by a jury in Fargo, North Dakota, to which his case had been mysteriously shifted. After evidence of FBI misconduct had been obtained through the Freedom of Information Act, Judge Paul Benson denied Peltier a new trial. In September 1986, the three-member panel of the United States Court of Appeals for the Eighth Circuit affirmed Benson's denial.

The court's opinion, which had been released to the press a week before it was received by Peltier's counsel, is a masterpiece of outrageous sophistry and intellectual dishonesty. The panel found that "the prosecution withheld evidence from the defense favorable to Peltier, and that, had this evidence been available to the defendant, it would have allowed him to cross-examine government witnesses more effectively." In addition, it stressed that the newly discovered evidence indicated "Hodge may not have been telling the truth" in his hearing and trial testimony. Moreover, it went on to point out that if the prosecution had not withheld the suppressed reports, key evidentiary rulings by Benson, which prevented the defense from adequately exploring the unknown inconsistencies, might well have been different. "In any event," it said, "the defense would have had substantial additional documentary evidence upon which to cross-examine Hodge, and would have had greater reason to pursue the inconsistencies more vigorously than it did."

Incredibly, however, although it expressed "discomfort with our decision," it refused to grant Peltier a new trial. "There is a possibility," it held, "that the jury would have acquitted Leonard Peltier had the records and the data improperly withheld from the defense been available to him in order to better exploit and reinforce the inconsistencies casting strong doubts upon the government's case." Yet, it went on to conclude that it was not convinced that "the jury probably would have reached a different result."

Sitting Bull and Crazy Horse had their Seventh Cavalry—Leonard Peltier his Eighth Circuit.

Part III
The Face of a Police State

Introduction to Part III

The image of a police state is one of a nation in which police act arbitrarily, violently, and with impunity against opponents of the state; in which the body politic is subject to surveillance and harassment by networks of secret police; and in which persons are interned, kept apart from others in prisons or concentration camps, for no reason other than their ethnic identity or their political views.

In the United States, our heritage of respect for civil liberties is rich, deep, and long-lasting. But for those perceived as a threat to the status quo, the reality has been different. Many dissenters have faced attacks that bear the unmistakable imprint of police-state repression. Police violence against Black activists in the 1960s was as unchecked and deadly as it was against labor organizers early in the century. The Everett and Orangeburg massacres are separated by more than fifty years, but both Jack Miller and Cleveland Sellers describe the fury of police violence that they—not the police—were held responsible for. Although the two attacks occurred in different times, in different contexts, and in different struggles, in both cases, as in other instances, police were able to run amok with impunity.

Political police have become secreted in bureaucracies that are virtually impenetrable. They are protected as well by a self-generated and self-righteous mystique of patriotism and infallibility. The proliferation of police and investigative agencies within many departments of the national government and within state and local governments, the variety of their methods and targets, and their collusion with vigilantes of one stripe or another testify to the depth to which they have permeated American political life. To borrow words from Harvey O'Connor (Part II), democracy is stood on its head when government agents can, without your knowledge, invade your personal life and study your every move, while they themselves operate beyond detection and even beyond the law.

The Federal Bureau of Investigation is the most well known and perhaps the mainstay of America's political police. The bureau sustained a campaign across several decades to disrupt Frank Wilkinson's political activities, to curtail his right to address his fellow citizens about matters that sharply disagreed with FBI policy—in this case, the abolition of the House Un-American Activities Committee. This campaign was conducted in secret. The FBI subverted Jack O'Dell's position within the Southern Christian Leadership Conference and used him to weaken the force of Martin Luther King's leadership of the civil rights movement and to divert the movement itself. This was also done in secret. The implications are ominous: In the cases of both Wilkinson and O'Dell, state power was secretly directed against the constitutionally protected activities of citizens seeking changes in government policies, changes that, ironically, most now accept as proper.

In recent times, grand juries have been used to expand the FBI's considerable authority beyond its legal mandate. Converted from a tribunal to protect the accused from unwarranted arrests, the grand jury became a powerful weapon to quiet dissent. When Jill Raymond and others refused to answer the bureau's questions, a right guaranteed by law, the Justice Department that houses the FBI subpoenaed them before a federal grand jury where they could be—and were—imprisoned for refusing to answer the same questions. "It is not too much to say," Frank Donner commented, "that during its heyday, the period from 1970 to 1974, the grand jury became a police-state instrument."[1]

Whatever local political police may have lacked in sophistication, compared to their federal big brothers, they have made up for in zeal. Federal agencies were complemented by local "red squads" that also pursued their political intelligence work in secret. In Los Angeles, they did more. Seymour Myerson tells of the seemingly limitless illegal harassment of his political activities and of the frustration he encountered in trying to get the Los Angeles Police Department to examine its own violations. His story makes an additional point: the problem of police overseeing police activities.

Some occasions seem to attract an extraordinary concentration of political police. FBI informants were joined by local, state, and national undercover agents who converged on the Vietnam Veterans Against the War as this group prepared to demonstrate at the Republican Convention that renominated Richard Nixon. Opposition to the Vietnam war by combat veterans was as impermissible as it was embarrassing to a Nixon administration that was not at all averse to the use of secret police. "Before, I used to be so open that anybody could come to my house," Scott Camil, the VVAW leader, said. "And they just filled the place up with cops."

The power of secret agencies is extended by their connections with the political right. J. Edgar Hoover cultivated conservative journalists to whom he leaked secretly garnered information about political opponents such as Frank Wilkinson and Jack O'Dell. Jay Paul, an agent of the same Los Angeles red squad that harassed Seymour Myerson, handed over many of the squad's files on political activists to Western Goals, a right-wing communication network with ties to the John Birch Society. Western Goals then circulated that and other information about radical and liberal political activists to local police forces.[2] The story related by Paul Bermanzohn is one of police collusion with the Klan and American Nazis, this time involving agents and informants who were supposedly monitoring the right-wing groups. In this case, the resulting violence took the lives of five anti-Klan demonstrators and almost cost Bermanzohn and others their lives as well.

As perhaps one of the most glaring examples of police-state actions, the arbitrary and wholesale internment of citizens by the military flies in the face of American ideals. Nevertheless, during World War II, a time of both great patriotic fervor and intense racism against Asian Americans, such internments took place. In what Minoru Yasui called "Watergate before Watergate," the War Department deceived the Supreme Court about the seriousness of the military threat and the danger Japanese American citizens and noncitizens posed to the national defense. One hundred twenty thousand people were rousted from their homes, deprived of their livelihoods and possessions, and shipped off to camps; they were imprisoned without trials or convictions, without even having charges filed against them. Few now are proud of that moment in our history. In 1988, Congress apologized and partially reimbursed internees for their financial losses. But when Minoru Yasui and several others like him fought the horrendous constitutional violation in the 1940s, they were imprisoned.

JACK MILLER

Police Unleashed

The Everett Massacre, 1916

Jack Miller

The violence of company police, deputized vigilantes, and local and state police, frequently acting as employer agents, made the efforts to unionize American workers a risk to life and safety. Sometimes, violent events were so outrageously brutal that they came to be known in labor history and lore as massacres.

May 30, 1937—the Memorial Day Massacre. A thousand persons gather in support of striking steel workers at Republic Steel's South Chicago mill. Men, women, and children assemble for a parade to the plant. Suddenly, there is a roar of gunfire. Then uniformed police charge with nightsticks and tear gas. Ten are dead. Scores are wounded.

April 20, 1914—the Ludlow Massacre. Striking miners, evicted from their company-owned homes, live in a tent colony at Ludlow, Colorado. During the night, company gunmen and members of the National Guard drench the tents with oil, set them afire, and machine-gun the miners and their wives and children as they try to escape. Thirteen children, a woman, and five men die that Easter night.

March 7, 1932—the Dearborn Massacre. Unemployed auto workers begin a hunger march to the Dearborn, Michigan, plant of Ford Motors to present petitions to get their jobs back. From a bridge and the roadside, they are met with fire hoses, tear gas, and then the pistols of the Dearborn police and Ford's private security force. Three men are

*killed. Retreating workers are sprayed with machine-gun fire. Another
is killed, and many lie wounded on the ground.*

*November 5, 1916—the Everett Massacre. The Puget Sound ferry-
boat* Verona *docks at Everett, Washington, with more than two hundred Wobblies on board. Before they can step ashore, a hail of gunfire
from Sheriff McRae and his deputies leaves five known dead and others
lost in the waters of the sound. The Industrial Workers of the World,
the Wobblies, faced assaults from state and local police throughout the
West, where they organized lumber, mining, and farm workers. Jack
Miller, a vigorous and enthusiastic Wobbly at ninety-five, is the last
living survivor of the Everett Massacre.*

I was a volunteer organizer for the United Mine Workers in 1908,
1909. The United Mine Workers didn't want the operators to know
what was going on, so it was very clandestine. I was an agitator, really,
and it was just as dangerous then to do something like that as it was to
belong to the Wobblies. I was either told to get out, or was escorted out,
or sometimes rather forcibly expelled from every coal-mining camp in
that Cumberland Valley division of Virginia.

Two of us would go into the camp as partners. When we got there,
we wouldn't "know" each other whatsoever. I was the one who did the
talking. Then, if I didn't appear in front of the company store between
five-thirty and six o'clock in the evening, my partner's job was to find
out where I was. He usually knew where to look first, down in the little
calaboose. We were taught how to defend ourselves in the "justice"
courts, because if they got hold of a union agitator, they loved to throw
the book at him. Even a vagrancy charge could lead to eleven months
and twenty-nine days.

The year Halley's comet was here, 1910, I became a Billy Sunday
convert. He had great powers of description. He was a master of slang
and would use it in all his sermons. He had a choir made up of all the
best voices in Danville, led by that great conductor Fred Fisher. Then he
had a building—it must have been two hundred fifty feet long by fifty
feet wide—with just benches. That was the tabernacle I was converted in.

Billy Sunday had come for six weeks, and I heard him every night he
preached. And honestly, I was fool enough to be quite sincere in this.
They organized a young men's Bible class, and I was elected president.

Well, if anybody had asked me to quote a verse from the Bible, I could have said, "Jesus wept," but I wouldn't have been sure of any other.

I started to study the Bible. The first chapter of Genesis didn't go down so bad. It seemed to me a reasonable story people would tell about creation. No orders, no rules were laid down except to "be fruitful and multiply." And I was quite willing. Then I started to read the second chapter of Genesis, and right away this plain creator had disappeared entirely. It opened up by calling him *Lord* God and *King* God. And rules began coming down on us like snowflakes in a Dakota blizzard.

I went back to the church and asked them questions. They'd say, "You have to pray for better pay. You have to pray for greater faith." Finally I got sore. "Listen, if I'm going to teach the Bible, I have to have some of these things that seem unreasonable explained, or I'm not going to do it." They said, "That's no attitude at all for a Christian." Well, I told them what they could do. I remember later, during the Palmer raids, Billy Sunday said, "Put radicals on ships of stone, with sails of lead, and make Hell the first port of call." That, I suppose, was the good Christian spirit.

I hit the road shortly afterward and wound up in Calgary. Now, I didn't know beforehand that you better have your stake made if you were going to spend a winter in Canada. There were very few jobs and, boy, was it cold and shivery! I was partnering with a guy in what they called a "crumborium," where people slept on shelves for fifteen cents a night and were sure to become lousy.

I felt like a big hunk of nothing, a lost soul with no place to go, no reason for existence. Then some Wobbly said to me, "Hey, Jack, let's get in here and listen to this Socialist spout off. We'll be out of the cold, anyhow." So we went in. That night the Socialist was starting a series of six weekly lectures based on the book *From Nebula to Man*. I took in those six lectures and was so impressed that I joined the Socialist Party. My education was carried on jointly by the Socialists and the IWW. They had a long hall. On one side the Wobblies met, and on the other side the Socialists met. They had a table sitting out there with literature from both organizations.

If they got anybody who they thought was interested—and they saw I listened to everything attentively—right away they would label him a "student." They had no mercy on me. Four or five of them would get around that little table, with me facing them, either the IWW or the

Socialists. They would throw questions at me that I had no idea how to answer. They told me it was my duty to find the answers. Well, I got a very good grounding in Marx. I also got Darwin, the various sciences, and a little smidgen of astronomy—enough to arouse my curiosity. From that time on, I was a student.

Down in Minot, North Dakota, my real education commenced. They were building a normal school there. The contractor just thought he had everything his own way, with all the harvest hands unemployed and hungry, waiting for work. But a few Wobblies got in there and organized a strike. Then, bingo! The city and the county officials declared war on the strikers, and they had a free speech fight on their hands.*

Well, I thought, "You're a hell of a rebel if you haven't had your baptismal, your first free speech fight. You better go up there and take part in it." That night I got on a freight train. When it stopped at Minot, I knew enough to dodge the authorities. I stayed in a big bin off in the coal yard till daylight.

Then I went down Main Street. They were paving it with wooden blocks and had them piled up alongside the curb. No free speechers were there yet, so I jumped up on one of those piles and said, "Friends, comrades, and fellow workers!" I didn't know what else I was going to say, but I didn't have to worry about it. Two cops came and dragged me off.

I asked, "Am I under arrest?"

They said, "No."

I said, "Don't you think you'd better take your hands off me?"

"Well, you can't talk up there."

"Why? Is it against the United States Constitution?" So they let go of me, and I went down a ways, and I got up on the blocks again. A few seconds later, there were five or six of them, all ganging up on me. Oh, I was a bloody sight! I got a scalp wound, and the blood came down my arm. I started to wipe the blood off with my hand and smeared it all over my clothes. Two ladies came up to the cops. One said, "You should be ashamed of yourself, mercilessly beating this man." I don't know why, but that turned the tide. Those people who had been indifferent to

---

* The IWW's organizing campaigns were often met with police harassment and city ordinances that forbade the Wobblies to make speeches in public streets or parks. The IWW resisted the restrictions by organizing free speech fights that brought hundreds of Wobblies to the offending town or city to exercise their rights: as soon as one soapbox orator was arrested, another would quickly take the speaker's place, until the jails were filled and the local police and the court system were strained to the breaking point.

the Wobblies or against them began heaving bricks down at these uniformed policemen. They took me to the can, and I was there until the free speech fight was settled.

That same year, I was in the harvest field. I joined Local 400 of the Agricultural Workers Union. We were fighting for four dollars a day in wages. Now I was ready for the IWW. I'd been trying to get a card all through Kansas. They had a branch open in Omaha, so I went in there, and Albert Prashner signed me up. I got my card on July 12, 1916, made out to Jack Leonard. My full name is John Leonard Miller, but that was too much of a handle for a Wobbly.

I stopped there to rest a day or two, and then went on to Council Bluffs. There were twenty-one of us who took possession of a flatcar attached to a freight train right there in the yards. When the head brakeman came through, he tried to collect money from us for the privilege of riding "his" train. When we refused, he invited us to unload. We told him he didn't own the train, to go back and do the job he was paid for. He swung a big braking stick and hit the guy sitting next to me. As the stick went past, I grabbed hold of it, jerked it out of his hands, and threw it into the swamp. He put down more feet than a centipede, running for help. Pretty soon he came back with the flame crew, the switchmen—everybody came. They were rather reluctant about it, but the brakeman started telling me what he was going to do to me.

I said, "I know you're big enough and dirty enough to do what you say. There's just one trouble—you don't have the guts to try it." He weighed about two hundred pounds, and I was skinny enough to haunt a house. I showed a lot of courage and not much judgment. But I had had a little experience as a wrestler, and there was swamp down there where his strength wouldn't count. I made up my mind that we were going to wind up in that swamp, and he was going to be on the bottom.

He put his head down, just as I hoped he would, and came in swinging. I put my knee under his chin, and then I hip-locked him. I threw him over, and we went down there, rolling in the swamp together. Then I gave that extra heave to put him on the bottom. We were in shallow water, but it was soft mud, and he couldn't get a purchase to get out of it. Every time he started to say something, I shoved his head under the water. And boy, that guy got seasick right there, a thousand miles from the ocean.

Later that afternoon, without any molestation, we got another freight train over to the Missouri Valley, where we did some harvesting. I was carrying what we called the "rigging," the IWW credentials.

I signed up fifty IWWs—that was no trick in those days—and was winding up the harvest and threshing at Chester, Montana. Some Wobbly came through: "All footloose rebels head for the free speech fight at Yakima."

The snow was on the ground already, and it was cold. That night it was thirty below zero, and we had to cross the summit where it got down to forty or fifty below. But these enthusiastic Wobblies, not knowing what they were up against, wanted to go right then. I said, "You better wait for good weather." No, they wouldn't do it. Well, I made them gather up enough food to last for a couple of days. We had one thin blanket between the six of us, so we exercised as much as we could to keep our blood in circulation. It was a terrible journey, but we made it to Washington. We got to Yakima one day late.

There, they suggested we go to Seattle and report for the Everett free speech fight. The shingle weavers were on strike in Everett. The sheriff, Don McRae, and his drunken deputies would take the strikers out to the woods, beat them up, and run them out of town. Don McRae took his orders from the Commercial Club. The Commercial Club was run by the lumber trust. And all these groups were organized against the shingle weavers.*

Well, the IWW always went to the rescue, especially of small unions. They would support them financially and give them help on the picket line. They opened up an office for the lumber workers. There was a speakers' corner in Everett, at Hewitt and Wetmore streets, where all sorts of groups spoke. But when the IWW came, they passed an emergency ordinance, overnight, that there would be no more speech making there.

On October 30, 1916, forty-one of us left Seattle on the ferry boat, the *Verona*, intending to exercise our freedom of speech at Hewitt and Wetmore. We were met at the dock by Don McRae and his deputies. I saw Don McRae about twenty-five times, and I believe he was sober on only two of those occasions. They took us off the boat and into a warehouse on the dock. I remember Don McRae saying, "Hah, I don't think these boys will come to Everett again."

Some fellow worker said, "Well, sheriff, we're only up here in pur-

---

* Shingle weavers were the sawyers, filers, and packers who worked as a crew to produce red cedar shingles. After 1900, mill technology introduced saws that made this a very dangerous and bloody occupation. The Shingle Weavers Union became the largest and strongest union in Everett.

suance of our constitutional right." "To hell with the Constitution," said McRae, the sheriff of Snohomish County. "You're in Everett now."

They loaded us into private cars and took us out to Beverly Park. Never at any time in Beverly Park did I hear the word "arrest" used. So we were not under arrest. We were being abducted. It was dark and it was raining, and we were right beside the interurban tracks. At least a hundred of McRae's deputies were lined up on each side of the roadway, armed with every kind of cudgel: billy clubs, baseball bats, ax handles, rifles. They ran us through that gauntlet, one at a time.

One of them said to me, "Oh, my God, if I knew what they were going to do, I'd never have come out here." I looked at him, and I remember saying, cold and unemotional, "Well, listen, mister, you can't play in shit without getting your hands dirty." I had nothing but contempt for those guys who made a living from something like that, people so lowdown they would have to get up on a high stepladder to shake hands with a snake.

I saw three men go through. Now it was my turn. I made up my mind: By God, I'm going to go through that standing up, or they'll have to drag me. I was just determined. I walked down to that first pair. They tried to shove me off balance, but I guarded against that. Both of them had big long clubs. When one of them swung, I ducked and stepped very quickly to the next. I got by him, using the same trick. The third one— now, don't ask me why I was wearing a necktie that night—grabbed me by the necktie, and I felt a blow come on the top of my head and another under my eye. I didn't remember another thing until I came to, down at the end of the line. I know there was a long lapse of time because I had been the fourth man to walk the gauntlet, but by now nearly everybody else was through.

Things began to register. They said, "Run, you son of a bitch, run!" I said, "I can't run."

"Run anyhow!" And they forced me across the sharp blades of the cattle guard. Thirty-one of us were treated at the hospital for injuries that we'd received because we wanted to exercise our right of free speech.

We decided that next Sunday a whole boatload of us would go up to Everett in daylight. We *were* going to hold that meeting up at Hewitt and Wetmore. Abe Rabinowitz, a delightful character with a sense of humor, said, "They may kill us, but they can't eat us. We're too tough for that." Abe was killed that day.

Practically everybody on the *Verona* was a Wobbly. There were so many of us that some followed in a second boat, the *Calista*. It was a two-hour run, and we sang all the way. We sang songs like "Hold the Fort" and "Solidarity." We were singing when the *Verona* whistled, coming into Everett. When the boat came to the dock, as many as could left the cabin to get out. There must have been a hundred or more men on the little forward deck. I was cold, so I'd been down below the freight deck, behind the galley. I came up on the port side in time to see everything of importance and hear everything of importance.

I saw Don McRae standing there with one hand in the air and the other on his belt, near his pistol. His belly wasn't hard to see. He called out to the boat, "Who's your leader?"

The reply came from the boat: "We are all leaders!"

He said, "You can't land here."

Someone said, "The hell we can't!" And at that McRae turned to face the deputies with a hand up in the air as if he were signaling. A single shot came first, followed by a volley. Now, all of the people on that forward deck, in that momentary panic, rushed to the starboard side. And the boat sharply listed. A railing broke, and several men went into the water. I guess nobody will ever know how many fell in. I know for sure that only one got back on the boat. Some people on the dock wanted to launch rowboats to rescue those in the water. They were not allowed to do it by those drunken bastards, the deputies who were shooting at the men swimming in the water and shooting toward the boat. Volley after volley came out in continuous fire off the dock.

After the shooting started, I went back down below. I saw Billings and Ben Legg go past the galley and into the engine room, where they found the engineer hiding behind the boilers. They pulled a gun on him. I could see this, but I couldn't hear it—there was too much shooting and screaming. Then I saw the engineer come up toward the engines. Shortly after that I felt the boat move. That's what saved the lives of the rest of us. As soon as that boat started moving, somebody went to find the captain. There were fourteen bullets that went through the port window by the wheel, any of which could have hit him. They found the captain in his quarters, hiding behind the safe with a mattress over his head. After we were out of immediate range, he took the wheel, and we turned around.

We had no first aid. The wounded just had to suffer it out till we got to Seattle. We couldn't save either one of the guys who died on the way back. Then we met the *Calista*. Jim Thompson, the most convincing speaker we had, the man who invented the clenched fist, was on that boat, along with some of the other speakers. We told them, "For Christ's sake, keep away from Everett! They're nuts up there." One of the important things we did was to turn that boat around.

In Seattle, we were met by the militia. They took us from the old Coleman Dock and marched us up Fourth Avenue. If you go along Fourth Avenue today, under the viaduct, you'll find an old boarded-up building. It's the old city hall. They booked us, put us on the elevator a few at a time, and sent us to the jail on the fifth floor. Our wounded went to the floor just below us. The city hospital was down there.

They had so many of us in one tank that there wasn't room for all of us to lie down on the floor. We finally managed to lie in a row with our heads against the wall. The second row would lie with their head and shoulders on the hips of those in the first row. The third row would lie with their head and shoulders on the second row. That way we made room for all of us, but of course it was awful inconvenient to turn over or do anything else. That was the way they housed us for three days.

Word had come down from Everett that we were to have bread and coffee once a day. That's all we got to eat until we were sufficiently organized to "build a battleship." And when the IWW built battleships, they were quite different from those that were built down at the waterfront.

To build this one, we got in the middle of the floor, twenty of us, and joined arms at the elbows. Then, on the count of three, we jumped as high as we could and all came down in one place. You take twenty people who average a hundred fifty pounds and you have a three-thousand-pound battering ram. It wasn't long before the other fellows around there wanted to join in the fun. We had everybody in that tank at that one place, all those feet coming down there at once. One, two, three, boom!

In a little while, they got wise in the other tanks to what we were doing and started to do the same thing. Finally, we got synchronized. The vibration could be felt all though the building. No building was ever made to stand such a stress as that. The first thing they did was come up and say, "You guys cut that out, or we'll turn the fire hose on you."

Somebody from our crew said, "Hurry up, or we'll soon have a hole in the floor for the water to go through." When that threat didn't work, they appealed to our "better nature." "You got comrades down in the hospital below. Some of them are almost dying, and this noise up here is going to kill them."

One of us said, "Don't you believe it. If those fellow workers hear us fighting up here, they'll get up out of their damn beds and join us."

Pretty soon they called the chief of police, and he brought the mayor, Hi Gill. Hi Gill said, "What are you complaining about?" By this time, somebody had pushed me up ahead. I said, "They're feeding us bread and coffee once a day." Gill turned to the jailer: "Who gave that order here?"

"It came from Everett."

He said, "Since when is the sheriff of Snohomish County running the city jail in Seattle? I want these men fed regular jail fare now." And he sent out for a good hot meal right then.

When they wanted to finger the IWW leaders, they put this Pinkerton stoolie and two others in a special cell with a four-inch opening. We couldn't see in, but they could see out. As we walked by them, they chose the "leaders" by putting up two fingers through the hole for "no" and three for "yes." I had been in the IWW for four months as a rank-and-file member. Yet I was picked as one of the "leaders." Happy Sopel, who had been in so many free speech fights and had been clubbed up so much that he wasn't mentally right, was one of the "leaders." There was a sixteen-year-old kid who was one of the "leaders." At least two who were picked were not even IWW members.

The prosecutor charged seventy-four of us who were fingered with first-degree murder of a deputy, Jefferson Beard. They took forty-one of us up to the Everett jail. The other thirty-three followed later. The age of the Wobblies in prison there ranged from the sixteen-year-old boy to men approaching sixty. There were migratory workers and resident workers; and some of them had worked at so many different jobs and at such a variety of crafts that I honestly believe that, given the tools and materials, they could have built a city complete with all utilities.

The jailers had been used to turning one prisoner against another by playing favorites. But we had no more than got into the jail when we organized. Every week we would elect a different committee of three, and they were the only ones who would speak to the jailer. Oh, yes, we were human beings. There were differences of opinion and some quarreling, but let any issue arise between any one of us and the jailers, then we were at once united and all personal differences forgotten.

The first clash we had was because they were feeding us worse slop than farmers threw their hogs. Our breakfast in the morning was moldy, half-cooked mush. One time, they fed us some beans that were sour.

During the night, we were all seized with cramps and diarrhea. We only had one toilet and some buckets for all of us. Do you know what that means, one toilet on the floor for seventy-four people with diarrhea?

We took the rest of the sour beans and plastered the wall of the brand-new jail with them. It made an awful mess. Then someone found that there was about three-quarters of an inch slack in the locking mechanism on our doors. So all twenty men on each side of the corridor threw their weight against this slack until nine of the ten doors were forced open. Then we bent the bars back with blankets rolled into rope, so the doors could never be locked again while I was there. That was our second "battleship." There were no two Wobbly battleships built the same way. From then on, we got pretty good grub.

We asked for a change of venue. They didn't fight it very hard because we were ready to prove that the two judges in Everett were down on the dock with McRae on November fifth. Then twenty-five of us, who were to be witnesses, were moved back to the Seattle jail.

On International Labor Day, 1917, people from all over the world were coming to Seattle. The Russian Revolution had just come into being, and many of them were going through Seattle and Vladivostok to get there. That May Day morning, they all congregated down at the Wobbly Hall, marched out through the main part of town, and went up to Mount Pleasant Cemetery, where three fellow workers killed on the *Verona* were buried.

Coming back, they headed to the King County jail at the top of Profanity Hill, where the twenty-five of us were incarcerated. They came marching up that hill. We felt the sounds before they became recognizable as such. Then we could tell from the cadence, somebody was singing. A minute later, when they came into good hearing, we could make out the air; it was the "Internationale," a good revolutionary song in those days. They were singing it in four distinct languages. We answered back from inside the jail with an IWW song. Back and forth we sang to each other until dark. That was one of the greatest thrills I ever had.

Under the law in the state of Washington, we could choose separate trials. Just imagine how long it would take and how much it would cost them, one trial at a time, for seventy-four cases. The state started with the trial of Thomas H. Tracy. The prosecution went first. They had a witness, a Judas among us, who was supposed to put the finger on Tracy as the killer. Instead, when they asked if he had seen anyone armed on the *Verona,* he pointed to someone other than Tracy. "There is the man," he said. After examination of scores of prosecution witnesses, no one was sure who had killed the deputy we were accused of doing in. We were convinced he had stopped a bullet fired by his own side.

Billings testified that he used his gun to force the engineer to move the *Verona* back from the dock, away from the volley of bullets. When George Vanderveer, our lawyer, asked him why he carried a gun on November fifth, he told of his beating at Beverly Park. Billings said, "I didn't intend to let anybody beat me up like I was beaten on October thirtieth." I was called to the stand to verify that Billings and Legg had gone and forced the engineer, who had left us at the mercy of McRae, to back the boat out.

It was a coincidence. That damned figure five kept going through everything. We brought back five dead men on the *Verona*. It happened on the fifth of November. The trial started on the fifth of the month. It finally came to an end on May 5, 1917, with the acquittal of Thomas H. Tracy. With Snohomish County broke, they dropped the charges on the rest of us and turned us loose. No one was ever charged with the murders of the Wobblies.

You lock a man up for the length of time we were in jail and that's not funny. There's far more bad things that happen than good. And if you let go of yourself, you could go crazy. You could come out with such an embittered hatred that your life would be miserable from then on. But we were a bunch of determined and spirited Wobblies. We laughed lest we weep.

The Orangeburg Massacre, 1968

Cleveland Sellers

The Constitution notwithstanding, local and state governments have re-
sorted to police violence to silence dissenters. Those organizing unions
felt its raw force in the first three decades of the century. Those in the
Black freedom movement lived with the knowledge that their lives were
constantly endangered by the complicity of vigilantes and police. As
Black and white students in the 1960s demanded fundamental changes,
they met with violent responses.

On May 4, 1970, after several days of demonstrations against the
U.S. invasion of Cambodia, Ohio National Guardsmen shot tear gas
into a peaceful rally on the Kent State University campus. Students pro-
tested, some threw rocks. The guardsmen advanced to a commanding
position on a nearby hill, turned, and without warning opened fire on
students who were the distance of a football field away. They killed
four, wounded nine, left one paralyzed from the waist down. Just ten
days later, on May 14, 1970, after students had engaged in demonstra-
tions and several confrontations provoked by frustration with the expe-
rience of racism in their daily lives, police and the state highway patrol
entered the campus of Jackson State, a Black college in Mississippi.
Again without warning, they fired a barrage of shotguns, carbines, ri-
fles, and submachine guns into a crowded dormitory. More than 150
rounds were spent. Two students were killed and twelve wounded.

CLEVELAND SELLERS

But these killings were not the first on American campuses. Two years earlier, state militia had fired into another group of Black students at the segregated South Carolina State College at Orangeburg. National attention was not focused on this tragedy, but its reverberations are still felt in the Black community. Three young men were killed and twenty-seven students were wounded. Cleveland Sellers, a national leader of the Student Nonviolent Coordinating Committee (SNCC), was among the wounded at the Orangeburg Massacre and was made its scapegoat.

———————

On the night of February 8, 1968, state troopers fired without warning into an unarmed group of students on the campus of South Carolina State College, wounding many and killing three. Shocked officials from a number of Black colleges wrote Lyndon Johnson: "Demonstrators seeking freedom were killed in the Boston Massacre in 1770: A Negro was the first to die there. In February 1968, freedom seekers led by Negroes were again fired upon and killed—this time in Orangeburg, South Carolina." [1] In a lot of communities in South Carolina, the Orangeburg Massacre and the memory of the three slain students are still very vivid.

My own origin with the civil rights movement goes back to the small rural town of Denmark, South Carolina. It was rigidly segregated, and my total existence—where I lived, where I played, where I went to school—went on in the Black community. To keep the schools segregated, the county had arranged for Blacks to attend high school at Voorhees College.

The college was founded by a Black woman, Elizabeth Evelyn Wright, and was built in the image of Tuskegee Institute. Emphasis was always placed on Black leaders such as Frederick Douglass, Booker T. Washington, George Washington Carver, and W. E. B. Du Bois. The school's objective was to prepare students to go out in the world to seek change, to dedicate yourself to the betterment of your people. But the underlying feeling was that we should be patient and not go too fast.

We used to discuss issues fairly openly during current events. When Emmett Till was murdered for whistling at a white woman, we talked a lot about it. Emmett was about the same age we were. *Jet* magazine ran pictures of him. One showed his bloated body after his murder, all distorted and disfigured. The act was so grotesque, so outrageous, that many of us felt something had to change and we had to see that it did.

Then came the sit-ins of 1960, and Voorhees students got swept up in that. The student union was jampacked each night after the sit-ins. We'd watch the events of the day on television. When I saw pictures of students being beaten and dragged through the streets by their hair, I became incensed. I had a burning desire to get involved.

We had our own sit-ins two weeks later. Although I was three years younger than the others, I was in on the planning of it. Seven students went into a drugstore in downtown Denmark. When they were arrested, another demonstration was planned. This time, seventy-five of us, dressed in our finest, marched three miles to town. State police and National Guardsmen watched as we passed hundreds of Black people who lined the route, mostly silent. We marched in silence, too. It was very dramatic.

I graduated from high school in 1962 and went to Howard University, which I thought would be throbbing with civil rights activity. I was terribly disappointed. Most of the students had a nonpolitical, social-climbing mentality. Through the Episcopal organization, I became part of a small group that later joined with NAG, the Nonviolent Action Group. Ivanhoe Donaldson, Stokely Carmichael, Charlie Cobb, Muriel Tillinghast, Cynthia Washington, and a number of others were part of NAG. We fought to bring people like Bayard Rustin and Malcolm X on campus. And we worked closely with the Washington, D.C., SNCC office. When people were murdered and atrocities committed during the voter registration drive, we would picket the Justice Department and the White House. In the summer of 1963, we helped prepare for the March on Washington.

We protested when George Wallace came to Cambridge, Maryland. They had had martial law there for about a year, and Blacks had been beaten and fired upon. As we marched, the National Guard used a nauseating teargas mix on us. My throat and stomach felt as if they were on fire. Some people were so disoriented they became hysterical. We were arrested by the military and held for three to four days at the Pikeville National Guard Armory. That was my first arrest for a civil rights activity.

I was losing time in my class work and had to make some choices. It wasn't hard. The summer of '64 was approaching, the summer of the Mississippi Freedom Project, which planned to register voters, operate freedom schools, and organize the Mississippi Freedom Democratic Party. We went around to all the major universities, trying to recruit people to go south. A group of about thirty of us from NAG went to Oxford, Ohio, for orientation, to get ready to go on the line.

Three civil rights workers, Michael Schwerner, Andrew Goodman, and James Chaney, had left a couple of days early to investigate a church bombing in Mississippi. They disappeared. We were afraid something very bad had happened. We put together a search team, eight or nine of us, and went to Philadelphia, Mississippi. During the daylight we would hide in a barn or under a house. At night we'd look for them. We wore dark clothes, no shiny stuff. We'd travel along dirt roads with lights out to avoid Klansmen and police who patrolled the main roads. We searched deserted houses, not knowing whether someone in there was holding them hostage. We searched swamps, creeks, and underbrush but couldn't find them. We knew at that point that we were not going to find those three alive.

When they were finally found murdered, buried in an earthfill dam, I remember the terrible pain I had in my stomach. It was hard to rest or forget what happened. I remained in Mississippi and ended up in Holly Springs, where Ivanhoe Donaldson was project director. Then Ivanhoe was transferred to Atlanta, and I took over his job. That summer we had another tragedy, a very suspicious automobile accident. One person was killed and another was badly injured. When we got to the hospital, we found it completely surrounded by police. Wayne Yancey, who died, was still in the ambulance, without any medical treatment. They had left him sitting there so long, his blood ran down through the ambulance. We saw it leaking from underneath. Charlie Scales might have died of neglect, too, if we hadn't moved him from that hospital to Memphis.

Once, three carloads of us got stopped in Oxford, Mississippi. The sheriff pulled each of us out of the car and was just ranting and raving. As he talked, the crowd got larger and larger and moved closer and closer. William Kunstler's daughter Karen was there, and the sheriff called her all kinds of nasty names: "Slut!" "Nigger lover!" He was really riling up the crowd, which was tremendously hostile. We were kept there about an hour and a half and then released.

When we left, there was a patrol car in the front of us and one in back. Once we got past the city limits, they pulled away, and as far back as we could see, there were car lights. We knew they would try to catch us on the way back. Sure enough, when we got five miles outside of Oxford, they had several cars blocking the right lane. We held our breath and squeezed through the left lane, speeding back to Holly Springs fast enough to beat our pursuers. It was a very close call.

It was not uncommon to have to run for your life. We were shown cars that were shot up in the back and sides and had all the windows blown out of them. We had to have elaborate security arrangements. We had CBs. No lights in the cars when we opened the door at night. In some cars, you could even switch off the tail lights. Others were made with larger engines. All that was not for play. It meant our lives.

Throughout Mississippi, there were bombings, fires, and beatings every day. People were getting blown out of their offices and homes. We probably lost about sixty or seventy Black churches from fires and explosions. Even in our area, which was considered "moderate," a school and a couple of churches were burned down. In McComb, Natchez, and many other places, it was very, very rough.

The Mississippi experience was almost like being in a war zone. You were constantly under attack. It forced us closer and closer together. We depended on one another so much we exhausted each other, giving so much we had nothing left for ourselves. A lot of folks ended up with the classic war neurosis.

The federal government and its agents would not intercede in our behalf in any incident that took place. They knew of the illegal brutality against us. The FBI even described it in their reports: "The Student Nonviolent Coordinating Committee (SNCC) was created in 1960 as a nonviolent civil rights movement primarily devoted to direct-action, voter-registration campaigns for the Negro in the Deep South. While attracting the most militant workers, both Negro and white, it practiced nonviolence despite repeated incidents where SNCC followers were clubbed, tear-gassed, beaten, whipped, shot, and even killed." [2]

They knew all of this, but they did not do anything to protect our human rights or civil rights. We saw that.

And we knew where the local law-enforcement people stood. The Chaney, Goodman, Schwerner murders, where the sheriff and the deputies were involved, made it crystal clear that we couldn't go to them for any kind of protection. Our protection was with the Black community. In a lot of instances when there was trouble or we had to stay low for a while, people would shelter us as we moved from house to house. They fed us, they consoled us, they tried to keep us straight when the pressures caused our commitment to weaken. That was our salvation.

I remember one time we knocked on an older woman's door. "We are civil rights workers, and the police are looking for us." She didn't say a word. She just moved to one side, let us in, and went to the kitchen to finish what she had been doing. Another time, I stayed with a very poor family in Marks, Mississippi. They had a two-room house with dirt floors. But I was not familiar with the house and didn't realize they were all cramped up in the back so I could have the front room.

It was not an easy thing for a family to take us in. To be associated with a civil rights worker could cost them their jobs. They might have their home shot up. But people would support us because they felt our work and activities were genuine. They saw our efforts to set up community centers and freedom schools for the young kids. We taught illiterate adults how to read. We investigated suspicious killings. We encouraged high school students to go to college. If a family needed help to bring in their crop, we would take two or three days and help them harvest it. Our involvement in the community was total.

I stayed in Mississippi about two years. And during those two years I became more and more active in the organization of SNCC. Then I became SNCC program director and worked out of Atlanta, trying to assess the weaknesses and strengths of the organization. Starting with the Democratic National Convention in 1964, we had begun to ask serious questions. Many of us had gone to Atlantic City to argue that delegates from the MFDP, the Mississippi Freedom Democratic Party, should be seated in place of the regular delegates. We did everything we could to make the issues clear. We experienced jailings, beatings, murders, to bring the voting voice of the Black people to the convention. There was no way for anyone to claim that MFDP delegates were not legally and morally entitled to the seats. So when the Democratic Party failed to respond, things could never be the same.

We began to do a lot of reflection. Questions arose as to the nature of man: At what level does he have compassion, does he understand the value of human life? Why could four kids be blown up in a church and absolutely nothing done about it? Why was it necessary to bring white students from the North in order to have some kind of insulation from the overwhelming violence and chaos that could have happened in Mississippi? *Why was a white life more important than a Black life?*

The Vietnam war brought up another question: Why do we have to go all the way around the world to fight for "democracy" when we are not permitted our basic freedoms here? The thing that triggered SNCC's statement against the war was the death of Sammy Younge. Sammy was a Navy veteran who had gotten a Purple Heart. He came home to Tuskegee and attended college there. Once, at the bus station, he asked for the key to the rest room. The man in charge told him he couldn't use it. Sammy reported it, but the police did nothing. When he went back to the bus station, that man just shot and killed him.

His murder brought back the memory of Emmett Till. It also said something about America, the double standards and contradictions and how democracy was, in fact, not working for Blacks. Our statement on the war came out because we saw that if there was going to be democracy, we had to fight for it here, where Sammy Younge died. Many of us refused induction then.

I filed suit against both Georgia and South Carolina, charging discrimination in the selective service system. Out of one hundred sixty-one draft board members in South Carolina, only one was Black. And the government was encouraging local draft boards to call SNCC people out of turn. That's when they told me to report. I refused induction and got indicted right after that. Two years later I was tried, found guilty, and sentenced to the maximum of five years. We appealed, and eventually my conviction was overturned on the grounds that there was discrimination in the selective service system. Winning felt good, but the irony was that I spent four months in federal prison before the reversal, because the judge had denied me bail. After my release, I had to turn in my passport and sign in weekly at the local U.S. marshal's office.

While all this was going on, the Justice Department, the FBI, and other federal police forces switched their tactics. When we had tried to open up a hamburger joint or a waiting room, the government appeared to be an indifferent observer. But their "impartial" behavior began to change. The trend of the movement began to change, too. We were not just talking about testing public accommodations. We began to talk about getting the vote, about economic boycotts, about resisting the draft. We were talking about real fundamental social change.

We were talking about more power for Black people, *Black Power.* There was such hysteria generated around our slogan of Black Power. You couldn't pick up a newspaper or a magazine or listen to the radio without a warning about its dangers. They distorted what we meant. We were not out to terrorize whites and take over the country. We just wanted the power to control our own destiny, the power to establish institutions that develop pride, self-respect, and self-determination.

J. Edgar Hoover used our call for Black Power as one excuse to put his COINTELPRO operation into full force. They invaded every bit of our privacy, every single corner of it. Their scrutiny was so close, it was like being in a glass house. They would plant provocateurs in SNCC to create conflict. They knew how to stir up difficulties in personal relationships, how to play people off against each other. An FBI document shows their plan to send a phony letter to Rap Brown "to plant seeds of distrust between Brown, Carmichael, and [James] Forman."

> Dear Rap, dig this man. I got it from inside. Stokely and Forman sent you to the West Coast so that the man would get you. This is a little too cool for you, Rap Baby. With you out of the way, they can have the whole pie. Soul Brother [3]

During the period from about 1966 to 1969, there was so much pressure from the federal government, it was like a series of forest fires. Every time you would get one halfway out, another would start up. You just could not get ahead of the game.

Anyway, after refusing to be drafted, I went to Orangeburg, South Carolina, in October 1967, hoping to organize students on Black college campuses. I was involved with BACC, the Black Awareness Coordinating Committee, made up basically of students at South Carolina State College. We tried to develop a Black history perspective, to talk about issues that were pertinent to Blacks, and to bring in speakers like Julian Bond and John Conyers. I gradually became aware that my activities were being watched by the local officials.

At the same time, the NAACP in Orangeburg had been trying to integrate the bowling alley. I was not involved, but some BACC students asked me to come down on the night of February 6, to see what they were doing. Faculty, staff people, and a few administrators were there. About nine hundred students were there, too. A number of them were trying to get into the bowling alley. The police sealed it off and arrested some of the students. The others wouldn't leave until they were released. The administrators were negotiating with the police and seemed to have worked out a compromise.

Just when the students were about to go back to campus, a fire truck rolled up. The students thought they had been tricked and were furious. They remembered when fire trucks had been used to break up a demonstration in the early sixties. Students had been knocked down and swept under cars by the force of the water from the fire hoses. Others were hosed down after they were locked up at the fairgrounds. It was very cold, and they almost froze. So when the fire truck showed up now, it had a special meaning. Everybody ran over and asked what it was doing there: "Where's the fire?" Even the administrators were saying, "Why don't they move the fire truck out?"

Most of the people were near the fire truck when a few students slipped inside the police lines and made a dash for the bowling alley. The police rushed over there. Now everybody went back to see what was going on. There was just a crush, with all of them pressed up against the glass, and it broke. At that point, the police went bananas and started beating everybody. They sent over twenty people to the hospital, a lot of them young women, with fractures and concussions. The students were frustrated and angry. On the way back to campus, they broke store windows.

The day after the bowling alley incident, there were meetings at the college. The administration told students not to leave campus. The National Guard took up positions nearby. That night, some kids went off campus. On their way back, someone came out in his yard and shot them. The police did nothing about it.

Some students retaliated by throwing bottles at passing motorists. The police sealed the campus off, but a car with two whites came into the area, shot up the campus, and sped back out. Everyone believed the cops let them through. The students' nerves, at that point, were really on edge. I thought it was a serious situation and talked to the administrators: "We've got to keep these kids from getting hurt real bad." They agreed.

On the day of the eighth, I woke up to find an army tank stationed right in the intersection, pointed directly at the house I was staying in. I moved to a dormitory on campus. Everything had been pretty quiet that evening. I was tired, so about nine o'clock I went to bed. The shouting of students woke me up: "There's a fire on campus!" We went down between the girls' dormitories. Some kids were sitting on the steps, casually talking and looking around to see what was going on. Down the street, you could see smoke like something had been burning but was out now. A group of students was standing in the middle of the campus in a huddle. I started toward them, hoping I could move them back. I crossed the street under a light, and you could see the silhouette of my hair. It was long then. By the time I got thirty feet from the light, I could see the helmets of the police.

As soon as I reached the group of students, state troopers opened fire. They were standing at the bottom of the hill, shooting up. It was more like skeet shooting. There were all kinds of weapons going off: shotguns, pistols, rifles, carbines. On the first volley, everybody turned to go in the opposite direction. At least ninety percent of the kids were shot either in the back of the head, the back, the back of the leg, or the bottom of their feet. I was shot in the underarm.

A lot of people went down. When they got up, bam! The cops were walking up the hill, still shooting. It sounded like it went on forever. I couldn't believe it was happening. I got behind a trash can and then behind a lamppost. When I looked back, that whole area down there was a cloud of smoke. I saw them still coming up that hill and thought: They'll kill those they haven't gotten already. Some people had been hit pretty badly and couldn't move. We dragged most of them back with us and got them into the infirmary. Samuel Hammond died. He was lifeless when they brought him in.

The two people we couldn't bring to the infirmary with us were dragged away by the cops. Delano Middleton was a football player in pretty good shape and might have had a chance to make it. Henry Smith, I knew very well. He had long hair and looked a lot like me. He was an up-and-coming, articulate young person. Delano and Henry were just rolled down the hill, lying there while the cops stood around and took pictures of them. When they finally got them to the hospital, it was too late.

The infirmary was a small area, and everywhere you looked there were people. Blood was all over the floor and walls. Even though some of the kids were badly wounded, it was very quiet. Everybody was in a daze. All the athletic trainers, the football, basketball, and baseball coaches were called. They started working on some people because the nurse wanted to check the more serious cases. Ambulances couldn't get up to the campus because the area was sealed off. So students who had cars took the injured to the hospital.

I didn't know how serious my wound was. I felt a numbness and a burning sensation. It was extremely painful, but the hospital was the last place I wanted to be. I knew the police would be there, and after what they had done that night, I was afraid they would kill me. But the nurse was concerned about my wound and insisted I go. When we got there, deputies were all over the place with their shotguns. One of them recognized me and brought the sheriff. "You come with us." They moved me ahead of a lot of people, kind of patched me up, and took me downtown to the county courthouse.

They put together the charges right there: inciting to riot, arson, assault on a police officer, destruction of personal property, grand theft, and housebreaking. This couldn't be happening. It did not seem real. The radio reported that a policeman was shot, and I was charged with the shooting. I thought to myself: Oh, boy, they've got this one rigged up to the very end. They were looking for a scapegoat, and they found one.

The bond was set at fifty thousand dollars, a lot of money in 1968. With it came a restriction that I could not go within five miles of Orangeburg. I had left a lot of records from Mississippi there, all kinds of records. I never saw them again.

Then I had to come back to be sentenced for refusing induction. That's when the judge denied the bond and sent me to the Atlanta city jail. In two days I was moved to the Fulton County jail. I stayed there several days, and the marshals said they were taking me to Arkansas, but I went to Cordelia, Georgia, instead. Howard Moore and the other lawyers came down that Monday. Tuesday, I was packed up again and told I was going to Arkansas, but I went to Rome, Georgia. When Howard finally found out I was in Rome, they moved me again, this time to the Tallahassee Federal Correction Institute. After three or four weeks, they moved me to the Atlanta federal penitentiary, then to Louisville, Lexington, and Terre Haute federal prisons. All this time I was kept in solitary confinement.

With each move, they tried to break my spirit. But the support I got from within the prison population and the continued activities outside the prison kept me alert and stimulated and more committed to the struggle for equality and justice.

I finally had my hearing in August, after Supreme Court Justice Hugo Black ordered that I be given bail. They took off the handcuffs, and I started smiling. But I turned around, and there were two deputies. They put a new set of handcuffs on me and said there was a charge outstanding from Louisiana. In 1967, they had stopped a fellow I was driving with and found a gun in the trunk of his car. He had the gun. I didn't. But when they figured they couldn't detain me any longer, the federal government managed to find this charge. They began to stack the cases.

The Orangeburg trial was next. The maximum time I could get if convicted of all their charges was eighty-five years. They had the courthouse completely surrounded with state trooper cars. The whole area was cordoned off. Twenty policemen lined the front row of the courtroom. It was just to keep the pressure around the trial at a high pitch. They consolidated all their charges into three: conspiracy to riot, inciting to riot, and riot.

The judge had to dismiss the conspiracy charge because I was the only one being tried. And they couldn't find one single person I had incited, so that charge was dropped, too. Now I was left with the charge of participating in a riot. But there was no evidence of any illegal activity on my part. They couldn't get anyone to testify that they had seen me riot. The sheriff said he saw me do absolutely nothing that violated the law. In fact, the states' witnesses admitted I was peaceful the whole time. That's when the trial judge ruled that my mere presence on the night of February 8, 1968, or the fact that I had been shot, was not sufficient to convict me of riot.

So the state of South Carolina had to violate its own code of jurisprudence by changing the indictment from the night of the massacre to two nights earlier, the night the police had beaten up the kids at the bowling alley. They claimed I went from one group to the other, trying to rile up the crowd. I was accused of climbing aboard the fire truck, flicking a lighter, and saying, "Burn, baby, burn." The only "evidence" the prosecutor had of that was the testimony of one South Carolina law-enforcement agent who said he had taken notes there. But when he was asked to produce them, he said he had destroyed them. And that was it.

Mine was the first case in the state's history where someone was convicted of rioting without having committed an unlawful act of violence. The judge even told my attorney, when the jury was out of the courtroom, that, according to the FBI, "thirty or forty agents investigated for four months and found nothing against your client." Yet that judge sentenced me to the maximum, one year hard labor. I served seven months in prison.

On the night of the shootings, one trooper said over his car radio, "You should have been here, ol' buddy; got a couple of 'em tonight." Nothing was ever done about the murder of those kids. The governor said I was responsible. I became the scapegoat for everything that happened. The police were not found guilty of any charges. As a matter of fact, the first thing the governor did was talk about how efficient and effective they were. Each of them was promoted as a signal that everything they did was fine.

But Black people did not accept that, because the fact is that the highway patrol killed those students. The Black educational leaders told

Lyndon Johnson: "We urge you to stop these invasions of college and university campuses by the American version of storm troopers. We urge you to stop wanton killing of young high school and college students. We urge you to bring to justice those who commit such murders."[4] There had been a terrible injustice done, and there has never been any restitution.

Secret Police:
American as Apple Pie

FBI Crackdown on
Opposition to HUAC

Frank Wilkinson

In the 1960s, surveillance programs were so widespread that virtually every form of dissent was targeted. By 1972, a significant number of the delegates to the Democratic National Convention were being surveilled, and many of the organizations they belonged to were singled out for disruption. Millions of law-abiding citizens were spied on. The secrecy that cloaks the FBI, the CIA, the National Security Agency, the Internal Revenue Service, the Bureau of Alcohol, Tobacco, and Firearms, military intelligence, and local red squads allows them to escape the restraint of public oversight. They have become a power unto themselves, a bureaucratic threat that undercuts the democratic society they are presumed to support.

When the scope of the Smith Act was limited by the Supreme Court in 1956,* the FBI secretly substituted a counterintelligence program, known as COINTELPRO, that executed the bureau's political agenda outside the law. The monitoring of dissidents entered a new phase: an institutionalized system where agents played an active role in harassment and disruption. Under COINTELPRO, the FBI's opponents lost their jobs, their apartments, their marriages; the bureau infiltrated and disrupted political organizations; it committed hundreds of illegal bur-

---

* The Smith Act is described in Gil Green's story (Part II).

FRANK WILKINSON

*glaries; its agents provoked violence and hostility; and on five occa-
sions, after COINTELPRO was officially terminated, they firebombed
cars.*

*The Communist Party was COINTELPRO's first target. Martin
Luther King, Jr., was its most notable one. Frank Wilkinson's FBI file—
some 132,000 pages—reveals that he was also a prime target. The fraction of the file he received is a twenty-year record of surveillance and disruption of his open and legal efforts to abolish the House Un-American
Activities Committee. Why, but for his outspoken opposition to the
FBI's political line, was he so attacked? By the bureau's own admission,
Wilkinson had not "shown the willingness or capability of engaging in
acts which would significantly interfere with or be a threat to the survival and effective operation of our national government."*[1]

I began my personal campaign to get rid of the House Un-American
Activities Committee in 1952. A national campaign to abolish HUAC
was launched in 1960. The committee was not abolished until January 14, 1975. And I know that if the free marketplace of ideas had been
left open for us to argue the cause of abolition with Congress or in the
field, we could have done the thing in five years or less.

The role of the FBI was to disrupt our opposition to repressive laws
and inquisitorial activities of government. That's clear from their own
documents. We got twelve thousand pages of my file, and they admitted
they had at least one hundred thirty-two thousand pages on me. The
more we got, the more damaging the material was. Just devastating,
what they've done to us. I took a pile of those documents to Loeb and
Loeb, a large Republican firm, and got them to do a pro bono agreement with the American Civil Liberties Union, the ACLU, to file a lawsuit against the FBI.

I had been part of a Los Angeles civil liberties group called the Citizens' Committee to Preserve American Freedoms. We defended victims
of HUAC. Whenever anybody got subpoenaed, we'd get them together,
get lawyers, hold a press conference, and have a public meeting. In December 1956, HUAC subpoenaed a group of people from the L.A.
Committee for the Protection of the Foreign-Born, and a Unitarian minister. We organized a fight-back. We invited Alexander Meiklejohn, the
philosopher, to come and speak. Meiklejohn had been a professor at
Brown and president of Amherst College.

I had never read any of his great works, so I was given a copy of his testimony before the Hennings Committee in 1955.* I read it that night, and for the first time I got a full appreciation of the First Amendment. Most people called before HUAC claimed the privilege of the Fifth Amendment, which is an honorable, important, and basic amendment to be protected. And while you walked away free if you used it, you lost your job, you were a pariah. But using the First Amendment only was considered a sure trip to prison. When I finished reading Meiklejohn's testimony, I was so impressed that I said, "If I ever get a subpoena, I'll rely on the First Amendment." That was eleven o'clock at night. Seven o'clock the next morning, I was served a subpoena.

The committee couldn't believe I was not using the Fifth Amendment. After I gave my name and address, I said my little statement on the First Amendment and then froze. They kept questioning me and then turned to each other—"He's not going to use the Fifth"—and then to me: "Are you using the Fifth Amendment, Mr. Wilkinson?" I said, referring to my statement, "My answer is my answer."

One committee member noticed, "He's wearing a hearing aid. Maybe he doesn't hear us." The chair came down and looked at my ears. "Mr. Wilkinson, we notice you're deaf. Do you hear us?" At that point I answered, "Yes." The crowd in the hearing room roared because for thirty minutes I would only say, "My answer is my answer." The committee threatened to indict me, but they never did.

Our work in Los Angeles had been so successful that Corliss Lamont, I. F. Stone, Carey McWilliams, Hubey Wilson, and James Imbrie, all with the Emergency Civil Liberties Committee, invited us to do the same thing nationally. I arrived in New York the first week of August, in 1957. By mid-September we had a mass meeting at Carnegie Hall with Dalton Trumbo as the keynote speaker. We announced that anybody called before HUAC could call us in New York and we would be there within twelve hours to organize a fight-back. I did that in Gary, Indiana, New Jersey, Boston, and Philadelphia, and that eventually led to the Committee to Abolish HUAC.

In July 1958, a number of people were subpoenaed in Georgia. HUAC was supposed to be investigating Communist influence in the South, but they were really trying to put the subversive label on Martin Luther King, Jr., and the Southern Christian Leadership Conference.

---

*The Senate Subcommittee on Constitutional Rights, headed by Thomas C. Hennings, Jr., examined the nation's loyalty-security program. Alexander Meiklejohn was one of four scholars who testified at its first session on November 14, 1955.

We got a telegram inviting us to come down. It said, "Meet us at the Atlanta Biltmore Hotel early tomorrow afternoon." On one day's notice, I said, "I'll go."

I went directly to the Biltmore, checked into my room, and within a minute there was a knock on the door. A federal agent was standing there: "Are you Wilkinson? I have a subpoena for you from the Un-American Activities Committee." I asked, "How did you know I was here? I didn't know I was coming until yesterday." He said, "They called me from Washington and said I'd find you at the Atlanta Biltmore Hotel early this afternoon." That was exactly the message I had gotten.

I immediately called the national ACLU and told them I got another subpoena. They wanted somebody to test the First Amendment in the courts, so I said, "Let's go." I was determined to make the challenge as a matter of personal conscience. I knew we could not save free speech if we were not ready to go to jail in its defense. I was prepared to pay the price.

The ACLU phoned all their lawyers in Atlanta. I went to see them, and in each case the lawyer would say, "I can't possibly represent you here in Atlanta at this time." At the hearing, I walked up and sat down next to an empty chair. I looked up, and there were many of the lawyers I'd been visiting for the last six days, just observing. Not one would move forward to sit with me as my counsel. It gives you an idea of how vicious it was down there.

There were indigenous southerners who were brave enough to stand up to the committee. Carl Braden* was one who was subpoenaed, and the two of us refused to answer the committee's questions, citing the First Amendment. They charged us with contempt of Congress. When I was indicted, the ACLU asked the government, "Where do you want the arraignment? New York? Atlanta? Los Angeles? Whenever you're ready, let us know." But they weren't interested in handling me in any reasonable way. They never made the call. Instead, they waited until I was due to have a private meeting with Eleanor Roosevelt, Aubrey Williams, and Hubey Wilson at the Princeton Inn. When I arrived, they arrested me ostentatiously.

The government insisted on a jury trial, but there was no factual

---

* Carl and Anne Braden challenged the segregated housing practices in Louisville, Kentucky, by buying a home and transferring it to a Black family who could not purchase it directly. The house was bombed. Instead of the bombers being brought to justice, the Bradens were indicted under the Kentucky state sedition law in 1954, and Carl was convicted.

material for a jury to decide. It was public record that Carl and I had refused to answer questions. The jury took only thirteen minutes to convict me and twenty-one minutes to convict Carl. I always kidded him that it proved how much more dangerous I was than he.

The night before we were to be sentenced, Rowland Watts, the ACLU counsel, came in my room and said, "Frank, I know what we've agreed to, but as your lawyer, I must inform you that if you allow me to tell the judge you're not a Communist, you'll never spend a day in prison." In those days, anti-communism got into every bit of your language. It was a protective shield for whatever political thoughts you might hold. If you were for integration of the schools, you would say, "I'm not a Communist, but I believe in integration of the schools." I had reached the conclusion that everyone should decline to answer whether they were Communists until a person who was could answer without suffering economic or other sanctions. I turned to Rowland and said, "Okay, you've told me. But you're not allowed to say that to the judge. I want this thing absolutely clean to the end." Then Rowland poured a tumbler of bourbon for each of us, and we drank a toast to keeping the case clean.

There was a time when I had answered those questions. I swore I was not a Communist in 1942, in an affidavit to the federal government. I took a loyalty oath every year when I worked for the housing authority. The higher I got, the more loyalty oaths there were. Then it was not just a piece of paper on your desk. We'd bring in the American Legion, the VFW, and get a battery of flags behind us, while the director and I swore our loyalty. I finally reached the point somewhere around 1952 when I was ready to regurgitate the stuff. I would not sign one more oath.

My downfall, my blacklisting, came from an eminent-domain proceeding concerning Chavez Ravine as a site for a huge thirty-five-million-dollar public housing project in Los Angeles. I had been charged with finding the site. And Chavez Ravine was a beautiful hillside above downtown L.A. where we could build homes. But by doing it there, we would be integrating areas that were not integrated. So the real estate lobby was after me.

I was called as the expert witness for the housing authority to testify on the necessity of using Chavez Ravine. I showed the correlation between delinquency, disease, crime, and the cost to the taxpayer for bad housing. The real estate lobby had been trying every conceivable way to kill the new public housing program since it was started in 1949. But they couldn't break me under cross-examination because I knew my stuff cold.

I'd been on the stand two days when the lawyer for the real estate interests pulled out a dossier on the table and said, "Now, Mr. Wilkinson, will you please tell us all the organizations you've belonged to since 1931?" I told them what universities I'd attended, what professional societies I'd belonged to, and what lectures I'd given. But he persisted. "And what political organizations did you belong to?" That's when I reached my regurgitation point. I refused to answer. This was in the atmosphere of what's called the McCarthy period, the fourth year of the Cold War. The housing authority suspended me, and I was out. My testimony was stricken from the record. The integrated housing program was destroyed. The housing authority made a complete switch and jammed housing into the old ghettos, the high-crime areas of L.A., and Chavez Ravine was turned over to Walter O'Malley as the home for the Brooklyn Dodgers.

I'd come a long way from the Youth for Herbert Hoover group I was part of in Beverly Hills High School. I was the fraternity-sorority candidate against the "radicals" at UCLA. And I was the first president of the Hollywood Young People's Chapter of the Women's Christian Temperance Union. Having been brought up in Beverly Hills, I didn't even know there had been a depression. This is my background.

My family agreed to send me on a trip to the Holy Land because I'd planned on the ministry. That summer, Jane Addams of Hull House died, and at a Baptist seminar I heard about her work with the poor. So on my way to Jerusalem, I went to Chicago looking for poor people. I was shocked by the poverty I saw, and from then on my life changed. I began to simulate the life of the poor. I lived in flophouses in Washington and New York. I traveled abroad, living with the poorest of the poor all across northern Africa. When I got to Jerusalem, I found I couldn't even get into the Church of the Nativity on Christmas Eve because there were so many beggars in front. I spent three months in Jerusalem and Bethlehem, struggling with my Trinitarian Christian beliefs, questioning why in two thousand years of Christianity or five thousand years of Judaism or twelve hundred years of Islam there is such a discrepancy between their teachings and their practices. And while I was there, I gave up the idea of becoming a Methodist minister.

I came back to L.A. and completely shocked my family, my friends, my church, everybody. I had gone through an unbelievable change, from a devout Methodist to an agnostic. The bishop of my own church would just pat me on the back and tell my family not to worry about me, that I'd be okay. By pure chance, a priest heard about me, the archdiocesan director of Catholic hospitals and charities, Thomas J. O'Dwyer. He came to my home, and I just ripped into him because the Catholic church seemed to me the most hypocritical of all. He let me talk, and when I finished, he said that I didn't need to go so far to get so excited. He took me to the Black ghetto of Watts and showed me slum conditions there equal to any I had seen in Jerusalem or Bethlehem. I'd lived in L.A. all those years and never knew it was there.

He hired me that afternoon as his secretary on a citizens' housing council, which promoted construction of low-rent, integrated public housing. We worked together to establish the housing authority and win state and city approval of the new sites. Then, in 1942, when the first projects were completed, the authority announced plans to segregate the projects into Black, Chicano/Hispanic, and white. To Father O'Dwyer, the citizens' housing council, and myself, this was morally wrong. Under the leadership of O'Dwyer, we set up picket lines to protest the segregation. They were a success. The housing authority officials hired me literally on the picket line. At twenty-eight years of age I became the manager of the first integrated housing project west of the Mississippi.

When you read the FBI documents, *that* was the month J. Edgar Hoover and the FBI began following me. From then on, my work in the housing authority was disrupted. Hoover was out to get me fired from the word "go." All of that is in my FBI files. And when I learned of their constant surveillance of me, it was no longer a mystery how a federal agent arrived the same time I did in Atlanta to serve me the HUAC subpoena that led to my conviction for contempt.

We appealed the conviction, and the case finally reached the Supreme Court. The Court chamber was packed that day in 1961 when the decision came down. I already knew we probably would lose. Earlier, Meiklejohn had come for the oral arguments before the Court. He was a close friend of all the justices. Hugo Black invited him to sit in the family section, and we sat together, nobody knowing who I was. In the middle of the arguments, Felix Frankfurter spotted Meiklejohn. He scribbled a note and sent a page to bring it over. Meiklejohn shook his head and handed me the note, which said: "Alex, can't you see how wrong you are?" We knew then that the swing vote of Felix Frankfurter was going the other way.

Now, six months later, the five-to-four decision was rendered. Potter Stewart got up and made the statement upholding our conviction. Before he began, he said that in rendering these opinions in no way was the Supreme Court majority affirming or denying the merits of the Un-American Activities Committee. Like Pontius Pilate, he washed his hands. Then Hugo Black got up out of his chair. He was angry.

He read:

> From now on anyone who takes a public position contrary to that being urged by the House Un-American Activities Committee should realize that he runs the risk of being subpoenaed to appear at a hearing in some far-off place, of being questioned with regard to every minute detail of his past life, of being asked to report all the gossip he may have heard about any of his friends and acquaintances, of being accused by the Committee of membership in the Communist Party, of being held up to the public as a subversive and a traitor, of being jailed for contempt if he refuses to cooperate with the Committee in its probe of his mind and associations, and of being branded by his neighbors, employer, and erstwhile friends as a menace to society regardless of the outcome of that hearing.[2]

It was very dramatic. Then Black said, looking at Frankfurter, "Which member of this Court has not been called a Communist?" Frankfurter had handled the Sacco and Vanzetti case in the 1920s when he was a Harvard law professor and, like so many others in their defense, had been labeled.

Black was so eloquent. "When they send Braden and Wilkinson to jail, who is next?" I'm sitting there, hearing my name thrown around and Carl's name thrown around. It's like you're really part of freedom's history. I began to cry, not about going to jail, but I was just so moved.

The *New York Times* gave three full pages to the majority and minority opinions. Suddenly Carl and I became national figures. Prominent people—Howard Schomer, secretary of the World Council of Churches; Dean Bennett, of Union Theological Seminary; Reinhold Niebuhr; Martin Luther King, Jr.; and others—initiated a clemency petition for Carl and me while we were in prison. It was a very impressive document. There were thirty-five hundred ministers and rabbis, writers, labor leaders, academicians of all kinds who signed it. Schomer and a delegation tried to deliver it personally to President Kennedy but were unsuccessful. Recently released FBI documents reveal that those attempting to win clemency for Carl and me were under surveillance for their actions.

After the Supreme Court decision, we were free on bond for several months. I was invited to speak at the University of California at Berkeley by a student group called SLATE. I asked Alexander Meiklejohn to go with me. I thought I had come up to speak to thirty-five students, a rap session. I didn't have a note with me. When we arrived at Sather Gate, it was jammed with five thousand people. A television reporter put a microphone in front of my face: "What have you got to say?" We were walking through the crowd, escorted by the police. And Meiklejohn was trying to help me get ready. I said, "I don't have anything to say to these people. Let me introduce you, and you tell them what you told the Hennings Committee. You're the one that got me in jail."

He was then eighty-nine years old and about eighty-nine pounds. A small man. He said, "Oh, no. This is your day, Frank. Tell them the anecdote about Thoreau and Emerson." It was about the time Thoreau went to jail, protesting the Mexican-American war, and Emerson came to see him. "What are you doing in there, Henry?" he asked. And Thoreau said, "What are you doing out there, Ralph?" Well, Meiklejohn looked at me, and I was blank-faced. He said, "You've read Thoreau, haven't you?" And I said, "No." You should have seen this dear scholar— Kennedy later gave him the Presidential Medal of Freedom. He looked at me and said, "Oh, Frank, oh, Frank. You get up there and make the best speech you can. And once you're in prison I'll send you the books so you'll know why you're in there."

When you read the FBI records, you find out that they knew I was invited to Berkeley and they were corresponding with those right-wingers who were pressuring the university president, Clark Kerr, not to allow me on campus. Only it didn't click, because Kerr refused to ban me. Instead, he had Adrian Kragen, the chancellor, invite a representative of the FBI to appear in rebuttal. Hoover's answer to this was: "I am absolutely opposed to this crowd of 'bleeding hearts' at Berkeley using the FBI to get 'off the hook.' I know Kerr is no good and I doubt Kragen is." [3]

When they couldn't get the president to ban me, a group of fundamentalist preachers formed a caravan of a hundred cars with signs plastered on the sides: "Ban Communist convict Wilkinson from speaking." They drove eighty-five miles to Sacramento and circled the capitol, honking horns. They tried to get Governor Pat Brown to ban me, but he upheld my right, too.

I was determined to step up the campaign to abolish HUAC and was drawing huge crowds wherever I spoke. There were the five thousand at Berkeley. There were five thousand at a Pete Seeger concert for us. The hall in Princeton was jampacked. They were hanging out the windows at Johns Hopkins and Northwestern. Everywhere were these huge meetings, sometimes three, four a day, all the way to jail. I was getting to the point where I could hardly wait to get there to start Meiklejohn's reading regimen. I really didn't have that much to say. My decision to stand on the First Amendment had been a matter of conscience.

Hoover was clearly upset about our attack on HUAC. He sent memos all over, declaring that I was a national security risk. The FBI had key newspapers around the country agree to be secret conduits for them. I'd arrive in town, and out would come these stories blasting me. When I got up to speak, people in the audience were holding copies of HUAC pamphlets and hopping up all over the room to ask me disruptive questions. Everywhere. And I never realized it was the FBI.

Carl Braden was much more skeptical than I was. He always thought it was the FBI. I argued, "Carl, we're in a McCarthy era. This is the Cold War atmosphere. You have to expect these things." He wouldn't hear of it. I remember once we were in prison, arguing across from each other, and I said, "Carl, you know you're absolutely paranoid about the FBI." At that point, lightning struck. I said, "I presume J. Edgar Hoover did that, too?" And he said, "Probably."

It turned out Carl was absolutely right. When you look into the FBI papers we received, you find that even after the Supreme Court upheld our conviction for contempt, Hoover wasn't satisfied. He wanted to know how much longer I was going to be allowed to travel around the country making speeches. When was I going to jail? In his own handwriting on a bureau memorandum, he insisted, "Can't we expedite that?"[4] Most disturbing of all was an FBI airtel from the bureau's Washington office that said our petition for rehearing "was furnished SA [censored] on 3/24/61, by [censored] U.S. Supreme Court."[5] It looked like the FBI had their own informant in the Supreme Court itself, something that's totally out of line.

Before we surrendered to go to jail, Martin Luther King, Jr., held a reception for us at Morehouse College with several hundred Black leaders. King got up and made a beautiful statement: "These men are going to jail for us. We will never achieve peaceable integration in the South until the Un-American Activities Committee has been abolished." He and Coretta King took us to dinner, and then we went to jail.

In Atlanta, Carl and I were handcuffed and taken from the courthouse to the Fulton County jail. Then, on the way to the federal prison in South Carolina, they chained our ankles and our waists. Even when we had to go to the toilet, they kept the chains on. I remember they had to unzip my pants for me. Petty, petty stuff.

We now know from the records that when Carl and I were in prison, every move of ours was recorded by the FBI. Every letter we wrote, everything that came in was photocopied and sent to them. When I first entered the prison, the warden said, "We know all about you, Wilkinson. We don't want any of your teaching here."

I was jailed with a wonderful group of moonshiners and bootleggers. Many were illiterate, but they loved to look at comic books. The only time inmates could get them was on Sunday, when the guards closed the library. Carl and I asked the warden to open the library, and he agreed. The guards had to come back to do that, and we could see the hate in their eyes. The following Tuesday our names were called out over the loudspeaker to report to control. Immediately, handcuffs were slapped on us. We were roughed up, pushed out the door, and put in a prison bus. I didn't even have my hearing aid batteries. Without them, I'm deaf.

In Virginia, we were stripped naked and put into a dark hole, still not knowing what the hell happened. The next day, we drove through Washington. Carl and I were alone, handcuffed on this barred prison bus. In a traffic jam, smack in front of the Jefferson Memorial, we rattled our handcuffs on the bar and hollered out, "Jefferson, we are here." Like "Lafayette, we are here."

From there, we were driven up to the Lewisburg penitentiary in Pennsylvania, where we were put in solitary. I couldn't hear anymore. I was in an all-concrete room with a little steel peephole. Carl was in the cell next to me. Finally, we found out why we were shipped out from South Carolina. After we got the library opened that Sunday, the hacks had gone to the Air Force base four miles away and claimed that Carl and I were looking out of the windows of our cells at the planes taking off. And we were getting this information to Russia. Crazy, crazy charges. That's how those days were.

One day, I got an ominous call to come to control. It's frightening to have your number called out, not knowing what's going to happen. The warden looked me in the eye and said, "You're going back to the hole. We caught you cold this time, teaching communism." I said, "What do you mean?" He said, "You know damn well what I mean. You've been teaching communism." I just knew I was going to be locked up in that concrete room without my hearing aid. My spirit was so broken at that point that I cried, "I haven't been teaching communism. I've never taught communism." That's something I would never have said before the committee.

I wondered what in the world could have caused this. Two days later, I walked into the john and an inmate came up next to me. "I can tell you what your problems are. It's that forum you tried to start." It was just a quick whispered thing. Suddenly it came to me—the forum, the forum. Another inmate had asked if I knew someone who could speak at their forum. I mentioned Martin Luther King and Reinhold Niebuhr. That's teaching communism!? It left me in absolute fear, afraid to look at anybody, to say anything.

We were hassled until the day we got out of prison. When you're released, you're usually freed at eight or nine in the morning. Knowing this, Pete Seeger and others in New York decided to have a welcome-home concert for us. We were literally honored into prison by Martin Luther King, Jr. And now, getting out, we were going to be greeted by Pete Seeger. But two days before our release, an inmate came up and said, "They know about that rally, and they're going to hold you till the legal end of the day, at five. Then they're shipping you to Los Angeles by Greyhound." We found out later that the change in plans came right after the New York FBI office reported the rally to Hoover.

We had to get word out to Pete and the others. Only one inmate was leaving before us, and he would be searched nude to be sure he wasn't carrying out one scrap of paper. So we got him to memorize some phone numbers. He called and told them our plan. The prison authorities took us out at exactly five o'clock by the watch and put us on the Greyhound. Then we were free. The driver went ten feet, and we yelled, "Stop the bus!" Behind us was a caravan of five automobiles. We got in and went honking off to New York City.

We didn't get to the meeting until eleven o'clock, but there were two thousand people waiting, still trying to sing, and Willard Uphaus was still trying to talk. I walked up on that stage and was so moved. Embraces from Pete and embraces from Willard, and everybody was cheering. I began talking. I talked straight through till one in the morning and nobody left. It was just unbelievable.

Again I toured the country, speaking out against the House Un-American Activities Committee. I was on a television talk show in Cleveland, and it was rough. They were asking me stupid questions to try to embarrass me. Now from the documents we find out that there was an FBI informant inside the TV station. And the questions that were asked me were written by the FBI.

Everything that happened was that way. I went out to speak at Knox College in Illinois, where the Lincoln-Douglas debates were held. I expected to speak to a small group. I got there and found hundreds of people, a hostile audience, waiting. Before I finished, a telegram was brought up from Fulton Lewis, saying, "I accept your invitation to deliver a rebuttal to Mr. Wilkinson." The FBI knew I had been invited. They had started a campaign to have me smeared over the local radio station and in area newspapers. When a conservative group brought in Senator John Tower to speak, the FBI tried to get him to immunize the students against me; Fulton Lewis was to come in the day after. Even articles in the Chicago papers about it were arranged by the FBI.

I was averaging at least a hundred fifty field trips a year. Every one of them was covered by the FBI. They had my plane schedule, my flight numbers, at whose house I would be staying, where I'd be speaking, who my contacts were. They kept detailed records of all my movements, as if I were doing something illegal. Here's a classic example: They have me coming into Ypsilanti Airport on an American Airlines flight fifteen minutes late. I was picked up by a woman wearing a brown plaid suit. I got into a 1949 Buick. I was seen driving east. This is the report.

Every time I left L.A. on a field trip, Hoover would send out a memorandum: Here is Wilkinson's travel schedule. Disrupt his meetings. Listen to this language: "Each office . . . should give careful consideration to possible counter intelligence plans to disrupt the efforts of Wilkinson to carry out these proposed speaking engagements in furtherance of the communist cause. Since Wilkinson's speaking engagements are scheduled to be held on college campuses, the utmost discretion will be necessary to avoid any possible basis for allegations that the FBI is interfering with academic freedom."[6]

They'd gone to Bowling Green in Ohio to get me stopped there. They'd gone to Ohio State to get me banned there. I was banned at St. Ambrose College. They'd gone to Wayne State to get President Hillberry to ban me. He did, and then, on appeal to the faculty senate, I was invited back to speak. But when I arrived, I was told, "The university canceled the hall. We'll have to meet someplace off campus."

As the years went by, the FBI never let up. Here's an airtel dated September 1968 from Los Angeles to Baltimore, Boston, Chicago, Cincinnati, Cleveland, Detroit, Indiana, Milwaukee, Minnesota, Newark, New Haven, New York, Philadelphia, Pittsburgh, St. Louis, and Washington, reminding them all that they were to keep up their interference with my right to speak: "For the info of offices who have not previously covered Wilkinson's appearances, the Bur. instructed by airtel 4/20/62 . . . that offices be alert for counterintelligence operations that might be effectively employed in connection with the speaking engagements of Wilkinson."[7]

They tried in every way to disrupt the Committee to Abolish HUAC and its successor, the National Committee Against Repressive Legislation, NCARL. Contributions received by our office were recorded at the bank, and then FBI files were started on each contributor. Sometimes they were more aggressive. Let me give you an example. We have a document that describes their plan to burglarize our Chicago office. The memo is marked "Not To File," a procedure the FBI used to hide records of their illegal activities.* It reads: "[Deleted—probably an employee at the building] has been contacted and displayed an extremely cooperative attitude. . . . [Deleted] has stated that at 12:00 midnight [NCARL's Chicago office] is closed. [Deleted] advised that the building is again reopened at 6:30 A.M. [Deleted—probably an officer of NCARL] will not have knowledge of this anonymous source† developed." And then they added, "In view of the maximum security, it is recommended that authority be granted to make contact with this source on or about 1/14, sometime during 1:00 A.M. to 5:00 A.M." And the break-in was authorized by Assistant Director William C. Sullivan.[8]

Burglaries of our office were carried out repeatedly in the 1960s. I'd come in the next morning and find the door smashed down, file cases completely removed, all my correspondence taken. The following year, people who were mentioned in the purloined letters were called before HUAC. I was sure HUAC was responsible. Our discovery of the FBI's

---

* The "Do Not File" file was a secret procedure to avoid detection of sensitive files in the bureau's central records system. It was used, according to Assistant Director William C. Sullivan, when an FBI "technique involves trespass and is clearly illegal" (Memorandum from W. C. Sullivan to C. D. DeLoach, re: "Black Bag" jobs, July 19, 1966, DO NOT FILE).

† A bureau code word for illegal breaking and entering. "Former FBI agents have admitted that it was not unusual for agents to stage bag jobs and then to report the information they obtained as having come from 'highly confidential sources,' 'anonymous sources,' or 'confidential informants'" (Anthony Marro, "FBI Break-In Policy," in Athan G. Theoharis, ed., Beyond the Hiss Case: The FBI, Congress, and the Cold War [Philadelphia: Temple University Press, 1982], p. 85).

part in this thing was purely accidental. One of our officers checked out the Watergate testimony and saw that G. Gordon Liddy had broken into Dan Ellsberg's psychiatrist's office the same week we had our last burglary. So I asked Archibald Cox, the Watergate prosecutor, to investigate it. Cox could find no evidence that the Nixon "plumbers" or Liddy had done it. He wrote back, suggesting I contact the FBI.

I asked the FBI, "Did you burglarize my office?" They came back with the strangest two words I've heard in my lifetime: "What date?" I gave them the dates. We began to receive the FBI surveillance and disruption documents. The four thousand pages of my file identified one burglary. When we get all one hundred thirty-two thousand pages of my file, we expect to learn of all their burglaries. So far, we've found out that forty-six of my meetings had been ordered disrupted. They had four teams of agents following me from seven A.M. to ten P.M. We found constant derogatory leaks about me to the newspapers. Every press article, every question, every disruption of a meeting came from an FBI plant. It began forty-two years ago.

From these four thousand pages alone, you can rewrite the history of the forties and fifties. People call it the McCarthy era. It should be named the J. Edgar Hoover era. There was no indigenous McCarthyism. It was not a spontaneous thing. Everything that happened to me was orchestrated right here in Washington by Hoover. Everything.

In February 1983, we got the most damaging FBI document. It showed they knew I was to be assassinated in 1964. The document is from the agent in charge in Los Angeles to J. Edgar Hoover: "[Deleted] contacted by an undisclosed source to assist in an assassination attempt on Frank Wilkinson . . . March Four Instant at eight P.M. while Wilkinson addresses a meeting of the American Civil Liberties Union . . . at the home of Dr. Allen Neiman. . . . will stake out residence Dr. Neiman. Matter will be closely followed and pertinent developments promptly reported."[9]

As people came in that night, they complained about two suspicious-looking men parked out front. Allen Neiman took down the license number and called the police. Within five minutes, the car drove off.

When they read the documents at the *Los Angeles Times,* they were shocked by them, as anybody would be. The paper gave it big coverage: "FBI Failed to Warn of Death Threat." Here is an agency sworn to protect life and property, that knew somebody was to be killed, and waited out in front for it to happen.

The FBI's Southern Strategies

Jack O'Dell

Publicly, the FBI kept a respectful distance from the violent and illegal work of southern vigilantes and law-enforcement agents, which was directed against the epic struggle of Blacks to integrate the lunch counters, the schoolhouses, and the voting booths. But behind the scenes, the bureau in effect undercut the mounting civil rights movement.

Chuck McDew testified to the public strategy (see Part I). It was when Martin Luther King, Jr., added his voice to criticisms of the bureau's ploy of "nonpartisan objectivity" that Hoover's vendetta against King intensified, unleashing the undercover strategy; the FBI would "neutralize" Dr. King. "No holds were barred," William Sullivan, the bureau's man in charge of the war against Dr. King, testified before the Senate Select Committee investigating the FBI in November of 1975. "This is a rough, tough business."[1] Hoover began by trying to paint King "red." To do that, the Senate Select Committee reported, he sought to associate King with an "Adviser B," and to associate "Adviser B," in turn, with the Communist Party. Jack O'Dell, one of the best organizers and fund-raisers the Southern Christian Leadership Conference had, was "Adviser B."

The inference in the FBI's frequent unsubstantiated memos to Attorney General Robert Kennedy, charging that Jack O'Dell belonged to the top echelons of the Communist Party, was not lost on the president,

JACK O'DELL

John Kennedy, and the attorney general, who themselves feared they
might be tainted by their support of Dr. King. That pressure was inten-
sified by the bureau's unsubstantiated stories, leaked to southern news-
papers, claiming a King-O'Dell-Communist nexus. The FBI timed its
news leaks to coincide with the Southern Christian Leadership Confer-
ence's campaigns to desegregate schools, colleges, and public facilities.
In the end, President Kennedy was persuaded to pressure Dr. King to
remove Jack O'Dell from the SCLC staff.

———————————

I think the attacks on men like Paul Robeson, W. E. B. Du Bois, and
Martin Luther King, Jr., show that this system is not tolerant of Black
leadership with something to say to the American people. J. Edgar
Hoover was not the first or the last in power to try to disrupt and discredit a "Black messiah." All COINTELPRO did was formalize a policy
of repression that's been in existence since the anti-slavery movements—
frame-ups, character assassinations, sometimes out-and-out assassinations, a broadside attack upon our leadership. When you look at what
happened to those who tried to serve with integrity from the Afro-
American community, you are led to conclusions about the United
States that are not compatible with the fantasy of America as the land of
the free. Mrs. Fannie Lou Hamer, who was savagely beaten in a Mississippi jailhouse, once summed up this experience as "land of the tree and
home of the grave."

The modern phase of the civil rights movement grew out of the
Montgomery bus boycott, which gave birth to the Southern Christian
Leadership Conference in 1957. SCLC's first national demonstration
was a Prayer Pilgrimage to Washington to demand the right to vote. On
May 17, twenty-five thousand people, southern-based, insisted: "Give
us the ballot!"

In 1958, on the first anniversary of the events at Little Rock, we
again held a national March on Washington, urging Congress to pass
legislation to implement the Supreme Court's desegregation decision.
We repeated the mobilization in April 1959. Those mass actions were
led by A. Philip Randolph and Jackie Robinson, along with Dr. King.

I volunteered to be southern coordinator for the April march, using
my contacts with my college fraternity, Alpha Phi Alpha, to circulate the
petition to Congress. Some of the activists who were putting into place a
northern support center for SCLC noticed my work. What attracted me

to SCLC was the emergence of an activist leadership centered in the Black church. Upon concluding my work with the Kennedy for President campaign in the Bronx, in November 1960, I agreed to become director of the New York office of SCLC, located in Harlem, at a salary of a hundred dollars a week.

New York was mainly responsible for fund-raising. That was one way the North could participate in helping the southern movement. Earlier that year, we organized a big benefit at the Armory in Harlem for the sit-in movement, with Sidney Poitier, Dorothy Dandridge, and Harry Belafonte. We raised ten thousand dollars, which at that time was a nice piece of change. I directed the fund-raising for much of SCLC's budget. Martin raised about one half in speaking engagements, and the rest came through our direct-mail operation. I also became director for voter registration, in charge of coordinating a staff in seven southern states.

That was about the time of the movement in Albany, Georgia. It started in December 1961. The whole community was involved. People from age seven to seventy were going to prison. For the first time, we literally "filled the jails" peacefully, in the Gandhian tradition of non-violent protest, and established our validity as a mass movement. We didn't focus on any *one* manifestation of segregation. The Greensboro sit-ins focused on public accommodations; the Montgomery bus boycott focused on public transportation; Albany said: Hey, *segregation* has got to go. That idea gripped the minds of the courageous women and men of Albany.

But we weren't able to desegregate Albany. And the reason was that the federal government did not fulfill its responsibilities to uphold our First Amendment rights. Our right to peacefully protest was violated by the local police. Chief Laurie Pritchett was able to break the back of that movement by just locking everybody up. He should have been charged with violating the constitutional rights of the citizens of Albany, but the federal government just dillydallied. We said, "We have a mass movement here. The Black citizens, forty percent of the population, are demanding an end to racial segregation, which the Supreme Court has condemned." The federal government did nothing.

We brought together a committee of prominent attorneys, headed by Clarence Jones, who drafted a document that showed there was civil rights legislation already on the books adequate to abolish segregation. President Kennedy could have wiped out segregation with a stroke of the pen, just by issuing an executive order. But it became clear that this

administration was long on rhetoric about how they abhorred segregation. Of course, even that was a change from the previous Eisenhower-
Nixon administration. In 1959, Charles MacParker was lynched in
Mississippi. The FBI investigated to see if his "civil rights" had been violated. It's almost like your civil rights were part of your anatomy, like a
piece of vertebra that had been broken. You know, mobs are chasing
you down the street, whipping your head. You are lying there dying, and
they want to know whether your civil rights have been violated. It was
ludicrous.

I know there's a great portrayal of John Kennedy having been actively for civil rights. Well, he was smart to pick up that phone in 1960
and call Mrs. King to inquire about Dr. King's jailing. But when it came
to exercising the power the office carried with it, the administration was
reluctant to do it. It was only when our movement embarrassed the
president internationally that they decided to act. Then they just made
token gestures. The FBI would routinely show up and take notes about
whether your civil rights were being violated. It never resulted in any
prosecution. It never put a stop to the atrocities. So they took notes.
Who cared?

And yet what did it mean? It meant that the role of the FBI was to
express some token concern for your rights by their presence. They were
never there to protect you. And they would argue—the attorney general's office and Hoover would argue—that they were not a federal police force. But when they were locking up Communists in the 1950s,
they were a federal police force. So you see, it was sheer hypocrisy.
Their definition of themselves as not being federal police meant that
none of these Klansmen had anything to fear, that the FBI wasn't going
to bother them. All of the violence directed against nonviolent marchers
was associated with this do-nothingness on the part of the federal government. There's a point at which you've had enough.

The Southern Regional Council's criticism of the FBI came out in
1962. The council was one of less than a handful of organizations made
up primarily of white southerners who recognized segregation was a
moral liability. They were on the side of any movement, any action that
addressed any piece of the segregation problem. It was very helpful to
have that kind of southern voice speaking out, a voice of moderation
and a little bit beyond.

Dr. King, of course, supported that criticism and added his voice to
it. He said, "The FBI is not doing anything." He pointed to things we
knew all along: They drew their FBI recruits from the southern milieu.

They had a bunch of born and bred segregationists running the southern offices. Their culture and politics conflicted with any objective role of the federal government as an anti-segregation force upholding the Constitution. That was the essence of the charge, and of course that put Dr. King and all the rest of us in bad stead with the chief mogul, J. Edgar Hoover.

Surveillance by the FBI and for the FBI and the whole range of dirty tricks were constantly part of our problem. I mean, I can remember in Albany when we used to hold meetings at Dr. William Anderson's house. Dr. King had to get out of that house to talk about what we were going to do. He operated on the assumption that the place was bugged and the phones were tapped and the house was under surveillance and that any information they got would be used against us. We were always operating in a treacherous environment.

Martin brought about nine of us together every January to discuss and lay out the program for the year. We used to meet in a little town near Fort Jackson in Georgia, in a school that the United Church of Christ had. We had come out of Albany with a sense of both victory and defeat. Where's our next target? Birmingham. Birmingham. People are ready. Of course, we knew how dangerous it would be, with Police Chief "Bull" Connor. Then Reverend Fred Shuttlesworth described the possibilities: "Martin, the people *are* ready. They want to move." We planned Birmingham that January of 1963.

Martin said, "We've got some bills left over from Albany. If I have to hit the road for the next five months to raise money, we'll have to postpone Birmingham." He turned to me and Stan Levison and asked about the status of the direct-mail fund-raising. And because I could lay out the volume of mailings that we were planning and what revenues we could expect to get from them, he knew he didn't have to hit the road. He said, "We're going to Birmingham as planned."

I'm obviously not looking for accolades, because I wouldn't have kept quiet for twenty years, but that is a fact. Now, if you were interested in putting the dampers on a movement, logic would tell you that if you moved some key persons out of the way, the thing would kind of slow down some. And I submit that anybody in my position could have been a target. I wasn't just instrumental in raising money. I was directing voter registration in seven states. All the Strom Thurmonds and Eastlands down in Mississippi and South Carolina were looking at that Black vote. And we were organizing it. Of course, Hoover and other adversaries were unaccustomed to Blacks voting or even demanding the right. If there had been a mentality in this country against eating vege-tables, they'd have called me a vegetarian. All I'm saying is, we don't need to be naive about the move they made.

Most of the books on this period proceed from the premise that here was this nice administration up there in Washington that loved the Negroes. And they were just looking for some way to help us out. And here this Communist had infiltrated. Why, the way I'm treated in all this scholarship, you would think I was white—you know, Jack O'Dell is Irish. But you'll never see me as a person. You'll never see why I got into the movement and what I was doing.

I was born and grew up in the ghetto of Detroit. I went to an all-Black college, Xavier University, in New Orleans. During World War II, I was in the merchant marine. I managed a Black insurance company in Montgomery. I had lived in Louisiana and sat behind the screens on streetcars and buses; couldn't eat in a Walgreens Drugstore restaurant; couldn't go to a public park. *That's* why I was in a movement to abolish segregation. Yet you read all those books and it's like the only reason I'm there is because I'm trying to "infiltrate" the thing and pick up slips off the desk, I guess, and pass them on as an agent of a foreign govern-ment. It's ridiculous. It's ludicrous.

As absurd as it is, this mentality was and remains the official out-look of the United States. You see, the anti-communist, McCarthy syn-drome was the undercurrent of everything. It's true the movement for civil rights and racial justice broke the back of McCarthyism by giving people an issue they could speak out on with enough moral authority for them not to get blacklisted from jobs or otherwise intimidated. That was its historic contribution on that issue. But in the early 1960s, there was enough sickness left over from the McCarthy period to make it un-comfortable for anyone to confront anti-communism head-on.

We first knew they were going after me in September 1962. The Kennedys had a friend who published one of the leading "moderate" newspapers in Nashville. They told him to call Reverend Kelly Miller Smith, pastor of the First Baptist Church, and express their concern that there was Communist infiltration in SCLC. Kelly Miller Smith was a very prominent board member of SCLC, whom all of us were fond of. Kelly called Martin, not out of consternation, and said, "We all like Jack, but this friend just called me." They took it seriously because they knew the real source was the attorney general.

Meanwhile, the FBI was pressuring the Justice Department with memos about me every other week. They kept it up. Then the Justice

Department put pressure on Dr. King. They ran that whole thing on Martin—you know, "O'Dell's one of the top Communists." First they told him I was on the national committee. The next time they talked with him, I had moved up to "one of the top five." We both laughed. We were in a hotel room, and Martin said, "I don't know what Jack's politics are, but I don't see when he has time to be a top Communist because I assume they require some things of you, too. He's got two jobs at SCLC, and he's running back and forth between New York and Atlanta." It was comical, you know. Then again, it was serious.

I said, "Now, I have Communist associates, and I'm not going to cross the street to keep from talking to them. But this 'top Communist' business is ridiculous." I told Martin, "Look, ask for my file and let them show you they have evidence for what they're talking about. I'd like to see it, too." I knew there could be nothing in that file to substantiate what they said, unless they manufactured it and, of course, you can't put that past them.

Meanwhile, I had temporarily resigned. We realized I was under surveillance. I mean, the federal police had been following me around all the while. But my colleagues in SCLC knew my work. They said, "We need you." That's why they hung on from September to June, trying to see if the pressure from the federal government would ease and they could go about their business without having to make this surgery.

But Bobby Kennedy, through Burke Marshall, head of the Civil Rights Division of the Justice Department, kept telling Dr. King to get rid of me. When Martin asked to see my file, they put him through a rigmarole. First, Marshall said, "Okay, come down to Washington." So Martin asked the executive director of SCLC, Reverend Wyatt T. Walker, to go to Washington to meet with them. And the head of the Civil Rights Division, working directly with Bobby Kennedy, told him, "I can't get O'Dell's file from the FBI." *He* couldn't get hold of my file from Hoover. Now, doesn't that seem strange?

Andy Young was executive vice-president of SCLC. They called him. "Burke Marshall has got to be in New Orleans. Come down there and we'll talk about it." Andy went to New Orleans and got the same answer: No file. As far as I know, no one has seen that file yet. So you see, they ran a game on the SCLC leadership. "O'Dell must go, but we can't get the file from the FBI." Now, I know there's such a thing as bureaucracy, but if getting rid of me was so important, certainly the attorney general of the United States could get evidence to prove his allegations.

The FBI never offered any proof to anybody, but it freely passed out its disinformation. The Church Committee of the U.S. Senate quoted an FBI memo saying they were going to leak their stories about me "in such Southern states as Alabama where Dr. King has announced that the next targets for integration of universities are located."[2] Identical stories appeared in papers in the South and the East: While I was "acting executive director of SCLC," I was "a concealed member of the national committee of the Communist Party." Each paper got the story from "a highly authoritative source." We saw those articles appear, but we didn't know where they came from. I don't think any of us suspected they were planted by the FBI. On the other hand, when you hear that now, you are not surprised.

When Kennedy was getting ready to go to Europe in June 1963, he took Martin out on the White House lawn for that walk through the Rose Garden, telling him I was an agent of a foreign government. There had just been a big scandal in Britain called the Profumo affair. Profumo was on the prime minister's staff and had been caught with this alleged prostitute, Christine Keeler. It had come out in the House of Commons, and the prime minister's future was at stake. Kennedy said, "I'm going to see a man whose political career has been ruined by scandal. You don't want any scandal around your staff because of Communist infiltration." He told Martin that Strom Thurmond and the segregationists on the Hill had said they would publicly denounce his civil rights legislation if O'Dell remained on the SCLC staff. He was saying that if he were red-baited it would be comparable to the prime minister's demise, politically. God, that was the worst thing you could be accused of, being soft on communism. McCarthyism was very much alive.

This latest pressure move was coming from heavy sources, the president of the United States. It went from Bobby Kennedy calling a publisher in Nashville and, over seven or eight months, from there to Burke Marshall, and then to the president of the United States. It was put on his agenda to deal with Martin on this issue.

We had a meeting because of that walk on the White House lawn. On June 25, I got a call that Martin wanted to meet with Wyatt Walker, myself, Clarence Jones, Walter Fauntroy, and three or four other people in his hotel room here in New York. A few days before, there had been a big demonstration in Detroit, the largest civil rights demonstration in any single city. More than one hundred twenty-five thousand people, led by Dr. King and Walter Reuther, marched down Woodward Avenue. It was clear the movement was growing. Of course, we were all very happy about that. And Martin said, "The people are with me right now." It was like saying, "I don't want this Communist issue to torpedo the momentum, and these guys will use it to do that."

I didn't disagree with him, because I understood the practical requirements. Here we have the opportunity and momentum to pass civil rights legislation that we've needed for a hundred years. There's a groundswell. Do we attempt to confront this anti-communist mentality and take the gamble to allow it to derail us? Or, given the sickness and paranoia that were still left from the McCarthy era, do we yield tactically to the premise of anti-communism? You have to realize that a lot of our support wasn't that solid. It was contingent on a certain "purity." It would pain labor leaders that Martin didn't preface every speech he made with some Cold War disclaimer. Their rule was to always slip in some kind of Cold War stuff to make it more "American."

It wasn't Martin's desire to let me go, but it was his decision not to get embarrassed by this issue. He held on as long as he could, hoping that the pressure from the federal government would ease. But they kept the pressure up. I left SCLC in July 1963. I stayed in touch, and I didn't have to make the effort. If any of their staff came through New York, they would "stop and see Jack." And they'd tell me what was going on. But if Martin was speaking somewhere, I'd stay clear because I'd figure they were surveilling it.

The surveillance of Dr. King increased after I left. The record shows that. And I know it. People from the staff told me what was going on. Martin would go to take a rest in some apartment, and firemen would break the door down, thinking they were going to catch him with some woman. Oh, man, just all kinds of dirty tricks. No, the surveillance did not stop after the "great menace" moved out. It increased. Despite these many harassments and provocations, Martin Luther King, Jr., continued to give splendid, creative leadership to our movement for justice.

I went on working for *Freedomways* magazine, writing articles as associate editor. I kind of plowed a whole new career for myself. By the time of the Poor People's Campaign in 1968, Martin was discussing with his staff bringing me back. He said, "We've got a lot of administrative problems, and I know who can solve them." That's what Andy Young told me after Martin died. Andy said, "He wanted you to come back, but it was just a question of timing." I did go back to SCLC in 1969 by invitation and remained for three years.

The struggle continues. . . .

The Grand Jury: An Extension of FBI Authority

Jill Raymond

The FBI, an agency of the Justice Department, has no legal authority to force anyone to answer its questions. The Justice Department itself, however, can arrange to subpoena a reluctant citizen before a federal grand jury, where refusal to answer the same questions can result in an indeterminate jail sentence. The effective authority of the FBI can therefore extend far beyond its legal mandate.

Historically, the Supreme Court has said, grand juries were intended to stand "between the accuser and the accused." They were created to protect the innocent against "hasty, malicious, and oppressive persecution."[1] The traditional function of grand juries was to vote on indictments after consideration of the adequacy or inadequacy of the prosecutor's evidence; they were not intended as inquisitorial bodies. It is an abuse of grand juries' considerable powers when prosecutors use them improperly as investigative tools to coerce testimony or to seek fugitives. Senator Edward Kennedy described modern grand juries as "a throw-back to the worst excesses of the legislative investigative committees of the 1950s."[2] The description is apt when grand juries are used to harass political opponents or compel witnesses to reveal their personal or political beliefs and associations.

During the administration of Richard Nixon, one hundred grand juries in eighty-four cities subpoenaed more than a thousand witnesses

JILL RAYMOND

from groups that included New Left radicals, opponents of the Vietnam war, and members of the Catholic left, as well as members of the Puerto Rican, Native American, and women's movements. "I am going to read you a list of names," one witness was told, "and I want you to tell the grand jury every occasion during the years 1971 and 1972 when you have had any contact with the individuals whose names I give you, describing for the grand jury when the contact was, where it was, and what was said and done on each occasion." [3]

In January 1975, FBI agents descended on the feminist and gay communities of Lexington, Kentucky, in search of two fugitives, Susan Saxe and Katherine Power. Jill Raymond was one of those who refused on principle to cooperate with their sweeping interrogations. She spent fourteen months in prison for declining to testify before a grand jury, a grand jury that failed to produce an indictment, or even a report.

All six of us who ended up jailed in Lexington in 1975 were at some point in our undergraduate college years. Some of us didn't know each other at all before the grand jury subpoenas came up. In other cases, we had been close buddies through women's study groups or just general hanging out together. We all had a wide assortment of interests in political activities and political causes.

By that time, a certain amount of antiwar consciousness and feminist consciousness had sunk in at large campuses in the United States. Many people were exploring alternative health care, alternative business enterprises, and alternative lifestyles, something that's become kind of a cliché, but at the time was not. It certainly wasn't the case that Kentucky was a great bastion of radical activities. But I've always found it interesting that in Lexington, where you might think only right-wing and entrenched traditional values would survive, there was a lot of activity around social justice causes.

People in Lexington, whatever else they might have thought about feminists and lesbians, certainly felt strongly about individual rights and individual privacy. And that aspect of what happened to us hit home more deeply than the government attempt to make us look bad. I think the majority of the Lexington community ended up seeing us not necessarily as people they would personally identify with, but definitely as people who were getting rapped by an overly zealous prosecutor, by an overly powerful judiciary maneuver. Sometimes I attribute the fact that I got out of jail at all—and was able to stay out without getting resub-poenaed—to the fact that the community was far more supportive of us than the government ever counted on.

During the summer of 1974, I was getting ready to go into my last semester as an undergraduate. There were a couple of women's study groups that I was involved in. There were gay groups and various other little enclaves. That was the summer when, among other comings and goings that seemed perfectly normal to us, two women named Lena and May blew into town and checked out the feminist bookstore, checked out bulletin boards, and asked around where the local femi-nists hang out.

They got the names of a couple of people who were the most active, which included the name of my very close friend Marla. Marla had been very visible in the lesbian community. Lena and May said they were traveling around the country, just visiting feminist communities. They were planning, as they said, to set up a feminist press of their own.

None of this seemed out of the ordinary to us. I emphasize that now because later on, when Marla eventually agreed to testify before the grand jury, they asked her about the entrance of these two people into Lexington and how she met them. One of the grand jurors could not fathom the idea that if two strangers came to your door, you'd not only talk to them but you'd let them in. You might let them stay overnight at your house. The idea of two lesbians from out of town traveling on a shoestring and living out of a backpack was a little beyond some of those grand jurors. It was like two cultures really not understanding each other. And for them, it was cause for suspicion. For Marla, it was a normal occurrence.

Anyway, I met Lena and May in a study group that Marla and I had been a part of. In that group or in the group house Marla shared with Lena and May, we, like others in those days and at that age, spent hours and hours talking politics and arguing. There were also, as friendships developed, the ordinary things. You know—you drive somebody to the grocery store because they don't have a car—that kind of thing. I re-member thinking about all those very mundane activities that we would do together and how bizarre it would be if they were recited in the grand jury room and were considered evidence.

When looked at from the knowledge that people had later on, it's very hard to believe that nobody around these two women who were wanted by the FBI—on the Ten Most Wanted list, for crying out loud, and evading God knows how many different kinds of police and intelligence agencies—noticed anything weird. It's hard to imagine that the behavior of people who were fugitives wasn't obvious. Well, we didn't have an inkling.

In fact, we felt that they made a fairly important impact politically on our group and on different ones of us personally. I had spent a great deal of time with them individually, hanging out and talking politics. We were right in the process of developing a political philosophy, sharpening political arguments. We hadn't agreed on everything, but each of them helped me a great deal. I and some of the other members of the study group that had included Lena and May felt, more than you might expect, that these two people whose stay had been so brief, so transient, had become important to us.

By mid-fall of 1974, both of them had left, and we didn't question their leaving any more than we questioned their coming. I was battling out my last semester in school. Then, at some point in late fall or early winter, somebody made the connection between the faces on the FBI's Most Wanted poster and Lena and May. That was really like the bomb dropping.

It was enough to throw everybody in a turmoil. We were concerned about what was going to happen to us and to Lena and May. Who were they, really? Nobody had proven anything with respect to that. There was a lot of doubt about those posters. After all, Susan Saxe and Kathy Power had been underground for five years, and the pictures were from high school. I myself said, "Oh, it can't be."

The Lena and May we had known in Lexington were not preaching the wisdom of robbing banks or shooting policemen. They weren't preaching the immediate violent overthrow of everything by any means necessary. In fact, we found them thoughtful, astute, careful, and caring people who, if they *were* the people who robbed this bank in 1970, had made a mistake in their lives that any of us might have made under certain circumstances.

Then, somebody who was not particularly close to the situation decided she should go to the FBI. After that, there wasn't a whole lot any of us could do. We talked among ourselves and tried to prepare psychologically for what might be, hoping that nothing would come of it. At Christmas time, when school got out, I drove across the country with a friend of mine. When I got back, the first week in January, I was greeted by the news that half my friends around town had been questioned by FBI agents. Rumors were flying all over the place.

For anyone who has ever been approached by the FBI, it is a very bizarre experience to have in your life—period. I guess the overriding feeling is that somebody out there who you can't see is focusing their attention on your life: on what you're doing, what you're saying, the mail you're getting. And if they're not, at any given moment they might be. It gives you a different perspective on how you live your day, how you view doing very normal things, like driving over to a friend's house and calling someone on the phone.

The first wave of FBI investigations took place in January of 1975. They questioned everybody whose names they could get hold of who might have had the remotest connection to Lena and May or to anything Lena and May were interested in, like the local gay bar. Hundreds of people were questioned in Kentucky and nearby, in Cincinnati. The FBI asked for the membership list of the Cincinnati chapter of the National Organization for Women. They asked an officer of the chapter to single out the lesbian members for them. Very courageously, she told them, "Not only can't you get a list, but we don't keep track of who is a lesbian and who isn't."

There were a lot of things that made us feel we didn't want to talk to the FBI. It was somewhat different for each of us. I had been pretty active all my years at school. I got very involved in a third-party movement in the early 1970s, called the People's Party. It ran Dr. Benjamin Spock for president. I'd been very involved in antimilitarist, anti–Vietnam war activities. Antiwar activists on campuses were sitting ducks for the FBI. The FBI, certainly under J. Edgar Hoover, had seen them as primary targets, somewhat below the Black Panthers in importance, but still right up there as "threats" to our nation.

I had long since looked at agencies like the FBI and CIA as very sinister, very untrustworthy, frightening intelligence organizations. I was unsure at the time, and I'm still unsure, whether they serve any really valid purpose in this country. By then, they had begun to fall into disrepute. I don't remember how much had come out publicly from congressional hearings about COINTELPRO at that time, but certainly we all had a suspicion, even if it hadn't been documented yet. So I was really disinclined to do any talking to FBI agents.

Besides, the FBI has a perfect right to lie to you in order to get information, and they certainly exercise that right. Talking to them, in and of itself—even if you have no information to give them, as in our case—talking to them without an attorney present is a dangerous enterprise. You have an absolute right to refuse to answer questions for the FBI, an absolute right to not talk to them. That, it seemed to us, was the safest option.

I was questioned the week after I got back from my trip. My first interview with the FBI was a very polite exchange. They said, "We'd like to ask you about these two girls. You know what we're talking about." They tried to bait me a little bit and show they knew something about me: "If you were going to describe your political philosophy in one word, would it start with an 's'?" I assume they were getting at "socialist."

I said, "I'm sorry, I just don't have anything to say to you. Here's my attorney's name and phone number." They were fairly nonpressuring at that moment. The pressure came at the next "interview." When the six of us refused to talk after the second attempt, they told us that they were going to seek grand jury subpoenas.

The FBI is not the issuing authority for subpoenas. The fact that they would make arrogant little comments like, "Well, okay, if that's how you feel, we may be seeing you outside the grand jury room next week," revealed their confidence in being able to get the U.S. Attorney to issue subpoenas. That, of course, is exactly what happened. The subpoenas came out within a week.

By February, the FBI had obtained lists of our long-distance phone calls for the last year or two and was approaching people all over the country. We found this out when we started getting calls from these people saying, "What gives? The FBI was just here." A friend of mine had recently moved to Detroit. The FBI went to see him and assumed, somehow, that we had had a romantic relationship. They tried to get him to talk about me. They said, "Did you know Jill is a lesbian?" Of course he knew I was a lesbian, and he was so indignant that they would use that to influence him. He called me right away. And he, among other people who had similar sorts of experiences, wrote affidavits for us that we tried to file in court as evidence of FBI harassment.

When they visited my sister, they told her I was already in jail, which, of course, was not true. Sometimes they offered people money to travel to Lexington and talk me into testifying. They went to my eighty-year-old grandmother, who lived in an old people's home. With her, they tried to emphasize the politics, that I was a socialist, and wasn't that awful? They asked friends of mine if they knew that I was playing around with Weather Underground members. They would dredge up any piece of the Old or New Left and tie me in to it.

For the most part, our families and friends stood up for us and told the FBI to go jump in the lake. My sister in Seattle was threatened with a subpoena herself, for telling them that. My grandmother was very polite and hostess-like with them, but she backed me up: "I trust that Jill is not in any trouble. She's a thoughtful person."

I think the FBI had known at some point during those five years when Susan and Kathy were underground that they had become involved in the women's movement and that they had become radical lesbians. That became an opportunity for them to find out about those communities, as well as about Saxe and Power. It was clear from comments the FBI made that they thought, "There's something really important here going on that we should know about, and this is our golden opportunity."

The FBI created a hard time for a few people who were not "out" to their parents, whose parents didn't know they were gay. For them, it was infinitely harder. It made a difference that most of us were not hiding in the closet, trying to live secret lives. I found a real lesson in that.

The first subpoenas came out about mid- to late January, for us to appear on February 3. Cary was the one man in our group of six. The FBI called him in the middle of the night, and he said, "Are you guys crazy?" The next thing he knew he had a subpoena. Marla and Gail never flat-out said no. "Call our lawyer, set up an appointment," they said, "and we'll see what you have to say." But the FBI didn't take them up on their offer, and they got subpoenas anyway. In my case, I was coming home late one night after being out to dinner with a friend. It was after midnight and the U.S. marshals were, just then, walking away from the front door of my apartment. "Here it is," they said.

Our attorney, Bob Sedler, was general counsel of the American Civil Liberties Union in Kentucky, a professor at the law school, and a pretty well known constitutional lawyer. First he called the FBI and said, "Look, this is a nothing case. Who are you kidding?"

They gave him the cold shoulder. "We're in this. We're serious." He hadn't believed subpoenas would come out, even after they threatened us with them. None of us did. None of us believed at any point in the process that it was going to go any further. Your logical faculties go into play, and you say, "It's not reasonable for them to pursue this. There's nothing here. We have no information for them." And we certainly didn't believe we were going to go to jail, even though we talked about it and tried to prepare for it. By the final days of the contempt hearing, we took bags of clothes, but we really couldn't believe we would be in jail that night.

A person has a right not to divulge the details of his or her personal life to the FBI. But if the FBI can go to the United States prosecutor and get a subpoena to a grand jury, and then the Justice Department can get a grant of immunity that effectively removes the use of the Fifth Amendment before the grand jury, then the law that protects you from having to talk to the FBI in the first place is worthless. It's all a little charade. So we didn't talk to the grand jury for the same reasons that we didn't talk to the FBI. The six of us had decided that we would follow that strategy through as long as we could.

What we tried to do in the grand jury room was connect with the grand jurors and circumvent the prosecutor. We each wrote out little speeches that we were going to present. We tried to say, "Look, this is a bogus hearing. There's nothing indictable here. We're just some students who were nailed because we didn't want to cooperate with the FBI." We tried to discuss the original purpose of the grand jury with them, that grand juries are supposed to protect people from overzealous prosecutors. But each time we got shut up by the prosecutor as soon as we started.

Each of us went in individually. It was a tiny room, with people crowded around an L-shaped table. I was sitting in the middle, among all of them. The prosecutor was right up there in front, the only one standing and asking questions. The grand jurors themselves didn't say anything. With each question, I'd ask to consult with my attorney outside the room. Then I came back with a statement explaining why I refused to answer. The prosecutor stopped asking questions as soon as he established for the grand jurors that I wasn't going to answer. Then he dismissed me.

We got our second subpoenas and went back to plan more legal strategy. At this point, the strategy was to fight the immunity grant, the legal linchpin everything else hangs on. Once we were granted immunity, we knew we did not have the right to assert the Fifth Amendment anymore. Now if we didn't answer, we would go to jail. We refused to answer their questions a second time and were charged with contempt.

Our attorney argued that we should have a full hearing on the legitimacy of this grand jury inquisition. The battle between the prosecutor and our lawyer boiled down to how far you could get into the grand jury's purpose, how far you could pull away the curtain of secrecy around grand jury activity. But there wasn't much we could do. We weren't even allowed to dig out of the prosecutor the grand jury's *official* purpose in subpoenaing us. And of course we had no way to get at—in the form of evidence—what may have been their *real* purpose: that they were on a fishing expedition to find out what they could about radical movements in Lexington and/or that they wanted to track down two fugitives.

At the hearing, we tried to show that the real purpose of that grand jury was to catch people who were already under indictment. For example, during her appearance before the grand jury, Linda asked the grand jurors point-blank, "What do you want to know? What are you trying to ask me?" And the foreman popped out with, "We want to know where those two girls went." The prosecutor made the same kind of slip when he argued against setting bail for us. He said, "The more time that passes and these people don't testify, the more time there is for Saxe and Power to escape." De facto evidence that he wanted our testimony to help catch them. And that certainly is *not* within the legitimate purview of a grand jury.

We tried to show that our subpoenas to the grand jury originated with the FBI when we refused to answer their questions. They wanted to get us in the grand jury room with immunity. It was a fishing expedition in which the prosecutor's offices and the FBI had worked hand in hand. But we were not allowed to question FBI agents. The minute our hearing started going in that direction, the judge and the prosecutor both said, "That's not relevant."

At some point we were confronted with the question, "Why are you protecting those bank robbers?" People in the mainstream didn't necessarily know that we hadn't knowingly harbored fugitives. But we knew it. And at the contempt hearing our attorney read a statement to the court, signed by us. It said, "We state that we do not know the whereabouts of these two individuals. We also state that when they were known to us in Lexington as Lena Paley and May Kelly, we had no knowledge of any other identity of theirs."

We were claiming that once we said, "No, we didn't knowingly harbor fugitives; no, we didn't have knowledge of a felony being committed and not reported," our personal lives were our personal lives. If you have the right to ask me what Lena Paley and I discussed on the night of October 3, 1974, when she and I went out to X bar and drank beer for three hours, if you have the right to quiz me about everything she said and I said, then I must surrender any privacy that would attach to that relationship.

There's a judicial concept to the effect that the law has the right to everybody's evidence. That may be, but to say that the law has a right to everybody's evidence is not the same as saying the law has a right to everybody's *everything*: everybody's experience, the sum total of their knowledge and their personal acquaintances, lifestyles, and everything else.

Going to jail was a lot to sacrifice if it was just a matter of withholding information that we really didn't have in the first place. But it was quite a bit easier knowing that we were protecting our privacy—and possibly that of others—from the abuse and arrogance of those agencies. It was a principle I felt at one with. When it's a matter of sitting in jail and having the choice every day to testify, ambivalence would be just crushing.

Being in jail when you know you could walk out of it any time you talk to the grand jury takes will power, as opposed to serving out a sentence. But in a perverse kind of way it makes it a little less frightening, too. You're able to take it one day at a time more easily. There are moments when the claustrophobia is overwhelming. Literally being locked in someplace that you don't have a key to is a bizarre experience that is truly something you can know only when you've been through it. And when that hit us, that panic, we could say to ourselves: "Well, I can wrestle with this today. And if I can't stand tomorrow, then I can get out."

The first one of the six of us who testified was Debbie. The prison experience was especially horrible for her. She said, "Okay, that's my limit. I'm going." And we all thought, "Good for her that she knew when to do it." And we had the power to do it, too. As time went on and our appeals failed, others testified.

There was a point at which I was about to testify, I'll be very frank. Two months after we went to jail, we were all trucked back to court for another hearing because the appeals court had ruled that the judge never made the finding that the grand jury investigation was legitimate. The prosecutor submitted a sealed affidavit to the judge that nobody else, even our attorneys, was ever able to see. Supposedly, it stated the official purpose of this grand jury investigation. And that's all it took. The judge ruled that the grand jury's purpose was legitimate. At that point, the remaining three people agreed to testify.

Now I was alone for the first time. They took me to a different jail in Franklin County, a frightening and more confining place. There was a whole litany of conditions that were just harder to live with, like the much more stringent visiting regulations. The worst part was that the one women's cell, which I occupied, directly faced the elevator that brought everybody into the jail: visitors, jailers changing shifts, or anybody. When they opened up the elevator door, there I was, whether I was undressing or anything else. The shower had two walls. People couldn't see me while I was in there, but they could when I got out. It was hideous for women. And I was beginning to despair.

We had a very sympathetic reporter on the daily Lexington paper who was covering our story. And I'm sure that had a great deal to do with public opinion. She came to visit me to talk about jail conditions. With her next story on our case, she wrote a separate article about the jail and how awful it was. Well, you would have thought something horrible had happened. The judge who had ruled on our case ordered me moved immediately to another jail, supposedly as punishment for having given this interview. The next jail had a perpetual reputation as an especially terrible place. It had an official rating as "poor."

This was all a little frightening, given that I was barely hanging on at the time. But as things happened, this next jail, which was indeed a dump, had a larger area for women, more people, and much broader visiting privileges, and that helped to deal with the effects of the isolation. There was a female matron, and she and I became pretty good friends. I mean, given the givens, she was a real human being. The combination of those things made a difference. And I, psychologically, came back. I felt like I was coming up from drowning.

The jailer himself was a big, fat, illiterate man who looked like your old southern sheriff type. His wife was this perfectly kind, warm human being, who was raising thirteen kids while she was the matron of the jail and cooked for the prisoners. The jailer's sons were the deputies. His father was often an inmate on Saturday nights when he got drunk. It was a family affair. Their house was literally attached to the jail building. On holidays, once in a while, they'd cook up some big turkeys. Some of the same things that made these jails horrible and frightening and un-regulated and sort of "anything goes" sometimes made them more humane environments than the super-modern, high-tech, institutional-type places. It was a real irony.

The defense work kept going. On the one hand, the case got quieter after six or eight months and wasn't in the paper every week. But on the other hand, what reaction you did hear was more and more vehement: "This is six and eight months this woman's been in jail!"

It seemed to me at that point the purpose of keeping me imprisoned was purely punitive. After I'd been in jail that long, any "information" I had was useless. Susan Saxe had been caught and was already on her way to trial. The trail had to be fairly cold for Kathy Power, or at least it certainly wasn't very hot in Lexington anymore. By then everybody else had either talked to the FBI or testified before the grand jury, so they had whatever information against me that was available. Obviously, it wasn't enough to come up with an indictment.

Actually, if they had indicted us, we would have had the full protection that a trial by a jury of your peers provides, the right to cross-examine and present witnesses and the right to present more complete evidence. We probably would have never spent a day in jail. We certainly would have been granted bail, as a matter of course. The irony of all that is fantastic, because without ever being so much as charged with a crime, we spent a great deal of time in jail.

Other grand jury cases sprang up around the country. The Connecticut grand jury case was going on at the same time. Joanna LeDeaux, on the Pine Ridge Indian reservation, had a subpoena related to the Wounded Knee uprising. Maria Cueto and Raisa Nemikan were going to jail.* We didn't know any of those people before this happened, but we all got together. Our defense committee worked with their defense committees. It was as if the FBI had put together the very network that they claimed had already existed.

Very literally, they created an alliance that lasted for many years. We all used each other's networks for publicity. People held rallies in New York against grand jury abuse that tied together this whole laundry list of victims. The weight of public awareness that all of those networks produced made it hot for the Justice Department in a way that our little defense committee couldn't have.

---

*In New Haven, Connecticut, Ellen Grusse and Terry Turgeon were also subpoenaed to a grand jury on the Susan Saxe and Kathy Power case. They were jailed for the term of the grand jury when they refused to testify. Upon release, they were given new subpoenas for a reconvened grand jury and again imprisoned.

Maria Cueto and Raisa Nemikan, director and secretary, respectively, of the National Commission on Hispanic Affairs of the Episcopal Church, were jailed for eleven months for their refusal to testify before a grand jury that was attempting to link the commission with bombings conducted by a Puerto Rican independence group known as the Armed Force of National Liberation (FALN). Called before another grand jury, Maria Cueto again refused to testify. This time she received a three-year sentence to a federal penitentiary.

After fourteen months, the grand jury was dismissed. I was released at midnight on that day, not a minute earlier. The matron took me downstairs, once the marshals brought the order. There were reporters and friends of mine and defense committee people. We waited in the lobby and watched for the clock to strike twelve. It was quite a scene.

The first few days I was out of jail were phenomenal. I went to get my driver's license renewed and have my picture taken all over again. The people down at the motor vehicle department knew all about me and said, "Oh, we're so glad you're out of jail." I went to the bank to deal with my account. The teller smiled, "Oh, you're out of jail. I read about it." I went into a bar downtown with a friend, a very ordinary, straight Lexington bar. And the waitress there recognized me and brought us our drinks on the house. I think a large proportion of ordinary citizens sympathized with me to the point where they thought there was something wrong that I was in jail.

And then I thought, "God, this succeeded. That's what this was for." If it hadn't changed any minds, if it hadn't made anybody else able to identify with us other than the same old political crowd, then it could leave you thinking, "Well, to hell with people if they don't want their constitutional rights," or wondering if, in fact, it's you who is nuts. But people from out of nowhere were saying, "Whoever she is, what she's doing is all right."

The Lawlessness of the LAPD Red Squad

Seymour Myerson

During a 1976 lawsuit against the Chicago Police Department, it was
discovered that the department's security section, or "red squad," kept
files on eight hundred organizations, including the PTA, the League of
Women Voters, the NAACP, the Jewish War Veterans, and Planned
Parenthood. The red squad had assigned hundreds of agents to infiltrate
targeted organizations, often as leaders; burglarized the organizations'
files; passed intelligence reports of lawful political activities to the FBI
and the CIA; infiltrated the legal team of those who had filed the lawsuit
against the police department; and assisted a paramilitary terrorist
group, the Legion of Justice, in physically attacking dissidents.

"The evidence has clearly shown," concluded a Cook County grand
jury, "that the security section of the Chicago Police Department assaulted the fundamental freedoms of speech, association, press, and religion, as well as the constitutional right to privacy of hundreds of
individuals." [1]

In 1982, the American Civil Liberties Union filed suit against the
Los Angeles red squad, which was called the Public Disorder Intelligence
Division, for spying on, infiltrating, and harassing 131 law-abiding organizations. Later, a report prepared for the city cited "pervasive" violations that came from the highest levels of the department. The activities of the Los Angeles PDID were first challenged by Seymour (Mike)

SEYMOUR MYERSON

Myerson, who was one of the subjects of its campaign of harassment. The harassment began in connection with his radical and antiwar activities and intensified to startling proportions when he publicly proposed stricter guidelines for the PDID itself. His story is presented largely through his notes, correspondence, and a brief he eventually filed against the police.

———————————

Early in the 1970s, I became aware of the fact that I was being followed and being photographed at various meetings and demonstrations. And then the harassment began that eventually led to this complaint against the police department and the city:

> On or about April 21, 1974 at Pershing Square, located in the City and County of Los Angeles, California, Defendant Ruff . . . and other unknown agents of Defendant City of Los Angeles, operating under the express or implied consent, permission, authority and direction of Defendant [Police Chief] Edward M. Davis . . . acted so as to prevent, deter, inhibit, suppress and render less effective a peaceful and lawful expression of social, political, and economic views and beliefs held by Plaintiff and others of his companions.[2]

First, this guy stepped in front of me and told me: I don't want you to be involved in this meeting. And he got aggressive about it. I tried to avoid him, but for a while he held me back bodily.

> Subsequent to the termination of the assembly . . . Defendant Ruff and [others] assaulted the Plaintiff with his motor vehicle so as to cause Plaintiff apprehension of great bodily harm.[3]

The car these agents were in wheeled the corner and almost clipped me from behind as I was walking across the street on the way to my car. Then:

> Defendant Ruff stated a future intention to do great physical harm to Plaintiff. Defendant Ruff and [others] further harassed, intimidated and threatened Plaintiff by maliciously tampering with and destroying a portion of Plaintiff's motor vehicle so as

to render it immobile. At this time and place, the name and occupation of Defendant Ruff [were] unknown to Plaintiff.[4]

Some of these same police agents followed me to North Carolina,
where there was a big demonstration for the Wilmington Ten.* There
they were in Raleigh, these agents from the *Los Angeles* Police Department, giving us a hard time.

> Defendants did so by gaining and exposing private and confi-
> dential information about Plaintiff, shouting obscenities and in-
> sults, and by publicly harassing, intimidating, threatening and
> undermining the public credibility of Plaintiff and those per-
> sons and groups engaged in such expression, association and
> assembly. At this time and place, the name and occupation of
> Defendant Ruff [were] unknown to Plaintiff.[5]

On April 26, 1975, a public meeting of the Police Commission was
called to hear citizens speak pro and con on revisions in the police
guidelines. Most complaints were about the red squad, the Public Disorder Intelligence Division. The PDID was supposed to get information
on terrorist activities. Instead, they used terrorist activities against left-
wing organizations. I spoke there on behalf of the National Alliance
Against Racism and Political Repression and the Los Angeles Committee for the Defense of the Bill of Rights.

I said: "The 'new guidelines' are designed to continue the un-
justified surveillance of citizens and maintain noncriminal files to harass
and victimize citizens of this community. Several book stores, offices,
residences were bombed and vandalized. These criminal acts include the
latest widespread practice of the slashing of automobile tires of cars belonging to individuals attending meetings, social affairs, and at places of
business, and their residences. We have information to prove these allegations, that the files are used to perpetuate violent and criminal acts
against individuals and organizations. Therefore, we demand the immediate abolishment of all noncriminal files."

After the public hearing, the police made targets of those they
thought were key people in this protest against their activities. In my

* See the story related by the Reverend Ben Chavis (Part II).

case, it resulted in a series of threatening and violent actions covering several years. They seemed like retaliations for my perfectly lawful activities as a citizen. With each one, I sent letters of complaint to the police commissioner, to the chief of police, to the mayor, to our congressperson, to everybody.

May 15, 1975

Samuel Williams, President
Los Angeles Police Commission
Dear Sir:
The undersigned, a resident of Los Angeles for the past thirty years, appeared before your commission and spoke on the subject of "New Police Guidelines," on Saturday, April 26, 1975.

On the following Tuesday, April 29, at almost 9 P.M., while my wife and I were watching TV, a boulder of 4–5 inches in diameter was hurled through the plate glass window of our living room, striking my wife on the shoulder and ricocheting off the side of her face.

Then, on Thursday, May 8, at 1:55 A.M. a loud explosive noise came from the front of my house. I rushed out to my front porch and discovered a partial brick of 2½″ × 2¼″ × 5″ in size which had been hurled at my newly installed plate glass window of my living room. This incident followed a Trade Union May Day event held at the Breakfast Club on Saturday, May 3, which I had attended.

It is my considered opinion this is part of a planned program of intimidation, harassment, and violence on the part of directed agents of law-enforcement. I urge you to conduct an immediate investigation of this matter.

Very truly yours,
Seymour A. Myerson[6]

May 22, 1975

Hon. Samuel Williams, President
Los Angeles Police Commission
Dear Sir:
On Tuesday, May 20, at about 4:45 P.M. I attended a meeting and demonstration on the Spring Street side of City Hall. I observed police cars, motorcycles, and unmarked cars parked across the

street. I drove my car to the front of 501 New High Street and parked. I walked to the demonstration.

At about 5:45 P.M. I left and headed north. About 100 feet away I heard my name called from one of the unmarked cars. I recognized the voice as that of a known agent provocateur. I followed the car to First Street hoping to note the license number. The car made a sharp left turn heading east. I watched it make another left turn heading north on Main Street in the direction of the area where my car was parked. I hurriedly made my way back to see if the car might return to its original station (it did not).

I rushed down Spring Street and crossed the freeway bridge and cut to 501 New High Street in a matter of minutes. There I found all four tires were slashed. No other parked cars on the entire block were touched.

> Very truly yours,
> Seymour A. Myerson

This letter got us a routine response from the police chief: "All criminal occurrences which are reported to this department are thoroughly investigated."

Two months earlier, on the night of March 26, 1975, we had had the tires slashed on both of our cars, which were parked in our driveway. All four tires on each car! This happened after I was in a demonstration that very afternoon in front of the Federal Building in downtown Los Angeles.

On June 11, 1975, at my initiative, Mr. Richard Eiden, an attorney, and I met with Commander Ruddell and Sergeant John W. Ensign of the LAPD Internal Affairs Division. Commander Ruddell was unimpressed with the facts stated in my May 22 letter and considered them as being "insufficient evidence" and "unsupported" by my "failure to get a license number."

By now, I was confident I could identify the guilty agents if he would just show me the personnel photos. But Ruddell and Ensign made no commitment as to making any reports, files, or photographs available to us. Sergeant Ensign did state, however, that they would "start an investigation into these matters."

The very next day, Sergeant Ensign called. He told me he and his colleagues had decided there were insufficient grounds for an investigation.

November 19, 1975

Hon. Samuel Williams, President
Los Angeles Police Commission
Dear Sir:

This morning at 9:50 A.M. I parked my car in the parking lot of
the California Bar Association Building. My presence was occa-
sioned by my attendance at a hearing concerning the Echo Park
Peoples Law Center. At 12:15 P.M. the hearing was recessed for
lunch and I, along with about 50 other observers, court attachés
and attorneys, went our separate ways.

I went to my car and to my consternation saw all four tires
slashed. Mine was the only one of over 50 cars parked on the
facility which was singled out for this criminal abuse. I proceeded
to process a police report by making a call to LAPD Central Division and requested a patrol car to implement an on-site investigation and report. I was abruptly told to contact Rampart Division,
which I did. They advised me to call Downtown LAPD. They in
turn referred me to Central LAPD. I spoke to Officer Reed who
said he would make a telephonic report. I again asked about an
on-site investigation and report. He referred me to Rampart Station which I then called and spoke to Officer Ortega. He advised
me that having made a telephonic report Rampart could offer no
further assistance.

Very truly yours,
Seymour A. Myerson

This is the run-around I got. What happened next is cited in my
complaint.

> On or about December 26, 1975, Defendant Ruff, operating
> under the expressed or implied consent, permission, authority
> and direction of Defendant Davis and others telephoned the
> home of Plaintiff.

My notes of the conversation are as follows:

> The phone rang. Mrs. Myerson answered.
> VOICE: Is Seymour there?
> MRS. MYERSON: Who's calling, please?

> VOICE: Jeff Watson.
>
> MRS. MYERSON: Hold the phone, please.
>
> MIKE: Hello.
>
> VOICE: Merry Christmas, you motherfucker. I'm going to cut your throat.

I recognized the voice of the police agent who seemed to make a career of harassing me. It wasn't long afterward that we were able to get the specifics on him that the police asked us to supply.

February 3, 1976

Hon. Samuel Williams, President
Los Angeles Police Commission
Dear Sir:
On Sunday, February 1, 1976, between 1 P.M. and 5 P.M., a cultural affair sponsored by the Los Angeles Institute of Marxist Studies was held at Larchmont Hall. Between 12:30 P.M. and 3:30 P.M. an unmarked 1970–71 Oldsmobile Cutlass avocado colored sedan, California License No. 360 FOS, with two "lawless agents" was observed cruising on Larchmont. The agent, not at the wheel, was taking note of the license numbers of all vehicles belonging to those attending the affair. Further, a lady who had parked her car around the corner was shouted at and frightened by these persons as she was leaving her car to make her way to the Hall. She also observed the license No. 360 FOS.
  On Monday morning, February 2, 1976, I went to the Department of Motor Vehicles in Hollywood and secured the ownership under License No. 360 FOS. It turned out that the plates were phony and were procured and/or stolen for unlawful use. This raises an interesting question. What violations of law, number and kinds of crimes are committed by agents of law enforcement operating vehicles under cover of false license plates and identities? Another interesting question—why does the LAPD refuse to uncover the identity of the criminal agent operations in its midst so clearly pointed out in my letters to you?

Very truly yours,
Seymour A. Myerson

The teletype report 2276 from the Department of Motor Vehicles named the most recent owner of the car. And then it said, "Status: Junk. Make:

Chevy. License No.: 360 FOS." But the car I saw that license number on was not a Chevy. It was an avocado green Oldsmobile Cutlass. The police used phony plates that belonged to a car that was no longer in existence.

We were also able to photograph the agents who were harassing me. And just one week earlier I had left copies of the photos with Commissioner Williams. They had said there was insufficient evidence. Now they had photos of the agent, a license plate number, and evidence that the plates were phony, and still they didn't act. I was to see the persons in the photos, the car, and the phony plates again.

June 19, 1976

Hon. Samuel Williams, President
Los Angeles Police Commission
Re: Terrorist Activities and Police Violence
Dear Sir:
On Friday, June 18, 1976, at 7:30 P.M. I was seated in my living room with Lincoln, my 13 year old grandson, watching TV. Lincoln called my attention to a car stopped in front of our house and a man calling out my name "Mike." I was in my blue bathrobe, having just taken a shower, and peered out from behind the screen door. The voice came from the driver, whose face and voice were only too familiar. See references to this individual in my prior letters to you dated February 3, 1976, July 31, 1975, June 16, 1975, May 22, 1975, and related correspondence.

The driver started to yell some taunts like "How did you like Cuba?" "We're from the CIA," "The CIA will get you, Mike." I advised him to get off the block and get lost. I did not have the presence of mind to just close the door and call the police. After a few choice obscenities and threats by the driver he continued north from the middle of the street. I then made note of the color of the car (an avocado 1970–72 sedan) and rear license plate (360 FOS). This is precisely the same person and vehicle as cited in my letter to you dated February 3, 1976. The vehicle proceeded north to the corner of Coronado Terrace and Scott Ave., a dead end, made a U-turn and came back in front of my house and then made a sharp right turn onto my driveway, another sharp right turn with tires screeching across my front walk and lawn and headed north across my next door neighbor's lawn at 1431, cutting across the lawn at

1435 and over the parkway onto the street continuing north to the corner. In its reckless course of travel the vehicle narrowly missed a neighbor, an elderly lady in 1435, who was walking her dog. This lady was ushered into 1431 and safety by its occupant, Mrs. Irene Grannell, who was on top of the situation. The car then turned left, then apparently circled the block, when the car and its driver and passenger again headed north, stopped and shouted more taunts and threats and then proceeded north and vacated the area, or at least the street. By then, I had gotten a good look at the passenger, who also looked very familiar to me. All this transpired within a period of ten minutes or so.

Hardly another ten minutes had gone by, when the following harrowing and incredible situation occurred. My living room door was open and I heard some shouts like, "Get out of there!" or "Come out!" "Walk out here with your hands up!", or such. I couldn't believe my ears. I thought it was coming from the TV.

I looked through the screen door, and then I couldn't believe my ears *or* my eyes. A uniformed policeman, with the rifle aimed at me, was crouched behind the tree near the street next to my driveway and ordering me to come out of my house with my hands up. I was stunned. He repeated his order about three times and I stepped out to the porch, barefoot in my robe. I then turned to my right and was looking down the barrels of rifles and revolvers, held by four or five uniformed police, all aimed at me, and at least two other officers on the lot, ordering me to raise my hands and place them behind my head. I looked at my left and a similar scene was performed by officers stationed in the driveway, next door north. This has got to be a Class D movie. I still can't believe it's for real.

By now, I was off the porch and on my lawn and was ordered to get on my knees with my hands behind my back. I was then frisked and patted down. Then I was lifted to my feet and per-mitted to drop my arms. I then shouted out, "What the hell's going on? What's this all about?"

An officer responded, "Where's the rifle?"

I replied, "What rifle? What the hell are you talking about? I don't believe in guns, not even toy guns." Meanwhile these two armed uniformed police had entered my house and made a quick search and came up with a small Little League baseball bat, which was in my house for such times as my grandson comes to visit.

The officers had interrogated Lincoln about guns and rifles. I don't believe he ever saw one in his life, let alone in my house.

I then took note of the fact that the street, sidewalk, and side-yards were crawling with police cars and armed police on foot. Also my neighbors and people down the block were out in great numbers. We were playing to a very large audience. By now, I had collected my thoughts somewhat and made some loud demands for an explanation. Four officers, Curiel, Sanchez, Sergeants Van Vetzer and Freedman, all from the Rampart Division, with Curiel leading, explained that they "had received a call that a man in a blue bathrobe, armed with a rifle, was shooting or threatening to shoot at people on the street or in automobiles. Therefore, we responded with the six or eight units."

It was here that I described to the police the activities involving the agent-provocateurs. They were still curious about me having guns, rifles etc. I asked them by what right police have to break into my home without a warrant and scaring the hell out of a youngster. There was no probable cause except this trick phone call, which was obviously a device for these agents-provocateurs to set me up. I'm quite certain that were it not for the large number of neighbors and citizens observing this crazy scene, I may well have ended up as another LAPD statistic labelled, "justifiable homicide."

Further, there are witnesses to the above described fascist-like activities. To my knowledge the police took no photos of tire marks, records of witnesses, their identities or their statements.

Very truly yours,
Seymour A. Myerson

I came close to getting killed. Things can't get more serious than that. I demanded an investigation. In response to my letter to her, the council-woman from my district, Peggy Stevenson, wrote to Commissioner Williams:

> Mr. Seymour A. Myerson, a constituent of mine, has sent me a copy of his communication addressed to you dated June 19, 1976.
>
> Apparently a meeting scheduled for March 29, 1976, in your office, failed to take place and he is now requesting a meeting be arranged with him as soon as possible.

I certainly understand his concern and I would therefore
very much appreciate your communicating directly with him in
an effort to arrive at a solution to the problems described in his
letter.

Finally, on February 10, 1977, I was served a subpoena to a hearing
about the incident on my front lawn. The day after that, I had a telephone conversation with Lieutenant Woodruff of Internal Affairs. It was
the first admission by the police of their involvement in the acts against
me. My notes record our conversation:

> MYERSON: Lieutenant, a subpoena was served on me yester-
> day in the matter of Clifford E. Ruff. What is
> this about?
> WOODRUFF: It is in reference to the incident in front of your
> house last June.
> MYERSON: Who is Clifford E. Ruff, named in the subpoena?
> WOODRUFF: The LAPD officer under investigation.
> MYERSON: Is he the guy in the avocado-colored car?
> WOODRUFF: Yes.
> MYERSON: How about the guy who was with Ruff, his
> partner?
> WOODRUFF: That will come out in the hearing.
> MYERSON: Would it be advisable for me to have an attorney
> appear with me?
> WOODRUFF: No, it will not be necessary.
> MYERSON: Will I have the opportunity to identify these
> guys?
> WOODRUFF: Yes, provided they are present.
> MYERSON: Will I be given a copy of the proceedings?
> WOODRUFF: No.

It was only later that we learned Ruff worked in the PDID as a su-
pervisor over two other police officers who had secretly infiltrated three
organizations I belonged to. They even became leaders. And for years
they reported to Ruff on the lawful activities of those groups and the
people in them, including me.

The day of the hearing, my neighbor, Mrs. Irene Grannell, and my
wife, Vivian, and I appeared at Room 508, Parker Center, at 9:30 A.M.,
as the subpoena required. About seven or eight police officers and our-

selves were sworn in and identified as witnesses. Also present were the accused officer, Clifford E. Ruff; Lieutenant Woodruff; and a stenotypist reporter, Thelma Karpf. Mrs. Myerson noted that Ruff was now clean-shaven, with short hair and a short mustache. Even so, she readily identified him as the person in the photographs.

We sat around waiting for the proceedings to start. At about 10:15 Lieutenant Woodruff announced a one-hour recess on the grounds that the charges had been "amended" and the amended charges required the chief's review and signature. I doubted that this hearing would get to the bottom of what happened. At 11:15 A.M. we returned to a locked hearing room. At 11:20 Thelma Karpf arrived, and while we were waiting, I asked her: "Ms. Karpf, what are the charges against Officer Ruff?" She replied: "As near as I can recall they are charges of driving on the lawn unnecessarily, giving inaccurate reports to Communications, and giving misleading information to Internal Affairs."

Finally, at 11:40, the hearing was called into session. Lieutenant Woodruff came to where I was sitting and asked me to join him in the corridor outside the hearing room. I followed him into the hall where this conversation took place:

> WOODRUFF: The accused, Officer Ruff, pleaded guilty to the most serious charge of giving an inaccurate report to Communications, and we dropped the driving charge since it is a less serious charge than the first to which Ruff pleaded guilty.
>
> MYERSON: You mean phoning in the phony report that I was a guy with a rifle and thus setting me up for a hit?
>
> WOODRUFF: Yes.
>
> MYERSON: What is the penalty for these guys?
>
> WOODRUFF: Ruff was transferred out some time ago.
>
> MYERSON: You mean he's still on the force?
>
> WOODRUFF: Yes.
>
> MYERSON: He won't even be fired?
>
> WOODRUFF: That remains to be seen.
>
> MYERSON: Did this inquiry cover the activities going back to Raleigh, North Carolina, in 1974 and before and since?
>
> WOODRUFF: No, it did not. We dealt only with the charges involving the June 18 incident. Since Ruff

pleaded guilty, there will be no need for your
testimony.

Woodruff then told Mrs. Grannell that there would be no need for
her as a witness. We left the building at approximately noon. Some
weeks later, on March 24, 1977, I learned from Lieutenant Woodruff's
office that Ruff had been given a five-day suspension. That was the action taken against him!

Later, the *Los Angeles Times* reported that two members of the city
council, Marvin Braude and Zev Yaroslavsky, expressed surprise and
concern that Ruff got only a five-day suspension. Yaroslavsky said, "He
should have been fired and prosecuted. . . . Why would we want to have
him on the force at all?"[7]

It was clear to us now that Ruff would never be prosecuted. So we
retained the services of attorney R. Samuel Paz and his co-counsel from
the American Civil Liberties Union, and we filed our complaint against
Ruff and the others:

> By their intentional actions carried out under color of state law
> as alleged above, Defendants Davis, Ruff, and [others] and each
> of them, and their agents and employees and those acting in
> concert with them, whose identities are presently unknown to
> the Plaintiff . . . unlawfully, willfully, willingly, corruptly, mali-
> ciously, discriminatorily, arbitrarily, and in bad faith combined,
> conspired, confederated, and agreed together and with each
> other to deprive Plaintiff of his rights, privileges, and immu-
> nities secured to him by the Constitution of the United States.[8]

We filed our complaint in 1977, against the city as well as the police
department. The complaint held the chief of police and police agent
Ruff of the red squad responsible for interfering with my attendance at
public meetings, vandalizing my car, slashing its tires, following me to
North Carolina to harass me, threatening me over the phone, and for
that terrible night of June 18, 1976, when Ruff drove across my lawn
and then set me up for a hit by the police.

As soon as the complaint was filed, five years of harassment ended.
There were another five years of legal maneuvering. Then, in 1982, the
Los Angeles Police Department agreed to pay me twenty-seven thousand five hundred dollars in damages. By virtue of that settlement, they
admitted their guilt. It was the first time the city police department

agreed to pay damages to a victim of political spying. The city council approved the out-of-court settlement, and that news made banner head-lines in the *Los Angeles Times*.

We filed suit as a political act to stop police harassment and violence against us and others. The proceeds from the settlement, adjudicated by the judge, were contributed to individuals and organizations devoted to bringing about peace and social change in our "free" America.

SCOTT CAMIL

Undercover Agents' War on Vietnam Veterans

Scott Camil

Patriotism moved Cril Payne to join the FBI in 1969. He became a "hippy agent," immersing himself in the anti-establishment youth culture. In 1972, he and other FBI undercover agents announced they would transport protesters to the Republican National Convention in Miami. They crossed the country in a caravan organized by the Vietnam Veterans Against the War (VVAW). "It was the unanimous opinion of the four agents who'd traveled with them for many days," Payne said, "that the Vietnam Vets were deeply committed to ending the war, not to senseless violence."[1] At the Miami convention, Payne himself was beaten so severely by police that he required several operations.

Even before the convention that would renominate Richard Nixon, VVAW had become the target of intense undercover operations by local, state, and federal police agencies. Agents infiltrated and became leaders. They gathered great amounts of information about the political activities and personal lives of the veterans, but in the end they were unable to demonstrate anything more than what Cril Payne had already observed. Undaunted, Guy Goodwin, Nixon's man in charge of indicting the antiwar movement to distraction if not to death, brought charges in Gainesville, Florida, against eight of the veterans for conspiring to disrupt the Republican Convention.

At the center of this vortex was Scott Camil, a recipient of nine medals for his service in Vietnam, a veteran who had volunteered for a second tour of duty because he, like Payne, was moved by patriotism. "A few times I thought my time was up," he wrote home from Vietnam, "but I fought hard and was lucky. Some of my buddies aren't so lucky and when one of them dies, a part of me dies with them. I can't see going home and leaving them here by themselves." [2]

Scott Camil and the others of the Gainesville Eight were eventually acquitted, but VVAW was severely weakened. Later, Scott Camil was in for a more personally devastating display of the power of federal secret police.

I grew up in a right-wing house. My stepfather was a policeman and very big in the John Birch Society. You dialed FRE-EDOM and you'd get a recorded message in his voice on the communist conspiracy, why we should invade Cuba, or that Martin Luther King attended communist meetings. In our house, I was taught that everybody owed a duty to their country. I had faith in the government. I looked up to authority and figured they knew what was going on. We were the smartest people in the world, I figured, our country was the best, and everything we did was right. So why not make the whole world like us? When I graduated high school, I joined the Marine Corps.

The Marines landed in Vietnam in September of 1965. Six months later, in March of 1966, I got there. I learned early that war was for real; you didn't get a second chance. I'd lost good friends, and it made me hate the Vietnamese intensely and consider all of them the enemy. Any time we'd go in a village and our people would step on a mine or get hit by a sniper, we'd burn the place down and kill everybody. It was an example to other villagers.

The rule for measuring success was dead human beings. It sounds crazy now, but we competed for body count. There'd be a beer party for the company or platoon with the highest score. Any dead body was considered a confirmed VC. I bragged about my body count. I wrote home how I was killing all those "commie gooks," and my parents wrote back saying, "We are proud of you."

Right before I got out of the Marine Corps, I spoke at Western Carolina University in Cullowhee, a real pretty place near Asheville, about why the war in Vietnam was right. The people said, "Well, you all kill women and children." I said that I didn't make the decisions and it wasn't my job to question them. I just did what I was told to do.

And they said, "But you killed women and children."

I justified killing women and children on the grounds that they could shoot you, they could throw grenades at you. Besides, they were communists, and it was important to exterminate communists. If we killed the women, they couldn't have any more children. And if we killed their children, they couldn't grow up to fight our children.

When I got out of the Marine Corps in 1969, I went to Miami-Dade Junior College under the G.I. bill. I learned about ethnocentrism, that you don't judge other cultures by your own. I studied about Indochina. It made me lose respect for the politicians and the government when I learned about the half-truths and lies they told. And that was very up-setting, but I didn't know what to do. I didn't like the peace demonstrators. In my mind, they were all communists. When they marched, I'd wear my Marine shirt and bump into them.

After I graduated from Miami-Dade, I transferred to the University of Florida. Jane Fonda came to speak. She said there was going to be a public inquiry into U.S. war crimes in Vietnam. Afterward, I talked to her. Since I had firsthand knowledge, I felt I should take part in it. So I went to the Winter Soldier Investigation in Detroit.* All I had really known about was what I and the guys with me had done. But then I saw all these veterans, some even from the Air Force and Navy, testifying that things like My Lai weren't just a fluke. All of a sudden, we saw the broad scope of what had happened.

My opposition to the war before that had been mostly because we were lied to and because we weren't fighting to win: "Why not go to Vietnam and just kick their ass and get it over with?" But now I asked, "What's it mean to win?" Do you have to have a higher score? Capture their flag? The only way to "win" was to kill all the people. As a boy, I'd heard about family members who were killed in Europe just for being Jews. I couldn't understand how soldiers could do that. I didn't stop to think that when I was a soldier I was doing basically the same thing. For the first time, I realized for sure that we were wrong and that what we had done to the people of Vietnam was bad. I wouldn't have done those

* The Winter Soldier Investigation of February 1971 borrowed its name from Tom Paine, who made the distinction between "sunshine patriots" and truly committed "winter soldiers." At that investigation, veterans testified about atrocities committed in Vietnam.

things had I known the truth. It made me sick that I had been used in this way.

We started an organization called the Vietnam Veterans Against the War. We testified before Congress. We spoke in schools, churches, synagogues, and had demonstrations all over the country. We expanded the Winter Soldier Investigation. It was local veterans who were telling people who knew them and their families what the hell the truth was. We grew from two thousand to fifty thousand members.

I was the VVAW coordinator for Florida, Alabama, Georgia, and South Carolina. It was very exciting: the planning, the work, and the movement. We used guerrilla theater to get our point across. One time, the VVAW carried a casket with an American flag in the homecoming parade, a big event for the University of Florida. People from the Quaker and Unitarian churches were at main intersections with blood packets under their clothes. Two squads of men carrying toy M-16s threw smoke into the crowd, then grabbed the people they had practiced with beforehand, threw them on the ground, and stuck them. People were screaming and yelling. Nobody knew what was going on. The last squad handed out leaflets saying, "If you were a Vietnamese, this could happen to you or your family."

We organized a march of two thousand veterans in Washington, D.C. Seven hundred of us threw away our medals in front of the Capitol. That was really hard, because my medals had been very important to me. The first time I got wounded, I thought about how I would have a Purple Heart to wear. But I came to see the medals as tokens for something I wasn't proud of anymore. It was like cutting the umbilical cord between myself and the government.

The government had been calling those against the war draft dodgers, punks who didn't know what they were talking about. But the government couldn't say we weren't willing to serve our country, because we'd been to Vietnam. Combat veterans are the epitome of patriotism. They couldn't claim we didn't know what happened in Vietnam, because we did it. So they had to make us look like violent, crazy people. We got tear gas, billy clubs, and police violence for doing things we felt were our constitutional right. The cops even beat the hell out of reporters who were taking pictures of them beating up demonstrators. Of course, we weren't pacifists, and we weren't afraid of the police. If we saw them hitting you at a demonstration, we'd help you. It's pretty hard to push around Vietnam veterans, especially once they realize they've been used and tricked.

But the government has a lot of power and a lot of money. They can be very disruptive to your life. They got people thrown out of school. They went to the employers of ex-G.I.s in the VVAW and got them fired for being "communists." I started getting phone calls: "Hey, man, I can't come to meetings anymore. The FBI went to where my mom works. She almost lost her job." It made me mad. I met with the FBI. I told them what we were doing so they could see we weren't doing anything wrong. And I told them they didn't have any right to get our members' parents in trouble at work.

I thought that if I just laid things on the line, they'd understand. What I didn't realize then was that the government had been infiltrating our organization all along. Some of them were informers. Some, like William Lemmer, were agent provocateurs who tried to play upon our Vietnam experiences, to manipulate us into some violent response, some confrontation with the authorities. In places like Oklahoma and Arkansas, he would help organize demonstrations, set vets up to get busted, and then tip the police off.

They began arresting VVAW people all over the country. They can destroy you without even winning a court case: getting bonded out of jail, paying for lawyers, having to go to court all the time. Without finding you guilty, they can bankrupt you financially and every other way. The government became very intent on arresting me. It didn't seem to matter for what. My FBI files showed me that. All it took for them to start keeping a file on me was a newspaper article about what I said at the Winter Soldier Investigation.

> Jacksonville: February 22, 1971
> "The Detroit News" dated February 1, 1971, carried an article on Page 3 regarding the WSI, which was described as "a three day mock trial of United States leaders accused of ordering war crimes against Vietnamese civilians." This article states that Scott Camil, a former Marine sergeant, "told of men in his unit cutting the hands off of slain enemy soldiers." Camil stated that "they had orders to stop such practice when newsmen were present." [3]

They kept track of me through that spring and summer.

> Jacksonville: August 2, 1971
> Subject continues to be very active in his capacity as South-

eastern Regional Director of the Vietnam Veterans Against the War and has maintained his non-violent approach in his anti-war activities. Subject has shown no propensity for violence.[4]

After the interview I had with the FBI, they wrote that I was "very cordial and friendly." In a November 24 memo from Jacksonville, they even considered "the possibility of development of Camil as a potential security informant."[5] I can't think of anything that would explain the sudden change on December 9.

> Director to Jacksonville: December 9, 1971
> A review of Bureau files notes subject's activities and alleged statements are such as to definitely warrant investigation of his activities, under current Bureau instructions, pertaining to New Left extremists. In this respect, you should place this case in an active status and promptly intensify your investigation.
> All individuals involved in New Left extremist activities should be considered dangerous because of their known advocacy and use of explosives, reported acquisition of firearms and incendiary devices, and known propensity for violence.[6]

The pressure was not coming from the bottom, from the people who had direct experience with me. It was coming from the top down. Somebody else was saying, "Do something about this guy."

> Director to Jacksonville, Miami, New York:
> December 10, 1971
> Information being developed by Jacksonville on continuing basis regarding subject indicates absolute necessity for full scale aggressive investigation be pressed in order that subject's activities can be neutralized and he can be prosecuted for criminal violations if warranted.[7]

> Jacksonville to Director, Miami, New York:
> December 11, 1971
> The Florida Alligator daily student newspaper, on December two last, carried an article which reflected an interview with Scott Camil, regional coordinator Vietnam Veterans Against the War. Camil said the VVAW has requested permission from the North Vietnamese government to send six veterans from all over the country to Hanoi. The purpose of the trip will be to

attempt to coordinate between the North and South Vietnamese governments and design a more effective way to end the war.

Will maintain continuous liaison with local state and federal law enforcement authorities re instant matter and direct logical investigation toward neutralizing Camil at earliest logical date.[8]

As much as I disliked what the government was doing, and as bad as I thought they were, deep down inside me there was something that wanted to believe that I'd just blown this out of proportion—that it was really not that bad. But when I read the memos saying "Neutralize him," it just did something to me. And it confirmed that they really are this bad.

> Director to Jacksonville: December 22, 1971
> Information developed to date regarding subject indicates clearly subject is extremely dangerous and unstable individual whose activities must be neutralized at earliest possible time. [Censored] Press U.S. Attorney for advisory opinion only as to whether facts to date warrant prosecution.[9]

When you pin the government down, they'll say, "Well, 'neutralize' just means to render useless." But if you talk to guys in the field, they say it means to kill.

> [Censored] to [Censored]: January 13, 1972
> Purpose: To recommend authority be granted Jacksonville Office to [Censored].
> Background: This refers to intensive investigation being pressed of subject, leader of Gainesville Chapter of VVAW [Censored].
> As previously reported, Jacksonville Office has [Censored]. Jacksonville has requested authority to [Censored].
> Action: Attached for approval is teletype to Jacksonville authorizing [Censored].[10]

Ten days after that memorandum, I was arrested for kidnapping. In Florida, it carried the death penalty. I was charged with kidnapping two seventeen-year-old kids for one hundred dollars' ransom. And the proof of the charges was a receipt I gave one kid. But kidnappers don't write receipts. It was so stupid. I knew that I didn't kidnap anyone, but there was nothing I could do. I was locked up. And all I heard on the radio every hour was "He could get the death penalty."

The head of Young Americans for Freedom, Mike Carr, lived across the street from me at the time. He allowed the FBI to use his house to spy on me. He testified later that he had been at meetings with the FBI agents in Gainesville. They said that pressure was being put on them from Washington to bust me for anything and to get it done quickly.

Six months later, they had to drop the kidnapping charges. In the meantime, I got arrested for possession of marijuana. I was eventually acquitted of that. I got arrested again in July. All of a sudden it was a pattern. Everybody was hassling me. The IRS came to arrest me for not paying an eleven-dollar phone tax. Naval Intelligence was hassling me. The Gainesville police, the Alachua County Sheriff's Department, the Region II narcotics squad, and the FBI were all spying on me. My house was broken into; my files were taken. My lawyer's office was burglarized, and only her file on me was missing.

When the Democrats and Republicans decided to have their conventions in Miami in the summer of 1972, we planned to go down there and demonstrate. But twenty-four of us, all in leadership positions, were subpoenaed to appear before a grand jury in Tallahassee. Our lawyers argued: "Hey, we need more time. There's only nine lawyers, and twenty-four of them." But the government wanted to keep us up there so we couldn't go to the convention. And the judge allowed them to do it, even though eleven of us were never called to testify.

After the Democratic Convention, the grand jury let us go. But then six of us were immediately indicted for conspiracy to disrupt the Republican Convention with the use of violence. Warrants were issued for our arrest. I had gone to the airport to pick up Mike Oliver, from the national office. On the way back, Stanley Michelson pulled us over. "We got a call from someone who said he was a government agent. He warned us the police were going to raid the house looking for you, that they were going to kill you and say you tried to escape."

The house we had been staying in was raided. About forty cops sealed off both ends of the block. They broke in with shotguns and ripped the place apart looking for me. I spent the night at a friend's. Then I called up the press and told them I was going to turn myself in. I arranged to meet my lawyers first, so I would have them and reporters with me for protection.

Two more guys were indicted, and we became known as the Gainesville Eight. We were made to stand trial together for charges of conspiracy that could have brought between ten and thirty years in prison. I represented myself. I wanted those who were going to judge me to get to feel my vibes and know me as a human being. I wanted to show the jury that the real reason the government was prosecuting us was to silence the VVAW.

The U.S. Attorney was Guy Goodwin. He was sent down from the Justice Department in Washington by John Mitchell and Robert Mardian. Goodwin's job was to get indictments on antiwar people like the Berrigans.* He issued over a hundred indictments around the country but got very few convictions. He just wanted to tie up people's time and money to keep them out of the way. For a year and a half, all our energy was taken away from the antiwar movement and turned to the courtroom for survival.

We got help from Philip Berrigan; Arthur Kraus, whose daughter had been killed at Kent State; and Anthony Russo, who was indicted with Daniel Ellsberg.† I went on a speaking tour around the country with Jane Fonda. We raised about two hundred eighty thousand dollars. Lawyers from the Center for Constitutional Rights defended us.

I was still naive enough to think there were rules that everybody played by and that everything was going to be fair and square. But the government just cheated all the time. The judge gave us a room in the court to work in with our lawyers. Somebody happened to look through the louvers of the closet and saw feet. We called the marshals, and when they unlocked the closet door, two FBI agents were in there with tape and equipment. We complained that our lawyer-client relationship was being violated. But the judge said we were making a mountain out of a molehill.

No matter what the government did, they were allowed to get away with it. When we were before the grand jury, our lawyers worried that some of us might be government agents. The judge put Guy Goodwin on the stand. He asked just one question: "Are any of the people sub-

---

* Guy Goodwin, an attorney in the Internal Security Division of the Justice Department, was instrumental in bringing indictments against Philip Berrigan and other antiwar Catholic activists for conspiring to kidnap Henry Kissinger and blow up heating pipes in federal buildings. Evidence for the bizarre charges was so thin that even some government lawyers felt there was no case. The Harrisburg Seven, as they came to be called, were acquitted without the defense presenting any witnesses.

† Daniel Ellsberg and Anthony Russo were charged with conspiracy to steal the Pentagon Papers and make them public. The Pentagon Papers, a copy of which was given to the *New York Times* by Ellsberg, detailed the secret history of American involvement in Vietnam and showed how the American people had been misled about the war. Ellsberg and Russo were freed when a mistrial was declared after government misconduct was revealed.

poenaed before the grand jury government informants?" Goodwin said, "No." So we picked the people to help us plan our strategy for the Gainesville trial from that group. But Goodwin had lied under oath. At least three government agents had been allowed to be in the meetings between us and our attorneys.

Emerson Poe was one of my best friends. My girlfriend and I used to babysit for his wife and him. When she had a miscarriage, we took care of his kid while they were at the hospital. We were that close. Poe had been right with me as assistant regional coordinator of VVAW. He worked with us when we met with the lawyers, talked strategy, and he even helped us select a jury.

And then we're sitting there near the end of the trial, and Jack Carrouth, the prosecutor, calls him. Emerson Poe gets up, and he's one of them. It blew me away. I couldn't believe he could be an informer. Poe testified that the FBI came to him when he worked at the Veterans Administration and told him we were violent communist sympathizers and he could do a service for his country by spying. So he joined our organization. Once he got in, it had to be obvious that we were doing good things. But the whole time, he was reporting back to the FBI. I don't understand why he went along with them. I don't understand.

When I cross-examined him, he wouldn't look me in the eye. He looked down at the table like he was ashamed, and he would talk quietly. My questions were all framed the same way: "Isn't it true that you gave a surprise birthday party for my girlfriend?" "Isn't it true that we decorated your Christmas tree together?" To all these questions, Poe said, "Yes." I asked him, "Poe, are we friends or not?" He answered, "No."

Before, I was so open that anybody could come to my house. And they just filled the place up with cops. There were over eleven government agencies in our organization. There was the Treasury Department, the Federal Bureau of Investigation, the Secret Service, the Florida Department of Law Enforcement, the Miami Police Department, the Dade County Metro Police Department, the Gainesville Police Department, the Alachua County Sheriff's Department, the New Orleans Police Department. At times, more than half of those at our meetings were government agents. One Miami police informant said, "Darling, the spies were spying on the spies that were spying on the spies." [11]

The government tried every way they could to provoke us. William Lemmer, the FBI informant, told us that he had seen government plans:

They were going to shoot a leader of the New Left at Miami Beach and blame it on the demonstrators; the bridges from the beach were going to be raised, and people killed; and national security measures were going to be put into effect. And Lemmer asked, "What are we going to do about it?"

We realized the government might be provoking us, but since we couldn't be sure, we figured we'd plan for the worst. After all, things like that were going on. People were getting killed—Kent State, Jackson State. So we made contingency plans to defend ourselves. We considered all the alternatives, and violence was one we discussed, to protect our lives and our rights, if necessary.

Lemmer lied to us, and then he came into court and lied to the jury. He told them we were going to the Republican Convention to fight, to attack and kill people. He said we had formed political assassination squads.

The fact was that we were going to Miami to exercise our right to protest the war. We remembered the police violence at the Chicago convention in 1968, so we took every precaution we could not to have it repeated. We had many meetings with the police in Miami and Miami Beach. We had meetings with the Miami Beach City Commission. We met with the city manager, the head of civil defense, the senior citizens, and the Governor's Task Force. We played a softball game, VVAW against the Miami Beach motorcycle police. We met with other organizations to ensure that there was *not* another Chicago.

We even met with the most militant right-wing Cubans in order to be assured of nonviolence. That turned out to be another government set-up. Undercover agents led us to believe that anti-Castro Cubans were planning to attack us and that we'd have to make a deal with them. When I tried to contact them, I was put in touch with Pablo Fernandez, a Cuban refugee. I didn't know he worked for the FBI and the Miami police and was part of the Cuban Watergate crowd.

I arranged a meeting with Fernandez in Hialeah. I told him there was no reason for them to attack the VVAW. We wanted self-determination for the Vietnamese, just as they wanted it for the Cubans. The next thing I knew, he was trying to sell me all these weapons: mortars, machine guns, bazookas. But their set-up didn't work; I wasn't interested. Afterward, Fernandez admitted to a reporter for the *Miami Herald* that he came to our meeting wired with a body bug.[12] When we tried to get him to testify, he disappeared.

Later, Adam Klimkowski of the Miami police said, "We are hoping for the overt act necessary to produce a conspiracy."[13] But there were no illegal acts. All they had were people crossing state lines or people talking on telephones and coming to meetings at my house.

Our lawyers felt the government hadn't proved anything. They said it would be a big political statement if we were found not guilty without even putting on a defense. I didn't want to do that. We'd gone through the work of researching all the dirty things the government did. We were able to get the original statements their informants turned in. Since they didn't know each other as agents, they lied about each other as well as about us. Now that we had international media attention, I felt this was our chance to put them on trial. But the vote was six to two against continuing. Six guys were tired of their lives being tied up. They wanted to be done with it.

In less than four hours, the jury returned with a verdict of not guilty. They came out of the box and hugged our lawyers and the defendants. It was really great. And the prosecutors just sat there, shaking their heads. A taxi driver who took two of the prosecutors to the airport told us he overheard them saying they would still get Scott Camil.

After the Gainesville Eight case, I moved out of town. Then I came back in quietly. I needed to have some privacy. I got a friend to rent me a house and turn on the electricity and gas in his name. One day, a woman came to the door. She said her name was Barbara Ives and that she was looking for my friend. She came in, and we got to talking. We soon developed a very intimate relationship. And we did drugs. She drove up every weekend from Orlando and stayed with me. This went on for about three months.

Once, she introduced two people to me as her friends. I was selling office supplies, and she said they were opening up a first-aid supply house and might be in the market for business equipment. One Friday, they came in town and said they were going to get some drugs, and did I want some too? They told me I needed some good stuff because Barbara was coming up and wanted to have a good time that weekend. So I went with them. On the way back, the guy in the back seat grabbed me around the neck, pinned me to the headrest, and stuck a gun there. He said, "If you move, I'm going to blow off your fucking head." Then he started hitting me with the gun.

I didn't know who these guys really were. I knew I wasn't going to let them take me anywhere. On TV, you see the bad guy walk into a bar with his hand in his pocket. He says, "You come with me." He takes the guy out to the woods somewhere and kills him. And I always thought, "Damn, why do they leave a crowded place? If the guy is going to commit murder, make him do it in front of all these other people."

The third or fourth time he came up with the gun to hit me, I grabbed his wrist and pinned his hand to the headrest. I unlocked the car door. We were in traffic, and I was going to jump out. The driver hit the brakes, and we all went forward. He pulled my one hand off the door, pulled my other hand off his partner's hand, and held my arms up while his partner shot me. The bullet went in my back and came out the front. It was such a shock, like being back in Vietnam again. There was no second chance here, either.

The shot knocked me out of the car. I hit the pavement in front of a restaurant. People looking out the window called the police station, a couple of blocks away. The guy who shot me jumped out of the car and stood over me with his gun. The Gainesville police came just in time. The guy flashed his badge, and at that point I knew Barbara Ives's two "friends" were cops. The Gainesville police took them into custody and got separate statements before they had time to collaborate on their stories. It turned out these two worked for the Drug Enforcement Agency: Dennis Fitzgerald, who shot me, and William Roy Porter.

It really hurt my head a lot when I found out Barbara Ives had been assigned by the government to sleep with me. The government shouldn't be allowed to invade your privacy like that. I was the kind of person who thought that if I had been intimate with somebody, there was a friendship, a closeness that shouldn't be violated. And here she had set it all up and was part of those cops trying to kill me.

The bullet went in behind my heart. It shattered some ribs. It collapsed my lung and caused kidney and liver damage. I was in the hospital for two weeks. I came home, and my lung collapsed again. I don't have the stamina that I used to have, and I don't have the twisting ability. I don't have any feeling in one leg, and there's shrapnel in my other leg and in my shoulder. But it doesn't keep me from doing what I want to do. You're going to have to hit me pretty hard to stop me.

After I was nearly killed by those two cops, I was charged with assaulting federal agents and with possession and delivery of drugs. I never understood why they took me to trial. What they should have done after they shot me and I didn't die was drop it. All they would have had was "this crazy guy with the beard" running around, bitching about them trying to kill him. As it was, Jack Carrouth, who was now head prosecutor, brought a second case against me, and in this one, too, his witnesses contradicted the evidence.

All our evidence came from FBI and police labs, stuff I couldn't tamper with and they couldn't discredit. It proved that Fitzgerald and Porter were lying. They said I grabbed the gun and tried to pull it from them, and it went off. But my fingerprints weren't on the gun. A paraffin test proved my hands weren't anywhere near the gun when it went off. An FBI ballistics test on the powder burns on my shirt and on the entrance and exit wounds determined that the gun was fired from a place that I couldn't reach. A witness I didn't know, so his credibility couldn't be tainted, said he didn't see me strike either of the two agents: "They were grabbing for him, and he was trying to get away." He said one of the federal agents told him, "We don't need any witnesses. We have all the witnesses we need."

We learned Fitzgerald and Porter had told the Gainesville DEA agent, Lloyd Vipperman, they were going to do a case on me. Vipperman said he didn't think I was involved in drug dealing, but if they had a good case they should return with a warrant and he would arrest me. Instead, they contacted their headquarters in Orlando and arranged to have Vipperman leave town. Then they came in without an arrest warrant and blasted me. The gun they shot me with was not their service revolver. It was unregistered. They came all the way from Orlando to try to kill me with a gun that couldn't be traced to them.

The jury found me not guilty on all charges. Then they did something that never happens. They recommended that the DEA agents be indicted for attempted murder. The jury foreman even went to the state attorney's office to tell him Fitzgerald tried to kill me and should be tried for it. They were never indicted.

When I think back on it, I'm still angry about what I had to go through in Vietnam. I was there two years and was wounded twice. The things I did to people who didn't do anything to me bother me a lot. The anger I have will never be gone. I'll always be mad at the government for lying.

A democracy can't live on lies. During the days of the antiwar movement, I wanted to tell the truth about the war, and I think I was intelligent and effective. I figured I was invulnerable, too. If they didn't like me, tough. But look what the government did. They arrested me for kidnapping, and that would have meant the death penalty; then they arrested me on conspiracy charges that would have meant years in jail.

They lied under oath. They burglarized my home and my lawyer's office. They surrounded me with spies, having one become my best friend. They invaded my deepest privacy. They tried to kill me.

There's a song that talks about coming home from Nam and still having the guns pointed at us. When the police shot me, it really changed my attitude. And now I have too much to lose—the joy I get from my family is more than I can explain—and I'm not willing to pay the price of being in the front lines. They've effectively silenced me.

PAUL BERMANZOHN

The Greensboro Massacre: Police-Vigilante Nexus

Paul Bermanzohn

All-white juries on two occasions refused to convict Klansmen and Nazis for the public murders of five anti-Klan demonstrators in Greensboro, North Carolina, in 1979. And public they were: four television crews had filmed the methodical murders that were later aired for nationwide audiences in PBS's "Eighty-Eight Seconds in Greensboro," a "Front-line" program. Six years after the massacre, a civil suit on behalf of the survivors and injured, alleging government complicity with the Klan and the Nazis, was partially won. "At last!" Dr. Martha Nathan wrote in June 1985, "Klansmen, Nazis, Greensboro police, and police informant Edward Dawson were finally held accountable for the death of my husband, Dr. Michael Nathan, and the assault of Dr. Paul Bermanzohn and Tom Clark." [1]

The apparent participation of undercover police in the planning and execution of the murders makes them all the more shocking. This was not the first time police operatives had been implicated in the criminal acts of violent, right-wing organizations or had refused to act on knowledge that could have prevented the crimes. Such was the case in the beatings of the first Freedom Riders, the bombing of a Birmingham church that killed four children, and the assassination of civil rights worker Viola Liuzzo. In the Greensboro Massacre, agents of the Bureau

of Alcohol, Tobacco, and Firearms and the Greensboro Police Depart-
ment had a hand in different aspects of what could be called a domestic
death squad.

Our daughter, Sandy, was in Sally's belly, three months from being
born, at the time of the massacre. She was named after Sandi Smith,
who was murdered there. Frankie Powell was eight months pregnant.
She was shot in the back of the legs and buttocks. We were very worried
she would lose her kid, but her son was born okay. The kids who made
it through those times became a rough, tough bunch.

My own mother and father were in concentration camps during
World War II. They were Polish Jews, and both their families had been
killed off. They met during an artillery battle, while the Russians engaged the German troops who were fleeing. They got married quickly,
as many people in that situation did. Then they went to Germany to
wait for a flight to the United States. Meanwhile, I was born. We came
to this country when I was about seven months old. And I was raised
with a lot of stories about the Holocaust. It was a big influence in my
thinking.

I went to City College and became politically active during the war
in Vietnam. That was an important period in my life, in many people's
lives. I was the president of student government in 1968 and, as you can
imagine, was involved in a lot of student movement stuff. After City
College, I went to medical school at Duke University, down in Durham,
North Carolina. That did a lot to radicalize me.

We started the Medical Committee for Human Rights in the 1960s
to provide medical presence for civil rights demonstrations. As the sixties became the seventies, we moved from simply providing support for
other things to fighting for improvements in the health system. We ran a
neighborhood clinic, one of those alternative clinics that had no facilities at all. We tried to get the university hospital to keep their clinic open
at night. They had the building; all they had to do was turn on the lights
and have a few doctors in there. But it was impossible to make any
headway because the administrators all gave us the run-around.

I became an expert in byssinosis, or brown lung, as it was called.
Byssinosis is a vast epidemic in the textile mills. Breathing in cotton dust
causes a kind of emphysema or chronic bronchitis that can be deadly
after a while. When I graduated from medical school, Jim Waller and I

became the medical wing of the Brown Lung Association. Marty and Mike Nathan worked on it, too. Our biggest job was to let people know that brown lung existed, because the textile industry kept it quiet. Their doctors had been diagnosing it as asthma or bronchitis or blaming it on smoking. We conducted screening clinics and educational sessions.

We spoke all over North and South Carolina to textile workers' groups. I'll never forget the first meeting of the Carolina Brown Lung Association. Jim and I went down to Columbia, South Carolina, to talk to about one hundred fifty retired textile workers in the union hall. There wasn't a silent breather in the crowd. They were all wheezing and hacking and coughing. But those workers were tremendous. Even though they knew they couldn't get rid of their brown lung, they were ready to help prevent others from getting it.

That was our first connection with textile workers. Later, some of our group went to work in the mills and became rank-and-file union leaders. Jim Waller led a strike of textile workers, increased the union's size from twelve to two hundred fifty, and then was fired from his job. He was enormously popular. After he was fired, the workers thought enough of him to elect him president of their local. Bill Sampson was about to be elected president of his local just before the massacre. And Sandi Smith was the head of a rank-and-file organizing committee at her mill; at their first public meeting, two hundred fifty or three hundred workers came, from a plant of about six hundred.

By that time, a series of collectives had spontaneously emerged around the country, people like ourselves who were trying to figure out what to do politically. There were very intensive polemics, debates, forums, studies, articles exchanged among them. It was an exciting time, and it culminated with our group in Durham, which was all-white, merging with an all-Black collective in Greensboro. Eventually, our two groups became part of the Workers Viewpoint Organization. The Communist Workers Party, the CWP, was actually founded in October of 1979, out of the various collectives that were merging with the Workers Viewpoint Organization.

In the summer of 1979, we were contacted by people in China Grove, a very small town outside of Kannapolis. Most of the people there are textile workers. Eighty percent of the town is Black. The Ku Klux Klan was going to show *Birth of a Nation* in the white community center to recruit new members. We organized a militant demonstration against them. About a hundred fifty people, some with sticks and other implements, marched right up to where the Klan was meeting. The Klan came out, very heavily armed, up to M-16s. I was as close to the Klan leadership as I am to you. It was intense, I'm telling you.

Then they backed up. Some people grabbed their Confederate flags and burned them in front of their eyes. We had confronted the Klan and humiliated them. It was all over the state. No one had stood up to them like that in quite some time. A Black lady, a real hard-fighting woman who was with us, said to me, "Oh, Paul, I wish my grandmother had been there. The Klan ran, and they had the guns."

People started asking us to do other things. That was why the November third demonstration in Greensboro was organized. It was supposed to be a march, followed by a conference at a church. Speakers were to talk about what the Klan stood for and who their secret supporters were. The punch of the anti-Klan campaign was to show that the Klan was not just an isolated entity, just a bunch of right-wing kooks with guns, but rather that they were pawns in a larger game. They were used by the police, many of whom were Klansmen themselves. They were used by people in high places who covered themselves in three-piece suits.

Prior to November third, the police kept tearing down our posters. They were harassing our people so much that on November first we had a press conference on the steps of the police station. We announced our anti-Klan march and said that what the police had been doing for the last few days showed that they supported the Klan.

Eddie Dawson, who later achieved fame as one of the leaders of the caravan that killed our people, showed up at the press conference. Eddie introduced himself as a businessman. He said he couldn't believe that in this day and age there was something like the Ku Klux Klan in Greensboro, North Carolina. He smelled funny, but I didn't make anything more of it.

Two days later, we went to Morningside Homes for the start of the march. People were gathering there, many of them with children. Some were singing civil rights songs, and others were packing up signs and posters. It was the mixture of exuberance and tension that always precedes a big demonstration. Camera crews from four television stations were setting up their equipment.

A minute or two before the caravan pulled up, Sandi Smith came up to me and said, "Something's weird."

I asked, "What's that?" She said, "There's no cops here." I looked around and, sure enough, there wasn't a police officer in sight. Now, for a veteran of a few hundred marches down South, this looked very unusual. But I had things to do, so I made no more of it.

The next thing I know, there's this caravan of cars driving up. At first, all you see is the lead car. Then you see there's a whole line of cars. It looks like a funeral cortège. And some guys are leaning out the windows. One guy is yelling, "Kill the kikes, kill the niggers!"

Another leans out of the window and shouts, "China Grove! You asked for the Klan, you've got it!" Some people who don't like Klansmen coming in like that kick a couple of the cars. And one or two guys take picket sticks and hit some of the cars to answer their "Kill the kikes, kill the niggers."

The lead vehicle in the caravan is a pickup truck. It stops about twenty feet from me. A young, neatly trimmed fellow—Mark Sherer is his name—leans out of the passenger side, all the way, so he is up to his waist out of the window. He picks up a long-barreled pistol—I'm close enough to see that the barrel is unusually long—and he fires a shot into the air. He waves his pistol, yelling, "Move them out, move them out!"

Suddenly, we are attacked from two sides, from the front and the back of the caravan, by guys with sticks. A lot of people run back into the housing project where we are assembling. I turn around and run with everybody else for maybe ten or fifteen steps. I stop for a second and look behind me. Cesar Cauce is over there, and they're hitting him. About six guys are around him, hitting him with sticks, and he's fighting back. So I look at that and think: "That's the right thing to be doing." I'm carrying a picket sign, and I kind of heft it to get the feel of it, like a batter does before going up to the plate. I turn around to run back to help Cesar.

I take about three steps. And zip, zip. I'm hit in two places. By what, I have no idea. You don't see bullets. You usually don't feel bullets. It's like a jet of high-pressure air. It just knocks me off my feet. I can't get up, and I can't figure out why.

One bullet shattered my forehead. You could feel all the fissures in the bone in the front of my head. It went through my brain, and it started to come out of my temple. The other bullet went into my arm, inches from my heart.

I am conscious through all this. I look up and see Cesar still fighting them. I continue to watch Cesar from the lawn and try to get up, but I can't. When I try, when I sincerely make an effort to get up, but I can't, then I figure I don't have any more responsibilities. I can relax. I have this strange sense of peacefulness. I probably pass out one or two short times, but I'm not really unconscious.

While the Klan and the Nazis are shooting, it makes a very loud, almost continuous roar of noise. It is impossible to distinguish individual gunshots. As I'm lying there in the little alleyway, the sound reverberates. It doesn't seem like there is any letup.

Suddenly, it's quiet. The Klan and Nazis have taken off. And the silence is almost as deafening. It is such an incredible contrast from the vast noise that had been pouring down on us.

People are yelling, "Doctor! Doctor!" Again, I'm trying to get up. I feel really tired. I feel I am very old, very, very old. I remember thinking, "Jim and Mike could handle it." I didn't know they were dying.

Sally comes over to calm me down. I hear people. I can't tell whether they are yelling or they are close up and talking. By this time, my eyes are swollen shut. I hear, "Jim's dead. Sandi's dead." It's like—What! I mumble a few things to Sally.

The ambulance finally came, after a long time. I remember my leg was kind of splayed out over the stretcher, stiff and shaking. They wouldn't let Sally in the ambulance. I was very fortunate that when I got to the hospital the best brain surgeon in central North Carolina happened to be in his greens just then, just there. I was in the operating room about six hours. They had to remove a section of my brain that was destroyed. They didn't know if I was going to live or die.

Right before they wheeled me into the emergency room, I said to the nurse, "Don't tell my parents." I figured they were going to be pissed off because now I'd gone and done it. And the last thing I wanted to do was to get them mad.

Afterward, I was lying in bed. My eyes were purple and still swollen shut. I must have really looked a mess, a frightful scene. My head was all bandaged up, and my arm was all bandaged up. I had tubes running into various orifices in my body, doing different things. Suddenly, I hear a voice that says, "Paul."

I'm telling you, that was the first time I got really scared during the whole thing. It was my mother.

I said, "Mom?"

My mother is a tough lady. She escaped three times from the Nazis in Europe, twice by jumping from moving trains. And she didn't lose any of that. Now she came over to me. Evidently, she had surveyed the scene and concluded that the only place she could grab me was around my chest. She hugged me, and she said, "Son, I'm proud of you."

When I heard that, I really choked up.

Oh, it was so heavy, because my parents' experience had a lot to do with my political development. But they hadn't exactly wanted it to turn out the way it did. They would have preferred some kind of a socialist-zionist or something like that. Instead, they got a communist. But my mother immediately began drawing connections between Weimar Germany, before the rise of Hitler, and this incident. "People could do this in broad daylight!" And "Where were the police?" And "What the hell was going on here?" She's been tremendous, just tremendous.

I was hospitalized for several months, two weeks in the Greensboro Hospital and two and a half months at the rehabilitation center in Durham. My left side was totally paralyzed. I couldn't move anything. One day, I was trying to put my legs under the sheet. The way you do it is you hook your good leg under your bad leg, then pull on it. I was about to do my little flip routine when my left leg jumped up. I said, "Welcome back!" I couldn't believe it.

For a while, I couldn't read. The top of the orbit of my right eye was blown away, and the part of my brain that controls focusing the eyes was pretty much ruined. People would give me only watered-down versions of what was happening. Every day the papers had stories about the massacre. It was outrageous garbage. We were being accused of having brought the murders on ourselves. Just lies, slander. Newspaper articles were coming out accusing Sally and Joe Waller's widow, Signe, of having organized the whole thing for publicity.

Later, *Time* magazine blamed me. They ran an article with the headline "The Dare That Ignited a Slaughter."[2] They were trying to blame me for shooting off my mouth. I had stated to the press, before the demonstration, that the Klan was nothing but a bunch of punks and cowards. I still say that and will continue to say that, because it's a fact. But saying that was no justification for the death squad. And that's what I believe it was.

When we saw five leaders of the CWP hit in the head and the heart out of a crowd of a hundred fifty people, we knew this was not a random shooting. It was as random as going into Grand Central Station at rush hour, opening fire blindly, and killing only people who were born in April. And who would have the ability to pick these five out, or the interest in doing it? We maintained that this was a political assassination and that the government was behind it. They had done this kind of thing in the past. COINTELPRO is a matter of record. The CIA does this all over the world. So why would the government have any more respect for revolutionaries who are American citizens than they have for anybody else—Nicaraguans or Vietnamese or whatever people they go around massacring?

So we said to the press straight out: The FBI was behind these murders. Immediately, all the liberal defenders of the order, the meticulous research types who use that as a cover for never doing anything, jumped up and said: "You're all paranoid, you're crazy; there's no evidence."

But shortly before the Klan-Nazi trial opened up, in June of 1980, an exposé came out on Bernard Butkovich. Bernard Butkovich, an agent of the Bureau of Alcohol, Tobacco, and Firearms, was exposed in the *Greensboro Daily News* as having been part of the planning sessions for the massacre. The BATF had sent Bernard into Winston-Salem to infiltrate the Nazis in July of 1979, after the China Grove confrontation. Butkovich helped arrange the coalition of the Nazis and the Klan, called the United Racist Front. The only thing the Racist Front ever did was carry out the massacre in Greensboro. It was Butkovich who incited them to violence and offered to train them in commando tactics. And, interestingly enough, this federal firearms agent offered to provide them with explosives, including grenades.

It didn't stop there. The day after the murders, Bernie was allowed to visit Roland Wood, the arrested Nazi, in jail. He told Wood he wanted to give sanctuary on a farm in Ohio to the other three Nazis who were wanted by the government for the murders. He also proposed to burn down Wood's house and plant evidence to make it look like the CWP did it. We know this because the Nazis fingered Butkovich.

The local papers carried the thing about Bernie. It was picked up by the *Post* and the *Times*. Government involvement was no longer a matter of wild communist paranoid fantasy. Butkovich was a member of the Bureau of Alcohol, Tobacco, and Firearms, part of the Treasury Department, which, as an intelligence agency, puts it very close to the Secret Service. That's high up.

Now there were names and faces of government agents to be associated with the actual commission of the murders.

Edward Dawson had been a longtime informer for the FBI. Dawson was the guy who, at our press conference, told us he couldn't believe that the Klan existed in a city like Greensboro. Dawson was the same guy who organized and recruited Klansmen for the caravan. He was a leader of the group. He confessed to that. During the Klan-Nazi trial in Greensboro, several Klansmen testified that Dawson showed up at the rendezvous point with maps. He kept walking around looking at his watch, they said, hurrying everybody up.

Dawson was in the lead car. He yelled out of the window something like "you communist son of a bitch" to me. Our eyes met, and at that moment I remembered him from the press conference two days before. I told the police about this guy later, after I got out of the hospital. But they never brought any charges against Dawson. Why should they? This was their boy. There is not a shadow of a doubt that Dawson was working with the Greensboro police while he organized this murderous caravan. On the morning of November third, Eddie Dawson talked two times on the telephone to his police contact, Jerry Cooper, alias "Rooster." He warned Cooper that the Klan was heavily armed—"everybody had a gun"—and that they were planning a confrontation. The police record shows that Dawson reported this at ten-thirty on the morning of November 3, 1979. The murders took place at eleven twenty-two.

Where were the police? The police were sent for sandwiches. The police assigned to duty for the march were ordered to go to an early lunch, only to arrive on the scene too late, minutes after the murders.

Earlier, Cooper himself had gone out to the rendezvous point of the Klan. Cooper watched them a long time. He photographed them. He followed them seven miles through Greensboro. The caravan consisted of nine cars of Klansmen and Nazis and one unmarked car with Detective Cooper. One block from the site of the murders, Cooper turned away from the caravan. He never made any effort to stop them. When he was later asked why, he said he didn't want to violate their civil rights, God forbid.

The Greensboro police were very well aware there was murder in the works. Police Chief William Swing admitted he had advance notice from Dawson that the Klan was coming to Greensboro with guns. It is obvious the police were, at the very least, allowing the thing to happen, giving them grace time for it to happen, if they were not directly carrying the thing out.

The first thing the police did when they came on the scene was to arrest some demonstrators, while the Klan was tearing off. They made no chase. In fact, the transcript of the police radio communications shows that Officer Burke, arriving on the scene, called in: "The guys are taking off. Shall I give chase?" It seems highly odd that a police officer, arriving on the scene of five murders, where the obvious perpetrators of the crime are taking off at sixty miles an hour, would stop to ask for instructions. Nevertheless, he never got an answer and never chased.

They arrested Rand Manzella on the spot. His best friend, Bill Sampson, had a revolver with him and had fired back a couple of shots. Bill was hit in the chest and tossed his gun to Rand, who was right next to him. Now, Rand was dazed by the whole thing. Gunfire was coming in waves. After the Klan and Nazis pulled out, Rand kind of wandered out into the open and knelt over Cesar's body. He was carrying this empty revolver, and he was looking at Cesar, just dazed. The cops ran up and arrested Rand for "being armed to the terror of the people," which is an old anti-Klan statute in North Carolina. By then, they had allowed the Klan to escape.

We didn't know that we had been under intensive FBI scrutiny for about a month and a half before the massacre. It ended November second. At first, the FBI admitted there was a report of that investigation. Then they denied it, then they steadfastly denied it. But Daisy Crawford, a textile organizer from Kannapolis, filed an affidavit that two FBI agents had visited her home the week before the murders. They showed her a photograph of Sandi Smith, whom she had known for a long time. She thought the other pictures were of Bill Sampson, Mike Nathan, Jim Waller, and me. Then, after years of FBI denials, Agent Penfield let slip that the investigation of the CWP had taken place and that a report of it had been written. It was a matter of record.

The FBI also denied having any knowledge before the massacre of the plans of the Nazis and Klan. Yet, on October 31, four days before the assault, Dawson warned the FBI that the Klansmen would be armed. There was more evidence. H. M. Michaux, a former United States Attorney, stated under oath that a Greensboro FBI agent told him about the plans for the attack before it happened.

Most incriminating of all was an affidavit from Mordechai Levy of the Jewish Defense Organization. When Levy got his FBI file through the Freedom of Information Act, he found an entry dated November 2, 1979, the day before the massacre. In it, the FBI reported that Levy told one of their agents: "I have information that Harold Covington of the National Socialist Party of America is up to heavy illegal activity. Covington has been training in the Jefferson County area with illegal weapons. He and his group have plans to attack and possibly kill people at an anti-Klan gathering this week in North Carolina."[3]

Well, that was evidence from the FBI's own files that showed they knew about the attack before it happened. They knew about it. The Greensboro police knew about it. The Bureau of Alcohol, Tobacco, and Firearms knew about it. But they did not warn us and did nothing to prevent the violence. And some of them were even in on planning the attack and took part in it.

Of the forty men in the assassination caravan, only sixteen were arrested. Of those sixteen, only six were brought to trial for the murders. In a murder trial, the district attorney becomes the lawyer for the victim. That meant we couldn't have our own personal lawyers. Although we petitioned for a special prosecutor, we had to rely on the North Carolina prosecutor, who we knew would not make a case against these guys. Before the trial, he told the press: "Most of the people in Greensboro think the communists got what they deserved." He also said, "I fought in Vietnam, and you know who my adversaries there were." Well, they weren't the Klan or the Nazis; they were the communists.

The jury selection was unbelievable. It's still unbelievable to talk about it. They asked questions like: Do you believe it's less of a crime to kill a communist? The potential jurors would answer yes. And they would be accepted by the prosecution, by those who were supposed to be our lawyers. They excluded Black jurors because Black jurors might, God forbid, be prejudiced against the Klan. Meanwhile, they admitted the next-door neighbor and close personal friend of the head of the North Carolina KKK. Two officers of the Greensboro Police Department were on the jury. Also on the jury was a certain Octavio R. Manduley, a right-wing Cuban immigrant who admitted being an active member of the Twentieth of May organization. That's the group that had participated in the Bay of Pigs invasion. These were his blood brothers on trial before him. And he was the foreman of the jury.

Now, when you have an anti-communist jury and an anti-communist prosecutor in a trial like this, you have to ask the question, In which direction are they going to turn their guns? It was very clear that this was going to be a kangaroo court, in which we would be on trial. That was confirmed when the prosecutor didn't even call Butkovich or Dawson as witnesses after the public revelations about them. So we refused to testify. In the end, they acquitted the Nazis and the Klan for murders that millions had seen them commit on national television. Justice!

But what if they had been found guilty? Secret Agent Michael Sweat, another BATF guy, conspired during the Klan-Nazi trial with the

Nazis to firebomb four sites in Greensboro in the event of a guilty verdict. Sweat convinced the Nazi leader to go ahead with the bombings, saying any moron could do it. And that was all recorded on tape.

It's sometimes said that in order to adequately monitor right-wing groups, the police informant has to get into the good graces of those he's observing. Consequently, he can't disdain violent activity completely. And, they say, to do that, he has to walk a thin line—which is nonsense. I mean, what kind of thin line is organizing firebombings and death squads?

The American Experience with Concentration Camps

In Defense of the Constitution

Minoru Yasui

During World War I, governors of four western states proposed to the federal government that members of the Industrial Workers of the World be interned for the duration of the war. In 1939, the Hobbs "Concentration Camp" Bill, which sought to detain aliens before or instead of deporting them, passed the House by an overwhelming majority but failed in the Senate. In 1950, the McCarran Act contained provisions allowing the establishment of concentration camps for "subversives." And through the 1960s, the FBI kept secret lists of more than two hundred thousand Americans it proposed to detain immediately upon the declaration of a national emergency. Concentration camps in America may seem inconceivable. But they have not only been proposed—they have in fact existed. One of the sites designated as an internment center by the McCarran Act was the notorious Tule Lake camp, where Americans of Japanese descent were imprisoned during World War II.

Without being charged with or convicted of any crime, one hundred twenty thousand Japanese Americans, most of them citizens of the United States, were ordered into internment camps shortly after Pearl Harbor. Minoru Yasui's defiance of that military order was driven by a fierce devotion to the Constitution. His challenge, turned back by the Supreme Court at the time, has been reopened. Now, forty years later,

MINORU YASUI

government misconduct has been discovered in his and two similar cases that set the disturbing precedent for the internment of civilians by the military.

As children, we grew up in the small town of Hood River, Oregon. I guess until about the third grade I thought I was like everybody else. I can remember fighting with a good friend of mine, Kenny Abraham, whose father was a doctor. We were rolling around in the dirt. And the father came by and said, "Kenny, get away from that goddamn Jap."

My grandfather came here in the 1890s. He went to work on the railroads, both in Idaho and in Montana. He got a few dollars and called for his eldest son, my uncle. Between the two of them, they brought in another uncle, and between the three of them, they brought in my dad.

Dad came in 1903, at the age of sixteen. Since he was young and not very strong physically, they made him a water boy. He resented that job and left for Portland. He worked as a domestic for fifty cents a week while he went to school. Dad wanted to become a lawyer. He soon found out, though, that as a Japanese, as an Oriental, the laws of the United States did not permit him to become a citizen, and therefore he couldn't be a lawyer. He left Portland to go east but got only as far as Hood River, and there he settled. The countryside reminded him so much of his home in Japan.

As I grew older, I realized more and more how the restrictions against persons of Japanese ancestry impinged upon our lives. A number of our nisei friends, second-generation Japanese Americans, who were engineers, were having an extremely difficult time getting jobs. In 1939, I graduated from law school, passed the bar examination, and looked for a job with a large law firm. There just were no good jobs for Japanese Americans in Portland. But among dad's personal friends was Hiroshi Acino, then the Japanese consul-general in Chicago. Being able to speak English and having a law degree, I was hired in the Chicago consulate for a hundred and a quarter a month. That was considered fairly good money in those days.

I was there in Chicago at the outbreak of the war, staying at the Dearborn Plaza. And a friend of mine, Suma Tsubo, called and said, "They're bombing Pearl Harbor."

I said, "Go back to sleep." I just couldn't believe it.

On the very next day, I resigned my job at the consulate. I held a commission in the reserves, second lieutenant in the infantry. A week later, I received a telegram ordering me to go back to the West Coast and report for duty on January 19, 1942. But when I went down to the railroad station, the agent wouldn't sell me a ticket. The first thing he said was, "You're a Jap."

"I'm an American citizen," I told him. "I've got Army travel orders." I had to go to the Union Pacific attorney to point out that the Fourteenth Amendment provided that any person born within the United States is a citizen thereof. Eventually, I did get a ticket to Portland, Oregon. I reported for duty at Vancouver Barracks, but I was told I was unacceptable for service and ordered off the base. I went back eight times and offered to serve, but each time I was told, "We'll call you." They never did.

After Pearl Harbor, only two or three newspapers counseled moderation. In the rest of the papers and over the radio, it was just constantly, "Slap the Jap," "Remember Pearl Harbor." Twenty-four hours a day. And they didn't distinguish between the Japanese in Japan or the military in Japan and the people here in this country. In California, you began to hear reports of night riders shooting into homes of Japanese Americans. It got so bad in Hood River, the sheriff I had known for twenty years told me, "Yasui, keep off the streets. Somebody's going to shoot you." Even to this day I hear, "How come you bombed Pearl Harbor?"

The FBI picked dad up in mid-December 1941 and shipped him out to Missoula, Montana. My mother and sisters never knew where he was for sure until February 1942, when we were told that there would be a hearing for him. I went there to act as his legal counsel.

At the hearing, the prosecutor produced a bunch of maps of the Panama Canal, with diagrams of how the locks worked. He asked dad why they were in our home. Those drawings were very obviously childish and, when I saw them, I knew they had been drawn by my brother or myself as we went through school. The government prosecutor said, "Mr. Yasui, we think you had the intent to bomb the Panama Canal, and you had your children draw the maps to throw us off the scent." Dad said, "No, no! That's not true."

"Then," the prosecutor said, "prove that you didn't intend to blow up the canal." Now, that's impossible! You can't prove a negative fact. But what could we do? It was with "evidence" like this that dad and so many others were placed in internment camps, and there they were kept until the end of the war.

Dad never felt free enough to go back to his home in Hood River. It was a feeling many of us had: Where do we belong in this whole scheme of things? Dad had once been a prominent member of his community, a member of the Rotary and a director of a bank. In 1906, he had begun a mercantile store with his brother, and together they grubstaked other Japanese families, helping them with start-up capital. They pioneered in growing asparagus and gradually acquired substantial land holdings.

Many Japanese farmers pioneered in making useless land productive. They dug canals in swampland and put in drainage. They scraped off sand from wasteland to expose the soil underneath and make it productive. They dynamited stumps where forests had been cleared, leveled the ground, and started producing. Much of that land was lost to the Japanese after they were ordered to evacuate.

The evacuation came out of Executive Order 9066. The president of the United States, as commander-in-chief, delegated to the secretary of war and his subordinates the authority to take whatever measures were necessary to secure and protect the United States. That delegation of authority certainly was within the competence of the commander-in-chief. But the administration of the order was absolutely racist. The knowing intent was to apply it only to Japanese, not to Germans or Italians.

The first thing General John L. DeWitt did was to order a curfew along the entire West Coast, for all persons of Japanese ancestry. It was raw prejudice on his part. This stupid general—and I'll continue to say stupid—was distinguishing between citizens on the basis of ancestry. Why should I have to abide by a curfew when it was clearly racist? I take you out to dinner and it's seven-thirty. Eight o'clock comes around. At one minute after eight, I'm guilty of a crime and you aren't. And we're doing exactly the same thing, except my parents are Japanese. It's crazy. I still can't get over it.

Remember, the civil processes of government were continuing to operate on the West Coast, and yet a *general* was telling you what to do! Look, I've studied the Constitution. And the thing that struck me immediately was that here the military, without imposing martial law—and that's the critical point—is ordering the civilian to do something. In my opinion, that's the way dictatorships are formed. And if I, as an American citizen—a loyal, patriotic American citizen—stood still for this, I was derogating the rights of all citizens. By God, I had to stand up and say, "That's wrong."

I was twenty-six years old then and very idealistic. I was going to go out after curfew hours to test the order. I notified the military, and I notified the U.S. Attorney's office. At eight o'clock, the curfew hour, I began walking up and down the streets of Portland, deliberately violating the law, knowing I was going to be put in jail. That was scary. But I walked for three hours, and no one bothered me. I talked to a policeman. He wouldn't arrest me.

Eventually, after eleven o'clock, I went to the Second Avenue police station, talked to the sergeant, and got myself jailed. I was thrown into the drunk tank, a terrible place. I laid over on Saturday night and Sunday and got bailed out on Monday morning.

The Portland paper came out with a front-page headline about me: "Jap Spy Arrested." I knew mother would be worried. After all, her husband was out there someplace in Montana, one of her sons was up in Michigan, and here I got thrown in jail. So I called her, and I said, "Gee, mother, I hope you're not worried." Her response was, "Worried? Nonsense. I encourage you."

About a month later, military orders for evacuation in Portland came out: "All persons of Japanese ancestry, aliens and nonaliens, will be evacuated." Think about it. What's a *nonalien*? I tell you, they played with words.

If there were certain dangerous people, and they could prove that, fine. Lock them up. But why lock up everybody? We all had to report for internment. The military order also said: "Evacuees must carry with them for the assembly centers the following property: bedding and linen, toilet articles, extra clothing, sufficient knives, forks, spoons, plates, bowls and cups. Size and number of packages limited to that which can be carried by the individual." It's crazy. There was nothing in the executive order or in any public law that allowed the United States government to keep Americans within any restricted area. The War Relocation Authority, by fiat, pure executive fiat, detained us under their jurisdiction and sent us to their camps.

I refused to report for evacuation. I called up the military police and told them: "I'm not going to abide by the order. I'm going home to Hood River." Sure enough, within the week, I got a telephone call saying, "We're coming to get you." I can still see the military police. The lieutenant was in a sedan, with an enlisted man driving. A jeep followed with four MPs. And they were sitting there with tommy guns. The lieutenant came up to the door. "Are you Min Yasui?"

I said, "Sure."

"Come with us."

I left my mother and younger brother and sister in the house. I got in my car, and we drove on down to Portland. What are you going to do? You're alone against the world. The United States government and all its military power is a very awesome thing.

Shortly afterward, the Japanese were ordered to evacuate Hood River. They were given five days to pack up everything and leave. Dad had interests in over a thousand acres of fruit lands. We had a store and a big house. Mother was home alone with two younger children. She had five days.

My family was completely scattered. My father was interned. I had been taken away. Two brothers had taken off for Denver. Another brother went off to Montana. To this day, I am amazed at how my mother was able to hold that family together. You talk about strength. And they say the Japanese woman is compliant. Boy, I saw what they did, and it's remarkable. My mother, who spoke very little English and had no business background, disposed of the family assets to support the kids in college. Mother was selling off property at whatever she could get. Sure, we lost a lot. They knew we, like other Japanese, were at their mercy. All our farms but one were sold. They're gone. Today, that land is worth millions. Well, what's happened, happened.

When the army took me from Hood River, I was thrown into the North Portland Livestock Pavilion, where Japanese Americans had been put. In stalls where horses and cows were kept, people now lived. Others lived in a large hall where thin plywood partitions had been put up. Of course, it had been calcimined and asphalted, but it was still literally a barn, an arena for exhibiting animals. And hot! It was sweltering, but we had no way to escape it. They wouldn't let us outside. I was there from May to September.

In September, they started moving us out to the desert camps. When we arrived in Minidoka, Idaho, the camp was not completed. They were building "theater of operations barracks" that were intended for single men. But they assigned whole families to live in those cramped quarters. There were no partitions separating them, no privacy whatsoever. The entire concept of home and family—the Japanese family had been close-knit—was just obliterated.

Egress and ingress were controlled by the military. Unless you had a pass, you could not come in; you could not go out. You were surrounded by barbed-wire fences. There were armed guards and search-lights. There were machine-gun nests. The whole atmosphere was just threatening.

When we were brought into these camps, we wondered how long we were going to be there. What was going to happen? By then, we had heard rumors of the forced labor camps in Germany. Were they going to separate us—the men and the women, the adults and the young people? No one knew. Were they indeed, as Westbrook Pegler and others were suggesting, going to castrate the men and ship them back to Japan? These things were in the papers constantly: Make them suffer. Make them hurt.

And you keep thinking, "What did I do?"

I had hardly gotten settled when a U.S. marshal came to take me back to Portland for the judge's decision on the curfew violation. The trial had already taken place in April. I rode in the back seat of the marshal's car, like an ordinary passenger. But when we got to Portland, I was locked up in jail. The next morning, I was led through the streets—handcuffed and with a chain around my waist—to the courtroom. There, the judge announced he had found me guilty and would not grant bail pending appeal. I was a "dangerous Jap," an "enemy alien."

My trial had been the first time the constitutionality of Executive Order 9066 was tested. During the trial, the judge had surprised me by questioning me directly:

> "What is Shinto?"
>
> "Shinto? As I understand, Shinto is the national religion of Japan."
>
> "Do you give adherence to its precepts?"
>
> "My mother and father were Methodists in Japan, and I myself have been a Methodist in this country, and I don't know about the precepts of the Shinto religion."
>
> "Was not Shinto practiced in your household?"
>
> "No, sir." [1]

I thought they were a bunch of stupid questions. I didn't know anything about Shintoism. But the judge pushed on: Were food offerings placed on the graves of members of my family? Did I accept the divinity of the emperor of Japan? Despite my denials, he seemed to insist that I was a believer in the Shinto religion, in a way that cast doubt on my loyalty. He wanted to find me guilty, and he was searching for any basis by which he could. I'm sure he was under tremendous pressure to rule in favor of the government.

When the judge issued his ruling in my case, he found DeWitt's curfew order unconstitutional when applied to American citizens in the absence of martial law. I thought: Boy, we won this one! Then he continued, "However . . . ," and he ruled I had forfeited my citizenship by "choosing" allegiance to Japan—that I was an enemy alien, in spite of all the evidence to the contrary—and therefore the curfew applied to me. No one ever made such a claim before or since. It was so obviously foolish—even the Justice Department never disputed my citizenship before the appeals court and the Supreme Court.

I was perfectly convinced that by the time my case went to the Supreme Court the war would be over and that, in calmer times, they would rule in our favor. I never expected when the judgment was handed down in November that my attorneys would be arguing in the Supreme Court by April. That's unheard-of speed. It takes four and five years normally, but they sure rushed that one through. The military wanted this thing to be ruled upon, and in their favor, and they applied every pressure possible. The Supreme Court ordered the lower court to rule on it in accordance with their decision in the case of Gordon Hirabayashi, another Japanese American who had tested the evacuation order. Their decision sustained the curfew and the evacuation.

I've gone through the exercise where lawyers go to the state penitentiary to "find out how it feels to be locked up." They put you in a cell, and they slam the door, and they turn the key. But you know in the back of your head that they are going to open it up and you can leave. Well, I went into the Multnomah County jail on November 16, 1942, and I heard that door slam. I didn't know when they were going to open it again. That's a different feeling.

I was in there for nine miserable months. In isolation. You're in a cell eight feet long and six feet wide. Have you ever been locked up in a broom closet? Nine months, two hundred seventy days and two hundred seventy nights, alone. My hair grew long and unkempt, my fingernails got long. They wouldn't let me take a bath for several months. "Damn dirty Jap. Keep him locked up in the hole" was their attitude.

But being a stubborn guy, I was convinced I was right. And as long as you have that kind of conviction, they can't touch you. If you don't have a guilty conscience, you can put up with almost anything.

I got out of jail in August of 1943 and went back to the Minidoka camp. I hadn't seen my family since May of 1942, so I applied for a temporary leave. Harry Stafford, the director, told me point-blank, "You're never going to get out of this camp." There was a charade of a hearing. After sixty days of haggling—and only after I threatened a lawsuit of habeas corpus—I was given a temporary leave. You left camp as a matter of privilege, at the behest of someone else, not as a matter of right. Why should I have had to ask anybody to go any damn place I pleased?

The military began a recruitment program to form a segregated Japanese American unit. But first they wanted to separate those who were loyal from those who were not. Certainly you don't do that by a loyalty questionnaire, but that's what they tried. Two questions became notorious. Question 27 asked, "Are you willing to enlist in the United States Army and to go on combat duty wherever assigned?" It was applied to all persons over the age of eighteen—females, too. And that created such resentment.

Question 28 was worse. It read something like "Do you swear unqualified allegiance to the United States of America . . . ?" Most people would say yes to that. Some would resent it. But then it went further to ask, ". . . and foreswear allegiance to the emperor of Japan?" You ask that question of me, and it's a catch-22 situation. If I say, "Yes, I foreswear allegiance to the emperor of Japan," that means I had allegiance before. If I say, "No," that means I still have loyalty to the emperor. It's like saying, "Have you stopped beating your wife?" It's an impossible question, so we had a lot of qualified answers. But qualified answers were considered to be inadequate, unacceptable, disloyal.

There was a bitter situation everywhere, but especially at Tule Lake, a camp of well over ten thousand people. That was to be where all the "No-Nos," the persons who answered no to questions 27 and 28, were to be segregated. Many of the people who already lived in Tule Lake— and it literally went into the thousands—felt that if you're settled into one place, why should you say "yes-yes" and be moved out to some other camp. I knew the Takeshita family there. The father got so bitter that he absolutely refused to respond. The Takeshita family couldn't desert their father. So they all had to "no-no" to stay with him. All these people were branded as disloyal, but they weren't. They just didn't want to be separated or uprooted again.

The people at Tule Lake got an undeserved bad reputation. The idea was "treat 'em rough," and they did. I can remember Ben Takeshita's brother, one of the "no-no" boys. MPs picked him up with a group of others, brought them to some darn place, and lined them up facing a firing squad. Did they want a cigarette? To be blindfolded? He said, "You know, those guys actually said, 'Ready, aim, fire!'" He heard the clicks of their rifles. It was a farce; their rifles weren't loaded. Why did they put people through that kind of thing? And people respond to the treatment they receive. The tougher the administrators got, the tougher the inmates got. And there was bitterness, terrible bitterness.

Many young men didn't want to answer the questionnaire or register for the draft. About that time I was on leave, and I visited various camps with Joe Grant Masaoka from the Japanese American Citizens League. We talked with hundreds of young men in prison for resisting, saying, "Look, if you resist the draft, you're going to have a criminal record. It's a felony. It's going to be with you all your life."

I can still remember one eighteen-year-old kid at a federal corrections institute in Englewood. He said, "My mother is in a camp with my fourteen-year-old sister. The government took my father and interned him. We don't know where he is. The government has locked us up like a bunch of criminals. I just can't register for the draft." We told him, "You don't bargain with the United States government. You perform your duties, and having performed your duties, you're in a better position to demand your rights." This kid gripped the bars, his knuckles showed white. Tears rolled down his face, and he said, "When the United States gives me my rights, I'll perform my duties."

Thirty-three thousand Japanese Americans did fight in the segregated 442nd Infantry Battalion of the U.S. Army, the highest percentage of any nationality. The casualty rate was truly amazing. They were used to spearhead battles and for rescue missions. The "lost battalion" of the Texas division was cut off in Vosges forest. They brought in the 442nd. You talk to Wilson Makabe; he was one of those guys. He said, "Look, Company K went in—two hundred fifty-five men went into the line. The Germans had all our positions targeted. They were shooting constant artillery barrages. They had the place mined. Only seventeen men walked out. And then they sent in Company I—my company—into the line. Four days later, only eight of us walked out."

It was that kind of casualty rate that they suffered. But they were trying to prove a point—their loyalty. And I think that they did, beyond any question.

Wilson Makabe was hit by an artillery shell. He lost the use of both legs; one was amputated and the other put in a brace. He went back home, with decorations, to face the hostility that still remained. His house had just been burned down, and there was no question it was arson. Not long after that, in his car, he picked up a young fellow who used to run a service station. He looked at Wilson, with tears in his eyes, and told him, "Do you remember those bastards that put up the big sign, 'No Japs buy gas here'? I was one of them."

That's what I want now from the United States government. I want them to acknowledge that they were wrong. My current suit is based upon the fact that the United States government withheld information, falsified information, and in doing that deceived the Supreme Court when my case and the cases of Fred Korematsu and Gordon Hirabayashi, which also challenged the curfew and evacuation, went before it.

John L. DeWitt was the general who ordered the evacuation. His final report to the War Department, in which he explained what he did, was issued just as my case was about to go before the Supreme Court. DeWitt said the mass evacuation was necessary not because there wasn't enough time to examine the individual loyalty of people of Japanese descent, but because he thought there was no point in doing so. "A Jap is a Jap," as he later put it, meaning Japanese Americans are so devious and so treacherous that you couldn't determine their loyalty. Now, that's the most racist argument you could possibly make.

John J. McCloy, the assistant secretary of war, worried about how that would look to the Court, but he was more concerned about something else. McCloy pointed out that the moment DeWitt admitted there would have been time to examine the loyalty of Japanese Americans, the government's argument that the mass evacuation was a military necessity would be destroyed. He called DeWitt's righthand man to Washington and told him: You've got to say "time was of the essence," that on the basis of the urgency you had to do something, so you moved them all. That's when the acknowledgment that there was sufficient time changed to the claim that there was *not* sufficient time.

Then, all copies of DeWitt's report were ordered destroyed. One warrant officer in the War Department reported, "I certify that this date I witnessed the destruction by burning of all galley proofs, galley pages, drafts, and memorandums of the original report of the Japanese evacuation." [2] A new "final report" was published in its place that included McCloy's changes, and it was presented in a brief to the Supreme Court. Now that's falsifying testimony.

DeWitt also claimed that Japanese American citizens had been engaged in actual acts of espionage. He said there were nine hundred seventy-four illicit shore-to-ship radio transmissions before the evacuation was ordered in May 1942. But James Fly, the head of the Federal

Communications Commission, reported—and we have the documentation—that they checked every one of the nine hundred seventy-four so-called transmissions from shore to ship. *Not one* was laid at the hands of the Japanese Americans. And DeWitt was told that by the FCC *before* he wrote his report.

When Edward J. Ennis of the Justice Department saw the reference to the radio transmissions, he immediately got in touch with DeWitt's office, saying, "You can't say things like that." He knew of the FCC findings. But DeWitt wouldn't change it. That's falsification, clearly. In fact, it's a damn lie, and Ennis said as much about the report in 1944: "It is highly unfair to this racial minority that these lies, put in an official publication, go uncorrected." [3]

Ennis told the Justice Department to admit these facts to the Court, but the solicitor general would not put them in the record. So what McCloy said about the lack of time and what DeWitt said about Japanese espionage were used to shape an argument before the United States Supreme Court that the evacuation was a military necessity. This was Watergate before Watergate. Dangerous. There was gross injustice done to one hundred twenty thousand people. By reopening our cases, we want the government to acknowledge it.

Over three thousand hours were put into the preparation of my case. My petition set forth in great detail how the government misled the Supreme Court. The documentation was three hundred-odd pages. Then the judge, a fellow by the name of Belloni, came in, looked at all that work, and said, "I haven't even read this stuff." When a judge does that, what is he there for? The government said that after forty years there's no point in reopening all these matters, and they conceded to vacating my conviction. Well, the judge did vacate my conviction, but he dismissed my petition.

I'm not satisfied. Forty years later, it isn't crucial whether I was convicted or not; it just isn't important any longer. I want a declaration from the Court that the United States government committed misconduct and that therefore the case is vacated. This should never be done to anyone else, but the sad thing is that it could happen again. If we have a court record saying the government was wrong, the government officials will be less apt to repeat it. But if you say, "Well, forty years have gone by, and we'll forget about it," they can intern others and forget about *that,* too. Unless we are all vigilant to protect the rights of others, it can happen to us.

Part IV
The High Cost of Winning

Introduction to Part IV

There are some who respond to a victory in a civil liberties case by saying, "The American system of justice *does* work." To take issue with
that view is not to deny the legacy of freedom in the United States. But
to see only that positive side ignores many who were not vindicated,
who were jailed for their beliefs or political activities because they
lacked adequate resources to defend themselves or because the times
were harshly biased against them. It ignores countless others who suffered repression in silence. And it suppresses the record of cruelties experienced even by those victims of repression who did, in the end, win.

In this final part, we look at the cost of victories. Here are the stories
of three who eventually won vindication for themselves and, more
important, for a principle that had been subverted. But in each case
the price paid was inordinate. Civil rights worker Margaret Herring
McSurely won back the personal papers that had been illegally confiscated by government officials, overturned a state sedition law, and exposed the workings of Senate witch-hunters; but she and her family and
friends were terrorized, profoundly private aspects of her life were invaded, her marriage broke under the strain, and her work in Appalachia
was effectively quashed. Labor lawyer Edward Lamb won his right to
operate radio and television stations and exposed those who plied their
trade as informers, but he was publicly vilified in the press by absurd

FCC charges, lost ground to his competitors, and spent a fortune to defend himself. Broadcaster John Henry Faulk won a landmark case against the self-appointed superpatriots who set standards for loyalty in the entertainment industry and dealt a mortal blow to the blacklist, but he lost access to a devoted nationwide audience, was virtually denied his livelihood, and forfeited a promising career in national radio and television.

Through it all, the determination to prevail shown by these three individuals was remarkable. If eternal vigilance is the price of liberty, these three demonstrate that the price of vigilance itself is measured in deeply personal terms.

Turning the Tables on Government Raiders

Margaret Herring McSurely

Pike County, Kentucky, where Alan and Margaret McSurely came in 1967 to work in an antipoverty program, was run as the personal fiefdom of wealthy coal barons. With the consent of the county's elite, Thomas Ratliff, a millionaire coal operator and commonwealth prosecutor, arrested Margaret Herring McSurely and her husband under the Kentucky sedition law, seized their books and personal papers, and created a climate of hysteria around them. To regain their papers, the McSurelys went before the Supreme Court several times, took on the U.S. Senate, and fifteen years later won a million-dollar jury award for damages.

It was about eight o'clock on an August evening. I was out in the kitchen cooking, and Al was writing a political paper. This was before women's lib got hold of me. I looked out of the window, and there were these men prancing through the grass. Some of them had uniforms on and some of them didn't, but they all had guns. I said to myself, "My goodness, they must be looking for an escaped convict." Then I told Al to look out the window, that there were a bunch of cops outside. The next thing I heard was a knock. Men burst in the front and back doors.

MARGARET HERRING McSURELY

One of them, Sheriff Justice, yelled, "Where's Alan McSurely?" Al said, "I'm right here." They had rushed past him in their hurry to get in. They told him to sit down, but before he could, he was shoved onto the couch. The sheriff pulled out a search warrant and read it to Al in a loud voice: "You are commanded to search, in the day or night time the house now occupied by Alan McSurely, which property is located at Pike County, Kentucky, and if you find in or upon said premises seditious material you will seize and take possession of it, and deliver it, together with the body of said Alan McSurely." Then Al was placed under arrest for sedition.

I couldn't believe my eyes or ears. The thing that unraveled was so bizarre, if you can imagine. One of the men, who was taking pictures, said to Al, "Hold your head up. I want to see how you'll look when you hang." It was frightening. I didn't know what was going to happen next.

The commonwealth's attorney, Thomas Ratliff, directed the raid. He sat down on the chair next to the bookcase and began going through our books, one by one, putting them in piles. Other men went into the bedroom and took the bed apart. They went through the dresser drawers and the closet. They just took everything. These men rooted through Al's desk and boxes of our papers in the bedroom. They would bring them in to Ratliff and say, "Hey, Thomas, here's a paper about organizing in Kentucky." And, "Lookie here, Thomas, the *Village Voice*. That's where all them beatniks are."

I went over and sat down next to Al. It was bizarre, comical, and terribly frightening at the same time. I mean, it was like the Keystone Cops, but they were deadly serious. I was horrified that Al would be killed, after the threat on his life, and I was near a state of panic.

I knew that what they were doing was unconstitutional and that I could count on the movement lawyers to help out, if we could just get word to them. I was about five months pregnant at the time, so I made an excuse of having to go to the bathroom. When I got up, I stood straight and held my shoulders back. I learned from having been with Miss Hamer* and the SNCC people that when you're about to be attacked, you never let on you're afraid.

I reached for the phone and called the local attorney, whom we had

---

*The courage and steadfastness of Fannie Lou Hamer, a grassroots leader from Ruleville, Mississippi, inspired young SNCC workers. Her eloquent account of the lives of poor people in the South and the brutal beating she received from police moved the nation when her speech was televised from the Democratic National Convention in 1964.

befriended, and told him what was going on. I was also able to get a call through to the Bradens.* Then I went back into the living room. There was a clump of men there, and they had some papers which showed that I had worked for the Student Nonviolent Coordinating Committee. Thomas Ratliff said, "Let's get her, too." In a way, I was relieved, because I felt like I would be safer in jail than left at home alone after this nightmare.

Ratliff commandeered a pickup truck from a neighbor, and they took all of our personal papers, every scrap we had, and about six hundred books. They took them all, and they locked them up in jail. And then they locked us up in jail for sedition.

According to the Kentucky law:

> Any person who by word or writing advocates, suggests or teaches the duty, necessity, propriety or expediency of criminal syndicalism or sedition, or who prints, publishes, edits, issues or knowingly circulates, sells, distributes, publicly displays or has in his possession for the purpose of publication or circulation any written or printed matter in any form advocating, suggesting or teaching criminal syndicalism or sedition, or who organizes or helps to organize, or becomes a member of or voluntarily assembles with any society or assemblage of persons that teaches, advocates or suggests the doctrine of criminal syndicalism or sedition shall be confined in the penitentiary for not more than twenty-one years, or fined not more than ten thousand dollars, or both.[1]

What did they mean by sedition? I knew they used that law against the coal miners when they organized. And I knew Carl Braden had spent time in jail for sedition after he bought a house for a Black family in a white neighborhood. Now we had to face the same charge.

Ratliff held a press conference while we were in jail. He told reporters that all evidence pointed to just one thing—the McSurelys were trying to stir up "turmoil among our poor." He said he found a "communistic library that was out of this world" and that he would make our materials available to congressional investigators. When Sheriff Justice

---

* Carl and Anne Braden were organizers for the Southern Conference Educational Fund, a group that sought to win white support in the South for the cause of Black rights. Margaret Herring McSurely had joined the Bradens on the staff of SCEF. Also see Frank Wilkinson's story (Part III), and note on page 267.

was asked for an example of one of the books in our "communistic library," his answer was *"Catch 22."*

It made no sense at all, but Ratliff's purpose was accomplished just by arresting us. He was running for lieutenant governor of Kentucky on the Republican ticket at the time, and this raid put his name in the papers. But for us, the publicity and the hysteria it created was awful. Ratliff spread wild rumors about us: that we had organized "Red Guards" to rescue us, that there was going to be a riot. Some people secretly admired our standing up to Thomas Ratliff, but they were afraid of us. We were being called communists, and to them that meant somebody who was anti-God, atheistic.

Actually, I was the youngest child of a southern Baptist preacher. I was born in Kentucky and raised in North Carolina. My father was very religious, almost a fundamentalist, and he had a kind of populist politics. So I was aware of political things that were happening, but we weren't really involved in them. I went to Wake Forest College and met my first husband down there. I guess it was around 1960 that we moved to the Washington area, where he went to medical school.

I went to work for Drew Pearson * as his secretary. Part of my job was to open Pearson's mail, so I read all the press releases the Student Nonviolent Coordinating Committee sent out. Then I went to the Democratic Convention in Atlantic City. I got to meet some of the SNCC people and some people from Mississippi like Fannie Lou Hamer, who really made an impact on me. I listened to their stories, how they risked their lives to do the fundamental things most Americans take for granted, like registering to vote. I felt an integrated movement like this was never going to happen again in my lifetime. I decided to go south to work with SNCC and the Mississippi Freedom Democratic Party before history passed me by.

Pearson didn't quite know what to think. He was proud of me, but he didn't want me to go. We were having an affair after my husband and I separated. When I went south, Pearson sent me love letters, trying to get me to come back to him.

But I'm glad I went. I met a lot of courageous people, and I found out what it was like to really do grassroots organizing for political justice. I committed myself to that struggle. I stayed until 1965. By then, I

* Author of a syndicated column, the "Washington Merry-Go-Round," Drew Pearson was most famous for his muckraking style. Over the years, Pearson and his colleague Jack Anderson had, for example, repeatedly attacked Senator John McClellan for supporting legislation that would lead to the congressman's financial gain.

had decided that Black people should run their own programs, since white people, no matter how well meaning they were, ended up by taking over. I wanted to organize poor, working-class white people, but I wasn't sure just how to do it.

Back in Washington, I tried working for an antipoverty agency. That's where I met Alan McSurely, my second husband. We went on a trip across the country, visiting movement people and seeing what was going on. We knew we'd be organizing, but we didn't know where. Then, in April 1967, we moved to Pikeville, Kentucky. Pikeville is in the heart of a billion-dollar coal field, but its people are among the poorest in the country. I went to work for the Southern Conference Educational Fund, which used to be known as SCEF and was headed by Anne and Carl Braden. Al worked for a government-funded antipoverty group called the Appalachian Volunteers.

The Appalachian Volunteers were working on whatever problems the local people felt they had, like bad roads and dilapidated schoolhouses. A big problem around Pikeville was strip mining. The coal operators pushed the land over the top of the mountain onto the farms and homes, such as they were, and flooded and polluted the rivers with silt. The mountain people were resisting them. Jink Ray was one example in Pike County. For weeks he stood in front of those bulldozers on the hill above his house to stop them. They say people watched from the woods with rifles in case anything happened to him.

After about a month, Al got red-baited out of his antipoverty job with the AVs and joined me on the staff of SCEF. He had written this paper calling for a new coalition outside of the Democratic and Republican parties. People inside the AVs thought it was too radical. But I think what really scared them was Al's idea of democratizing the AV staff. Al felt that the local people should have the same rights and salaries as the regular staff members.

After Al left, he still had contact with some of the AVs. We lent them our big house for a week to train poverty workers and Peace Corps volunteers. We worked out rules for them beforehand with the landlord to avoid any trouble. He agreed. But not long afterward he made us move, with the excuse that his daughter needed the house.

About a week later, there was a meeting in the Pikeville courthouse, where they planned the raid on us. Ratliff was there, along with the head of the chamber of commerce, Robert Holcomb; Sheriff Justice; our landlord, James Compton; and other officials—the magistrates of county districts, the county attorney, and more. It was a star-chamber proceeding. The landlord told them a story different from his statement to us. He said he kicked us out because he thought a nest of communists was there, when those Peace Corps trainees used our house. He didn't like all those young people coming, mixed races, and male and female. He thought that wasn't Christian. And he said he saw pamphlets, "communistic" books, and race mixing and that kind of stuff. They wrote the warrant to search our house—right there at that meeting—based on what he said.

When we had had to move, the only place we could afford was a tiny house up on Harold's Branch. By August, we were in our new home, and people were coming by to say hello. We were just getting to know them when our house was raided. But after we got out of jail, after all that publicity, it was frightening being in Pikeville. Nobody would have anything to do with us. It was just a very tense atmosphere. A cross was burned on the front yard of the lawyer who defended us. I always felt like people were watching me. It was scary even to go to the grocery store. Our closest friends in the community said, "Please don't come over for a while." They had been getting death threats and warnings that their houses would be dynamited.

Meanwhile, the Kentucky sedition trial was hanging over us. Our attorneys went to federal court to stop it until the judges could hand down a ruling on its constitutionality. Ratliff promised them he would not prosecute, but the grand jury went ahead and indicted us anyway. And they indicted the Bradens, too. It was then that the federal court ruled the Kentucky sedition law was unconstitutional. Judge Combs wrote a strong opinion:

> The statute in question is clearly unconstitutional under even the most flexible yardstick. It is too broad and too vague. It contravenes the First Amendment to the Constitution of the United States because it unduly prohibits freedom of speech, freedom of press, and the right of assembly. It fails to distinguish between the advocacy of ideas and the advocacy of action. It imposes the penalty of imprisonment for advocating an unpopular political belief. It would turn the courts into a forum for argument of political theories, with imprisonment the penalty for the losers.
>
> In addition, the conclusion is inescapable that the criminal prosecutions were instituted, at least in part, in order to stop plaintiff's organizing activities in Pike County. That effort has

been successful. Not only has there been the "chilling effect" on freedom of speech, there has been in fact a freezing effect.[2]

We thought that we had won a great victory and that we were going to get our papers back. But we didn't. The judge had trusted them to Ratliff for "safekeeping." The next thing we knew, this man, John Brick, came to the door early one autumn morning with a subpoena from Senator McClellan's committee.* He said, "The Senate doesn't want you. It just wants your papers. We can get them from Thomas Ratliff."

I thought: Why would the Senate want our papers? Suddenly, I remembered something about the name Brick. The psychiatrist I had been going to for therapy when my first marriage was breaking up, and later when I was seeing Drew Pearson, had a secretary named Mrs. Brick. I asked Brick if she was any kin to him. He said yes, she was his wife. I thought: Good God, that was kind of an odd connection. Maybe information had come from my therapy to the United States Senate.

When Brick left, we called our lawyers. They went immediately into court to stop Ratliff from giving McClellan our stuff. There were months of legal wrangling. Finally, in November of 1968, more than a year after they were taken, the court of appeals ordered Ratliff to return our books and papers. When we went to the courthouse in Pikeville to pick them up, guess who was there with another set of copies—John Brick. Ratliff had allowed Brick to go over our personal papers and had given him copies to take back to Senator McClellan. Brick took more than two hundred of them without our knowledge. When he had served us with the original subpoena, it had been just a formality.

Brick brought the photostatic copies with him now because the appeals court had ordered McClellan to return them to us. He gave them to Al one by one, making humiliating comments about what was in my love letters from Pearson. I had to walk away. Then Brick warned us that a federal marshal would serve us with the second subpoena he had brought from the McClellan Committee. This time, we would be ordered to come with our papers. And Brick told us, "If you destroy any of those papers, you'll be in contempt of Congress." Al answered, "We're *full* of contempt for Senator McClellan and his committee."

Outside the courthouse, just as Brick promised, a marshal did serve

---

* Senator John L. McClellan of Arkansas succeeded Joseph McCarthy as chairman of the Senate Permanent Subcommittee on Investigations. Under authorization to conduct a congressional inquiry into the causes and cures of urban rioting, he sought to connect the unrest to "subversive influences" and "militant agitators."

us with another subpoena. We loaded our things into our VW bus before a very hostile crowd—"We don't want your kind in Pikeville"—and then we left.

At home, we went through our documents and were able to see for the first time everything they had taken. There were address lists of civil rights organizers and other movement people we had met throughout the country. We knew that we couldn't in good conscience turn those over to the Senate. There were our birth certificates and marriage license and many very personal things. I was really horrified to see my love letters that McClellan had taken. And my diary—which I had never intended for anybody to read. What they had done was so outrageous that even if it meant we would go to jail, we would not allow anyone else to ever get hold of them. And we were afraid we might be killed, and we didn't want the papers scattered after our deaths. We felt we had to destroy these things, though some of them were very precious to us. We went right out in the back yard and burned them.

We were living there in Pikeville under constant threat, and we were effectively stopped from doing any organizing at all. The judge said the raid and arrests had a freezing effect on us. I can tell you from my personal experience that they really did. I was frightened. I was afraid that we were going to be killed, almost every day that we were in Pikeville. I cried every day for our safety, especially for the baby.

A month after our papers were returned, our home was dynamited—people did indeed try to kill me and Al and our baby, Victor. It was about midnight. We had gone to bed, but I wasn't asleep yet. Victor was in the crib near our bed. I heard a car go by slowly up the road and stop, turn around, and come back. Then a thud on the screen, and something dropped to the ground. Suddenly, there was this big implosion—air seemed to be sucked out of the room—and then an explosion. Everything was all in the air—dirt and clothes—and it was real dark. And Victor was screaming. When I picked him up, he was covered with broken glass.

We packed up and left Pikeville that night. That was in December 1968. Subpoenas were hanging over our heads, and our house was dynamited, and we didn't have a place to move. The subpoenas said we had to be in Washington in January. So we went there and lived for a while out of the trunk of our car.

On the day of the McClellan hearing, we stopped at the federal district court and filed a civil lawsuit against Senator McClellan and the other senators on the committee. In the suit, we claimed that they had conspired with Kentucky officials to intimidate us, to stigmatize us, and to stop us from organizing.

McClellan was supposed to be investigating the causes of riots. He saw this as his chance to blame them on SNCC leaders like Stokely Carmichael. Stokely had spoken at a SCEF board meeting in Nashville that we had attended. McClellan took that board meeting and made something sinister out of it, trying to connect it to riots that took place later.

At the hearing, McClellan opened with a long statement about how riots were caused by subversives. We tried to tell him that we thought some of the causes of the riots were right in that room, up behind that mahogany desk. But he wouldn't let us talk. McClellan would say things like: Let the record show that the witness is conferring with counsel. Let the record show that the witness is smiling. "Let the record show . . ."— that was supposed to really scare us. Not knowing we had already destroyed our papers, he told us that if we didn't turn them over, we would be in contempt. Well, instead of giving him our papers, we gave him the complaint we had just filed in the federal court.

After that, Al and I started to put two and two together. Maybe McClellan was after Pearson, and not us at all. Pearson often attacked the senator bitterly in his columns, and McClellan very much wanted to stop him. Was the riot investigation camouflage to get at our personal things? Was McClellan trying to use them for his own ends? When Pearson found out McClellan had copies of his letters to me, he was worried frantic that they could be used as blackmail. And he never wrote about McClellan after the raid.

Everything they say "can't happen here" had happened here to us. Now we were indicted for refusing to give the Senate our papers that they had already taken illegally. We got blocked again and again by the trial judge and became more and more frustrated. Then, when he would not even allow us to tell the jury *why* we refused to obey the subpoenas, we began to wonder if we had any hope of escaping prison.

We were convicted. Al was sentenced to a year, and I got three months. We and our attorneys from the Center for Constitutional Rights appealed that decision. In the meantime, we made arrangements for Victor in case we had to go to jail. Finally, two and a half years after our trial, we were vindicated. The appeals court said that the search warrant Ratliff used was invalid. They said that it was illegal for Brick to look at our papers and copy them for McClellan. All that violated the Fourth

Amendment. So, McClellan's subpoena was based on illegally seized evidence, and we were acquitted. I was relieved we weren't going to jail, but what could make up for all the pain and fear and frustration? We paid a terrible price.

Al and I started to prepare for our civil case against them, which claimed that Ratliff and McClellan and his aides conspired to violate our rights and had to pay for what they did to us. Every step of the way, the Justice Department would block us. Their main argument was that the defendants were protected by the Speech or Debate clause, which says that on the floor of Congress a legislator can say anything and not be liable for it. According to them, that clause extended to anything Senate employees did while working for the legislature.

That particular question was litigated to the Supreme Court, and we won. The Justice Department attorney argued that all employees of the Senate were immune from civil prosecution. Justice Potter Stewart leaned over the bench and asked: "How far does that reasoning take you? Let's say its purposes were very clearly to aid the legislative process by aiding the congressional committee, and in the pursuance of that pristinely protected purpose he simply burglarized a house and stole things out of a locked drawer or safe. Is he protected under the Speech or Debate clause for that? By 'he' I mean the aide to the committee."

And this Justice Department lawyer said, "Mr. Justice Stewart, that question raises a number of complexities. My answer to it ultimately is yes, probably he is protected."

There was a big silence. Then Justice Stewart said, "Including murder, I suppose?"

The lawyer said, "That, too, falls within my yes, probably, answer."[3]

The Supreme Court sent the case back to trial. When they decided McClellan and the others were not absolutely immune from prosecution, the Justice Department lost its most important argument.

Our trial began in November 1982, before a jury of six people. The jury upheld us. They said that we were right. And they made a judgment of 1.6 million dollars. Most of that was to come from Ratliff.

A *New York Times* editorial on January 15, 1983, stated: "At long last a jury in Washington, D.C., has delivered a ringing verdict: the late Senator John McClellan of Arkansas conspired with Senate aides and Kentucky law enforcement officials to rob the McSurelys of their liberties. . . . Considering the depth and range of official misdeeds, the award may be too little and is certainly too late. No American should need fifteen years to claim political and civil rights. Yet the judgment, and the moral condemnation it carries, are a welcome deterrent to officials who would value liberties cheaply."

Since Al and I were involved in this fight, the pressure on us was so great that our marriage broke up. It was a tremendous strain on our relationship. But we were together on this particular issue. We endured. And people around the country supported us. It never occurred to me— and I'm sure it never occurred to Al—not to do this or to give up on it.

Exposing the Informer Racket

Edward Lamb

"Somewhere in my childhood I had learned that you don't tell tales on people," philosopher Barrows Dunham recalled. "It felt to me as something laid way deep in my psychology." Historically, informers have enjoyed an unsavory reputation, but as the crusade of anti-communism touched every aspect of American life, the informer became the instrument for its success. Congressional investigations; trials of conscience; loyalty, deportation, and other administrative proceedings; secret police—all required informers. They were made into heroes, held before the people, John Henry Faulk says, like icons. By 1954, one poll found that 72 percent of Americans would report to the FBI acquaintances they suspected of being Communists.

Being a professional informer emerged as a lucrative and ego-boosting calling for a special type of person. James V. Blanc recruited his brother-in-law into the Communist Party and then turned his name over to the FBI.[1] Barbara Hartle named both her former husband and a former common-law husband.[2] David Brown padded his reports to the FBI with names of people he didn't know.[3] Matt Cvetic, the glamourized FBI spy, had abandoned his children and had a history of alcoholism, assault, and mental illness.[4] The perjury of Paul Crouch, Manning Johnson, and Harvey Matusow was so blatant that the Supreme Court ordered their testimony stricken from the record.[5]

EDWARD LAMB

The Immigration and Naturalization Service had eighty-three infor-mants under contract in the early 1950s, paid to perform on demand at trials and hearings. Among them were the witnesses whose false testi-mony was exposed by Edward Lamb. Denied licenses for his radio and television stations because of charges that he was a Communist, Lamb demolished the "liars for hire," as he called them, who testified against him in a trial that lasted four years. All that time, his income from the stations was curtailed, and his defense required out-of-pocket expenses of nearly one million dollars. It was a bittersweet victory.

One afternoon in 1953, when I was at the National Press Club in Washington, a friend handed me a wire service bulletin that said my name had been dropped by a witness before McCarthy's committee. Senator Joe McCarthy had a one-man show in New York that sup-posedly was investigating the United Nations. John Lautner was his wit-ness. Without any relationship to anything that was said before or after, McCarthy asked, "Do you know Edward Lamb, the broadcaster?"

"I don't know Lamb, but I can say that he was highly respected by the top Communists. I wouldn't be able to say whether Lamb himself was ever a card-carrying Communist."

I soon learned that Lautner was one of a large pool of professional witnesses maintained by the U.S. Immigration and Naturalization Ser-vice and on loan to other agencies. The tale he told was pretty thin stuff on the face of it, but vicious nevertheless. Lautner had done what Sena-tor Joe McCarthy knew very well he would do. In that time of national hysteria, Lautner's otherwise innocuous statement was enough to link me to the "Communist conspiracy" in headlines across the country. New ammunition was handed to powerful men in politics and business, including those who were already gunning for me.

Before this happened, I had filed a number of applications to the Federal Communications Commission to renew licenses for my radio and television stations. Although these were ordinarily routine matters, my applications lay on the desk of FCC Commissioner John C. Doerfer, and there they remained for months. Doerfer was an Eisenhower ap-pointee from Wisconsin and a rabid lieutenant of McCarthy. He had close ties with the White House, where he spoke with the powerful word of McCarthy in back of him. Doerfer made no bones about the fact that they were going to get me.

I decided to see him personally, hoping that we might be able to talk our problems out in a face-to-face discussion. He immediately asked me about a book I wrote in 1934, *The Planned Economy of Soviet Russia*, although the work had nothing to do with my application. Then, he launched into a line of questions about my vigorous defense of trade unions in the 1930s. He couldn't understand why a lawyer of my background would defend "colored" people, Communists, or trade unions. "It's too bad," he said, "that you aren't still a Republican."

In the beginning of my career, I had been a Republican and a corporation lawyer. Then we had this terrible, violent Auto-Lite strike hit us, in my hometown of Toledo. It was during the Depression. City workers were paid in scrip. The courthouse lawn was filled with hungry people living in tents and blankets because they had been thrown out of homes and work. By 1934, Electric Auto-Lite was one of the few plants still operating. Conditions there were unbelievable. And the AFL union that represented them sold out the Auto-Lite workers on every wage demand.

Finally, the workers went on strike, not just against the company but also against the conservative union leadership. The company brought in strikebreakers and provided them with guns. Things got very tense. The company sought an injunction against the strikers, and I was asked by a committee of workers to represent them. The trial judge was so drunk I had to help him on and off the stand. He issued an injunction that limited the pickets to twenty-five at each gate. The workers left the courtroom outraged and went right back to the picket line. The National Guard was called in from Columbus, several thousand strong. Toledo was in the midst of a revolutionary crisis. In the days that followed, there were shootings and pitched battles, and several strikers were killed.

A strike of onion workers in McGuffey followed and became equally as violent. The owners brought in farmhands from Kentucky during the planting and harvesting seasons, and then kicked them out. The standard wage was ninety cents a day from sunrise to sunset. All the kids worked, too. As many as ten or fifteen in a family lived in tarpaper hovels. The poverty, the disease, the hunger, and the lack of housing were outrageous. I saw misery in the midst of plenty. I was moved to continue my representation of workers, even though I knew some of my corporate clients would back away. When the onion strikers were arrested and I was asked to be their counsel, I was happy to join them.

In 1937, John L. Lewis put me in charge of the Little Steel strike litigation. The Steel Workers Organizing Committee had already reached agreements with the Big Steel companies. But Little Steel, composed of Republic Steel, Bethlehem Steel, Inland Steel, and Youngstown Sheet and Tube companies, refused to follow suit. Their attack against the unions became a "patriotic" crusade in defense of Americanism and Christianity.

When the strike broke out, there were thousands of arrests. At times, one hundred fifty workers a day were jailed. We were so well organized that sometimes we could get pickets out of prison within minutes of their arrest. I defended dozens of Little Steel strikers in Youngstown, Canton, Massillon, and elsewhere, sometimes several cases in different courts in one day. One of my favorite arrested clients turned out to be Gus Hall, then the leader of the Steel Workers Organizing Committee and later the leader of the Communist Party, U.S.A.

I have never been convinced that certain steel interests were not behind my later troubles with the Federal Communications Commission in Washington and before that, with the court at Portsmouth. In 1937, there was a shoe workers' strike in Portsmouth that led to an attempt to get me out of the legal profession.

The shoe workers at the Shelby and Williams companies were being paid wages that were shockingly low, even in those days before unionization. When the workers went on strike, the police and sheriffs attacked them. In the midst of the crisis, the companies sought a temporary injunction to restrain picketing. Judge William R. White of Gallipolis, a power in Ohio Republican politics, presided over the hearing. The first thing he said was, "I have an injunction to issue, and we had better get the business over with, as I want to get back home."

I demanded a chance to argue against the injunction. The judge grew red in the face. The company lawyer piped in that he had a noon appointment and asked for the injunction without further ado. We all became involved in loud argument. The judge said over and over again that I would not be allowed to present testimony. Finally, I lost patience: "Oh, for heaven's sakes, the corporation attorney makes his objections, and they are always sustained." "Keep still!" the judge roared. I asked to say a few words. "Keep still," he repeated. "I want this gentleman," he said, pointing to the company attorney, "to have the floor." "I thought so," I said.

The next day Judge White issued the injunction. A few days after that, he appointed the lawyers for the shoe companies as a committee to start disbarment proceedings against me. It was a disgusting frame-up. They leaked their charges to the press and tried to convict me in the headlines before I had a chance to defend myself. This was a harbinger of what I was to experience during the Washington witch-hunt.

The National Lawyers Guild organized my defense. Morris Ernst and Judge Ferdinand Pecora formed a large committee of federal judges and prominent lawyers all over the country to help. Robert Jackson, who was solicitor general of the United States and later a Supreme Court Justice, came to my defense: "I know of no adequate explanation of this fierce and vindictive proposal except that Lamb is a labor lawyer."[6] The day before the trial, ten thousand people gathered at the Portsmouth baseball field to support the strikers and defend me in my disbarment proceedings: "We're not going to let them disbar Ted Lamb!" In a packed courtroom the next day, Judge Young dismissed the charges.

The labor case that brought me the greatest notoriety arose because of a strike at the Mount Clemens Pottery Company. The company ruthlessly fired strikers, shut off their utilities, foreclosed on their homes, and closed out their grocery accounts. Pickets were being arrested wholesale. None of the local lawyers would defend the pottery workers. After late-night, clandestine visits to workers' homes, I learned that the company expected them to be at their workbenches ready to work for long periods each day without pay.

In April 1941, I filed the portal-to-portal suit in the U.S. district court in Detroit for the workers to be paid while on the employer's premises and under the employer's control, doing company work. The trial stretched out for almost a year. During that time, I virtually abandoned my regular law practice. I didn't receive a dime at any point along the line for the case, and I even paid the court expenses, more than ten thousand dollars.

The trial judge was the colorful, wisecracking Frank A. Picard. Picard and his family formerly had a circus act called the "Flying Picards." Here was a federal judge who could still straddle almost any issue. He ruled that the workers should be paid, but for only a fraction of the time they were required to be on the job before and after the whistle. The case was appealed to the Supreme Court, and I won. The majority opinion held that a worker must be reimbursed for the time spent on the employer's premises and under the employer's direction, including the travel time from the plant gate to the workplace.

After the portal-to-portal decision, thousands of lawsuits totaling billions of dollars were quickly filed across the country. A wave of panic gripped the chambers of commerce and the manufacturers' associations as they recognized their new liabilities. After fierce debate, Congress voted to outlaw portal-to-portal suits for back wages, effectively over-turning the Supreme Court decision. In the meantime, portal-to-portal pay began to be incorporated into almost every union contract. It be-came a fact of life. Somehow, American corporations survived the expe-rience of paying their employees fairly.

Although I continued as a labor lawyer, by 1951 I also had accumu-lated between eight and ten million dollars in newspaper, radio, tele-vision, and other stocks. How did it come about that a lawyer for labor also could acquire corporate interests? I found the acquisition of assets was not a difficult job in those days. My own luck—and it was luck—came from a fee of twenty-five thousand dollars I collected for the sale of a patent in my beginning year of practice. I smelled blood financially and was off on my acquisitive career.

But I was not an ordinary owner of radio and television stations. I had defended workingmen against their corporate employers. And some of those cases attracted widespread publicity. That made me an attractive target of Republicans, even before the FCC affair.

In March of 1954, the FCC sent me a letter informing me that I must face charges that I had misrepresented my qualifications on my ap-plication for a television license. I received the letter only after the offi-cials released its contents to the press. The letter stated that I had falsely sworn I was not a Communist and that the FCC had evidence that "for a period of years, particularly the period 1944–1948," I had been "a member of the Communist Party."

Naturally, I was dumbfounded and outraged. No one could say in truth and with a straight face that I was ever a member of the Communist Party. No one at any time had any such evidence. By making the charge public, the FCC had invited my rival applicants for the valuable Toledo television license to use the Communist issue against me. They must have known their false accusation would be played up in my hometown of Toledo. And they were effective; the Toledo TV grant was given to a local politician and congressman.

I answered the FCC letter, categorically denying all their charges and requesting an early hearing. The FCC said in response that I could try to "disprove the charges." That's quite a trick, proving a negative, but I set out to do it if it took my last penny. We built up our defenses by hiring detectives, accountants, and lawyers. I retained J. Howard McGrath, who was attorney general under President Truman, as my counsel. He had been a United States senator, a governor of Rhode Island, and chairman of the Democratic National Committee. He knew his way around Washington.

At the very time the FCC said it had proof I was a Communist, it spent large amounts of money trying to *get* evidence to back up the verdict it had already made public. They sent their agents to Toledo, Erie, Columbus, and elsewhere in search of such evidence. Drew Pearson, the columnist, reported that these men caused a professional ex-Communist stool pigeon in Toledo, one William Garfield Cummings, to offer another ex-Communist, Emmett L. Wheaton, the sum of ten thousand dollars if he would "remember" that I had attended the opening of a Toledo Communist bookstore in 1944.

Every day, the FCC's press releases about new secret "evidence" against me sparked national headlines. To answer them, I placed an advertisement in the *New York Times* and many other newspapers and magazines throughout the country. In it, I offered ten thousand dollars to anyone who could disprove a single one of the many non-Communist affidavits I had sworn to. Of course, there were no takers.

The FCC wouldn't provide me with details of their charges against me even after the U.S. Senate Interstate Commerce Committee directed them to. It gives one an eerie feeling to go into a trial without knowing exactly what you are being charged with or even who your accusers are. I found myself a defendant before an agency of my own government, forced to answer anonymous charges involving possible perjury and disloyalty. I would not be tried by a jury of my peers, but by innuendo, by smear, and by headlines.

The trial before the FCC started in September 1954. The trial rules ran contrary to every normal legal practice I had been accustomed to in my years in the courtroom. The prosecutor, Walter Powell, was free to introduce any new charge against me he saw fit, with the burden of disproving his accusations falling upon me. The most shocking aspect of the case was that early in the trial the prosecution shifted its ground of the "indictment." The original charge, that I had been a *member* of the Communist Party, was changed. Now they took out a new hunting license, one virtually without limits, claiming that a dozen or more years before I had *associated* with Communists.

The FCC's case rested heavily on the nineteen professional witnesses lined up against me. The first was a Black man, William Cummings, who had been mentioned in Drew Pearson's column. Cummings was paid twenty-five dollars a day by the Immigration and Naturalization

Service. Being a professional witness was his only employment. On the stand, he said he had seen me at the opening of the Communist bookstore and that he knew I had made cash contributions to the Communist Party. He made the first big headlines, and the FCC lawyers were ecstatic.

By this time, I had accumulated a staff of detectives, and we thoroughly searched the backgrounds of witnesses as soon as we learned who they were. This was one of the prerogatives of a person who had the means to do it. Our detectives were able to quickly discredit Cummings. They showed that he had falsified several affidavits, even such items as his marriage certificate and his application for a driver's license. We learned he recruited his friends, and even members of his family, into the Communist Party and turned their names over to the FBI. During the course of my trial, he was arrested for perjury. His testimony was worthless.

Another witness, Clark Wideman, swore that when he was seventeen, in the early 1930s, he heard me talk in southern Ohio for two hours about the Soviet economy. Although he "remembered" every word I said, he could not remember one other person who was at the meeting. Wideman's great value to us was that under cross-examination he admitted what we believed to be true of all the witnesses—that his questions and answers had been prepared for him by the FCC staff. We began to realize that the trial judge was not to be a hanging judge and that our exposure of the professional witnesses would bear fruit.

Ernest Courey was another one of the Immigration Service's professionals who testified against me. He said he was a "respected summer resort operator" in a Wisconsin town and that he had joined the Communist Party at the behest of a private detective agency. He said he was in my office in 1938 and received two dollars for a ticket to a Communist picnic.

We made him look like a fool. He said that he'd never been convicted of a crime, but under cross-examination he admitted he had just gotten out of the Ohio penitentiary after serving a sentence for murder. He couldn't remember being in prison for murder, but he "remembered" being in my office twenty years earlier for a two-dollar contribution. Courey gave us the opportunity to learn how the Immigration Service worked. We found out he was a Syrian, facing deportation. He had every reason to assume that he must tell the "right" story or be shipped back to Syria.

We knew the witnesses were lying. We knew they were coached by the FCC. We obtained copies of scripts and the tapes of rehearsals. We actually had some tapes where the FCC staff said: Here's the question and here's your answer. Once, we turned a script over to reporters and spectators in the courtroom. When one especially confused witness began to recite his lines, the reporters took turns giving the answers before he could get them out.

Louis Budenz was America's number one professional witness. At the time of my trial, he was at the height of his glory, testifying for the government for big pay. When we questioned him about his income, he said he had earned seventy thousand dollars by 1953 from being on the witness chair. He did know how to arrange the wildest story to make fodder for headlines. He was a master of innuendo and an expert in showing guilt by association. Unlike the others, Budenz did know me, for he had once been my client in a picketing case during the bitter Auto-Lite strike in Toledo. But his "evidence" against me didn't come from our brief association.

It was Budenz's claim that the names of four hundred persons given to him by a high Communist official named Jack Stachel were etched solely and secretly in his own mind. He claimed that after he had memorized the list, he and Stachel tore it up. He said that this mythical list was a super-confidential catalog of hidden Communist Party members in the United States.

For the purposes of this trial, Budenz cheerfully placed me on his secret list. Why not? As a government witness, he had practical immunity from libel action. Budenz admitted under cross-examination that he had written several books and articles and delivered hundreds of speeches without once having mentioned my name as an associate or friend of Communists. He had no explanation for this oversight. We were able to suggest that it might be because no one had previously hired him to do a job on me.

I was really laughing at Budenz while he testified. And he was conscious of my laughing. I'm sure we both remembered the days when I got him out of jail in Toledo. He realized that I knew what he was up to now. He was engaged in a dirty, despicable trade—a witness for hire.

The FCC's prize witness was Marie Natvig. She wanted to make a name for herself, like Elizabeth Bentley, the premier informer of the day, or Whittaker Chambers, the turncoat in the Alger Hiss case. Mrs. Natvig said that she came from a very wealthy family in Cleveland, Ohio. She said she first met me at a Communist meeting of agricultural workers in Chicago in 1936. She claimed she had seen me again at a Communist Party conference in Columbus. She told how "Comrade Lamb" led discussions of intricate problems of dialectical materialism and claimed that I was the architect of the future Communist movements of the world. She recalled I described the course of events to come in Asia, including the hot and cold wars.

"Didn't those terms come into existence years later?" the trial examiner asked. "No," she replied. "Comrade Lamb invented them." Then Mrs. Natvig claimed that I proposed to seize communications, then transportation, and finally to prepare for insurrection in the armed forces.

This seemingly mild little lady had already produced a first-class newspaper sensation. But on the second day of her testimony, she found a way to make even larger headlines. Testifying about the meetings I was supposed to have attended in Columbus, she shyly confided, "Mr. Lamb and I had a 'liaison' in the Chittenden Hotel." Then, with head bowed, she added movingly that this was "my first infidelity and led to my divorce." After she told of our trysts at the best hotels around the country, my wife, Prudence, was asked by reporters what she thought of the testimony of Mrs. Natvig. She answered, "Ted couldn't be guilty of that. She's no blonde!"

Newspapers all over the country feasted on this sex scandal. A lot of reporters were there. The FCC had a practice of timing their press releases just before the noon press deadline. They would make the afternoon papers before we had a chance to answer the scandalous charges.

The revelations of a revolutionary conspiracy and a sex scandal should have been enough, but Mrs. Natvig was encouraged to bring her adventures up to date. She said that a railroad yard worker, just the night before, had offered her fifty thousand dollars if she would stop testifying against me. All hell broke loose! There were big headlines: "Government Witness Offered Bribe!" The *Washington Post* carried over eight full columns on her shocking bribe story.

As Mrs. Natvig testified, her stories became more fanciful. She said she was a close friend of Langston Hughes, the poet, "during his Cleveland days." It was the trial examiner who pointed out that Hughes had never spent time in Cleveland. At first, we thought the man she claimed offered her the bribe was another figment of her imagination. But, as luck would have it, she used his right name, and our detectives located him and brought the very embarrassed railroad man into the hearing room.

Then, with his wife present, he told the true story of what happened that night. He was at a Washington bar, where he picked up this lone woman. He had intended to entertain her. They were getting a little high, and she excused herself to make a phone call. When she returned to him, she insisted he take her to her hotel, where he left her in full view of two FCC lawyers. My name was not mentioned the entire romantic evening.

Our detectives were able to learn more about Marie Natvig's colorful past. Instead of being a super-rich woman with servants, a penthouse, and a Rolls Royce at her disposal, she was the daughter of a used furniture dealer in Cleveland. She had an honest, hard-working father, incidentally—a very decent man, who had severed all connections with his daughter. In 1928, years before Mrs. Natvig's "first infidelity" with me that led, she said, to her divorce, she had been arrested in Madison, Wisconsin, for soliciting. We learned she had faced embezzlement charges in Florida and that she had sworn in affidavits to the government that she had never "at any time or place" been a Communist, contrary to her testimony at my hearing.

Mrs. Natvig had been thoroughly prepared by three FCC lawyers. But when my lawyer's questions got too hot, she refused to answer them, claiming "personal privilege," a right generally reserved for members of legislative bodies. She shrugged off affidavits given by courts as "vicious falsehoods." When we asked about her children, she said, "I'll kill you if you ask me another question about that." At times, she became downright hysterical on the stand; she became loud and vulgar. She once threatened to throw a water bottle at one of our attorneys.

Her testimony covered more than eight hundred pages. Attorney General McGrath said there was at least one glaring contradiction on each page and sometimes within one sentence. When Mrs. Natvig later looked at her testimony, she said it was like awakening from a nightmare. She finally called Howard McGrath and said she wanted to set the record straight.

She came back on the stand, this time to say under oath that she had been browbeaten and brainwashed by the FCC staff into going along with the prepared script. She told of her enforced confinement in Washington hotel rooms to prevent access to her by outsiders. She swore that her original testimony was a fabrication bought and paid for by the prosecution: "We were manufacturing evidence which I was forced to memorize." Actually, she said, she had never been a member of the Communist Party. She had never known me in Chicago, Columbus, or anywhere else. Even the bribe hoax was plotted by the FCC lawyers. She said she had been coerced by FCC lawyers to lie about having sexual relations with me. The prosecutor had dreamed up the romance between us. "Make it gory," she quoted prosecutor Powell as saying. "It's good for big headlines."

When she told the FCC lawyers she wanted to repudiate her original testimony, she said they offered her new incentives. When she refused, they threatened her with arrest for perjury. After she recanted, the government did bring a perjury charge against her during my trial. Then, in an unprecedented move, they recessed my proceedings while they tried their own witness, Natvig—not so much for her lies about me, but as a lesson to warn others not to recant. In the end, she was convicted for saying the things they told her to say and sentenced to nine months in prison.

The government wanted to force witnesses to think long and hard before recanting. They were successful with some, but others returned to the stand. The real estate agent, Clark Wideman, recanted. He said that he had falsely uttered words that were put into his mouth by the FCC lawyers.

A farmer from Kansas, Lowell Watson, recanted in a big way. Watson had originally testified that in 1931 he and Gene Stoll, an Ohio Communist leader, visited my Toledo office and received contributions to the Communist Party. But Stoll had told Watson the night before he testified that he'd never seen me until 1934, so he couldn't have been with Watson in 1931 to visit my office. That disarmed Watson. Then we brought out that Watson, some years earlier, had been found guilty of contributing to the delinquency of a minor girl. We led him through a series of embarrassing questions. He soon confessed that the FCC attorneys had given him a prepared script when he arrived in Washington and had ordered him to memorize it down to the slightest detail.

Now Watson testified: "I spent many restless nights worrying about the subject and finally concluded that the only fair thing to do, the only truthful thing to do, the only thing that I could possibly do and continue to live with my conscience the rest of my life was to return to the stand and tell the real truth as I know it. My previous testimony was false. It was the result of constant and consistent coaching by legal representatives of the FCC."

Watson was specific: "When I was asked about conversations which were supposed to have taken place in Lamb's Toledo offices, I couldn't remember anything about them. . . . So Powell sat down with me and began suggesting what conversations could have occurred, so that when I returned after lunch I was able to testify as to those conversations— falsely, of course. For instance, when I said that Mr. Lamb once said, 'If it had not been for the Communist Party, the Scottsboro Boys* would have burned long ago,' it was not true. Mr. Powell and I, looking through literature, found this statement made by some unnamed person, so Powell suggested that we say Lamb said it."[7]

It was very embarrassing for the FCC to be in the headlines now. That's the trouble with frame-ups. When you start them, you can't stop. You've got to lay it on. Just like Marie Natvig—she told fanciful stories. And when we found weaknesses, we sure as hell were not going to let her go. So she told more and more fanciful lies. Rigorous cross-examination quickly exposed such witnesses.

I was eager to take the stand myself. I knew I was innocent and that I could destroy any picture they had of me as a Communist. Also, I was anxious to explain my philosophy. I stood for a planned, sharing society where there are limits on greed and private profit and the personal acquisition and control of wealth. I still do believe in an international, humane, sharing society for all peoples.

In my opening statement to the FCC, I told of my early days as a labor lawyer, days of the Depression and social upheaval, bitter strikes, economic disorder, and hungry men. "Most of all," I testified, "I don't want anyone to get the notion that I appear here on this public stand to withdraw from my past associations or activities on behalf of the underprivileged."

Then, referring to this FCC hearing, I added, "You are the ones who hired the liars to repeat your manufactured slanders, and now we have the spectacle of your same people in the FCC passing judgment on the truth or falsity of your own manufactured evidence."

Old friends, on their own motion and without subpoena, began to come forward to testify as witnesses to my loyalty and character. Estes Kefauver led the parade. During all my difficulties, I enjoyed most my friendship with this truly great senator.

In December 1955, one year after the hearings began, the trial ex-

---

* In 1931, nine Black youths, one barely twelve years old, were accused of raping two white girls in Alabama. Eight of them were sentenced to death in the electric chair. They became known as the Scottsboro Boys, and their case gave rise to massive demonstrations and aroused protests in the United States and abroad that served as a prelude to the modern civil rights movement. Although they escaped execution, five served long terms in prison, despite the recantation by one of the supposed victims during the trial and medical testimony that a rape had not been committed.

aminer completed his decision. It was one hundred forty pages long. Every finding of fact was decided in my favor. "Mr. Lamb possesses the qualifications necessary for a broadcast station licensee," he concluded. Then he added that my request for a license "would be in the public's interest, convenience, and necessity."

But the FCC lawyers were able to further delay the final decision by the commission. Until they renewed my licenses, we couldn't even replace worn-out equipment. We lost advertisers and untold amounts of business. It exercised a slow stranglehold over our entire operation—no doubt about it. McGrath forced the issue with a brief: "These licensees, as well as Mr. Lamb's family, have suffered and continue to suffer economic harm beyond calculation. The economic and social damage done to Mr. Lamb personally can never be repaired, and it is extremely doubtful if the expenditure of hundreds of thousands of dollars by the government can ever be justified."

The Lamb case finally came before the full Federal Communications Commission. There it remained for more than another year. On June 14, 1957, the FCC grudgingly gave me clearance and renewed my radio and television licenses. Their final judgment had the element of saving my personal integrity and reputation. Perhaps the greatest victory I can claim may be that the Immigration Service's pool of several hundred informers-for-hire—"consultants"—was disbanded. They were riding high and wide at the time. At least we exposed their racket and slowed down the persecution of radicals.

By temperament, I am a fighter for social causes. I always will be. But to take on the FCC successfully, a will to fight was not enough. One also had to have the financial means. I hate to ascribe it to affluence, but I was one of the few victims of that sordid era who could afford to mount a full-fledged counterattack against the massed resources of the government and stand by the guns for four long years. That was the difference between my trial and that of my friend Alger Hiss. It cost me, first to last, more than nine hundred thousand dollars to clear my name and protect my properties. That's a sum that was far beyond the reach of the hundreds of minor officials, hapless intellectuals, honest progressives, and innocent bystanders who were run down by the McCarthy juggernaut during his dastardly witch-hunting days.

JOHN HENRY FAULK

Bringing the Blacklisters
to Account

John Henry Faulk

*The underhanded coercion of the blacklist so violated democratic prin-
ciples that superpatriots could not endorse it openly. Ronald Reagan
said, on behalf of the Screen Actors Guild, over which he presided, "We
will not be party to a blacklist."* [1] *Then the guild banned from membership both Communists and anyone who had been an unfriendly witness before the House Un-American Activities Committee. "As long as I
live," vowed producer Eric Johnston in October 1947, "I will never be
party to anything as un-American as a blacklist."* [2] *In November of that
year, the Association of Motion Picture Producers, led by the same Eric
Johnston, resolved to dismiss the Hollywood Ten, to never knowingly
employ a Communist, and to seek the assistance of the Hollywood
guilds to eliminate "subversives" in the film industry. "No right-thinking
person believes in 'blacklists,'" wrote Roy Brewer in the* American Legion *magazine.*[3] *But he and the Legion were as deep in the business of
blacklisting on the West Coast as Vincent Hartnett was on the East
Coast.*

*Hartnett's Aware, Inc., sought to purify East Coast theater and
television in the 1950s by publishing lists of "subversives." When they
listed John Henry Faulk, they got more than they bargained for. He
sued them for libel and won a judgment for damages that at the
time was the largest ever awarded in a U.S. libel case. But in shed-*

ding the light of day on their blacklisting operation, he lost a promising career as a radio and television personality. "In my very considered opinion," testified producer David Susskind, "John Henry Faulk, had he been allowed to continue as a performer on television, would have become a star of the first magnitude."[4]

I had a professor by the name of J. Frank Dobie. He was a folklorist, a great writer in Texas. He had but one goal: the liberated mind. Dobie and I came from the same milieu, a white, Protestant kind of primitive egalitarianism. But he and I both pronounced the word "Negro" as "nigra" and called Black people "colored folks" or "darkies," without any thought of the implications of using designations like that. We had never challenged the notion of segregation or the Jim Crow laws that were fixtures in our society.

In a way, it was old Hitler who opened our eyes. Hitler's treatment of the Jews outraged me. I was raised an Old Bible Methodist. My father, a biblical scholar, was pro-Semitic and thought the Jews had hung the moon. But it took a fellow English instructor from Yale, who sympathized with Hitler's persecution of the Jews, to point out, "You're so damn self-righteous. Don't you know Hitler could have taken all his race laws from your laws in Texas? Hitler says the Jews have to sit on separate benches, to ride in separate conveyances. Well, that's exactly the way you treat your colored people right here in Austin."

It hit me like a ton of bricks. Dobie and I got to talking about it. "By God," Dobie said, "I hate to admit it, but he's right." We began to see what an injustice was being perpetrated on the Black portion of our population, the indignities they were subjected to twenty-four hours a day. And I became much more sensitive to them.

When World War II boiled up, Dobie and I were all asweat to get after the Nazis. They represented the ultimate in arrogant destructiveness. But Dobie had been in World War I and was too damn old. And the army wouldn't let me in at first, because I'm blind in my right eye. So we felt part of our function should be to help bring a bit of democracy to Blacks, especially since they were being asked to serve.

Dobie and I were regarded as authorities on folklore. I had a keen ear and was good at southern dialects. By 1942, I was in great demand as a kind of entertainer-educator before civic clubs and women's study groups. I got to interjecting into my speeches the injustice practiced against Blacks. Well, this was considered absolutely out of bounds. It was like bringing up the subject of sex in front of my mother. You just didn't discuss matters sexual in mama's presence. Anyhow, when I agitated that Blacks be allowed to vote, the attitude was, "Isn't it a shame the Communists have gotten hold of Johnny?"

I had seen two Communists in my entire life. They came drifting through Texas and stayed in daddy's office. His place was a center of tolerance for all the various sects. They would headquarter there, from Judge Rutherford's World Bible Organization to Jehovah's Witnesses. Daddy had been a Socialist then. The Socialists in Texas were a decent bunch of fellows who were going to bring about the millennium. Once they had a "mass" rally, consisting of fourteen people. There was a lot of hostility between the Socialists and Communists, and those two Communists picketed it. I was pretty disgusted with them.

So in 1942, when I agitated for Black rights, I wondered why I was called a Communist. I didn't even like Communists, from those I'd seen. Certainly it didn't take a Communist to feel that justice should be done. Then I made a fascinating discovery: The word "Communist" was a catchword and had nothing to do with reality. It was used to discredit an opponent without rational dialogue. You could just say, "He's a damn red," and win your point.

Later, I got to know a few Communists at the University of Texas. I remember one fellow was trying to sell me on the Communist Party. He sounded just like my Aunt Ella. She tried to get me into the foot-washing Baptist church because they had the only truth. Aunt Ella's group was the only one who knew that women with bobbed hair and lipstick smeared on their face were works of Satan. Well, this guy was like her in that he wanted me to tap into his source of truth. I felt the same kind of discomfort being around him that I felt being around Aunt Ella.

But common sense and plain facts taught me that most, if not all, of the loud denunciation of reds and the threat that they were taking over America was utter nonsense and political hogwash. So I never had the inclination to join those who sought to gain political or social advantage by denouncing Communists. Members of the Communist Party had as much right as Republicans and Democrats to speak their piece.

In 1942, I joined the Southern Conference for Human Welfare. When I heard Clark Foreman, Palmer Weber, and Eleanor Roosevelt all holding forth, I was profoundly impressed. And there was Mary McLeod Bethune, a genius of a human being, whom I just adored. They all felt there were enough good people in the South to do something about the injustice that was visited on Blacks.

The House Un-American Activities Committee attacked the Southern Conference as a Communist transmission belt. In 1947, the House Committee came yapping out of the woods and was made permanent by that sterling American patriot John Rankin of Mississippi. He was the soul of vulgarity and viciousness. He referred to Congressman Vito Marcantonio and Mayor La Guardia of New York as "those two dagos," to Walter Winchell as a "kike," and to a certain Black leader as the "big nigger up in Washington." He would give subpoena powers to the House committee and call anybody a red who was for allaying the racial conflicts in the South.

Then, in 1948, the Alger Hiss trial came off.* It was pretty obvious that it was an attack on Roosevelt's New Deal. Roosevelt had for years been called a bolshevik. They tried to beat him in 1936, 1940, and 1944. Hell, he just handed them their heads each time. But with Roosevelt gone, the Republicans' weapon—namely, that of charging a Communist threat—began to work. They declared to the country that the Democratic Party was the party of treason. It all added up to a carefully orchestrated anxiety.

It was a day of complete madness, and nothing was going to slow it down. First, you had poor old simple-minded Harry Truman chirping and barking. Then Joe McCarthy was heaving over the horizon. McCarthy and Roy Cohn, his running dog, spread a kind of fury and hysteria through the land and a quaking in Congress. Courage wasn't an attribute of Congress or our national leadership. Eisenhower sat up there and grinned like an old possum laying up on a limb. Everybody said: He's too noble to go for McCarthy's crude tactics. But he never objected to them.

And the whole damn rotten shootin' match of them sold this country down the river by introducing into the political dialogue, into the very lifestream of a democratic society such as ours, the term "treason." The founding fathers, when they framed the Constitution, very carefully defined treason, because they knew that for five hundred years tyranny had used "treason" to shut off opposition. You could freeze it tight when you hit it with a blast of "treason." And when McCarthy and the Republicans introduced this "vast conspiracy that had its cold bony hand on the very highest levels of government"—including even Mrs.

* See note on page 41 for information on the Hiss trial.

Roosevelt and Harry Dexter White—they injected a deadly disease into the political dialogue. God, it was a grim period.

Any crackpot who sobered up enough or was let out of jail long enough appeared before the committee: "I used to be a Communist. I'll tell you all about it." Regardless of how unstable their personalities had been in the past, they were carried around like icons to show the people. It sounds idiotic, but there were alcoholics, hot-check artists, and everything else coming before the committee, fantasizing their damn hearts out. All this was played out in bold headlines. The hysteria took the form of a frothing insanity.

The House Un-American Activities Committee was sweeping over the land, punishing schoolteachers, professors, librarians, and ministers of the gospel. The committee had been playing havoc in Hollywood and the rest of our industry. I despised them with a quaking fury for what they were doing to our society, just as I despised J. Edgar Hoover. Where did he come off, joining in with McCarthy and those other weirdos who disgraced our Senate at the time? But Hoover had been elevated to sainthood, and to criticize him publicly was to get blacklisted. He pronounced like a prophet. Every other week, in *Reader's Digest* or some other magazine at the supermarket, he was telling you how to judge your neighbor's patriotism.

This caused a proliferation of these self-appointed vigilantes throughout the land. Damn near every community in the country had its anti-communist group. Even Cousin Snodgrass had a Committee to Combat Communist Infiltration in the Third Precinct of Washtub County. "By God, Johnny, come down here and see how we've held them Communists at bay. There ain't one in our government today in Washtub County." He made his money by clipping off those damn fool bankers, who would give him a stipend to "save America from Communism."

This is how Aware functioned in the entertainment industry. Aware, Inc., was a self-appointed vigilante group in New York. It had as its declared purpose for existing combating the Communist conspiracy. The way they combated this "Communist conspiracy" was to publish a bulletin and circulate it in the industry. It listed individuals who in the past had done something that violated Aware's notion of what a patriotic American should be. Vincent Hartnett was the executive secretary. The networks and advertising agencies would send him lists of people they wanted to hire, and he'd let them know who was safe and who wasn't, for a fee.

People who got blacklisted were never charged with violating any law. If they appeared at a function, signed a petition, or marched in a parade—all of which were perfectly legal, constitutionally protected activities—they were charged by innuendo with being part of a Communist conspiracy. Hundreds of decent, law-abiding citizens in the radio and television profession, who cared very deeply—cared enough to take political stands that were unpopular—were punished for it, cast out, blacklisted, and became unemployable. It was a wicked, wicked operation. John Randolph and Sarah Cunningham, Madeline Lee, Jack Gilford, and good old Zero Mostel were decent, nice people. Yet you weren't even supposed to be seen publicly with them. Well, I admired all those people who stood up to it, who looked them in the eye—like Myrna Loy did—and said, "The hell with you." They were people of strength, of character, and, to me, the ultimate patriots.

Most of the leadership of AFTRA, the American Federation of Radio and Television Artists, supported Aware completely. A number of them were officials of Aware. In fact, the clique of people who ruled the union, like Bud Collyer and Ed Sullivan, used this anti-communism to keep control of it. Bud Collyer owned interests in several production companies, and he was the damn president of the union. Ed Sullivan was a producer, for God's sake, and had been rehearsing people over-time and not paying them anything. Anybody who complained was "a red troublemaker."

In 1954, a slate of candidates ran against the entrenched board of directors in AFTRA and lost. After the election, Aware put out a bulletin attacking the patriotism of those who lost and circulated it to all employers in radio and television. It served as a warning to others who might want to oppose them. Then, in 1955, a resolution to condemn Aware was gotten up in the union. The board charged it was a Communist plot and warned, "If you vote to condemn Aware, the House committee will come up here and investigate." It was an open threat. But Aware was despised, and the union membership voted to condemn it.

Sure enough, HUAC announced it was coming to New York. It called about nineteen people. The board of directors of the union immediately passed a resolution that anyone who did not cooperate with the House committee, which meant naming names and being one of their lackeys, would be subject to suspension from the union.

It was a terrible period, and one that aroused a great deal of shame in me for not being more outspoken. I was doing awfully well, sailing along chopping in the tall cotton. I had a radio show on WCBS, a one-hour show, five days a week. I talked, told a few stories, and commented on the news of the day. I also had a weekly television show. My manager and everyone else in the business said, "Don't stick your neck out. Don't sign anything. Don't be showing up at no damn meeting where they can take your picture."

But I'd been watching this Aware crowd. A bunch of us, including Charlie Collingwood and Orson Bean, got to talking one night about these wicked rascals. We decided we ought to run our own slate of officers. Charlie and Orson and I ran. It became a passion with me, but it was hard as hell to get others to run. Faye Emerson, a hell of a good gal, had the guts to do it. Garry Moore and Janice Rule ran, too, along with twenty-eight others on a platform condemning Aware. We called ourselves the Middle-of-the-Road slate. We said we were opposed to Communism but we were also opposed to the terrible practice of blacklisting. We were swept into office, winning twenty-seven of the thirty-five seats.

We took office on January 1, 1956, and by God, we were going to put a stop to blacklisting. Then came the reaction. On January 10, the House Un-American Activities Committee published a statement. It was on the front page of all the papers: "House Committee Condemns New Faction in Union." The committee's counsel, Frank S. Tavenner, said the Communist Party was making a new assault on the entertainment world, that it was taking the form of anti-blacklisting, and that this group had recently taken office in New York.

About a week later, here comes Aware out with a bulletin. I'm sitting home, and old Val Adams of the *New York Times* calls me: "Have you seen this bulletin Aware put out on your slate? It's got some pretty rough stuff in it." I found myself getting nervous, my throat tightening.

I went down first thing in the morning to get a copy of it. It said: The Middle-of-the-Road slate claims it is anti-communist, and this might well be the case with some, but let's look at the leadership. Let's look at Charlie Collingwood; he attacked the House committee. Let's look at Orson Bean; he appeared at a function that ridiculed the House committee. Let's look at John Henry Faulk. It denounced me in particular, listing seven things I was supposed to have done, places I entertained or spoke at, or something I sponsored.

It gave me a terrible sinking feeling; some of the crap was from ten years back. One item said: A John Faulk was scheduled to appear at the

Astor Hotel at a dinner under the auspices of the Independent Citizens Committee of the Arts, Sciences, and Professions. And then, parenthetically, "Officially designated a Communist front."

Well, I looked through old diaries and telephone logs and found that, sure enough, I was at the Astor Hotel. I got furious when I read that damn thing. It was a dinner for the United Nations. The Security Council had a birthday party sponsored by the American Association of University Women, the American Bar Association, the YMCA, and others. The principal speaker was Edward Stettinius, then secretary of state. I'd been sent by CBS to entertain.

I took the bulletin to my agent, Gerald Dickler. He was a damn good guy, and he knew the business very well. He said, "This is it. You've had it." I said, "Hell, most of this stuff is false. The rest is unimportant." Gerry said it made no difference whether it was true or false. "You've been named. You're now controversial."

"CBS is going to stand behind me," I said. "I can promise you that. I'm making them an awful lot of money." He said, "They may stand behind you for a while. But if they are pressured, they'll make a decision to fire you. And they're not going to say it's because you became a hot potato. They'll give you half a dozen other reasons why." He knew that blacklisting was all done underground.

I called a meeting of our slate. They were outraged and indignant. "By God, this can't happen to Johnny Faulk! That's what we ran against." There was a great deal of bravado, but I could tell there was a lot of nervousness, too. I began getting calls at night from members: "Listen, Johnny, you know I'm behind you one hundred percent. But I was at a dinner party tonight, and a guy there—I can't name him—said they had the real goods on you and that you really sucked us into a deal. I know it's a damn lie, Johnny. But were you ever a member of the Communist Party?" I'd say, "Wait a minute. Did you think they were going to let us kick them out and not even respond? This is McCarthyism at its best."

The union's chief counsel, Henry Jaffe, was so closely identified with Aware that many members of our slate felt he should be replaced by another lawyer. Jaffe agreed to announce his resignation at a union meeting. When that got out, it was like an earthquake. I got calls from unnamed persons who told me they knew for a fact that Jaffe's dismissal was ordered by the Communist Party. Ed Sullivan, in his *Daily News* column, beat the drums for AFTRA members to come to the meeting to support Jaffe.

There was a huge turnout. One person after another got up to support Jaffe. Then Dick Stark, a wheeler and dealer and windmill fixer, "confessed" that he had been deluded into running on the Middle-of-the-Road slate. It was obviously a put-up job. Two or three other members of our slate got up and denounced us, too. Aware's bulletin and supporters had succeeded in panicking them, and they fell all to pieces. Fear is an effective weapon; it can make you do irrational things and take actions that are very unworthy of you.

I went back to CBS that afternoon, very dejected. The station manager, Carl Ward, told me that Laurence Johnson from Aware was going to my sponsors, demanding they withdraw from my show. "They've gotten to you. Libby's Frozen Foods is canceling." Libby's was on five times a week, twice a day, and represented a lot of money. This man, Johnson, a supermarket owner from Syracuse, threatened the sponsors: "We're going to put a sign over your goods that you endorse Stalin's little creatures." That's all he had to say to the board of directors of Borden's Milk or Pillsbury Flour. A nice, big-jowled Republican gentleman would say, "Good God, tell us what to do to stop it."

There was nothing more reprehensible to Ward than losing an account. He told me, "Look, you made us a lot of money in the past. Maybe you can take Aware's charges and answer them. You can say how you were duped into it, that you had no idea you were being used as a pawn by the Communists. You can say, 'I'm willing to make a confession of anything I've done that was wrong.'" He was very sincere. This was the way you sought to get out of trouble. That's the way Kim Hunter got the heat off her. Those who didn't give in paid for it. Hell, you've got to see some of the faces of people who had been hit and were out of work.

So when CBS gave me this thing to answer, I was going to do just that, take it home and answer it. At that moment, I felt utter defeat. I had a wife and three children. I needed eighteen hundred dollars a month just for rent on my Manhattan apartment. I didn't want to lose it or my job. But when I looked at Aware's bulletin again, I realized there was no way it could be answered without losing my self-respect. I made up my mind right there I could never do that. It made me tingle all over, because I had decided to fight them and not to go through the rigmarole of apologizing and explaining.

I wrote CBS a letter. I told them that they knew good and well who I was and what I stood for, since I'd been there for ten years and was known to every officer; that the men who'd made the charges were a faceless group and I would answer none of their allegations; that this was simply a way to destroy my effectiveness as a union officer; and that if CBS had any questions, I was perfectly willing and anxious to answer them. Then I served notice on CBS I would hold them as responsible as I held Aware for whatever happened to me.

It was a smashing fine statement. I remember vividly the sense of self-worth and self-respect I felt. My God, this is the way you do it. You look them in the eye. You don't give in to these birds. They have only one weapon—fear. Once you've confronted it, you have an enormous sense of relief.

I wanted to sue the hell out of Aware, but I had no hard evidence that I was suffering anything. CBS hadn't fired me yet. Then one day, an account executive with the Grey Advertising Agency, a sweet old guy named Tom Murray, got a call from Laurence Johnson threatening to boycott Hoffman beverages if they didn't drop my program. He also got a vicious letter from Johnson, attacking me. Murray was furious and sent me a copy of the letter, concrete evidence of blacklisting. Now I had something I could go to a lawyer with.

I talked to Ed Murrow, and he thought it was a smashing idea. He said, "Of course, this will destroy you. You know that. This will be a battle unto death. Their roots run right into the FBI and the House Un-American Activities Committee." I told him, "I think they got the wrong sow by the ear when they got me."

We decided to try to get Louis Nizer to represent me. He was a good, tough operator who I knew would protect me at all costs if he took the case. Nizer went over my background with a fine-tooth comb. He asked me if I'd ever signed a hot check, if I'd ever been a Communist or had kinfolk who were Communists. I told him I hadn't been one and didn't intend to be one, but that I did not share the "Communist conspiracy" notion. I felt it was a bunch of hogwash. He didn't argue that. Nizer deliberated several days and decided to take my case. It lifted my spirits and reassured me. We had a great handshaking.

Later, he asked me for ten thousand dollars for out-of-pocket expenses, which, as he pointed out, was a very modest sum for him. But it was a hell of a jump for me because my savings didn't nearly cover that amount. I went to Ed Murrow about it. We were having breakfast, and I said, "Damn, I've got to scare up some money." Ed said, "Wait a minute. The directors of CBS will pay for this. You're fighting a fight for them." The next day, he told me CBS wouldn't touch it with a ten-foot pole. So Ed wrote out a check for seventy-five hundred dollars and said,

"I am investing this money in America. Louis Nizer must try this case, and this blacklisting racket must be exposed." And we were into it.

The suit made headlines. People were full of congratulations. My friend Palmer Weber said, "Nizer will take you by the heels and flail them within an inch of their lives." But I was surprised at how many very decent people said, "Look, you're a damn fool. You have no right to jeopardize your career, your livelihood, doing something this idiotic." Nine months later, CBS fired me while I was off on vacation.

Lou Nizer knew how to draw up a lawsuit, if anybody did. We were suing Aware, Vincent Hartnett, and Laurence Johnson for conspiracy to libel me. We had a pre-trial examination. Godfrey Schmidt was the attorney for the defendants. He was a member of Aware and really believed all this claptrap. Vincent Hartnett was the first witness Nizer examined. I never will forget it. It was quite fascinating to watch him writhe. Nizer was able to find out how Hartnett had blacklisted people, who helped him with it, where he got his information, and how much he made from these "services."

Just before Hartnett was to testify, the House Un-American Activities Committee had subpoenaed me. I took the subpoena to Nizer: "What'll I do about it?" I was worried he would say, "Go before the House committee and answer any question they ask you." I would have had to tell him, "Hell, no, I won't submit to their damn subpoena."

But instead Nizer said, "They have no right to subpoena you. They work with Aware." He called their counsel. "Mr. Arens, if I have to turn Washington upside down you're not going to call John Henry Faulk now. If you force me to, I'll expose your complete unconstitutional pattern of behavior, that the House Un-American Activities Committee is leaking material to Aware and to the FBI. We will charge that you're doing it as an accommodation to the defendants." His voice dropped about three octaves: "We have sufficient evidence in our files right now to establish this." Arens told him to consider the subpoena postponed.

As soon as Hartnett found out I was not scheduled to appear before HUAC, he completely capitulated at the pre-trial hearing. He and Schmidt admitted that they had been fed a barrel of false information about me and offered to make any public statement we desired. Soon afterward, Roy Cohn replaced Schmidt as defense attorney and was able to force one delay after another.

Nizer warned it might take years to bring my case to trial. I was blacklisted during that whole time, about six years. At first, I felt that I was giving up a lot, the fame and popularity of the show world. After I reflected on it, I realized I was doing something far more important than all the success I could ever have. But I was also getting deeper in debt. Myrna Loy, my good friend, got together with a few other friends and planned a benefit party for me. Mrs. Roosevelt, Ed Murrow, and others came and contributed generously. It was a lifesaver.

I moved back down to Austin, Texas. Most of the people whose good opinion I cherished—like J. Frank Dobie, Roy Bedichek, and Dr. Walter P. Webb of the History Department—rallied around me very closely. They symbolized the America I had such a deep affection for.

In 1787, the founding fathers gathered in Philadelphia to frame their ideals into a constitution and pass them on to us. They spent all summer long slapping mosquitoes, swatting flies, and framing a charter of government that had never seen the light of day before. Then they said: We need a Bill of Rights to make sure these ideals and principles are never violated. These great rights of the people—freedom of conscience, speech, press, and the right of the people to peacefully assemble—must never be touched. It still makes a lump come to my throat. This is who we are. This is our strength.

You get an enormous sense of well-being and security once you understand how our society began and you know you're on the beam with it. That knowledge is what sustained me through my case. And it was the asininity of these jackanapes and scoundrels—those who pronounced those basic freedoms that were created and nailed into our Constitution as being somehow Communist-inspired—that showed how desperately far we'd come from our ideals.

Nizer constructed a brilliant case. He had gathered a library of information on who Aware had blacklisted, how they had blacklisted them, and the careers they had destroyed. I was able to get David Susskind, Tony Randall, Garry Moore, and Mark Goodson to agree to testify for me. Now we needed to get witnesses who had been victims. At first, no one wanted to come forth.

Then, I asked Kim Hunter, who had won an Academy Award. She had endorsed a peace conference and signed a petition asking for clemency for Willie McGee, so she was blasted by Aware. It had a dismal effect on her career until Hartnett got her to sign a series of affidavits to remove her name from the blacklist. He had her say that she had committed a grievous error by not realizing how sinister the Communist conspiracy was and that she hoped she would be forgiven. I didn't know how she would react, now, when I asked her to be my witness. She put her arms around me and said she'd testify, not just for my sake but for her own and her children's sake as well.

The trial went on for three months. We presented some twenty-eight witnesses. Each one told a pretty scorching story. Kim Hunter testified that when AFTRA was about to vote on the resolution to condemn Aware, Hartnett said that her affidavits were not enough to show she was a loyal American, that she must do something actively anti-communist, like publicly supporting Aware. She agreed to send a telegram to AFTRA.

Nizer asked, "After this date, did you get television appearances?"

"I worked quite frequently after that, and to the present date."

David Susskind told about a program he created, called "Appointment with Adventure." It ran for fifty weeks, every Sunday night. Nizer asked him, "Can you estimate for this one program how many names you submitted for political approval?"

"I must have submitted about five thousand names."

"For this one program?"

"For this one program. I had to submit the names of everybody on every show in every category."

"Can you estimate how many of the names you submitted came back rejected?"

"I would guess about one third, perhaps a little more, came back politically rejected." Then Nizer asked, "Did you also submit even the names of children?" Susskind said, "Even children," and told how he searched everywhere and finally found an eight-year-old child who could play a certain role. "That child's name came back unacceptable, politically unreliable." And, of course, Nizer made that look like the idiocy it was.

At one point when Hartnett was on the stand, I noticed he was writing down names. I told Nizer at lunch that day, "Son of a gun, he hasn't been broken of sucking eggs yet. That damn fool is still taking down names." That afternoon Nizer cross-examined him: "Mr. Hartnett, whose names were you writing down? Were you writing down names of people who come into a public courtroom so you can blacklist them in the future?" The jury looked at Hartnett as if he had been caught publicly molesting a child.

That night, his lawyer, Tom Bolan, hatched a way to get him out of this. The next day, Bolan asked, "Would you please tell the court whose name you were writing down?" Hartnett answered, "I wrote down

Elliot Sullivan, who was a Fifth Amendment Communist. He sat down next to the wife of John Henry Faulk, the plaintiff." The whole purpose was to have the jury associate my name with Communists. I said to Nizer, "I wonder who the hell he thinks is my wife? She's not here. She's in Texas."

That rang a bell with Nizer. He got up. "Mr. Hartnett, you said that Mr. Sullivan came in and sat next to the wife of plaintiff Faulk. Can you point out Mrs. Faulk in this courtroom?" Everybody was suddenly jolted. The entire press table sat up. The trial was being covered by the *Post,* the *Times,* and the *Herald Tribune.* The judge became interested, too. Hartnett was looking, searching for her. Then he pointed: "It's that lady right there." There was a hubbub. Nizer waited, took about ten beats until everything quieted down.

"Madam, would you be good enough to rise and state your name to the court and the jury, please?" The lady got up and said, "My name is Mrs. Helen Soffer."

The courtroom exploded. The jurors looked at each other and laughed. Hartnett looked like he'd just been stripped buck naked and was sitting up there absolutely nude. Nizer took another beat until it quieted again. He drew his hand back like he had a lance in it and was going to throw it all the way across the courtroom at poor Hartnett. He went up to the witness chair and said, "Sir, is that the accuracy with which you have named your victims and drawn the noose of starvation around the necks of countless American citizens?"

When we came to the end of the trial, Nizer did his summation, and it was a humdinger. By this time, he had decided to ask for two million dollars. I was embarrassed and thought he'd gotten carried away with his own rhetoric. The jury went out and came back in a while. The fore-man rose and asked, "Can we give more than two million?" Nizer looked like somebody had hit him between the eyes with a ballpeen hammer. Whatever mistakes he had made in the past, asking for too little was never one of them. I was just numbed by the whole thing. About thirty minutes later, the jury came back with a three-and-a-half-million-dollar judgment. I must say it has a therapeutic effect on your bruised feelings.

It headlined all over the country. That was a record judgment, the biggest in history for a libel case. And it struck a real blow at blacklist-ing, because it sent a message to CBS, NBC, ABC, and all the agencies: You get caught doing this, baby, and you might have to pay three and a half million dollars. In a way, it was a trial for all of the victims of the blacklist. A lot of them suffered far more than I did. I was the catalyst in the thing, and Nizer framed it and tore the hide off of them. He said, "Send a message to the world."

But we couldn't collect. A settlement was made for a fraction of it, and most of that went for legal expenses. I was middle-aged, almost, nigh on to fifty, and I had to scramble around to pick up what I could. I got a little radio show, and then I got on the lecture circuit. The networks were never friendly to me again. Some individuals were terribly nice and just as enthusiastic as ever, but when it came to corporate policy, I was persona non grata. After all, they'd been part and parcel of the whole ugly system of blacklisting. I was tainted because I'd brought the case against it.

In 1977, I was having lunch with a friend of mine, David Berg. He asked me if I'd gotten my FBI file. I said, "I don't expect that I have one." They had checked on me once. Two FBI guys had come to CBS in 1951 or 1952. Later, I reflected on that a great deal, because these were decent guys, really. What they were doing, I felt, was indecent. They were working for old man Hoover, who had been maneuvering in a fantasy world and selling the American people big doses, big bowel-moving doses, of fantasy and imagination.

I never had heard from the FBI after that. So when David Berg bet me that I had an FBI file, I didn't believe him, but I sent for it anyhow. They wrote back: Yes, they had information on me. I was perfectly outraged that an agency of my government would have information regarding my behavior behind my back. They sent about one hundred seventy pages, going back to 1943. My FBI report was a mishmash of gossip, distortion, and falsehood. One informant told them that I was a Communist and had recruited J. Frank Dobie into the Communist Party. Another informant told them that Dobie was a Communist and he had recruited me.

There were some very interesting things in my file. There was a memo from one of Lyndon Johnson's assistants to J. Edgar Hoover: "Can you give us any information on Faulk?" And J. Edgar Hoover turned over my whole file to him, all of this unauthorized claptrap. You see, in 1955, Lyndon Johnson had asked me to come work for him and then had suddenly lost all interest in me. He told me he was just dropping the whole project. But the dates were right there. Hoover's information had gone to Johnson on April 19. Johnson sent word to me on April 20 that he wasn't interested in carrying through the contract we had.

There were two or three instances like that. The FBI furnished information to Roy Cohn, the attorney for the opposition at the trial.

Then in 1964—two years after I had won the lawsuit against their buddy-buds in Aware—there was an exchange of memos between the House Un-American Activities Committee and J. Edgar Hoover: "We want to dig up some dirt on Faulk." Dirt! It's the actual term they used. They asked, "Will the director be cooperative?" And Hoover signed the memo, "Yes."

A Final Word

The experiences recorded in this book contradict the view that "it can't happen here." They show, as well, that political repression cannot be attributed simply to moments of national weakness or to the excesses of ambitious or zealous bureaucrats. There was, of course, the colossal arrogance of J. Edgar Hoover, who took it upon himself to determine the appropriate leadership for Black Americans by "neutralizing" leaders from Martin Luther King, Jr., to the Black Panthers. And it is true that political repression reached spectacular proportions in times of national hysteria: the red scare of the 1920s and the Cold War of the 1950s. Nevertheless, we believe that repression in America is a pervasive phenomenon that transcends specific persons and specific periods.

Political repression has appeared throughout the century in the actions of local, state, and national governments—including the administrations of liberal presidents. Scott Nearing escaped conviction under the Espionage Act used by the progressive Wilson administration to imprison hundreds of dissidents for their writings and speech. Pete Muselin was one of the many jailed for sedition or criminal syndicalism after the post–World War I red scare had subsided. The internment of Minoru Yasui and 120,000 others of Japanese heritage was carried out by the executive branch of the New Deal. And some of the harshest repressive acts of the century were visited upon civil rights workers and

Black Power advocates well after the McCarthy era, during the protest decade of the 1960s when the Reverend Ben Chavis, Chuck McDew, and Cleveland Sellers experienced southern "justice." Today, Leonard Peltier is in Leavenworth, denied the new trial he deserves, and Margaret Randall is threatened with deportation for what she wrote.

Attacks on dissenters, as illustrated by the FBI's campaign of political intelligence-gathering and espionage, have been tenacious, far-reaching, and foreboding. Once a target was fixed upon, it could be relentlessly tracked across decades. When a 1956 Supreme Court interpretation of the Smith Act precluded the prosecution of the Communists the bureau had been feeding into court dockets since the late 1940s, the FBI secretly initiated the illegal COINTELPRO as a substitute. Thus the attack continued unabated. And for another decade or more, Communists were subjected to intelligence operations that were unrestrained by legal or moral bounds.

The reach of domestic intelligence-gathering and surveillance extended well beyond the "extremes" at which it was supposedly aimed. Once initiated, COINTELPRO expanded to include others whose political activities were unacceptable to the FBI—Frank Wilkinson's National Committee to Abolish HUAC, for example, and the United Farm Workers Union, as well as Dr. Martin Luther King, Jr. The FBI's unbridled intrusion into the private lives of Americans has included such notable figures as John Steinbeck, Carl Sandburg, Albert Einstein, and Eleanor Roosevelt and such popular idols as Marlon Brando, Paul Newman, Joe Louis, Muhammad Ali, and Joe Namath. The bureau kept track of the political associations of many of the delegates attending the 1972 Democratic Convention, the private lives of members of Congress, and, as a recently uncovered memorandum reveals, the sexual preferences of the Washington press corps, information that was supplied to Richard Nixon upon request.[1]

The ominous function of political intelligence-gathering has been secured by its incorporation into federal bureaucracies; the agencies that conduct such intelligence operations have proliferated and expanded. The veil of patriotism they have drawn around themselves as the guardians of our national security and the glamorous self-portrait they have promoted in the popular culture have shielded their clandestine activities from both citizen and rigorous congressional oversight. "The intelligence community tends to become a sacred cow," writes Thomas Emerson, Professor of Law Emeritus at Yale, "untouchable by normal methods of control."[2] No less a body than the U.S. Senate was frustrated in its attempts to learn whether the FBI's illegal COINTELPRO operations had ended. A Senate report states that the Church Committee "has not been able to determine with any . . . precision the extent to which COINTELPRO may be continuing"; and Morton Halperin, a former National Security Council official, adds: "But all available signs do indicate that COINTELPRO by other names is still going on." [3]

Especially in this country, repression has been fed by a virulent anticommunism. We are not speaking of the serious criticisms many have of communism, but of a mania that suspends rationality. The mere term "communist" became, as John Henry Faulk notes, a catchword to brand an opponent and shut down debate. Any movement for social justice, for peace, for civil rights, for unionization could be painted red—labeled "bolshevik," "pinko," "fellow travelers," "communist-controlled"—and then attacked. Fear of communism has gained such a foothold in the American consciousness that gross abuses of civil liberties are tolerated as if they were in the national interest. These irrational fears have sustained repression across the century, confronting every generation with the problem of how to prevent the erosion of our freedoms. There is no resting easy.

The repressive techniques described in this book are inimical to democratic practice. Laws cannot prohibit speech or political activities without compromising democracy. When laws are used to arrest those who organize unions, to imprison those who advocate alternatives to the established power relationships, and to jail those who oppose foreign policy, democratic principles are among the victims.

Congressional investigating committees cannot require persons to reveal their political beliefs and associations in a democracy. When such a committee recklessly impugns reputations; when it parades witnesses whose false accusations are unquestioningly accepted; when it makes names of witnesses public, causing them to be hounded from their jobs or homes—or even driven to the point of suicide; when it interferes in the internal disputes of unions and other organizations; or when it attacks with subpoenas and slander anyone who opposes it, then the dissent that is so necessary for the practice of democracy is quieted.

In a democracy, loyalty tests cannot be a requirement for either employment or immigration. When persons are labeled disloyal because of their writings or their associations, and when disloyalty is determined by arbitrary standards and vague charges and the loyalty proceedings deny the accused constitutional protections such as the right to confront their accusers, the boundaries of democracy are constricted.

If democratic principles are to be honored, police cannot interfere with lawful political demonstrations. When demonstrators are subject to mass arrests or harassment for absurd infractions of the law; when police beat or intimidate demonstrators—indeed, even shoot or kill them; when police infiltrate violence-prone organizations and participate with them in violence against demonstrators, citizens cannot freely exercise their democratic rights to petition and to assemble.

If free expression is to survive, the FBI and other secret police cannot collect political intelligence or engage in political espionage. When secret police target their political opponents for prosecution; when lawful organizations are infiltrated and disrupted, their offices burglarized, their files and membership lists rifled; when police provoke violence among rival political groups; when the FBI opens people's mail, hounds them out of their jobs and apartments, and breaks up their marriages; and when all this is done in secret by agencies unaccountable to the electorate, then democratic institutions are subverted.

Repressive techniques have been selectively applied. Those who opposed one or another policy of established economic or political interests have felt the force of government power against them, whether they were involved in organizing Blacks to register to vote in McComb, Mississippi, in organizing lumberjacks and copper miners into "one grand industrial union," in opposing the internment of Japanese Americans, or in challenging an unpopular war in Vietnam.

By any measure, repression has been visited disproportionately upon the American left. The state has crushed indigenous radical movements from the Industrial Workers of the World to the Black Panther Party. Anyone who professes a belief in socialism and advocates it effectively within the bounds of the Constitution would be naive indeed not to expect to be a target of repressive state action. The tiny Socialist Workers Party suffered intense secret police surveillance and harassment for more than three decades, although no evidence of illegal activity by the party was uncovered in all that time. Yet political police agents and informers, for a number of years, constituted one out of every ten of the party's members; its offices were burglarized 193 times from 1958 to 1966; ten million pages of files on its members were amassed; and its perfectly legal political activities were sabotaged.

But the costs of these violations of democratic rights are borne by more than those who are directly attacked. The chilling effects of such assaults instill fear in others who, but for the abuse of grand juries, the

FBI visits to family, friends, and neighbors, the loss of jobs, the sub-poenas, the imprisonment, or the deportations, might have raised their voices in protest. Speaking of the sedition law used against Margaret Herring McSurely, the federal judge who overturned her indictment said: "The conclusion is inescapable that the criminal prosecutions were instituted, at least in part, in order to stop plaintiff's organizing activi-ties in Pike County. That effort has been successful. Not only has there been the 'chilling effect' on freedom of speech, there has been in fact a freezing effect."[4] Fear engendered by violations of constitutional rights becomes the instrument for what might be the worst intrusion of all: self-censorship.

Political repression in America has been consequential; it has had major, long-term effects. The brutality used to subjugate Black people in the South, for example, not only caused them to live for generations in poverty and misery, but it also affected the balance of political power in that region, allowing southern ultraconservatives to become entrenched in pivotal positions within the national government, affecting its poli-cies on issues from civil rights to foreign relations.

The use of local and state militia to break strikes, the harassment and mass arrests of unionists, the existence of private police in company towns, and the injunctions and other legal sanctions against strikes suppressed unionization until the mid-1930s. Historian Robert Gold-stein cites as evidence of the effectiveness of those repressive measures the dramatic upsurge in union membership when the Wagner Act pro-hibited much of the harsh treatment unionists had experienced. Af-ter the 1930s, the most severe attacks were reserved for left-led unions. As a consequence of government actions that curtailed or weakened union organizing, business gained disproportionate benefits from peri-ods of prosperity, and the possibilities of radical unionism never had the chance to be realized. Instead, bureaucratic and sometimes corrupt unionism flourished, with a corresponding loss of union fervor among rank-and-file workers.

Political repression also helped foreclose consideration of socialist alternatives in America. The left did not simply lose out in the free marketplace of ideas because of the weight of its own errors or because of the affluence of the American working class. Consider the example of the Communist Party: whether its political fortunes were or were not on the wane by the 1950s, the massive assaults directed against it and against so-called fellow travelers not only devastated the party apparently beyond repair, but also stigmatized the entire socialist left in such a way that it has yet to recover, in addition to opening the door to continuing repression against newly emerging radical views and organizations.

Finally, in part as a result of our experiences with the remarkable men and women whose stories are told in this volume, we've come to a greater respect for constitutional rights, which, as principles, are often honored but too often violated. Such rights are precious—the upside of America—and they are treasured most, perhaps, by persons who have had them denied. "Thank God for the Bill of Rights," said Harvey O'Connor, reflecting on his own encounters with congressional inquisitors. We absolutely agree.

Notes

PART I

Thou Shall Not Teach—Myles Horton

1. Rosa Parks quoted in *Highlander Reports,* Highlander Research and Education Center, New Market, Tennessee, December 1982.

Thou Shall Not Preach—William Howard Melish

1. Arthur Miller, *Father and Son* (New York: Churchman, 1952), p. 1.

PART II

Introduction to Part II

1. Jim Messerschmidt, *The Trial of Leonard Peltier* (Boston: South End Press, 1983), p. 54.

The Steel Fist in a Pennsylvania Company Town—Pete Muselin

1. Quoted in Richard Harris, *Freedom Spent: Tales of Tyranny in America* (Boston: Little, Brown, 1974), pp. 183–184.

Forbidden Books on Trial—Gil Green

1. Allen Guttman and Benjamin Ziegler, eds., *Communism, the Courts, and the Constitution* (Boston: D. C. Heath, 1964), p. 42.
2. *Yates v. United States,* 354 U.S. at 330–331 (1957).
3. Unsigned FBI memorandum (100–3–2642), July 23, 1948.

The Conspiracy to Oppose the Vietnam War—Benjamin Spock

1. Lynn Z. Bloom, *Dr. Spock* (New York: Bobbs-Merrill, 1972), p. 299.
2. Thomas Emerson, *The System of Freedom of Expression* (New York: Vintage Books, 1970), p. 411.
3. Richard Harris, *Justice* (New York: Avon, 1969), p. 58.

The Beginning: The Hollywood Ten—Ring Lardner, Jr., and Frances Chaney Lardner

1. Charlotte Pomerantz, ed., *A Quarter-Century of Un-Americana* (New York: Marzani & Munsell, 1963), p. 87.

To Swing a Union Election—Tom Quinn

1. Robert Justin Goldstein, *Political Repression in Modern America: 1870 to the Present* (Cambridge, Mass.: Schenkman, 1978), pp. 345–346; Pomerantz, *Quarter-Century of Un-Americana,* p. 123.
2. Goldstein, *Political Repression in Modern America,* p. 345.
3. Ibid.

To Smear a Professor—Barrows Dunham

1. I. F. Stone, *The Haunted Fifties* (New York: Random House, 1963), pp. 117–118.
2. *Temple University Alumni Review,* Fall 1981, p. 2.

There's No Business Like Show Business—John Randolph and Sarah Cunningham

1. Otto Nathan and Heinz Norden, eds., *Einstein on Peace* (New York: Simon & Schuster, 1960), pp. 546–547.
2. *Notable Names in American Theater* (Clifton, N.J.: James T. White, 1976), p. 1066.

He Said No to Joe—Harvey O'Connor and Jessie O'Connor

1. Frank Donner, *The Un-Americans* (New York: Ballantine Books, 1961), p. 3.

The Palmer Raids: The Deportation Mania Begins—Sonia Kaross

1.   Robert S. Murray, *Red Scare: A Study in National Hysteria, 1919–1920* (Minneapolis: University of Minnesota Press, 1955), p. 219; Goldstein, *Political Repression in Modern America,* p. 158.

The Ordeal of the Loyalty Test—Arthur Drayton

1.   Goldstein, *Political Repression in Modern America,* p. 300.
2.   L. A. Nikoloric, "The Government Loyalty Program," in *Loyalty in a Democratic State,* ed. John C. Wahlke (Boston: D. C. Heath, 1952), p. 55.

Forbidden Utterances: Reason Enough for Exclusion—
Margaret Randall

1.   Quoted in William Preston, Jr., *Aliens and Dissenters: Federal Suppression of Radicals* (New York: Harper & Row, 1963), p. 227.
2.   Arthur Miller quoted in Mark Schapiro, "The Excludables," *Mother Jones,* January 1986, p. 32.
3.   Immigration and Nationality Act (1952), Section 212(a)(28) (G)(v).
4.   Margaret Randall, *The Coming Home Poems* (East Haven, Conn.: Long River Books, 1986).
5.   Affirmation of Harold Fruchtbaum to Immigration Judge Martin F. Speigel in the Matter of Margaret J. Randall in Deportation Proceedings, March 13, 1986, pp. 2, 19.
6.   Testimony of Adrienne Rich at the Deportation Hearing of Margaret Randall Before Immigration Judge Martin F. Speigel, El Paso, Texas, March 19, 1986, p. 595.
7.   Letter from Norman Mailer to Immigration Judge Martin F. Speigel, February 26, 1986.
8.   Affirmation of Alice Walker to Immigration Judge Martin F. Speigel in the Matter of Margaret J. Randall in Deportation Proceedings, February 1986.
9.   Lines here and immediately above excerpted from the poem "Under Attack," by Margaret Randall, published in Randall, *The Coming Home Poems.*
10. Quoted in James Ridgeway, "Just the Facts," *Village Voice,* September 16, 1986.

The Wilmington Ten: Prisoners of Conscience—Ben Chavis

1. Anne Braden, "American Inquisition Part II: The McSurely Case and Repression in the 1960s," *Southern Exposure* 11(September/October 1983): 22.
2. Sworn affidavit by Allen Hall, cited in Michael Myerson, *Nothing Could Be Finer* (New York: International Publishers, 1978), p. 228.
3. Letter from Jerome Mitchell to the North Carolina Parole Board, cited in Travis L. Francis, ed., *Human Rights in the United States of America* (New York: United Church of Christ, 1978), p. 20.
4. Francis, *Human Rights*, p. 18.
5. *New York Times*, February 18, 1977, p. A3.
6. *New York Times*, May 21, 1977, p. 17.

War Against the American Nation—Leonard Peltier

1. "Letter from Leonard Peltier to Friends and Supporters," *Peltier Update Report*, North Carolina Leonard Peltier Support Committee, n.d., p. 1.
2. Authors' interview with Karen Northcott, Washington, D.C., June 12, 1985.
3. Interview with Roselyn Jumping Bull, conducted by Candy Hamilton, Oglala, South Dakota, September 1976.
4. Authors' interview with Hazel Little Hawk, Washington, D.C., June 12, 1985.
5. Remarks by Bruce Ellison at press conference, Washington, D.C., June 12, 1985.
6. Darrell Butler, Testimony Before Citizens' Review Commission on the FBI Hearings, Minneapolis, February 5, 1977, pp. 7–10.
7. Memorandum from William F. Muldrew, Equal Opportunity Specialist, to Dr. Shirley Hill Witt, Mountain States Regional Director, United States Commission on Civil Rights, July 9, 1975.
8. Trial testimony of Myrtle Poor Bear, quoted in Messerschmidt, *The Trial of Leonard Peltier*, p. 84.
9. Remarks by Bruce Ellison at press conference, Washington, D.C., June 12, 1985.
10. Trial testimony of Mike Anderson, quoted in Peter Matthiessen, *In the Spirit of Crazy Horse* (New York: Viking Press, 1983), pp. 331–332.
11. Quoted in Matthiessen, *In the Spirit of Crazy Horse*, pp. 333–334.
12. Trial testimony of Norman Brown, quoted in Messerschmidt, *The Trial of Leonard Peltier*, p. 77.
13. Norman Brown, Testimony Before Citizens' Review Commission on the FBI Hearings, Minneapolis, February 5, 1977, pp. 3–4.
14. Statement of Leonard Peltier to Judge Paul Benson before sen-

tencing, quoted in Messerschmidt, *The Trial of Leonard Peltier*, pp. 113–114.

PART III

Introduction to Part III

1. Frank Donner, *The Age of Surveillance: The Aims and Methods of America's Political Intelligence System* (New York: Knopf, 1980), p. 357.
2. Richard Hansen, "Police Files on Leftists Funneled to Birchite Group," *Guardian*, June 15, 1983.

The Orangeburg Massacre, 1968—Cleveland Sellers

1. Jack Nelson and Jack Bass, *The Orangeburg Massacre* (New York: World Publishing, 1970), p. 111.
2. Federal Bureau of Investigation, "Student Nonviolent Coordinating Committee," August 1967, unpublished, p. i.
3. Letter from SAC [Special Agent in Charge], New York (100–161140)(P) to Director, FBI (100–448006), April 1, 1968.
4. Nelson and Bass, *The Orangeburg Massacre*, pp. 111–112.

FBI Crackdown on Opposition to HUAC—Frank Wilkinson

1. Memorandum from SAC, Los Angeles (100–16439) to Director, FBI (Bufile 100–112434), September 20, 1974, p. 2.
2. Walter Goodman, *The Committee: The Extraordinary Career of the House Committee on Un-American Activities* (New York: Farrar, Straus & Giroux, 1964), pp. 420–421.
3. Memorandum from C. D. DeLoach (Hqs 100–112434–114) to Mr. Mohr, March 20, 1961, p. 2; Hoover's comment in his own handwriting on the memorandum.
4. Memorandum from J. F. Bland to A. H. Belmont (100–112434–107), March 21, 1961.
5. Memorandum from SAC, Washington (100–37787) to Director, FBI (100–112434–106), March 24, 1961.
6. Memorandum from FBI Director (100–3–104–9–80) to Chicago, Detroit, Indiana, Los Angeles, Milwaukee, and Springfield, September 27, 1962.
7. Airtel from Los Angeles to Bureau, Baltimore, Boston, et al., September 19, 1968.
8. Memorandum, Chicago with copy to bureau, Not To File, January 10, 1966.
9. Teletype from Los Angeles (100–16439) to Director, FBI (100–112434–165), March 4, 1964.

The FBI's Southern Strategies—Jack O'Dell

1. U.S. Congress, Senate Select Committee to Study Governmental Operations with Respect to Intelligence Activities, *Final Report—Book III, Supplementary Detailed Reports on Intelligence Activities and the Rights of Americans*, 94th Cong., 2d sess., April 23, 1976, p. 81.
2. Ibid., pp. 95–96.

The Grand Jury: An Extension of FBI Authority—Jill Raymond

1. Donner, *The Age of Surveillance*, p. 358.
2. Ibid., p. 356.
3. Ibid., p. 367.

The Lawlessness of the LAPD Red Squad—Seymour Myerson

1. Quoted in Nathaniel Sheppard, Jr., "How Chicago Red Squad Sabotaged 60s Dissidents," *New York Times,* December 2, 1980, p. B12.
2. Complaint for Damages Against the City of Los Angeles, Edward M. Davis, [and others] filed on behalf of Seymour Myerson by R. Samuel Paz and the ACLU Foundation of Southern California in the Superior Court of the State of California, June 14, 1977, p. 3.
3. Ibid.
4. Ibid.
5. Complaint, p. 4.
6. The letters reproduced in this story are the personal possessions of Mr. Myerson. Several of them have been excerpted from the full originals.
7. "Panel Urges Payment of $27,500 to Alleged Victim of Police Terror," *Los Angeles Times,* June 17, 1982.
8. Complaint, p. 10.

Undercover Agents' War on Vietnam Veterans—Scott Camil

1. Jeff Cohen, "'Hippy Agent' Found FBI More Dangerous Than Suspects," *In These Times,* April 23–29, 1980, p. 19.
2. "Message Center," *Miami Times,* November 24, 1966.
3. Excerpted from FBI memorandum (100–463962–1), February 22, 1971, p. 2.
4. Excerpted from FBI memorandum (100–463962–3), August 2, 1971, cover page.
5. Informative Note, Domestic Intelligence Division, November 24, 1971.
6. Excerpted from teletype from Director, FBI (100–463962–5) to SAC, Jacksonville (100–1731), December 9, 1971.

7. Excerpted from teletype from Director, FBI (100–463962–7) to SACs, Jacksonville (100–1731), Miami (100–16234), New York, December 10, 1971, p. 1.

8. Excerpted from teletype from Jacksonville (100–663962–9) to Director, FBI Miami, and New York, December 11, 1971, pp. 1–2, 6.

9. Excerpted from teletype from Director, FBI (100–463962–25) to SAC, Jacksonville (100–1731), December 22, 1971, p. 1.

10. Excerpted from FBI memorandum (100–463962–32), January 13, 1972, pp. 1–2.

11. Fred Cook, "The Real Conspiracy Exposed," *The Nation*, October 1, 1973, p. 301.

12. Rob Elder, "Spy Job Offer at Convention Revealed," *Miami Herald*, May 23, 1973, pp. 1, 21a.

13. David Harris, "Hogtown Justice," *Rolling Stone*, February 14, 1974, p. 50.

The Greensboro Massacre: Police-Vigilante Nexus—Paul Bermanzohn

1. "Letter From Martha Nathan to Friends," Greensboro Civil Rights Fund newsletter, Washington, D.C., June 1985.

2. "The Dare That Ignited a Slaughter," *Time*, June 30, 1980, p. 25.

3. *Workers Viewpoint*, May 11–13, 1983, pp. 3, 14.

In Defense of the Constitution—Minoru Yasui

1. Quoted in Peter Irons, *Justice at War: The Story of the Japanese American Internment Cases* (New York: Oxford University Press, 1983), p. 141.

2. Quoted in Irons, *Justice at War*, p. 211.

3. Ennis quoted in ibid., p. 288.

PART IV

Turning the Tables on Government Raiders—
Margaret Herring McSurely

1. Quoted in Harris, *Freedom Spent*, p. 147.

2. Quoted in ibid., pp. 183–184.

3. Questions and answers taken from Transcript of Oral Argument in the Supreme Court of the United States, *Herbert H. McAdams II as executor of the Estate of John L. McClellan v. Alan McSurely and Margaret McSurely*, March 1, 1978, p. 15.

Exposing the Informer Racket—Edward Lamb

1. David Caute, *The Great Fear: The Anti-Communist Purge Under Truman and Eisenhower* (New York: Simon & Schuster, 1978), p. 121.
2. Ibid., p. 131.
3. Ibid., pp. 120–121.
4. Goldstein, *Political Repression in Modern America*, p. 347; Caute, *The Great Fear*, p. 222; Cedric Belfrage, *The American Inquisition, 1945–1960* (New York: Bobbs-Merrill, 1973), pp. 120, 152.
5. Caute, *The Great Fear*, p. 132.
6. Edward Lamb, *No Lamb for Slaughter* (New York: Harcourt, Brace & World, 1963), p. 63.
7. Ibid., pp. 167–168.

Bringing the Blacklisters to Account—John Henry Faulk

1. Victor Navasky, *Naming Names* (New York: Viking Press, 1980), p. 87.
2. Nancy Lynn Schwartz, *The Hollywood Writers' Wars* (New York: McGraw-Hill, 1982), p. 266.
3. Eric Bentley, ed., *Thirty Years of Treason: Excerpts from Hearings Before the House Committee on Un-American Activities, 1938–1968* (New York: Viking Press, 1971), p. 196.
4. John Henry Faulk, *Fear on Trial* (Austin: University of Texas Press, 1983), p. 97.

A FINAL WORD

1. References to FBI files can be found in Donner, *The Age of Surveillance*, p. 115; Morton H. Halperin, Jerry J. Berman, Robert L. Borosage, and Christine M. Marwick, *The Lawless State: The Crimes of U.S. Intelligence Agencies* (New York: Penguin Books, 1976), p. 7; Athan Theoharis and John Stuart Cox, *The Boss: J. Edgar Hoover and the Great American Inquisition* (Philadelphia: Temple University Press, 1988), pp. 191–193, 409; and Herbert Mitgang, *Dangerous Dossiers: Exposing the Secret War Against America's Greatest Authors* (New York: Donald I. Fine, 1988), pp. 71–78, 87–91.
2. Thomas Emerson, "Controlling the Spies," *Center Magazine*, January/February 1979, p. 9.
3. Halperin et al., *The Lawless State*, p. 240.
4. Quoted in Harris, *Freedom Spent*, p. 184.

For Background Reading

The books briefly described below have been selected from the literature on political repression in America because they are particularly relevant to the experiences of the persons we interviewed. Extensive bibliographical lists are furnished in many studies of the topic, including David Caute's *The Great Fear: The Anti-Communist Purge Under Truman and Eisenhower* (New York: Simon & Schuster, 1978); Frank Donner's *The Age of Surveillance: The Aims and Methods of America's Political Intelligence System* (New York: Knopf, 1980); and Robert Justin Goldstein's *Political Repression in Modern America: 1870 to the Present* (Cambridge, Mass.: Schenkman, 1978).

Goldstein's *Political Repression in Modern America* is a comprehensive study that examines more than a century of government attacks on the rights of dissenters. Goldstein presents repression not as an exceptional phenomenon, but rather as an instrument of government policy that has been used consistently since the end of the 1800s, consequently altering the course of our national development. Thomas Emerson's authoritative *The System of Freedom of Expression* (New York: Vintage Books, 1970), a legal analysis of the First Amendment, examines court decisions from which doctrines of free expression have evolved. Emerson argues for an interpretation of the First Amendment that requires the full protection of expression with control only of subsequent illegal action.

In general, the study of repression in America has concentrated more closely on specific periods and events than on broader survey histories. William Preston's documented analysis of the events leading up to the Palmer raids, *Aliens and Dissenters: Federal Suppression of Radicals* (New York: Harper & Row, 1963), portrays the red scare of 1919–1920 not as an aberration but as an event grounded in a well-established antagonism toward both radicals and aliens that was transformed into policy—especially into immigration laws—and executed by all branches of the federal government. Directed in large measure against the Industrial Workers of the World, these federal actions foretold repressions that were to follow. Walker Smith's *The Everett Massacre: A History of the Class Struggle in the Lumber Industry* (Chicago: IWW, 1918) is a contemporary account of that event by an IWW historian. It sets the massacre in the context of the political-economic forces that ruled Everett and describes the massacre, and the trial of Wobblies that followed, in considerable detail.

Two works on the World War II internment of Japanese Americans are especially informative. Michi Weglyn's *Years of Infamy: The Untold Story of America's Concentration Camps* (New York: Morrow, 1976) reveals both the oppressive life in the camps and the resistance that developed, as well as documenting the hypocritical denial of civil liberties to Japanese Americans by a nation at war to defend democracy but nevertheless imbued with racist fervor. Peter Iron's *Justice at War: The Story of the Japanese American Internment Cases* (New York: Oxford University Press, 1983) is a careful legal history of government misconduct—and its subsequent cover-up—in the formation of the internment policy.

Two comprehensive reviews of political repression during the Cold War period are *The Great Fear,* by David Caute (mentioned above), and *The American Inquisition: 1945–1960* (New York: Bobbs-Merrill, 1973), by Cedric Belfrage. The first is a topical treatment that establishes the roots of the anti-democratic hysteria of McCarthyism in the Truman administration that preceded it. The second is a detailed chronological treatment that places the reader in the midst of the many-sided attacks on "heretics" as those events unfolded.

Congressional investigating committees spawned many studies. *Thirty Years of Treason: Excerpts from Hearings Before the House Committee on Un-American Activities, 1938–1968* (New York: Viking

Press, 1971), edited by Eric Bentley, includes extensive selections from testimony of notable witnesses before HUAC. Walter Goodman's *The Committee: The Extraordinary Career of the House Committee on Un-American Activities* (New York: Farrar, Straus & Giroux, 1964), perhaps the most encyclopedic history, is an account of HUAC from its origins in the late 1930s to its demise three decades later. In *Fear, The Accuser* (New York: Abelard-Schuman, 1954), author Dan Gillmor focuses on the year 1953 to examine the investigations of Harold Velde's HUAC, Albert Jenner's Senate Subcommittee on Internal Security, and Joseph McCarthy's Senate Subcommittee on Investigations. *A Quarter-Century of Un-Americana* (New York: Marzani & Munsell, 1963), edited by Charlotte Pomerantz, is a lively attack on HUAC, using cartoons, quotations, and essays by the committee's opponents. Telford Taylor's *Grand Inquest: The Story of Congressional Investigations* (New York: Simon & Schuster, 1955) presents a legal analysis of the origins of investigating committees, defending the use of the Fifth Amendment against the erosion it suffered from congressional inquisitors.

Nancy Lynn Schwartz's *The Hollywood Writers' Wars* (New York: McGraw-Hill, 1982) chronicles the history of the Screen Writers Guild, with special attention to the case of the Hollywood Ten. *The Inquisition in Hollywood: Politics in the Film Community, 1930–1960* (Berkeley and Los Angeles: University of California Press, 1979), Larry Ceplair and Steven Englund's history of the left in the film industry, places the case of the Hollywood Ten in context. The authors argue that the attack against the Ten and their successors on the HUAC witness stand took place because they had been an effective voice of the radical left. Victor Navasky's *Naming Names* (New York: Viking Press, 1980) uncovers the elaborate apparatus set up around HUAC to coerce submission to the committee's authority. Navasky looks behind the events themselves to study the motivations of both the informers and those who resisted HUAC's inquisition. In that regard, Sterling Hayden's fascinating autobiography, *Wanderer* (New York: Knopf, 1963), portrays the extraordinary pressures to cooperate with the committee and offers a remorseful account of Hayden's own surrender to HUAC.

Historian Howard Zinn studied the Student Nonviolent Coordinating Committee as a participant. His *SNCC: The New Abolitionists*, 2d ed. (Boston: Beacon Press, 1965) is an account of early civil rights struggles in Mississippi and Alabama and the brutal attacks against politically active young people by police in the Deep South. Clayborne Carson's *In Struggle: SNCC and the Black Awakening of the 1960s*

(Cambridge: Harvard University Press, 1981) is a more complete history of SNCC that includes the FBI's use of counter-intelligence programs to disable the once-vital organization. James Forman's no-holds-barred autobiography, *The Making of Black Revolutionaries* (Washington, D.C.: Open Hand Publishing, 1985), includes the dramatic story of SNCC as told by one of its foremost leaders. Michael Myerson's *Nothing Could Be Finer* (New York: International Publishers, 1978) examines the somewhat later case of the Wilmington Ten within an in-depth study of North Carolina's historical suppression of the Black and labor movements.

Peter Matthiessen's *In the Spirit of Crazy Horse* (New York: Viking Press, 1983) is an absorbing account of the events that led to the imprisonment of Leonard Peltier. Matthiessen shows that present-day Native American resistance is a continuation of the struggle to defend Indian sovereignty against longstanding white encroachments and violations of treaty rights. The Indian takeover of Wounded Knee and the massive military response are part of the contemporary background to the firefight at Pine Ridge several years later. An intimate glimpse of those events is recorded in the words of the participants in *Voices from Wounded Knee* (Rooseveltown, New York: Akwesasne Notes, 1974), edited by Robert Anderson and the Editorial Collective. Jim Messerschmidt's *The Trial of Leonard Peltier* (Boston: South End Press, 1983) contains a documented account of the government's drive to silence the Native American activist; Messerschmidt even presents evidence suggesting that Peltier was set up for an attempt on his life while in prison.

Richard Harris's case study of the ordeal of the McSurelys in *Freedom Spent: Tales of Tyranny in America* (Boston: Little, Brown, 1974) includes a historical essay on the Fourth Amendment's protection of "the right of the people to be secure in their persons, houses, papers, and effects against unreasonable searches and seizures." Another of his case studies in the same volume, this one on grand jury abuse, examines the sources of and reasons for the Fifth Amendment's protection against self-incrimination in a case similar in many respects to Jill Raymond's experiences.

Beyond the Hiss Case: The FBI, Congress, and the Cold War (Philadelphia: Temple University Press, 1982), edited by Athan G. Theoharis, contains essays on the FBI burglaries directed at dissidents, on the surveillance and disruption of political opponents such as the National Lawyers Guild and Congressman Vito Marcantonio, and on the connections between the FBI and congressional investigators. The last point was expanded into a full-length study by Kenneth O'Reilly in *Hoover and the Un-Americans* (Philadelphia: Temple University Press, 1983). By examining declassified bureau files, O'Reilly documents a symbiotic relationship between the FBI and HUAC.

The Senate's *Final Report of the Select Committee to Study Governmental Operations with Respect to Intelligence Activities* (Washington, D.C.: Government Printing Office, 1976), more commonly known as the Church Committee Report, made public the covert and frequently illegal activities of the military, the Internal Revenue Service, the National Security Agency, the CIA, and the FBI. Using testimony and documents, the committee examines the disruption of First Amendment rights of American citizens by these undercover government agencies. Drawing on material from the Church Committee and other sources, Morton H. Halperin, Jerry J. Berman, Robert L. Borosage, and Christine M. Marwick, in *The Lawless State: The Crimes of U.S. Intelligence Agencies* (New York: Penguin Books, 1976), sketch the extraordinary scope and severity of political surveillance: the computerized index of more than a million names; the opening of mail, the "black bag" jobs, the disinformation, and the illegal wiretaps; and the programs to disrupt and "neutralize" American citizens. They examine as well the thin reed of authority upon which these mammoth agencies operate and the difficulty of bringing them under public control.

Finally, Frank Donner's *The Age of Surveillance,* mentioned above, is essential reading. Donner places the sources of political intelligence-gathering in the exaggerated American fear of communism and in its nativist ethos; he traces the emergence of the intelligence establishment from its modest origins to its present state as an oppressive, institutionalized form of social control.

Compositor:	G & S Typesetters, Inc.
Text:	10/13 Sabon
Display:	Sabon
Printer:	Maple-Vail Book Mfg. Group
Binder:	Maple-Vail Book Mfg. Group